THE COURT
AT WAR

THE COURT
AT WAR

❧ ❧ ❧

FDR, His Justices, and
the World They Made

CLIFF SLOAN

PUBLICAFFAIRS

NEW YORK

PublicAffairs
Hachette Book Group
1290 Avenue of the Americas, New York, NY 10104
www.publicaffairsbooks.com
@Public_Affairs

Printed in the United States of America
First Edition: September 2023

Published by PublicAffairs, an imprint of Perseus Books, LLC, a subsidiary of Hachette Book Group, Inc. The PublicAffairs name and logo is a trademark of the Hachette Book Group.

The Hachette Speakers Bureau provides a wide range of authors for speaking events. To find out more, go to hachettespeakersbureau.com or email HachetteSpeakers@hbgusa.com.

PublicAffairs books may be purchased in bulk for business, educational, or promotional use. For more information, please contact your local bookseller or the Hachette Book Group Special Markets Department at special.markets@hbgusa.com.

The publisher is not responsible for websites (or their content) that are not owned by the publisher.

Print book interior design by Linda Mark.

Library of Congress Control Number: 2023938541

ISBNs: 9781541736481 (hardcover), 9781541736450 (ebook)

LSC-C

Printing 1, 2023

To the memory of my brother, Marty Sloan,
and my parents, Howard and Maryce Sloan

Contents

Photo section appears after p. 208

THE JUSTICES

Chief Justice Harlan Fiske Stone (associate justice 1925–1941, chief justice 1941–1946): Raised on a farm in Massachusetts, Stone excelled as a student and football player at Amherst, where his circle of friends included the future President Calvin Coolidge. He was a professor and dean at Columbia Law School, as well as a Wall Street lawyer, before Coolidge appointed him Attorney General and then Associate Justice in 1925. Expected to be a defender of business interests on the Court, Stone opposed the Supreme Court's pre-1937 pervasive rejection of social and economic legislation. In the summer of 1941, President Franklin D. Roosevelt promoted him to Chief Justice.

Justice Hugo Black (1937–1971): Black grew up in modest circumstances in Alabama and became a leading trial lawyer in Birmingham. Elected to the Senate in 1926, he emerged as a populist champion and then a New Deal supporter. FDR selected him as his first Supreme Court appointment in 1937. Shortly after Black's confirmation, a national controversy erupted about his past membership in the Ku Klux Klan.

Justice James F. Byrnes (1941–1942): Byrnes was a South Carolina Senator and close political ally of FDR when the President named him to the Supreme Court in the summer of 1941. Byrnes left the Court after only one year and joined FDR in the White House as "Assistant President" overseeing the wartime economy.

Justice William O. Douglas (1939–1975): Douglas spent his youth and college years in Washington State. He went east to attend Columbia Law School and became an acclaimed law professor specializing in business regulation at Columbia and Yale Law Schools. One of the first chairs of the new Securities and Exchange Commission, Douglas was named to the Supreme Court by FDR in 1939, when he was only forty years old. FDR favored Douglas to be his running mate in the 1944 presidential election.

Justice Felix Frankfurter (1939–1962): A native of Austria, Frankfurter emigrated to the United States at the age of eleven not knowing a word of English. After graduating from the City College of New York, he was a superstar student at Harvard Law School and then served in a series of high-level government jobs before becoming a Harvard Law professor. Frankfurter first got to know FDR when they both worked in the Wilson Administration in World War I. The ebullient Frankfurter became a close adviser to Roosevelt when FDR was Governor and President. Frankfurter placed his protégés, nicknamed "Felix's Happy Hot Dogs," in key positions throughout the Roosevelt Administration. FDR appointed him to the Supreme Court in 1939.

Justice Robert Jackson (1941–1954): A brilliant lawyer in upstate New York, Jackson attended only one year of law school and served as an apprentice in a law office before joining the bar. He met FDR when Roosevelt was a state senator. FDR brought him into his administration in a succession of posts, including Solicitor General and Attorney General, before appointing him to the Supreme Court in the summer of 1941.

Justice Frank Murphy (1940–1949): Murphy had been Mayor of Detroit, Governor of Michigan, High Commissioner to the Philippines, and FDR's Attorney General when FDR named him to the Supreme Court in 1940. Murphy was an outspoken social justice champion. A saying gained currency: "The Supreme Court tempers justice with Murphy."

Justice Stanley Reed (1938–1957): A leading Kentucky lawyer, Reed came to Washington in the Hoover Administration to work on agricultural issues and then joined the Roosevelt Administration. He served as FDR's embattled Solicitor General when the Supreme Court struck down many New Deal laws and regulations. In 1938, the President selected him to be his second appointment to the Court.

Justice Owen Roberts (1930–1945): The only Justice during World War II who did not owe his position to FDR, Roberts was appointed to the Supreme Court by President Herbert Hoover in 1930. A prominent Philadelphia lawyer, Roberts stepped into the national spotlight in 1924 when Coolidge appointed him as the Special Counsel investigating the Harding Administration's Teapot Dome scandal. On the Court, Roberts's perceived change, at the height of FDR's Court-packing fight, to vote in favor of the constitutionality of social and economic legislation became forever known as "the switch in time that saved nine."

Justice Wiley Rutledge (1943–1949): Rutledge was FDR's final appointment, replacing Byrnes when Byrnes resigned to join FDR in the White House. A former law professor and dean at the University of Iowa College of Law, Rutledge attracted FDR's attention as a prominent supporter of the President's controversial Court-packing plan. FDR named Rutledge to the District of Columbia Court of Appeals in 1939 and then elevated him to the Supreme Court in 1943.

PROLOGUE

O N MONDAY MORNING, DECEMBER 8, 1941, GEORGE HUTCHIN-son, an eighteen-year-old library aide, attended to his tasks in the Supreme Court's ornate building. The "marble palace," as it was widely known, had opened six years earlier, replacing the cramped room in the Capitol across the street that had long been the Court's home.

Suddenly there was a commotion. Hutchinson was startled to see armed soldiers burst into the Supreme Court. They quickly moved into sentry positions at the Court windows, weapons prominently displayed. Other soldiers roamed the building and mounted the roof. They had arrived as emergency security for President Franklin D. Roosevelt before his noontime speech to Congress, the address in which FDR would decry the "date which will live in infamy"—Japan's surprise attack on Pearl Harbor the preceding day.

The country was now at war. And the war had, quite literally, invaded the quiet precincts of the Supreme Court.

❖ ❖ ❖

JUST A FEW YEARS prior, FDR had been in a bitter battle with the Supreme Court. It had repeatedly struck down key pieces of New Deal legislation. Frustrated, Roosevelt had sought to enlarge the Court and pack it. His effort encountered bipartisan hostility. But a surprise switched vote flipped his fate. Justice Owen Roberts, an appointee of Herbert Hoover (the incumbent FDR had defeated in the presidential election of 1932), changed his tune, and the Supreme Court began upholding New Deal policy.

By the start of World War II, FDR, benefiting from a wave of retirements, had effectively packed the Court without having to add to the number of Justices. He had appointed seven of the nine and elevated an eighth to Chief Justice. It represented the most Justices appointed by a President since George Washington—and the most sweeping influence by a President on the Court since the first days of the republic.

FDR's Justices were a fractious crew, plagued by internal rivalries, bitter resentments, and behind-the-curtain feuds. But they were united in their loyalty to the President and frequently jostled for his favor.

The Roosevelt Justices included Hugo Black, an ex-Klansman from Alabama who had become a progressive force; William O. Douglas, a western iconoclast and New Deal wunderkind whom FDR would favor as his running mate in 1944; Robert Jackson, a legal superstar and FDR poker crony; Felix Frankfurter, the cocksure Harvard Law professor with a legion of strategically placed protégés; and Frank Murphy, a social justice champion who had served as Governor of Michigan and Attorney General.

The cases that came before the War Court—the identity the Roosevelt Court quickly assumed—required its Justices to weigh constitutional commitments to civil liberties in the context of a brutal global conflagration. The Justices were not—could not be—divorced from the war effort. Hugo Black had two sons in the military and a wife whose anxiety about them contributed to bouts of severe depression. Frank Murphy enlisted for a brief stint in the military while remaining a Justice. Robert Jackson left for Europe to prosecute the Nuremberg trials.

Felix Frankfurter frequently consulted with close friends at the War Department, including his mentor, Henry Stimson, whom he had helped install as Secretary of War.

All of them felt a deep allegiance to FDR. They regarded him as not only their President but also their friend and beloved patron, as he steered the nation through a war that was simultaneously grand, ugly, and profoundly momentous.

World War II was interwoven with every ruling. In some of the Court's most enduring decisions, the Justices decried the Axis powers' fascism and bigotry, and historically expanded American liberties as a conspicuous contrast. But in other rulings, particularly when FDR's actions were challenged, the Court demurred submissively. The Supreme Court and the Executive Branch, designed as two distinct forces in a system of constitutional checks and balances, emerged as allied institutions in wartime.

The Court struck down a forced-sterilization law in *Skinner v. Oklahoma*, a decision that would powerfully influence later landmark opinions on the right to sexual and reproductive privacy and other personal freedoms. It heard the *Barnette* case, in which two West Virginia schoolgirls refused to salute the flag out of adherence to their Jehovah's Witness faith. Ruling in their favor and against the compulsory nationalistic displays of America's enemies, the Court called the protection of basic liberties a "fixed star in our constitutional constellation." And the Court found for an African American crusader in Texas who bravely contested the constitutionality of whites-only primaries. His voting-rights victory established a key precedent for later battles for racial equity.

But in other rulings, the Court obsequiously deferred to the President's authority, citing the unique demands of war. In its most infamous decision, *Korematsu*, the War Court upheld the shameful incarceration of Japanese Americans. And in its strangest proceeding, spurred by private communications from FDR, the Court upheld a Roosevelt-ordered fast-track military tribunal that summarily tried a group of Nazi spies. The Justices offered no formal explanation until long after the accused saboteurs had been convicted and executed.

Alongside its pathbreaking leadership on civil liberties and civil rights, the Court offered another, darker message: "Discrimination which would ordinarily be abhorrent" to the Constitution was a permissible exercise of the broad war powers of Congress and the President. "Hardships," the *Korematsu* decision proclaimed, "are part of war, and war is an aggregation of hardships."

At the heart of these cases sat the individuals of the American mosaic. There was Jack Skinner, described by a law professor nearly seventy-five years later as "a one-footed chicken thief [who] laid the foundation for marriage equality"; Lonnie Smith, a Black dentist who insisted he had a constitutional right to vote, defended in the High Court by the young Thurgood Marshall; the Barnette sisters, Marie and Gathie, schoolchildren who practiced their faith against government opposition; William Schneiderman, a committed Communist represented at the height of the war by Wendell Willkie, FDR's Republican opponent in the 1940 presidential election. They would be vindicated, assured that the Constitution and the rule of law provide powerful protections for disfavored Americans.

And then there were the others: Fred Korematsu, who underwent eye surgery in an attempt to disguise his ancestry and avoid the cruelties of incarceration; Gordon Hirabayashi, prosecuted for refusing to obey anti-Japanese orders; and Albert Yakus, sentenced to jail for selling meat that violated wartime rationing rules—the inevitable casualties of war, in the words of the Court.

WHEN FDR DIED IN April 1945 a few weeks before the Nazi surrender, his Court unraveled and its infighting grew public and vicious. Less than five years after FDR's death, the Roosevelt Court was no more. Three Justices were dead and a fourth had resigned. Harry Truman had appointed four Justices.

The War Court left an indelible mark on the legal landscape. Its proudest and most enduring contributions vividly highlight the importance of protecting civil liberties in a time of national crisis. And its most objectionable and troubling decisions flowed from the unwillingness of Supreme Court Justices to stand up to the beloved President who appointed them. Both its accomplishments and its failings offer important lessons today, in a time of convulsive change at the Supreme Court.

· chapter one ·

WAR CLOUDS

PRESIDENT FRANKLIN ROOSEVELT AND JUSTICE FELIX FRANK-furter settled in for lunch at the White House on Monday, June 9, 1941. The previous week, Charles Evans Hughes had announced he would retire as Chief Justice. Roosevelt wanted Frankfurter's advice on the next Chief Justice.

Hughes would be a hard act to follow. With his regal bearing, care-fully groomed beard, and judicious manner, Hughes commanded great re-spect. He also had a wide-ranging and distinguished background. He was ending his second stint on the Supreme Court, having served as a Justice from 1910 to 1916 and then resigning to run as the Republican nominee against Woodrow Wilson in Wilson's reelection campaign—a race Hughes nearly won. Warren Harding had named him Secretary of State in 1921, and Herbert Hoover had appointed him Chief Justice in 1930. Hughes also had served as Governor of New York from 1907 to 1910; he and his fellow former New York Governor, FDR, teasingly called each other "Governor."

Public speculation focused on Roosevelt's Attorney General, Rob-ert Jackson, as the likely next Chief Justice. For good reason. FDR had told Jackson he would like him to head the Court, and FDR and Jackson were close. But Hughes, in a White House lunch with the President shortly after announcing his retirement, had recommended that FDR elevate Justice Harlan Fiske Stone. Stone was the longest-serving Justice, appointed in 1925 by Calvin Coolidge. Though a Republican, Stone had been one of the few Justices before 1937 who had often voted to uphold New Deal legislation. FDR now asked Frankfurter, whom he had appointed to the Court two years previously, for his thoughts.

In the back of their minds as the two men lunched was an all-consuming concern: the dire situation of the war in Europe.

IN JUNE 1941, NAZI Germany ruled Europe—from France to Poland; from Belgium to Greece; from the Netherlands to Czechoslovakia. Mussolini's Italy obsequiously supported Hitler. Since the fall of France in June 1940, England had stood almost alone in the face of Hitler's fury and onslaught. By the end of the month, Hitler would invade the Soviet Union as well. Japan, meanwhile, was on the march in Asia, attacking and invading China and Indochina.

FDR had been pushing the American public to support Britain while also navigating around isolationist sentiment. In September 1940, with the authority of a legal opinion by Attorney General Robert Jackson, the President announced a destroyers-for-bases deal. He directed the transfer of old American destroyers to Britain in return for ninety-nine-year leases on eight British military bases in the Western Hemisphere. That same month, the Roosevelt Administration persuaded Congress to pass the first peacetime draft in the nation's history, requiring conscripts to serve for one year. In March 1941, FDR convinced Congress to enact the Lend-Lease Act, giving him broad authority to provide Allies a wide range of supplies and materiel, with repayment terms set by the President.

But FDR knew that many Americans remained skeptical of foreign entanglement. At a campaign appearance in Boston on October 30,

1940, the President had made a promise to "you mothers and fathers": "I have said this before, but I shall say it again and again and again. Your boys are not going to be sent into any foreign wars." A Gallup poll in April 1941 reported that 81 percent of Americans opposed entering the war. But in a telling reminder that poll results can turn on a question's phrasing, 68 percent supported going to war if it was the only way to defeat Germany and Italy.

AFTER THE WAITERS LEFT the room, FDR pressed Frankfurter, a frequent visitor and close adviser. The President had been thinking of Jackson for Chief. But Hughes now had recommended Stone. What was Frankfurter's view?

"On personal grounds," Frankfurter replied, "I'd prefer Bob [Jackson]. . . . I feel closer friendship with Bob." And then Frankfurter lowered the boom. "But from the national interest . . . for me the decisive consideration, considering the fact that Stone is qualified, is that Bob is of your political and personal family, as it were, while Stone is a Republican. Now it doesn't require prophetic powers to be sure that we shall, sooner or later, be in war—I think sooner. It is most important that when war does come, the country should feel that you are a national, the Nation's, President, and not a partisan President. Few things would contribute as much to confidence in you as a national and not a partisan President than for you to name a Republican, who has the profession's confidence, as Chief Justice."

Characteristically, FDR did not commit himself. But he was persuaded. As Frankfurter well knew, the previous summer FDR had appointed two prominent Republicans to his Cabinet for precisely this reason: Secretary of War Henry Stimson, who had served as Secretary of War in the Taft Administration and Secretary of State in the Hoover Administration, and Secretary of the Navy Frank Knox, a Chicago newspaper publisher who had been Alf Landon's running mate on the Republican ticket against FDR in 1936. Frankfurter had played a key role in FDR's appointment of Stimson; Stimson had been an early and important mentor for Frankfurter, appointing him to key positions early in his career when Stimson served as US Attorney for the Southern District of New York and as Secretary of War.

In the days after his lunch with Frankfurter, FDR met with Stone and Jackson. FDR told his Attorney General that he probably would appoint Stone as Chief Justice in the interest of bipartisanship. He also would name Jackson as Associate Justice to take Stone's place. It seemed likely that Stone's tenure would be brief—he was sixty-eight—and that Jackson then would become Chief.

HUGHES'S SEAT WAS NOT the only Supreme Court vacancy on FDR's desk. On February 1, 1941, James McReynolds had retired from the Court. McReynolds had been the last of the "Four Horsemen" to leave the Court—the ultraconservative reactionaries who had formed a solid bloc rejecting progressive economic laws passed by states and the federal government. Public speculation predicted that FDR would appoint South Carolina Senator James F. "Jimmy" Byrnes, a highly effective advocate for FDR in Congress (and FDR's floor manager at the 1940 Democratic convention).

Byrnes had been a leader in the Senate's passage of the Lend-Lease Act. As columnists Joseph Alsop and Robert Kintner reported, "The lend-lease law came through the Senate so well as it did, chiefly because of the able management of Byrnes." Others had played a role as well. When Byrnes's colleague Senator Claude Pepper wanted advice about drafting the legislation, he consulted an old colleague: Justice Hugo Black, a former Alabama Senator. "We talked about it in his library," Pepper recalled. "He gave me some very helpful comments that were incorporated in the final version." Another sitting Justice—Frankfurter—participated even more extensively in shaping the Lend-Lease legislation, working directly with FDR and Stimson.

Byrnes also had memorably castigated famed aviator Charles Lindbergh, a leader of the isolationist "America First" movement. Lindbergh vehemently opposed FDR's foreign policy. He had argued, in testimony against the Lend-Lease Act, that it would be better for the United States if neither England nor Germany scored a decisive victory. Byrnes ridiculed the world's most celebrated pilot. Lindbergh knew as much about foreign affairs, observed Byrnes, as Wrong Way Corrigan, the national laughingstock who, in 1938, mistakenly flew to Ireland when he had intended to fly to California.

❧ ❧ ❧

ON JUNE 12, 1941, the President announced his Supreme Court appointments. Associate Justice Harlan Fiske Stone would become Chief; Attorney General Robert Jackson would take Stone's Associate Justice seat; Senator Jimmy Byrnes would fill the McReynolds vacancy. Public reaction was favorable. "All three appointments were received with enthusiasm at the Capitol," reported the *Washington Post.* "Mr. Roosevelt's selection of Justice Stone…was seen here as a bid for national unity comparable to the appointment last year of two Republicans as Secretary of War and the Navy."

In a sign of senatorial courtesy and friendship, within minutes the Senate confirmed their colleague Jimmy Byrnes on a unanimous voice vote (a vote by acclamation without the need for a roll call). After brief Judiciary Committee hearings, Stone and Jackson also were promptly confirmed by voice vote—Stone on June 27 and Jackson on July 7.

It was now, truly, Franklin Roosevelt's Court. He had appointed seven of the nine Justices—in order of appointment, Senator Hugo Black in 1937; Solicitor General Stanley Reed in 1938; Harvard Law professor and longtime FDR adviser Felix Frankfurter in 1939; Securities and Exchange Commission Chairman William Douglas in 1939; Attorney General Frank Murphy in 1940; and now Byrnes and Jackson. And FDR had elevated an eighth, Stone, to his current position as Chief.

It was an amazing turnaround. In the early years of his Administration, FDR had raged against the Justices' "horse and buggy" approach

and their invalidation of key New Deal programs. On the Supreme
Court at that time, only Justices Louis Brandeis, Benjamin Cardozo,
and Harlan Fiske Stone tended to support the Roosevelt Administration's position, occasionally joined by Chief Justice Hughes. FDR's
Court-packing proposal in 1937 had sought to add a seat for every Justice
over the age of seventy, but he had encountered fierce opposition, including institutional resistance from the Supreme Court itself, and the
bill had faltered. While it was pending, however, Justice Owen Roberts
voted to uphold progressive legislation by Congress and the states. His
change became forever known as the "switch in time that saved nine."
Although the timing and cause of Roberts's changed votes continue to
be debated, his perceived switch helped take the wind out of the sails of
FDR's Court-packing plan.

Though failing to adopt FDR's bill to enlarge the Court, Congress
passed a little-noticed important companion law. It provided full retirement benefits for any Justice who had reached the age of seventy and
served at least ten years. Over the next four years, five Justices retired, all
over seventy and all with more than ten years of service; two others died.
As a result, FDR was able to put his imprint on the Court in a way far
surpassing almost all previous Presidents.

They were not just Roosevelt's appointees. They had close relationships with him. This intimacy delighted the President but gave rise to
concern in some quarters. While generally lauding the three new appointments, the *Washington Post* editorialized, "All of his nominees,
except Justice Stone, have come from his own official family or his own
circle of advisers, and the current vacancies are to be filled by his Attorney General and his spokesman in the Senate.... So, in spite of Mr.
Stone's elevation to the Chief Justiceship, the President has laid this tribunal open to the charge of being a New Deal court."

❧ ❧ ❧

FDR IMMEDIATELY DEPLOYED HIS new symbol of national unity: Chief
Justice Harlan Fiske Stone. Stone was sworn in by a National Park
Service official at his vacation cabin in Estes Park, Colorado, on July

3, 1941. The next day, the Fourth of July, FDR gave a national radio address calling for national preparedness. Invoking the Pledge of Allegiance for inspiration, he said that the country could "never survive as a happy and fertile oasis of liberty surrounded by a cruel desert of dictatorship....And so it is that when we repeat the great pledge to our country and to our flag, it must be our deep conviction that we pledge as well our work, our will, and, if it be necessary, our very lives." And then, by prearrangement, the radio networks turned to the new Chief Justice in Colorado, who led the national radio audience in a recitation of the pledge. "It was a pulse-quickening moment," reported the Associated Press. "A vast unseen audience repeated the words pledging fealty to their flag."

The official swearing-in ceremonies of Byrnes and Jackson took place in FDR's White House office. Both were high-spirited events. Byrnes was sworn in on July 8. Although the Senate had immediately confirmed him on June 12, Byrnes had delayed taking his judicial oath so that he could serve as acting Majority Leader in the Senate until the ailing Majority Leader, Alben Barkley, returned. After Byrnes was sworn in, the President eyed the throng of Senators in attendance and boisterously cried, "The Senate is now in session, and galleries may applaud as much as they want." He said that he wished he could be Solomon and divide Byrnes in two, with one half remaining in the Senate and the other half going on the bench.

Jackson's White House swearing-in took place a few days later, on July 11, 1941. Immediately before his swearing-in ceremony, Jackson attended his last Cabinet meeting. FDR beamed as New Deal stalwarts and other visitors crowded into his office for Jackson's swearing-in. They included Roosevelt's close aides Harry Hopkins and Tommy Corcoran, Jackson's fellow Supreme Court Justices William O. Douglas and newly installed Jimmy Byrnes, and FBI Director J. Edgar Hoover.

❖ ❖ ❖

AS THE OFFICIAL SITTING of the new Court neared on the first Monday of October, it was clear it was a very different Supreme Court. In addition to the judicial philosophy of the Roosevelt Justices (which accorded far broader latitude for economic and government regulation), the average age on the Court now was fifty-six, compared with almost seventy-two at the time of FDR's Court-packing plan. Only two Justices had any judicial experience before joining the Court, and it was minimal. Black had served briefly as a police judge in Birmingham and Murphy as a municipal judge in Detroit, both before launching their political careers as Senator (in Black's case) and as Mayor and Governor (in Murphy's). Every detail of the new Court seemed a matter of public interest. With the retirement of the magnificently bearded Hughes, noted one Alabama newspaper, "the Supreme Court will be whiskerless...for the first time in 80 years." An AP headline summarized the new bench: "Young, Beardless, Liberal." Highlighting the sense of transition, iconic retired Justice Louis Brandeis died on Sunday, October 5, on the eve of the reconstituted Court's first official session on the first Monday in October.

Days before the start of the new Supreme Court term, on September 30, FDR hosted now Chief Justice Stone at the White House for a private meeting. The *Washington Post* reported that "Chief Justice Harlan Stone came in for lunch at the President's desk, stayed over time." There is no record of what they discussed.

It was traditional in those days for the President to host the Justices for an afternoon White House reception at the beginning of the Court's term. The 1941 gathering had an especially buoyant mood. In a sign of FDR's new ease with the institution he had battled, the President, for the first time, had designated it an informal affair. The Justices arrived in business suits rather than their black judicial robes, and the effervescent Roosevelt likewise wore a suit. "The President yesterday shattered another dressy, rigid precedent," reported the *Washington Post*. "Down through the years, the annual Presidential receiving of the Supreme Court justices has been held in the White House Blue Room with the justices in their robes and the President in his frock coat, striped pants and starched shirt. But this year Mr. Roosevelt...decided to rip off the frills."

The message of the friendly get-together was unmistakable: the war between the White House and the Supreme Court was over.

THE NEW COURT QUICKLY showed its receptivity to constitutional claims against oppressive government actions. Just weeks later, on November 24, 1941, the Supreme Court unanimously struck down a California law making it a crime to bring a nonresident to California if the nonresident was indigent. The Court's decision in *Edwards v. California* was momentous in a country still wracked by the Great Depression and its economic devastation. Twenty-seven other states had enacted similar statutes, commonly called "Okie laws" (a reference to the mass exodus from Oklahoma after the Dust Bowl of the 1930s).

The Supreme Court case involved a destitute Texas man, Frank Duncan, whose relatives helped him move to California. Duncan's brother-in-law, Frank Edwards, was criminally prosecuted for picking Duncan up in Spur, Texas, and driving him back to Edwards's home in Marysville, California. The Supreme Court opinion by Justice Byrnes—his first as a Justice—struck down the law. The Court ruled that a state's interference with an individual's travel from one state to another unconstitutionally interfered with interstate commerce; the decision established the constitutional right to travel. Byrnes's opinion pointedly rejected the notion that poverty reflected a "moral pestilence." "Poverty and immorality," stressed the former New Deal Senator, "are not synonymous."

Although the Court was unanimous in its result, four Justices indicated they would have taken a different approach. In separate concurrences, Douglas (for himself, Black, and Murphy) and Jackson stressed that they would rest the Court's decision, not on the interstate commerce ground, but on the principle that the ban on interstate travel for poor people violated the constitutional "privileges or immunities" guaranteed to every citizen by the Fourteenth Amendment. "The right of persons to move freely from State to State," wrote Douglas, "occupies a more protected position in our constitutional system than does the movement of cattle, fruit, steel and coal across state lines." And Jackson, immediately showing the style that would earn him a reputation as one of the Court's greatest writers, observed, "Unless this Court is willing to say that citizenship of the United States means at least this much to the citizen, then our heritage of constitutional privileges and immunities is only a promise to the ear to be broken to the hope, a teasing illusion like a munificent bequest in a pauper's will."

The war in Europe provided a dramatic backdrop for the Court's decision. Edwards's counsel contrasted the constitutional right to travel in the United States with "the non-democratic states of the world." Okie laws, he argued, risked turning the forty-eight states into "forty-eight economic concentration camps." In an amicus brief supporting Edwards, California Congressman John Tolan, chair of a House Select Committee on Interstate Migration, emphasized that "the suspicions, jealousies,...scheming and conniving of one country against the other on the continent of Europe" must not be replicated through interstate travel barriers in the United States; such a balkanized structure would interfere with the need to "prepare for national defense...without regard to State lines."

When the Court announced the *Edwards* decision, commentators also viewed it in light of the ongoing global crisis. At a time when "human rights are abridged throughout the world," the *New York Post* editorialized, "it is an invigorating fresh breath to find such re-assertion of rights here." The *Washington Post* hailed the Court's repudiation of such "un-American legislation." And a New Jersey newspaper editorial on the decision proclaimed, "Be Proud You're American."

ON MAY 27, 1941, FDR delivered a nationwide radio address, one of his trademark "fireside chats," declaring "an unlimited national emergency" and calling for "the strengthening of our defense to the extreme limit of our national power and authority." He emphasized that the United

States would "give every possible assistance to Britain and all who, with Britain, are resisting Hitlerism or its equivalent with force of arms." But the country continued to be ambivalent, with some bitterly opposed to involvement. In a sign of the continuing divisions, on August 12, 1941, the House of Representatives passed an extension of military draftees' one-year service by only a single vote in a dramatic 203–202 vote.

In the months after FDR's "national emergency" speech, the Justices made extraordinary public speeches strongly supporting FDR's war mobilization. On June 14, 1941, Owen Roberts told a Philadelphia audience that the nation should join in a "unity of sentiment" supporting FDR on defense mobilization; as the "darkness of tyranny spreads westward," the President "knows better than any of us the gravity of the threat to our security." Four days later, Frankfurter told students at Radcliffe that the pacifist and isolationist view that "war never settles anything" must be rejected: "The Civil War settled slavery. This war will settle the quality of your lives and your children's lives."

The Justices' speeches on the international situation continued. Stanley Reed exhorted a Bridgeport, Connecticut, gathering on July 14, 1941 that "force must be met by force" and that "now it is for us to show the world that we are a united people." At a national emergency rally at Madison Square Garden on August 19, 1941, Roberts proclaimed, "We subscribe to every word of the great declaration of the aims of democracy so recently made by our President and the Prime Minister of Great Britain" in the Atlantic Charter, a joint statement issued days before by FDR and Churchill after a secret shipboard meeting. "Every hour's delay," he continued, "is fraught with great danger. Now, not tomorrow, we must highly resolve to meet this threat by toil and sacrifice."

That same day, Frank Murphy, the Court's only Catholic, told the Knights of Columbus conference in Atlantic City, New Jersey, that its members should support FDR's "policy of aiding those countries which are offering resistance to the aggression of Nazi Germany"; the antireligious views of the Soviet Union, now fighting the Nazis after Hitler's June invasion of his former ally, are "not today the greatest danger." And, four days later, Black emphasized to University of Alabama students in Tuscaloosa that the United States must ensure the victory of freedom— "peaceably if we can, forcibly if we must."

At least some of these public statements were closely coordinated with the President and the White House. FDR, for example, had enlisted Murphy to speak to the Knights of Columbus and promptly let him know that he was "tickled to death" by Murphy's comments. Even when there was no direct coordination, the Justices knew that they were publicly and vigorously rallying support for the President on his highest priority.

The prospect of Justices taking to the hustings to advance the President's policy on a matter of intense public debate was an overt sign of political support unimaginable in later years. The Supreme Court—and the federal judiciary generally—is intended in our separation of powers to be an independent branch and an important element of checks and balances, not an auxiliary unit furthering political and policy goals, however laudable.

The Justices' public statements continued. On September 26, 1941, Douglas told the Civitan Club of Atlanta that "the sons of freedom are aligned against the hosts of tyranny"; the American defense initiative must be a "total effort, whether we are workers in an airplane factory, farmers, housewives, business executives or government officials." And Robert Jackson told the American Bar Association in Indianapolis on October 2, 1941, that twenty centuries of civilization would not be "worth a tinker's damn" unless "the sort of thing the world now witnesse[d]" could be stopped.

The Justices' families also became involved in support for victims of the attacks by the Axis powers (Germany, Italy, and Japan). Jackson's son William, according to a press account, "had been in England at the beginning of the Battle of London and had served in the British Ambulance Corps.... His duties were to go out after air raids to pick up casualties and bring them to hospitals."

Felix and Marion Frankfurter, who had no children of their own, had been hosting three lively English children—Ann, Venetia, and Oliver

Gates—since the summer of 1940. Their father, Sylvester Gates, was a barrister who had been a Frankfurter protégé at Harvard Law School; he and his wife reluctantly but gratefully accepted the Frankfurters' offer to care for the children and provide them with shelter from the Nazis' bombing raids on England. The Frankfurters regularly brought their British charges to see the President, who delighted in their antics.

The Justices' spouses threw themselves into war relief efforts— Agnes Stone in an organization providing relief for Yugoslav refugees; Elizabeth Roberts in a "Piccadilly Arcade" to raise money for the Royal Air Force Benevolent Fund; Winifred Reed in Bundles for Britain and Overcoats for Britain; Marion Frankfurter in an organization helping women serve in national defense. "What did we do with our time before there was a war in Europe?" Mildred Douglas asked a *Washington Post* reporter.

As THE YEAR PROGRESSED, it seemed that some Justices might move off the Court and into war-related government service. Reporters raised the possibility that Murphy might leave for a position as High Commissioner of the Philippines (a post he had held in the 1930s), or as Ambassador to Mexico, or perhaps back to his perch as Attorney General. But Murphy coveted the Secretary of War slot. He pressed FDR to jettison Stimson and appoint him to replace the distinguished elder statesman, a wildly implausible suggestion that FDR deflected with his usual deftness. Frankfurter, viewing Murphy's judicial skills as inferior, urged FDR to ease Murphy off the Court by enticing him with a lesser government job, and he even at times became an intermediary (perhaps self-appointed) in FDR's communications with Murphy on the subject. FDR and Murphy also directly discussed possible positions in meetings and lunches, but nothing came of it.

FDR and William O. Douglas, meanwhile, had serious conversations about Douglas leaving the Court and heading domestic war mobilization. But, after initially reaching out to Douglas, FDR seemed to back away from finalizing the arrangement.

The President seemed to see the Court as his personal bullpen rather than as an independent and impartial branch. And at least some Justices seemed to see their Court seats as possible launching pads for more compelling posts.

On Saturday morning, December 6, 1941, Douglas met privately with FDR at the White House for forty-five minutes. While there is no record of the conversation, it seems likely they were discussing the possibility of Douglas taking on a major war mobilization role. But whatever plans they might have been considering were overwhelmed by the events of the next day, Sunday, December 7, when the world would change for every American, and for every Justice.

· chapter two ·

PEARL HARBOR

O N Sunday afternoon, December 7, 1941, in his study on the second floor of the White House, President Roosevelt ate lunch at his desk with his closest and most trusted aide, Harry Hopkins. At 1:40 p.m., an urgent call came from Secretary of the Navy Frank Knox. Japanese bombers had attacked Pearl Harbor, the home of the Pacific fleet. Throughout a long afternoon and evening, the Navy updated the President with reports about the stunning damage and rising casualties.

By the time the Japanese attackers had completed their work, the toll was enormous. American deaths and injuries, military and civilian, totaled more than 3,500. The Japanese had destroyed or damaged eight American battleships, three destroyers, three light cruisers, and four auxiliary ships; they also had devastated the Pacific air fleet.

Justice Hugo Black and his wife Josephine enjoyed a relaxed Sunday lunch at the Maryland farm of Secretary of the Interior Harold Ickes. Senator Tom Connally of Texas, Black's former colleague from his

Senate days, was the life of the party, regaling the guests with amusing stories. As he was driving back to his historic home in Alexandria, Virginia, Black had the radio on and suddenly heard the bulletin with the astounding news of the Pearl Harbor attack.

At his sprawling estate in McLean, Virginia, Justice Robert Jackson was listening to classical music on the radio while reading. An emergency report about Pearl Harbor interrupted the musical program. Jackson felt "a deep sense of shock. . . . I had known that we were not far from war. Still, I was shocked by the boldness of the attack as well as by its success."

Shortly before noon that Sunday, Justice Felix Frankfurter talked on the phone with his former student John J. McCloy, now one of Stimson's closest aides at the War Department, about an American lawyer who was acting on behalf of the Japanese government. Afterward, comfortably ensconced in his Georgetown home, Frankfurter settled in to consider the Supreme Court cases to be argued in the coming week. He heard the alarming news, and his attention shifted from the Supreme Court briefs before him.

George Hutchinson, the eighteen-year-old aide in the Supreme Court library, was also sitting in his Capitol Hill home, listening to his radio and cheering on quarterback Sammy Baugh in the game between Hutchinson's beloved Washington Redskins and the Philadelphia Eagles, when a news flash interrupted the football game and reported the attack. Stunned, Hutchinson listened to the rest of the game, pleased to hear his Redskins defeat the Eagles in the final game of the year. When he left to get a loaf of bread from a local grocery, he found the streets eerily deserted. He realized that everybody was at home. They were glued to their radios, trying to follow the latest developments about the attack.

While many huddled at home, others gathered in a crowd outside the White House, looking up at the lights in the White House executive offices and waiting for word about how the nation would respond.

❖ ❖ ❖

UPON HEARING THE PEARL Harbor news, Frankfurter immediately swung into action. Concerned that legal issues would instantly arise, he left an urgent message at the White House: "If the President cannot get hold of the Attorney General or the Solicitor General he might want to have a good lawyer standing by in an advisory capacity." Frankfurter recommended Assistant Secretary of State Dean Acheson. A prominent Washington lawyer, he had been Frankfurter's protégé as a student at Harvard Law School and, on Frankfurter's recommendation, a law clerk to Justice Brandeis. (Acheson later would serve as Secretary of State in the Truman Administration.) Frankfurter gave the White House a phone number for Acheson to give to the President and, for good measure, the number of Acheson's housekeeper. The Justice separately sent FDR a letter assuring him that "the whole American people are behind you" and that "the God of Righteousness is with you—and you are His instrument."

Later that afternoon, FDR took a call from Prime Minister Winston Churchill. Churchill had heard the news about Pearl Harbor while dining in London with Roosevelt's emissaries, including U.S. Ambassador John Winant. Churchill immediately understood that the surprise attack meant that the United States would now enter the war—and that, at last, England would no longer be alone.

At Churchill's request, Winant called Roosevelt and, after initial pleasantries, handed the phone to the Prime Minister. "Mr. President," Churchill asked, "what's this about Japan?" "It's quite true," FDR replied. "They have attacked us at Pearl Harbor." And then FDR delivered the message Churchill had long been waiting to hear in words Churchill, like Roosevelt a former top Navy official, would truly understand: "We are all in the same boat now."

At 8:30 p.m. on December 7, Roosevelt met with his Cabinet in the Blue Room. He told them it was the most serious crisis any Cabinet had faced since Lincoln met with his Cabinet at the start of the Civil War.

At 10:00 p.m., the President, accompanied by the Cabinet, met with congressional leaders. Roosevelt reported on the extent of the casualties and the damage. The Senators and members of the House sat in stunned silence. Finally, Senator Tom Connally, Hugo Black's lively luncheon companion earlier that day, exploded. He castigated Secretary of the Navy Knox. "I am amazed by the attack by Japan," said Connally, "but I am still more astounded at what happened to our Navy. They were all asleep. Where were our patrols?"

The White House announced that President Roosevelt would appear before a joint special session of Congress at noon the next day to report on the attack.

In the House chamber of the Capitol, anticipation built for the President's arrival. Vice President Henry Wallace and Speaker of the House Sam Rayburn sat perched in large chairs just behind the Speaker's podium. FDR's Cabinet was present, with Secretary of War Henry Stimson, Secretary of State Cordell Hull, and Secretary of the Treasury Henry Morgenthau in the front row. Also close to the podium were congressional leaders and the nation's highest military officers, in their full uniforms. Sitting just behind the military men was the ubiquitous British ambassador, Lord Halifax.

The Supreme Court Justices sat prominently in the front row in the center of the House chamber, near the Cabinet Secretaries. They were arranged in order of seniority—Chief Justice Stone, then Roberts, Black, Reed, Frankfurter, Douglas, Murphy, and, finally, the two newest Justices, Byrnes and Jackson. The Justices had taken the unusual step of adjourning the Court so that they could attend the joint session and hear the President.

At 12:29 p.m. in the House chamber, a thunderous voice announced, "The President of the United States." A silence fell on the audience. "Then through the door," the *Washington Post* reported, "headed toward the Speaker's dais, came the President. He was leaning on the arm of his eldest son, Capt. James Roosevelt. The President wore a black frock coat and striped trousers. His son wore the uniform of a Marine Corps officer. A tremendous ovation rose up as the Chief Executive advanced to the dais to confront a battery of 12 microphones. He smiled, but it was a strained, sad smile."

Leaning on the podium, FDR stood and gazed out at the notables arrayed before him. In a seven-minute speech broadcast to a radio audience of eighty million, he set forth the facts of the Japanese attack with a cold fury. "Yesterday, December 7, 1941, a date which will live in infamy, the United States of America was suddenly and deliberately attacked by naval and air forces of the Empire of Japan." He recounted Japanese treachery in pretending to engage in negotiations with the United States while preparing for the surprise attack. He then related in blunt terms, "The attack yesterday on the Hawaiian islands has caused severe damage to American naval and military forces. Very many American lives have been lost." He described subsequent Japanese attacks, following the Pearl Harbor assault, on Malaya, Hong Kong, Guam, the Philippines, Wake Island, and Midway Island.

"Hostilities exist," he soberly reported. "There is no blinking at the fact that our people, our territory and our interests are in grave danger. With confidence in our armed forces—with the unbounding determination of our people—we will gain the inevitable triumph—so help us God."

He concluded, "I ask that the Congress declare that since the unprovoked and dastardly attack by Japan on Sunday, December 7, a state of war has existed between the United States and the Japanese empire."

The audience immediately rose in a roaring standing ovation. In the front row, Justice Hugo Black wiped tears from his eyes.

Within an hour, both houses of Congress voted to declare war on Japan. The vote in the House was 382–1. The only opposing vote was cast by Representative Jeannette Rankin, a Congresswoman from Montana who also had voted against US entry into World War I. The Senate vote was unanimous, 82–0.

Later that afternoon, the President signed the declaration. It was official. The United States and Japan were now at war.

Four days after the Pearl Harbor attack, on Thursday, December 11, Germany and Italy declared war on the United States. President Roosevelt immediately asked for reciprocal declarations of war. Congress responded with alacrity, passing its own declaration of war against those nations the same day. America's war with all three Axis nations was now official, and with it, the isolationist movement in the United States collapsed. On December 11, the America First Committee announced that it was disbanding. Its putative leader and hero, Charles Lindbergh, stated that he no longer opposed the war.

After the joint session of Congress on December 8, the Justices trooped back to the Supreme Court to take the bench and resume their business at 2:30 p.m. Sitting shortly after FDR's stirring speech, they heard arguments in a dry railroad case from Texas.

The Justices also announced eleven decisions. In the immediate wake of the President's call to arms, the cases must have seemed painfully prosaic. They addressed federal taxes; the rights of sureties under the National Bank Act; an Interstate Commerce Commission administrative interpretation; the Longshoremen's and Harbor Workers' Act; a property dispute involving a Native American tribe; the enforceability of a state's orders in another state; and two criminal cases. Black wrote his wife about FDR's speech at the joint session and the Justices' return to the Court: "It seems difficult to concentrate on individual disputes between Americans at a time when the entire country is participating in a world dispute."

One decision announced that day addressed important First Amendment principles, and for those paying attention, it was a significant bellwether about an emerging dynamic on the Court. In a 5–4 decision, the Court set aside contempt of court citations against controversial labor leader Harry Bridges and the *Los Angeles Times* for their public comments criticizing a judge. Black wrote for the majority, and Frankfurter for the dissenters. It was one of the first signs of a rift among the Roosevelt Justices. "The legend that a 'packed' court would mean a set of rubber stamps," editorialized the *St. Louis Star and Times*, "is dying a deserved death."

Behind the judicial curtains, the fight was far more intense than the public knew. Frankfurter was irate that he was on the losing side. Believing Stanley Reed to be his best hope in the five-Justice majority,

Frankfurter incessantly lobbied Reed at least to concur separately and not join Black's opinion, thereby denying Black a majority. Frankfurter even drafted a concurrence for Reed. But Reed held firm, to Frankfurter's dismay.

Frankfurter had assumed he would be the intellectual leader on the Roosevelt Court. But now it was Black, the Alabama populist Senator, rather than Frankfurter, the Harvard Law School professor, who was leading the Court on a fundamental First Amendment case, with Black taking a broad view of constitutional rights and Frankfurter failing to garner a majority for his narrower interpretation. For Black, the First Amendment was "a command of the broadest scope that explicit language, read in the context of a liberty-loving society, will allow." For Frankfurter, the speech had to yield to the need to respect the independent authority of courts, particularly "at a time when it is repudiated and derided by powerful regimes"; he chided Black, "We must be fastidiously careful not to make our private views the measure of constitutional authority."

It was a relationship—and a competition—that would, over time, become increasingly intense and toxic.

THE NEXT DAY, TUESDAY, December 9, the Court heard arguments in *United States v. Bethlehem Ship Building Company*, a case concerning federal payments for ships built by Bethlehem Ship Building Company during World War I.

Byrnes, until recently a powerful Senator, was struck by the incongruity. At the very time the nation faced the emergency of a new world war, the Supreme Court was poring over contractual payments from the last world war. "As I listened to the arguments," Byrnes recounted in his memoir, "my mind kept turning not only to 'the law's delays' but to the irony of our considering a case arising out of the construction of ships twenty years ago, when so many of our naval vessels had been destroyed only the day before."

Two days later, FDR summoned Byrnes to the White House. When they met that Thursday morning on December 11, the President was in bed surrounded by documents and newspapers, as he often was. "His appearance shocked me," Byrnes recalled. "As he told of developments since Sunday afternoon, he was more nervous than I had ever seen him. We continued our discussion as he dressed and wheeled himself into the bathroom to shave. I sat on the only seat in the room. He was worried about the steps to be taken immediately to put the nation on a war footing, saying we were not prepared either militarily or psychologically for the ordeal confronting us."

Roosevelt asked Byrnes for help on war-related legislation, and Byrnes immediately agreed. "I mentioned my thoughts while listening to the Bethlehem case," Byrnes wrote. "Jokingly, I told him that I had once thought him wrong in urging mandatory retirement of Supreme Court justices at the age of seventy; now it seemed preferable that in time of war only men over seventy should be allowed to serve on the Court." Men under seventy, Byrnes was saying, should be in the thick of the action, away from the Court. He then made an offer to FDR. Byrnes's extensive experience in government, he told the President, would allow him "in wartime to perform greater service than upon the Court; and if he ever concluded I could be of more value elsewhere, I hoped he would call upon me." In the meantime, he would be pleased to work on any tasks FDR assigned him while he remained a Justice, as the President had suggested.

Roosevelt promptly directed Attorney General Francis Biddle to confer with Byrnes on all emergency war legislation and executive orders and to have Byrnes work on getting the legislation expedited. Confirming the President's directive, Biddle reassured FDR, "All defense legislation is being cleared by the departments and then through Jimmy Byrnes, who takes care of it on the Hill."

Byrnes swiftly set to work on what became known as the First War Powers Act. It gave the President sweeping new authority to shape the government as he saw fit for the war effort. The President could "make such redistribution of functions among executive agencies as he may deem necessary" for "national security and defense, for the successful prosecution of the war, for the support and maintenance of the Army and Navy, for the better utilization of resources, and for the more effective exercise and more efficient administration by the President of his powers as Commander in Chief of the Army and Navy."

Byrnes played a major role in drafting the bill and securing its passage. He worked closely with Speaker of the House Sam Rayburn, Senate Majority Leader Alben Barkley, and other congressional leaders. The fact that Byrnes was now a sitting Supreme Court Justice did not deter him, nor did it bother the congressional leaders and Roosevelt Administration officials.

The new war legislation sped through both Houses. The President signed it on December 18, only a week after his shaving-in-the-bathroom conversation with Jimmy Byrnes. While the breathtakingly broad legislation can be justified by the war emergency, the immersion in the executive and legislative processes by a sitting Justice cannot be, especially because the Court might be called on to interpret its provisions or rule on its constitutionality.

Byrnes was not the only Justice, that Pearl Harbor week, who sharply felt the contrast between the gravity of the war and the nature of the Court's cases. Jackson later recalled, "It was a very depressing time to be on the court. I've never forgotten that the [week] after Pearl Harbor we heard argued two cases involving the question of whether country club members were taxable on their greens at golf courses. I sputtered much about hearing such a damn petty question all day with the world in flames." To make matters worse, the Chief Justice assigned him to write both opinions.

On December 29, Jackson wrote FDR, "I take this occasion to say what I am sure you already know—that if at any time I can serve you better elsewhere, I am glad to respond."

Other Justices also sought to contribute. Frankfurter sent the President a stream of war-related messages. Following an FDR fireside chat on December 9, Frankfurter telegrammed Roosevelt that the President's "soberly confident voice" would "bring confidence without complacency to our people" and "gird them for the gloriously grim task ahead." On December 17, he sent Roosevelt a memo detailing "a good many talks I have had since September 1939 with some of the best brains who were intimately familiar with the defects and inadequacies of the British and French war effort." On December 18, he wrote FDR that his presidential letter about a soldier killed in action would "live in history" with Lincoln's famous letter to a grieving mother. And on December 23, Frankfurter forwarded a suggested Christmas message from Dorothy Thompson, an acclaimed journalist who had been expelled from Germany in 1934 for her critical coverage of the Nazis.

Frank Murphy, meanwhile, was focused on the battle in the Philippines. He had served as Governor General of the Philippines and then as High Commissioner of the Philippines, appointed by FDR, from 1933 to 1936. Acquired by the United States in the Spanish-American War, the Philippines were now a commonwealth on the path to independence. But the situation in December 1941 was bleak, with the Japanese on the verge of control. "I actually wish I was back in the islands right now helping those people," Murphy told a reporter. "It seems awful to be so helpless when your friends are being ruthlessly killed by an army that knows no mercy. I feel that the things I helped to create—the democracy and the independence of the islands—are now being destroyed by the Japanese army." He broadcast a radio message of resistance to the Filipinos. "Show them that it matters not how greatly we love peace, for always we love freedom more," he proclaimed. "Shoot straight, never falter!"

Chief Justice Stone focused on civil defense. Stone and his wife Agnes participated in a neighborhood defense preparation meeting near their DC home. They listened intently as an air-raid warden set forth the procedures in an aerial attack, their attendance prominently reported by journalists. But Stone was not reassured. "We have no defense against an airplane attack so far as I know," he confided in a letter two days later, "and if one occurs we will have to sit and take it."

Despite Stone's misgivings, Washington had quickly become a war town. Blackouts at night were intended to make Nazi bombing sorties more difficult by shrouding the streets in darkness. The Associated Press advised, "If you don't want to bump into somebody in a blackout, take along a white handkerchief or a newspaper. Or draw a cigarette so that the glow will be a signal to the person approaching you. And walk slowly. Those tips come from Britain's blackout experiences." DC residents, reported syndicated columnist Jack Stinnett, "started runs on black cloth for use in blackouts, and adhesive tape to interlace house and shop windows to prevent breakage in air raids."

Even Washington's historic sites were darkened. "For the first time since floodlighting was introduced here," Stinnett continued, "the Capitol dome, the Washington Monument, the Lincoln Memorial, and the White House spend their nights in darkness." At the Supreme Court, hastily arranged heavy curtains blocked windows throughout the building.

But black cloth was not going to win a war. In the days after Pearl Harbor, concern about the lack of preparedness for the attack became a focus of national attention. Senators and members of the House discussed the creation of a special congressional committee to investigate. The President moved promptly to preempt a congressional inquiry.

The wily FDR thought that a presidential commission would do the job. To head it, he needed somebody who would be perceived as independent, fair-minded, and nonpartisan. He also wanted somebody who would be reliable for a sensitive mission. He settled on his candidate: Justice Owen Roberts, a Republican and the only man on the Court who did not owe his position to the President. Roberts also had investigative experience, having served as a special Deputy Attorney General in World War I prosecuting espionage in Pennsylvania and as an acclaimed special counsel investigating Teapot Dome, the Harding-era scandal about the leasing of national oil reserves. And in the months leading up to the war, he had vociferously backed the President and his war planning.

On Tuesday, December 16, at 5 p.m., FDR met with Roberts at the White House to ask him to head a presidential commission investigating responsibility for any lack of readiness at Pearl Harbor and reporting directly to him. Roberts would chair the commission, and his panel would have four other members, all military men—three retired military officers (a General and two Admirals) and one current Air Corps Brigadier General.

Roberts immediately agreed. He was not surprised by the offer. In another example of Frankfurter's wide-ranging role in Administration affairs, earlier that day, Stimson aide John McCloy had consulted Frankfurter about Roberts's possible appointment. After sounding out Roberts, Frankfurter had told McCloy of Roberts's willingness to chair the commission. That evening, the White House announced the President's appointment of the Roberts Commission. Stone granted Roberts a leave of absence from the Court until the Commission reported its findings to the President.

The next day, the new Commission on Pearl Harbor met for ninety minutes with Secretary of War Stimson and Secretary of the Navy Knox. The Commission announced it would head shortly to Hawaii for fact-finding. Roberts directed the Commission members not to give press interviews or make public statements.

Congressional leaders announced that, in light of the new Roberts Commission, they would not move forward with their own investigations. House Naval Affairs Committee Chairman Carl Vinson of Georgia said his committee would not undertake any inquiry because "the President has named such an outstanding board to conduct an investigation"; his Senate counterpart, David Walsh of Massachusetts, called the President's appointments "in every way commendable." Within days, Congress passed legislation giving the Roberts Commission subpoena power.

Commentators praised FDR's creation of the Roberts Commission. "The outstanding characteristic of the investigative board," wrote *Boston Globe* columnist Jay Hayden, "is that its stature and independence are such as to make it free to condemn even the President himself, if it should find that his actions or failure to act contributed to the unreadiness of the Hawaiian garrison.... Justice Roberts is one member of the Supreme Court who never before has received an appointment from President Roosevelt. More than that, he is the highest ranking Republican in the government, excepting Chief Justice Harlan F. Stone, who was appointed to his present position by President Roosevelt." The *St. Louis Post Dispatch* editorialized that "the board of inquiry appointed by the President is one which will command public confidence.... [The] Associate Justice of the United States Supreme Court is admirably suited to weigh facts and give them judicial appraisal."

But controversy also emerged. "Selection of Roberts rocked the capital tonight," the *New York Daily News* reported, "because the detaching of a Supreme Court Justice from his duties is without precedent in American history." That historical statement was erroneous. The first two confirmed Chief Justices, John Jay and Oliver Ellsworth, for example, both left the country for extended diplomatic missions while on the Supreme Court, at the request of Presidents George Washington and John Adams. But the criticism highlighted the unease some felt about this assignment for a Supreme Court Justice. Syndicated columnist Frank Kent, an arch FDR critic, was the most scathing. "Once a man ascends to... the highest court in the land," wrote Kent, "he should cease to be available for any other public or political post." Kent noted that Roberts's absence would strain the Court, leaving it shorthanded. "It does seem," he acidly concluded, "that among 130,000,000 people Mr. Roosevelt easily might have found some man of the required character and capacity without raiding the Supreme Court." But these were contrarian public views in a national chorus of praise for Roberts and the Commission.

Chief Justice Stone, not yet six months into his new job, was not pleased either. He may even have been a source for Kent, who noted in his column that Roberts's selection was a surprise "to the Justice's colleagues on the Supreme Bench." On December 18, Stone wrote his two sons, "You have probably seen that the President has appointed Justice Roberts to head the Commission to investigate the Pearl Harbor disaster. That puts a serious crimp in our work as his absence may cause all sorts of complications. The matter is made worse by the fact that the Government is drawing on Byrnes for advice in legislation which will cut down his writing." And then in a clear echo of Kent's column (or perhaps the comment in Kent's column was an echo of a point he had heard from the Chief Justice), Stone continued, "With one hundred and thirty million people in the United States to draw from to do these jobs it seems as though the Court might have been left alone."

❧ ❧ ❧

ON DECEMBER 22, A special visitor arrived at the White House. The excitement of his visit captivated the Justices, like all Americans.

Winston Churchill was a guest for the holidays. He and Roosevelt, now formal allies in the war effort, worked long hours, poring over military maps and discussing war strategy. Both leaders also enjoyed drinks and merriment. FDR presided at his usual cocktail hour each night, mixing drinks. Churchill was not a fan of the President's concoctions; he frequently snuck his own drinks in before and after the gatherings.

At one point during the stay, FDR wheeled into Churchill's room and encountered Churchill, fresh from a bath, without a stitch of clothing. The Prime Minister gleefully told FDR that he had "nothing to conceal" from the President. FDR delighted in the encounter, telling his secretary Grace Tully that Churchill was "pink and white all over" and his cousin Margaret (Daisy) Suckley that Churchill looked like a "pink cherub."

On Christmas Eve, before an enthusiastic crowd of fifteen thousand, Roosevelt and Churchill lit the national Christmas tree on the South Lawn of the White House. FDR asked his visitor to say a few words. "For one night only," Churchill announced, "each home throughout the English-speaking world should be a brightly-lighted island of happiness and peace.... Let the children have their night of fun and laughter. Let the gifts of Father Christmas delight their play. Let us grown-ups share to the full in their unstinted pleasures before we turn again to the stern task and the formidable years that lie before us, resolved that, by our sacrifice and daring, these same children shall not be robbed of their inheritance or denied their right to live in a free and decent world."

The day after Christmas, on Friday, December 26, at 12:30 p.m., Churchill spoke to a joint session of Congress in the Senate chamber.

Supreme Court Justices again took positions in the front row, prominent in the packed room with Senators, Representatives, Cabinet Secretaries, and diplomats. Lord Halifax, the British ambassador, again was on hand. So too was the Soviet Ambassador, Maxim Litvinov.

Throughout the Capitol, soldiers stood guard in full military uniform, bearing fixed bayonets and trench helmets. Squadrons of Secret Service agents supplemented the security. Outside, on the Capitol Plaza, thousands surged to try to get a glimpse of the Prime Minister.

Churchill charmed his audience by reminding them that his mother, Jennie Churchill, was American. "The fact that my American forbears have for so many generations played their part in the life of the United States, and that here I am, an Englishman, welcomed in your midst, makes this experience one of the most moving and thrilling in my life," Churchill began. And to gales of appreciative laughter, he continued, "I cannot help reflecting that if my father had been American and my mother British, instead of the other way around, I might have got here on my own." The Senators and Representatives relished the suggestion that he might have been elected to their ranks. He was a member of the club, not a foreigner.

But the Prime Minister had a serious message for the nation newly at war. He scorned the Axis nations and vowed victory: "What kind of a people do they think we are? Is it possible they do not realize that we shall never cease to persevere against them until they have been taught a lesson which they and the world will never forget?" Churchill had deftly established the inseparable and indissoluble bond between the United Kingdom and the United States—a single "people," a single "we."

The audience interrupted Churchill's thirty-five-minute address often with raucous applause. One journalist reported that "Supreme Court Justice Felix Frankfurter beat his hands together until they were red." Another observed that Frankfurter "fidgeted in his seat, made nervous gestures, and applauded with great vigor when the Prime Minister made a point."

As Churchill finished, the chamber rose in a standing ovation. Churchill looked out at the crowd and bowed. He flashed his signature two-fingered "V for victory" sign. From his front row seat, Chief Justice Harlan Fiske Stone immediately raised his own hand to the Prime Minister with his two fingers raised, a gesture widely reported by journalists across the country.

The message was clear: the Court was in the fight.

· chapter three ·

WAR

THE NEW YEAR BEGAN ON A SOMBER NOTE. PRESIDENT ROOsevelt proclaimed a National Day of Prayer for Thursday, January 1, 1942. The President and Winston Churchill attended services at Christ Church in Alexandria, Virginia, where George Washington had prayed.

In Hawaii, at high noon, Justice Owen J. Roberts participated in a prayer and memorial ceremony at Nuuanu Memorial Park, overlooking the Honolulu harbor. Roberts led a procession at the graveyard. Six Native girls recited an ancient Hawaiian chant for departed warriors, and a group of Hawaiians sang "Aloha 'Oe," a "hail and farewell" song composed in 1878 by then Princess (and later Queen) Lili'uokalani. The assembled crowd of several hundred people joined in patriotic hymns and "The Star-Spangled Banner." The wife of the Honolulu Mayor placed a wreath on a memorial for more than 350 sailors and others killed at Pearl Harbor, now buried at Nuuanu, and she placed another wreath on the graves of three Honolulu firemen who perished fighting the flames at Hickam Field, an Army post. Other sailors and soldiers killed at Pearl

Harbor were buried separately in a military cemetery, to which civilians were denied access for security reasons.

Thousands of flowers poured into the cemetery from around the territory, including an enormous wreath from Maggie's Inn, a waterfront café that sailors favored. At the high point of the ceremony, Justice Roberts approached the burial places and solemnly placed brightly colored leis on the graves.

Roberts and his fellow Commissioners had arrived in Hawaii on December 22 and would remain until January 10. Working through the Christmas holiday season, they held hearings from 9 a.m. until dusk; at that point, blackout restrictions required them to cease until the following morning.

The Commissioners began with private depositions of military personnel on Army and Navy bases. In early January, Justice Roberts formally requested testimony from any civilians with information that might shed light on military preparedness at Pearl Harbor the morning of the attack.

The Commissioners heard the citizens' testimony at the Royal Hawaiian Hotel, a magnificent pink Moorish-style hotel on the Waikiki beach that had opened in 1927 and now was heavily guarded. Far from the Supreme Court's marble palace in Washington, DC, the converted luxury hotel became the base of operations for the Justice spearheading the government's inquiry into its most sensitive issue.

OWEN JOSEPHUS ROBERTS WAS born in 1875 in the Germantown section of Philadelphia. His father was the son of Welsh immigrants and prospered as a hardware merchant and wagon dealer; his mother was of Scots-Irish descent. A prodigious reader, Owen attended Germantown Academy, where he excelled on the debate team. Entering the University of Pennsylvania at the age of sixteen, he thrived in his studies, with a focus on the classics, and graduated Phi Beta Kappa. He went on to the University of Pennsylvania Law School, where he again distinguished himself, finishing at the top of his class and serving as an editor of the law review.

Roberts became a leading lawyer at two Philadelphia law firms and taught commercial law courses at the University of Pennsylvania Law School. He quickly earned a reputation as a commanding courtroom presence and represented clients on all sides of legal disputes, plaintiffs as well as defendants. Roberts also served for three years in the Philadelphia District Attorney's office. Along the way, he married Elizabeth "Betty" Rogers of Fairfield, Connecticut. She had graduated from Mount Holyoke College, where she was a classmate and close friend of Frances Perkins, the woman who would be FDR's Secretary of Labor. Owen and Betty had one daughter, their only child.

After World War I, President Woodrow Wilson's Attorney General appointed Roberts to serve as "Special Deputy Attorney General," responsible for prosecuting Espionage Act violations in the Philadelphia area. Roberts gained several convictions as part of a wave of controversial prosecutions against war critics that raised troubling civil liberties issues.

Roberts came to national attention through the Teapot Dome scandal of the Harding years. Federal government officials had awarded lucrative government oil leases in questionable circumstances, including at Teapot Dome in Wyoming. A Senate investigation revealed tawdry and complex corruption at the highest levels of government. In February 1924, six months after Warren Harding's sudden death, Congress passed a law requiring that President Calvin Coolidge appoint a special counsel, subject to Senate confirmation, to investigate the scandal and bring appropriate prosecutions. Coolidge announced that he would appoint not one but two special counsels—one Democrat and one Republican. His choice for the Democratic counsel was Atlee Pomerene, a former Senator from Ohio.

Pennsylvania Senator George Wharton Pepper enthusiastically recommended Roberts for the Republican appointment. At a White House meeting with Roberts and Pepper, the notoriously laconic Coolidge commented, as he pointed to a picture of his own Vermont farm, that he understood Roberts was a farmer. The owner of a farm in rural Pennsylvania, Roberts replied, "Guernseys are my money crop and I've never shown a loss." Coolidge asked about Roberts's knowledge of public land laws. Roberts replied, "Nothing whatever." When Senator Pepper tried to interject, Coolidge rebuked him: "When I want an interpreter, I'll call on you." Roberts assured the President he had taught property law for several years and, while he lacked direct familiarity with public land laws, they would not present a difficulty.

That was the entirety of the interview. "Silent Cal" offered Roberts the position on the spot. "If you are confirmed," the President advised, "there is one thing you must bear in mind. You will be working for the government of the United States—not for the Republican Party, and not for me. Let this fact guide you, no matter what ugly matters come to light." The Senate promptly confirmed both Pomerene and Roberts.

Roberts received widespread acclaim as an effective counsel. Securing a conviction of former Interior Secretary Albert Fall, he also argued and won two unanimous Supreme Court decisions regarding Teapot Dome. Justice Louis Brandeis reported to Felix Frankfurter (then a Harvard Law School professor) that Roberts had made an "uncommonly good impression on our Court."

In 1930, President Herbert Hoover's initial pick for a Supreme Court vacancy—a US Court of Appeals judge from North Carolina named John J. Parker—ran into trouble in the Senate over a controversial antilabor opinion he had written and racist remarks he had made in his 1920 campaign for Governor. The Senate rejected Parker on a bipartisan 41–39 vote.

Hoover turned to Roberts as a consensus nominee. Roberts did not have a conspicuous antilabor record, and he had served as a trustee of historically Black Lincoln University. On May 20, 1930, the Senate unanimously confirmed him.

Roberts arrived on the Supreme Court at a fraught time. One wing of the Court comprised "the Four Horsemen"—archconservatives who claimed the Constitution required striking down a broad swath of

federal and state laws concerning economic regulation and social justice. With varying personalities and backgrounds, they shared a hostility to progressive political initiatives: Willis Van Devanter, a former US
Court of Appeals judge appointed by President Taft; James McReynolds,
a virulent antisemite and racist appointed by President Wilson; George
Sutherland, a former US Senator from Utah appointed by President
Harding; and Pierce Butler, a former railroad lawyer from Minnesota
also appointed by Harding.

The Court included a wing of three liberals: reformer Louis
Brandeis (a Wilson appointee, though that did not spare him from the
antisemitism of his fellow Wilson appointee McReynolds); Boston patrician Oliver Wendell Holmes (a Theodore Roosevelt appointee); and,
in a surprise to many that he was in the liberal camp, Harlan Fiske
Stone (a Coolidge appointee and a former Wall Street lawyer, law school
dean, and, briefly, Attorney General). The ninth Justice was the Chief,
Charles Evans Hughes.

In what was viewed as a momentous development during the spring
of 1937, Roberts sided with the liberals and Hughes to uphold Washington State's minimum wage law in the *West Coast Hotel Co. v. Parrish*
case. In sharp contrast, the previous year, Roberts had joined the Four
Horsemen to throw out New York's minimum-wage law in *Morehead
v. New York ex rel. Tipaldo*. Two weeks later, Roberts again joined the
liberals and Hughes in sustaining the National Labor Relations Act, a
major New Deal initiative, in *NLRB v. Jones & Laughlin Steel Corp.*
For many, it seemed the only thing that had changed with Roberts was
FDR's Court-packing threat earlier that year.

The historical reality is more complicated. Before the *West Coast
Hotel* decision in 1937, Roberts had sometimes voted with the liberals
and Hughes even while often voting with the Four Horsemen. Roberts
later contended that his apparently conflicting votes on the minimum-
wage laws had been about technical differences in the cases; evidence
has surfaced that Roberts voted to uphold the Washington law immediately after it was argued in December 1936, before FDR's proposal to
expand the Court. In addition, legal historians debate whether Chief

Justice Hughes had persuaded Roberts the previous summer, in a visit to his farm, that the Supreme Court needed to be more deferential in approving state and federal legislation—an explanation suggested by Secretary of Labor Frances Perkins based on her memory of discussions with her longtime friend Betty Roberts.

Whatever the reality, the public perception at the time was certainly that Roberts had "switched" his allegiances on the Court in the spring of 1937, with the "switch in time" becoming a commonly repeated quip. After the *West Coast Hotel* minimum-wage decision, moreover, Roberts frequently voted to uphold the constitutionality of economic legislation, and the threat to major New Deal undertakings seemed to have passed.

The Pearl Harbor Commission was not Roberts's first extrajudicial presidential appointment. In 1932, soon after he joined the Supreme Court, Hoover appointed him to be the "umpire"—the lead adjudicator—on the German-American Mixed Claims Commission for the "Black Tom" disputes. The cases concerned German liability for losses from alleged German sabotage against a munitions plant on Black Tom Island in New York Harbor in 1916 and 1917. Roberts led the Commission to a $50 million judgment against Germany in 1939, which Hitler promptly repudiated. But Roberts's service impressed observers. John J. McCloy, then a private lawyer in the case, recalled that "the towering figure of Roberts," with his "great power of expression and clear style," produced "a magic effect"; his "mind and character promptly took command of that confused situation and held it through many vicissitudes and attempted diversions to the very end."

The question now, in January 1942, was whether Roberts's work on the Pearl Harbor Commission—on a far more compressed schedule and on a matter of far greater national urgency—likewise would be viewed as generating a "magic effect."

❖   ❖   ❖

By mid-January, Roberts was back in Washington and working on the report with his fellow Commissioners.

Felix Frankfurter, always eager to be in the mix, wrote FDR on Saturday, January 17 urging him to meet with Roberts privately. "Owen Roberts," Frankfurter confided, "is, as you well know, the most forthright of men. But he is not only—thank God!—very modest. He is also truly shy. And so I venture to suggest that you get him alone, and not with the other members of his Board, to tell you of things that have no proper place in their report—particularly on matters of personnel pertaining not to the past but to what lies ahead." Roberts apparently had formed some views on military leaders or Cabinet Secretaries and Frankfurter, ever keen to have a hand in Roosevelt Administration matters, sought to make sure that Roberts shared them with the President.

The next day, according to White House logs, Roberts met with FDR alone at the White House for fifty minutes, from 5 p.m. to 5:50 p.m. Again, no record exists of a private, extended conversation between the President and a sitting Justice.

Roberts, meanwhile, continued his leave of absence from the Court. Ultimately, there were twenty-one Supreme Court cases in the 1941 term in which Roberts did not participate.

On Friday, January 23, at a session with reporters in his office, FDR commented that Roberts was almost done with his report. The next morning, Saturday, January 24, Roberts drove himself to the White House. He and the President met for two hours, beginning close to noon, in the President's study on the second floor of the White House, and Roberts presented FDR with his Commission's report. As Roosevelt carefully read every word of the document, Roberts recalled, the President made "a sort of running commentary." At one point, he asked Roberts "what reasons the officers out there . . . gave for having thought there would never be an air attack."

Always the master public strategist, FDR decided to release the entire report that night. After confirming with Roberts that there would be no risk of disclosing harmful information to US enemies, he reversed previous White House statements that the report would be partially withheld. The report noted that, in deference to national-security sensitivities, it did not include quotes from documents or witness testimony. The President summoned his aide Marvin McIntyre, tossed the report across the table, and directed, "Mac, give this to the Sunday papers in full."

As Roberts left the White House that Saturday afternoon, he was mobbed by reporters. He stood on the White House portico, garbed in his overcoat and derby hat, and spoke in generalities without revealing the content of the report. The report contained findings of fact and conclusions, he said. It fixed responsibility and named names. The President had read it carefully. All five members of the Commission had signed the report. His work was done, and the Commission would now go out of business.

The reporters followed Roberts to his car, positioning themselves between the Justice in the driver's seat and the open car door so that Roberts could not close his door. But he declined to say more.

White House Press Secretary Stephen Early announced that the Commission's report would be mimeographed and made public promptly. He told reporters that FDR considered it a "painstaking and most thorough investigation and report."

The White House released the entire document at 9:00 that evening. The fifty-one-page report sharply criticized the two most senior officials in Hawaii—the Navy's commander in chief of the Pacific Fleet, Admiral Husband E. Kimmel, and the Army's commanding general of the Hawaiian Department, Lieutenant General Walter C. Short, both of whom had been relieved of their command by FDR in December. It found them guilty of "dereliction of duty," a most serious offense. The Admiral and the General had received repeated warnings about a possible attack but had not taken appropriate actions in response. With devastating consequences, they also had failed to communicate adequately with each other. Accordingly, "the Japanese attack was a complete surprise to the commanders and they failed to make suitable dispositions to meet such an attack."

But the Commission absolved the most senior government officials. Secretary of State Cordell Hull had acted appropriately, passing on information to other departments as he had received it. So too had Secretary of War Stimson and Secretary of the Navy Knox. The President was not mentioned at all.

Junior officers likewise were exonerated. "Subordinate commanders executed their superiors' orders without question. They were not responsible for the state of readiness prescribed." And, contrary to rumors that excessive drinking and partying by sailors and soldiers on Saturday night had inhibited their response on that fateful Sunday morning, the Roberts Commission carefully noted that, "except for a negligible number, the use of intoxicating liquor on the preceding evening did not affect their efficiency."

The Commission's findings thus validated the approach of FDR and his Administration to Pearl Harbor. It blamed the two top military officials who already had been relieved of command and nobody else.

Commentators praised the report. Syndicated columnists Drew Pearson and Robert Allen proclaimed, "The nation will always be proud of and grateful to the five members of the Pearl Harbor board of inquiry, headed by Justice Owen J. Roberts, for their blunt and courageous report. It was a great tribute by true patriots to the honor and gameness of their country." A South Carolina newspaper agreed. "Many people, including a number of newspaper editors, thought the investigation would be another 'white washing job,' but evidently the investigating board undertook its task in a thorough business like manner and went to the very heart of the situation, placing the blame where it appropriately belonged." And an Illinois newspaper emphasized, "Only in a country which has the courage and the understanding to face the facts could a report so devastating and detailed be given to a public in wartime."

Congressional leaders of both parties hailed the report. Senate Democratic Leader Alben Barkley of Kentucky praised it for providing the "whole truth"; his counterpart, Senate Republican Leader Charles McNary of Oregon, commended the "frank report," and Republican Senator Warren Austin of Vermont said that it would "aid in establishing confidence."

Eventually, however, the Roberts Commission report was criticized for perceived failings and omissions. As early as 1944 and 1945, with the war still ongoing, the lack of preparedness for the Pearl Harbor attack was the focus of another Executive Branch inquiry and two congressional investigations. Controversies about the accuracy and completeness of the report continued after the war. Criticisms of the Roberts Commission varied: the initial discussions in Washington with high-ranking participants should have been transcribed and under oath; the Commission had too many conversations with principals, such as Stimson, outside the strictures of the investigation; the Commission's mandate was too narrow; the Commission had inadequate investigative resources. Students of presidential investigations and commissions later invoked the Roberts Commission as an example of what *not* to do—a "rush[] to judgments" and "an ill-considered effort to appease an impatient president and an angry public."

But in January 1942, the report, completed only six weeks after Roosevelt appointed the Commission and only seven weeks after the attack, brought some information and reassurance to a still-shocked nation. The aura of impartiality conferred by a Supreme Court Justice overseeing four Commissioners with military backgrounds provided an important stamp of reliability—exactly as FDR had hoped.

Four days after giving the President his report, on Wednesday, January 28, Roberts returned to Philadelphia to give a luncheon address at the Warwick Hotel to the United Charities Campaign Workers. In his first public remarks since the release of the report, Roberts issued a scathing call for mobilization and engagement. He warned that "complacency," "smugness," and a feeling that "it can't happen here" had contributed to the Pearl Harbor disaster. Now, Roberts told the crowd, the nation could not afford such laxity. "I don't have to tell you," he implored the luncheon guests, "that this country faces a crisis the like of which we have never known. You know that however much the burden grows heavier, how much the purse grows lighter, we civilians have got to bear the brunt of this thing." To a burst of vigorous applause, he told the audience that "what we must have is greater sacrifice for democracy."

And then, for Owen Roberts, it was back to work at the Court.

❖ ❖ ❖

ROBERTS WAS NOT THE only Justice working on war-related activities outside the Court. In early January, newspapers reported that FDR was likely to appoint a new domestic chief to oversee the war economy. FDR told Congress in his State of the Union address on January 6 that he wanted, on the home front, to "keep the wheels turning and the fires burning twenty-four hours a day and seven days a week." Appointing a domestic economic czar was a way to jump-start the economic effort.

Newspapers reported that the shortlist for the new post included Justices James Byrnes and William Douglas. Journalists speculated about whether Byrnes or Douglas would take a leave of absence from the Court, as Roberts had done with the Commission, or leave it entirely.

Douglas was eager to take on new war assignments. He wrote a friend in December 1941, "Now that we are in a life or death struggle...I have been turning over in my mind possibilities for a more active participation on my part. If the President should ask me to take over the Defense program, I would of course not hesitate....It's hard to keep one's mind in the work with the violent issues joined." Douglas acknowledged his Supreme Court work—"I suppose it is as important as anything else to keep important and essential domestic functions operating"—and then pivoted to his thirst for action: "I felt like joining the Marines...and taking a personal swat."

In mid-January, Douglas's supporters launched a public campaign for his appointment, circulating an open letter urging his selection and releasing it to the press. The President quickly ended the suspense. He announced that Donald Nelson, a former Sears, Roebuck executive (and, since the summer of 1941, head of one of the numerous overlapping defense mobilization agencies), now would be in charge of wartime production.

Frankfurter promptly wrote Roosevelt on Nelson's appointment with his usual effusive praise. "It took Lincoln three years to discover Grant, and you may not have hit on your production Grant first crack out of the box," Frankfurter gushed. "But the *vital* thing is that you have created the function—the function of one exclusive, 'final' delegate of your authority. It's simply grand—indispensable for *your* conduct of the war."

Byrnes, meanwhile, continued and intensified his war-related activities. White House Press Secretary Stephen Early told reporters that Byrnes had informed the President he would volunteer in any capacity, "even as a messenger boy."

Throughout the first several months of 1942, Byrnes worked closely with the President and his aides. In fact, it was Byrnes who pushed aggressively for a domestic economic czar. Byrnes sent a memo to Harry Hopkins, FDR's closest adviser, arguing for such a position. Byrnes pointed to the chaos and confusion of the overlapping federal agencies on war mobilization, many of which had been created haphazardly in the previous months and years as the possibility of war loomed. Power and authority needed to be centralized in one man, Byrnes urged. The individual should be somebody close to FDR, somebody FDR fully trusted. "Call him Hopkins," Byrnes said in a lighthearted reference to the President's associate as the ideal type of candidate. When Byrnes learned that Hopkins had not even forwarded his memo, Byrnes brought it directly to the President. Four days later, FDR appointed Nelson to the post.

Just as with the First War Powers Act, Byrnes played a major role in drafting the Second War Powers Act, enacted on March 27, 1942. The law provided FDR and his executive departments and agencies with sweeping powers on an astonishing range of subjects—from seizing property for "military, naval, or other war purposes" to compelling "the joint use of equipment, terminals, warehouses, garages, and other facilities"; from expanding financial power to relaxing the naturalization requirements for any noncitizen who "serves honorably in the military or naval forces of the United States during the present war"; from waiving "navigation and inspection laws" to using Civilian Conservation Corps workers "to protect the munitions, aircraft, and other war industries."

In the Senate, Byrnes had been a master tactician regarding the federal government's organization. Before joining the Court, he had successfully steered a massive government reorganization bill enhancing the President's authority. He now used that insider's knowledge in crafting a bill expanding war powers throughout the massive Executive Branch.

It was widely known that Byrnes was working with the President and his Administration on war legislation. News accounts included general references to his role. One article reported, "Justice James F. Byrnes has become an intermediary between congress and the White House." And one columnist noted that Byrnes was devoting so much "time to the war program at the request of the president" that "his secretaries at the court haven't had as much work to do as the secretaries of the other justices.... The latter group therefore are taunting the idle secretaries: 'They're fiddling while Byrnes roams.'"

Byrnes's White House activities were so consuming that they prevented him from being at the Supreme Court for the announcement of a significant opinion on January 12, 1942—even though the opinion was his own.

The case concerned Ira Taylor, a Black laborer in Georgia. He had been convicted of violating a Georgia law that made it a crime for a worker to receive advance payment and then either not complete his work or not pay the money back with interest. Routine employment disputes thus became a cudgel of criminal law, used to force involuntary labor by those who could not afford repayment.

The Supreme Court unanimously struck down the Georgia law as an unconstitutional "peonage" law that violated the Thirteenth Amendment's ban on slavery and involuntary servitude. Although race was never mentioned in the Supreme Court's *Taylor v. Georgia* opinion, it was an obvious subtext. Taylor's Supreme Court brief prominently noted his racial identity, discussed the effect of the law on African Americans in Georgia, and argued in the brief's concluding sentence that striking down the peonage law would be "a second Emancipation Proclamation for the present debtor slaves in Georgia."

The racial subtext made the identity of Byrnes as the opinion's author particularly notable. As a politician, Byrnes was not quite in the category of bombastic bigots like his colleague Cotton Ed Smith of South Carolina or Theodore Bilbo of Mississippi. But Byrnes was fully in step with the white supremacist mores and policies of the ruling party in South Carolina. Byrnes's *Taylor* opinion was short and to the point—and it delivered a fatal blow to the racially charged peonage law.

When the Court rendered the *Taylor* decision on Monday, January 12, Harlan Fiske Stone, rather than Byrnes, announced Byrnes's opinion. One South Carolina newspaper reported that Byrnes had been too busy at the White House: he was "conferring with President Roosevelt on the problem of coordinating the nation's war production." In fact, at the very moment the Court announced his peonage decision on January 12, Byrnes was meeting with FDR to discuss Byrnes's memo urging creation of a domestic wartime production czar.

A SHORT TIME LATER, the Supreme Court decided the case about World War I shipbuilding contracts that had irked Jimmy Byrnes when it was argued two days after the Pearl Harbor attack. But, ironically, the case turned out to have direct and immediate significance for the nation now in its second world war.

The issue was whether Bethlehem Steel Corporation could retain a lucrative 22 percent profit on its wartime shipbuilding activity for the government. Only six Justices participated in the case. Roberts was away performing his Commission duties, and Stone and Jackson had recused themselves because of their previous positions as Attorney General. A majority of the participating Justices held in a 4–2 decision by Hugo Black that the contract permitted the windfall: the government must be held to its bargain, and Bethlehem Steel could retain the profits, however exorbitant. But the Court had harsh words for wartime profiteering, which it called "scandalous." Black's opinion emphasized that Congress could mandate strict limits on profits. Even while rejecting the government's position in *Bethlehem* itself, the Court was inviting aggressive new congressional action targeting the problem.

Felix Frankfurter, who had worked in the War Department in World War I, disagreed with the ruling. He was furious that, in his view, the shipbuilder was permitted to reap the benefits from gouging the government during the war. He pounded his fist on the bench as he read his dissent and stated, "The law is not so primitive [as to allow the windfall]...It is not difficult in these days to appreciate the position of negotiators for the Government in time of war and to realize how much the pressures of war deprive them of equality of bargaining power in situations where bargaining with private contractors is the only practicable means of securing necessary war supplies."

Black's majority opinion, with its invitation to legislative action, caused an immediate stir in Congress. The previous month, a little-known Senator from Missouri, Harry Truman, had released a major report focusing on the emerging problem of war profiteering. The Supreme Court's opinion now directly sparked legislation addressing the problem. One Senator emphasized that, under the *Bethlehem Steel* decision, the country was "absolutely defenseless" unless it passed new legislation. Another confidently proclaimed, "If the provisions embodied in this bill had been the law at the time the Bethlehem Steel Co. made the contract, the decision of the Supreme Court would have been directly to the contrary." Black, the former Senator, undoubtedly knew that his harshly worded opinion would spur prompt action from his former colleagues on this sensitive and vital war-related issue.

Once again, although one Justice wrote the opinion, another released it. This time, Stanley Reed announced Black's decision. Black was two hundred miles away in Norfolk, Virginia, celebrating with Governors, Senators, Representatives, and high-ranking military and naval officials as they attended the launch of the *Alabama*, a new thirty-five-thousand-ton battleship named for the state Black had represented in the Senate.

❖ ❖ ❖

WHEN SENATOR HUGO BLACK became FDR's first Supreme Court Justice in 1937, the Alabama Senator had a secret: his relationship with the Ku Klux Klan. Revelations about that secret would rock the country soon after Black was sworn in as a Justice.

Black was the youngest of eight children, born in rural Clay County, Alabama, in 1886. As a child, he loved watching trials in the county courthouse, soaking up an atmosphere that included games of checkers and dominoes just outside the building. An avid bookworm, he attended Ashland College, went to Birmingham Medical College for one year, and then pursued his original passion, graduating from the University of Alabama School of Law in Tuscaloosa in 1906.

Black enjoyed a varied legal career in Birmingham—thriving in personal injury law, where he found it easy to connect with juries; serving as a police court judge for nearly two years; winning election as county solicitor (the public prosecutor position). In World War I he joined the Army, becoming a captain while serving stateside the entire time and then resuming his private law practice after the war.

In 1920, Black, then thirty-four years old, began courting a young woman who dazzled him from the moment he saw her. He soon married Josephine Foster, thirteen years younger than him and a glamorous descendant of prominent families in Alabama and Tennessee. In quick succession, Hugo and Josephine had two sons (Hugo Jr. and Sterling) and then, after a miscarriage and other frustrations over several years, a daughter (JoJo).

In 1926, Black ran for an open Senate seat. He won the contested primary and cruised to victory in the overwhelmingly Democratic state. Senator Black became a prominent populist, railing against corrupt businesses and unscrupulous lobbyists. Winning a second term in 1932, he enthusiastically supported the new President and his New Deal program.

In the midst of the 1937 fight over FDR's controversial plan to pack the Supreme Court, Justice Willis Van Devanter, one of the archconservative Four Horsemen, announced his retirement, opening up the first Supreme Court vacancy of the Roosevelt presidency. FDR had promised a Supreme Court appointment to the Senate Majority Leader, Joe Robinson of Arkansas. But in July 1937, a sudden heart attack killed Robinson.

A few weeks later, FDR summoned Black to his White House study. The President showed him a Supreme Court nomination form and said with a gleeful twinkle, "Hugo, I'd like to write your name here." Black responded, "Mr. President, are you sure that I'll be more useful to you on the Court than in the Senate?" "Hugo," replied FDR, "I wish you were twins because [the new Majority Leader Alben] Barkley says he needs you in the Senate, but I think you'll be more useful on the Court." Black accepted.

As always, FDR operated on multiple levels—what Frances Perkins called his "four-track mind." He knew that Black would be a strong voice for upholding the legality of social and economic reforms at a pivotal point in Supreme Court history; at fifty-one years old, Black was relatively young; the South had almost no representation on the Court. And most deliciously for FDR, at a time when he was feuding with some Senators over his Court-packing proposal, Black had been one of the plan's most aggressive and outspoken champions.

The next day, on August 12, in a surprise announcement on the Senate floor delivered by a White House messenger, FDR formally nominated Hugo Lafayette Black to replace Van Devanter. Four days later, the Senate Judiciary Committee approved Black's confirmation.

The following day, the Senate considered Black's nomination. Montana Senator Burton Wheeler later recalled that some Senators "felt Hugo went a little too far in support of Roosevelt and that on the Court he would vote the New Deal line." Conservative opponents raised a legal objection—that Black was ineligible under the Constitution because the compensation for a Justice had been increased while he served in the Senate—but it gained little traction. More attention was paid to a charge by eccentric New York Senator Royal Copeland, described by the *New York Times* as an "ardent opponent of the New Deal" even though he was a Democrat. Copeland repeated rumors that Black once had belonged to the Ku Klux Klan and that the KKK had strongly supported his 1926 Senate campaign.

William Borah, a prominent Republican from Idaho and the "dean of the Senate" as its longest-serving member, opposed Black's confirmation. But he rose on the Senate floor and rejected Copeland's Klan attack. "There has never been at any time one iota of evidence that Senator Black was a member of the Klan," Borah thundered. "Senator Black has said in private conversation...that he was not a member of the Klan." Although Black did not publicly address the accusation, it seemed that the issue had been put to rest. The Senate voted 63–16 to confirm Black, with the opposition coming from ten Republicans and six Democrats.

On August 19, 1937, Black took his oath and became the seventy-sixth Supreme Court Justice and the first FDR-appointed Justice. One week later, he and Josephine set sail for a celebratory monthlong vacation in Europe; they would return shortly before the start of the new Supreme Court term on the first Monday in October.

Beginning on September 13, 1937, Ray Sprigle, a reporter at the *Pittsburgh Post-Gazette*, published a bombshell series of articles. Sprigle reported that Black had been a member of the Ku Klux Klan and had quietly resigned before the Senate campaign. After he won the Democratic primary, the Klan awarded him a "golden passport" (a lifetime membership) at an event Black attended, and, Sprigle said, Black accepted it. Sprigle's series provided definitive proof—official Klan records—detailing Black's past Klan membership and his close relationship with the Klan in the years before his first Senate victory. Sprigle's articles would win him the Pulitzer Prize in 1938.

The Sprigle series ignited a political firestorm. Senator Royal Copeland, eagerly returning to the attack, announced that they must "keep this man from wearing the black robe of justice by day and the shameful white robe of the Klan in the dark of the night." Besieged by reporters in London, Black refused to comment. So, too, did the man who appointed him, President Roosevelt. FDR kept a watchful distance, gauging whether Black could survive the controversy. When Black and his wife arrived back in the United States by ship at Norfolk, Virginia, on September 29, reporters mobbed them. Black continued his silence on the revelations but suggested that he would give a radio address.

Two nights later, at 9:30 p.m. Eastern time on Friday, October 1, Black took to the airwaves on a national radio broadcast. Fifty million people listened. In an eleven-minute speech, Black admitted that he had joined the Klan "about fifteen years ago." But he maintained that he had resigned and cut all ties and that he had no continuing relationship with the Klan. He emphasized his progressive record in the Senate, voting with liberal Senators. He also professed support for "Negroes," Jews, and Catholics. And he proclaimed, without a hint of irony, that "some of my best and most intimate friends are Catholics and Jews." Although Black did not discuss his motive for joining the Klan, he later gave varying explanations, including that he was joining many organizations at that time for political purposes and that, for juries in his legal cases, he wanted to compete with opposing lawyers who belonged to the Klan.

Black's speech received sharp criticism. Massachusetts Senator David Walsh, a Democrat who had not voted on the Supreme Court confirmation, declared that Black should have announced his resignation in his radio address: "If the President had known all the facts, he would not have named him" and the Senate would not have confirmed him. The *New York Times* decried Black's nomination as a "tragic blunder," calling it "a deplorable thing that a man who has ever taken the oath of allegiance to a sinister and destructive organization should now take his place on the highest court of justice in this country." The *Pittsburgh Post-Gazette* editorialized, "The record of the past is unmistakable....No man with that record ought ever to sit upon the highest court in the United States of America." The *Washington Post* observed that Black "has now, too late, stripped off the mask to show the kind of man he really is"; resignation from the Court would be "the only adequate reparation which he could now make to the President, the Senate, and the Nation as a whole."

But three days after his radio address, on the first Monday in October, Black took his seat on the Supreme Court bench. As he hoped, the issue died down and the controversy blew over.

SHORTLY AFTER BLACK'S *BETHLEHEM Steel* opinion, the Supreme Court established a rare exception to the First Amendment's protection of speech. It concerned the insult of calling somebody a fascist.

In Rochester, New Hampshire, a historic town in the southeastern part of the state, residents complained to the City Marshal that Walter Chaplinsky, a Jehovah's Witness, was denouncing organized religion as he distributed his sect's literature on a public sidewalk in the center of town. At one point, when the Marshal approached him, Chaplinsky denounced the Marshal as "a damned Fascist" and "a God damned racketeer"; he added that "the whole government of Rochester are Fascists or agents of Fascists." Chaplinsky was promptly arrested and charged with violating a New Hampshire law banning "any offensive, derisive or annoying word to any person who is lawfully in any street or other public place." He was convicted and sentenced to six months in prison. Now he sought reversal on First Amendment grounds.

In an opinion by Justice Frank Murphy, the Supreme Court unanimously upheld Chaplinsky's conviction. Murphy emphasized that, under the New Hampshire Supreme Court's interpretation, the law prohibited only "fighting words"—"what men of common intelligence would understand would be words likely to cause an average addressee to fight"—and that such fighting words are not constitutionally protected. The First Amendment, Murphy continued, does not protect statements that "by their very utterance, inflict injury or tend to incite an immediate breach of the peace....Argument is unnecessary to demonstrate that the appellations 'damned racketeer' and 'damned Fascist' are epithets likely to provoke the average person to retaliation, and thereby cause a breach of the peace."

In early 1942, the Supreme Court needed little explanation to conclude that "fascist" was a quintessential "fighting word"—an early sign that the war would play an important defining role in shaping the Court's doctrine and decisions.

· chapter four ·

TAKING A STAND

B Y APRIL 1942, THE US EXPERIENCE OF THE WAR HAD BEEN bleak. Setback after setback unfolded for the Americans in the Pacific—at Pearl Harbor, at Wake Island, in the Philippines, and on and on. For America's allies, the war news was similarly grim. Britain had suffered major losses in Singapore, Burma, and Hong Kong. The Nazis, meanwhile, continued their brutal domination throughout Europe.

But on Saturday, April 18, Americans for the first time had reason to cheer when General Jimmy Doolittle led a daring aerial raid on Tokyo. The nation thrilled in response. While the actual damage of the Doolittle sortie was minimal, the psychological boost for a worried American public was enormous. A Pennsylvania newspaper observed, "The sky was gray and overcast in the Valley this morning, but the sun shone more brightly in our hearts than it has since Pearl Harbor. For with the dawn came the news...that Japan has gotten a taste of the bitter medicine she began to dose out on December 7." The excitement swept the capital as well. "It's Just the Beginning, Beams Smiling and Elated Washington," announced one wire service headline.

❀ ❀ ❀

SIX WEEKS LATER, ON June 1, 1942, the Supreme Court announced a decision drawing a sharp contrast with the Nazis' program of forced sterilization. *Skinner v. Oklahoma* became a foundational opinion in later Supreme Court decisions on personal privacy, reproductive freedom, and marriage equality.

Jack Skinner was a one-footed chicken thief. Born in Oklahoma in 1907, he lost his foot six inches above the ankle in a farming accident as a teenager. By the time he was twenty, he had been convicted of stealing chickens; by the time he was thirty, he also had been convicted twice of robbery with firearms.

In 1935, Oklahoma passed a law permitting the state's Attorney General to impose forced sterilization on any individual convicted three times of "a felony involving moral turpitude." Men would be subjected to a vasectomy, women to a salpingectomy (the surgical removal of fallopian tubes). The law excluded a broad range of white-collar crimes, including "embezzlement," "political offenses," and violations of "revenue acts."

The eugenics movement had surged in the United States in the 1920s and early 1930s. Proponents sought sterilization of the "feeble-minded"—those perceived to be "defective"—to improve the human race. Mainstream elites, including the American Medical Association and the American Bar Association, enthusiastically embraced eugenics. The Catholic Church was the only major national organization to oppose the practice.

In 1927, the Supreme Court, in an 8–1 opinion written by Oliver Wendell Holmes, upheld a Virginia eugenics law permitting the forced sterilization of nineteen-year-old Carrie Buck. In one of the most notorious statements in Supreme Court history, Holmes summarily dismissed Buck's constitutional challenge by harrumphing, "Three generations of imbeciles are enough." As later research established, Carrie Buck did not even have an intellectual disability, and her forced-sterilization procedure was maliciously instigated by a family whose nephew had raped and impregnated her. But Holmes's *Buck v. Bell* opinion provided an imprimatur for eugenics. By 1933, twenty-seven states had enacted some form of sterilization statute.

Oklahoma's sterilization law was notable in targeting convicted criminals for forced sterilization rather than, as in *Buck v. Bell*, "mental defectives." Also unlike the statute in *Buck v. Bell*, the Oklahoma law did not permit a targeted person to show on an individualized basis that he or she should not be subject to the procedure because the alleged objectionable traits would not be passed on to children. The only issues to be tried in the Oklahoma procedure were whether the individual had been convicted of three or more felonies involving moral turpitude and whether the vasectomy or salpingectomy could be completed "without detriment to his or her general health." If the answer to both questions was affirmative, the forced sexual sterilization would proceed.

As the 1930s progressed, parallels between the Nazis' program of sexual sterilization for racial superiority and the American eugenics doctrine became clear. As law professor Victoria Nourse relates in her definitive study of *Skinner*, as early as December 1933, in a story on eugenics, the *New York Daily News* featured photos of the Governor of Oklahoma, Justice Oliver Wendell Holmes, and Adolf Hitler. From the earliest days of his rule, Hitler aggressively pushed a far-reaching sterilization program to further his goal of race purification.

Oklahoma prisoners rebelled against the sexual sterilization laws—organizing a litigation committee and funding it with their canteen accounts; speaking to the press; even staging escapes. One prisoner's mother wrote Eleanor Roosevelt, who replied that she could do nothing to help.

In public statements, the prisoners explicitly drew comparisons to the Nazis, complaining of the "Hitlerization" they faced. After the first inmate chosen to be sterilized by Oklahoma escaped, the state turned to its next candidate: Jack Skinner.

Skinner's lawyers, funded by the prisoners' litigation committee, mounted a constitutional challenge to the forced vasectomy. But the

Oklahoma Supreme Court rejected the challenge. It split 5–4 in favor of the law and ordered the sterilization to proceed.

Skinner's lawyers then went to the US Supreme Court, which accepted the case on January 12, 1942. In light of the war and the difficulties of wartime travel, Skinner's lawyers and the Oklahoma Attorney General's lawyers agreed they would waive oral argument and submit the case on written briefs. But at its regular weekly conference on Saturday, April 11, the Court decided to require the Oklahoma Attorney General to appear for oral argument. Skinner's lawyers had the option to participate but were not required to do so. It was an ominous sign for the state because the Court did not even need to hear from Skinner's counsel.

On May 6, the Court heard argument from Oklahoma Attorney General Mac Q. Williamson. Skinner's lawyers had declined to make the trip.

At argument, the Justices seemed skeptical of the forced-sterilization law. Several asked Williamson why stealing chickens was a crime of moral turpitude triggering the possibility of a forced vasectomy, while embezzling money was not. He replied that stealing chickens involves "elements of violence." Stone sharply responded, "Not if done surreptitiously." Stone further pressed Williamson on whether the state had any scientific evidence "which indicate[s] that 'criminal propensities' are transmitted" by heredity—and, if there was no such evidence, shouldn't Oklahoma forfeit the usual presumption that its statute was constitutional? Williamson's answer was halting and confused: "I am not prepared to say that that presumption must be indulged here. But I don't know that the court should assume there was no such evidence."

In its private conference, the Court voted unanimously to find the Oklahoma law unconstitutional. Frankfurter took the lead in arguing that the Court should rely on equal protection grounds based on the Fourteenth Amendment's guarantee of "the equal protection of the laws." In Frankfurter's view, the law blatantly and impermissibly discriminated: it imposed forced sterilization on chicken thieves but not on embezzlers or other white-collar criminals. Chief Justice Stone assigned the opinion to Douglas, the onetime crusading chair of the Securities and Exchange Commission.

DOUGLAS ANNOUNCED THE COURT'S decision striking down the Oklahoma law on June 1, 1942. He began with the gravity of the right at issue: "This case touches a sensitive and important area of human rights...the right to have offspring." Douglas then emphasized the equal protection rationale—the unfairness of treating white-collar criminals differently. A "person who enters a chicken coop and steals chickens...may be sterilized if he is thrice convicted," but a clerk who repeatedly "appropriates over $20 from his employer's till" would not be sterilized despite the clerk's multiple felonies. Douglas, the scourge of corporate wrongdoers at the SEC, delighted in emphasizing that embezzlers and other corporate cheats had at least the same "moral turpitude" as those who steal chickens: If chicken thieves could be sterilized against their will for their multiple offenses, why not tax evaders, crooked politicians, and other white-collar offenders?

In the wake of the previous conservative Supreme Court's regular striking down of economic legislation, Douglas emphasized that legislative line-drawing is inevitable and that it generally should receive judicial deference. But the individual right at issue made this case far different from challenges to laws governing minimum wages and working conditions. A sterilized individual "is forever deprived of a basic liberty." Douglas introduced a new and important concept: courts must apply a rigorous "strict scrutiny" to the deprivation of a fundamental right, rather than the usual deferential review. It was the Supreme Court's first use of the term "strict scrutiny" in the equal protection context, a concept that would become a bedrock of the Court's equal protection jurisprudence. It reflected the principle, first articulated by Stone in a footnote to a 1938 opinion (*United States v. Carolene Products*), that courts should be deferential on economic legislation and yet vigilant in protecting fundamental liberties and guarding against invidious discrimination.

Douglas contrasted the protections of American liberty with the Nazi zeal for forced sterilization. "The power to sterilize...may have subtle, far-reaching and devastating effects. In evil or reckless hands it can cause races or types which are inimical to the dominant group to wither and disappear." Douglas's reference to "evil or reckless hands" was unmistakable. As the Oklahoma prisoners had emphasized, forced sexual sterilization was a well-known Nazi technique, beginning with the passage of its "Law for the Prevention of Hereditarily Diseased Offspring" in 1933 and used ever more aggressively by the Third Reich since then. By 1935, the year the Oklahoma law was passed, the Nazis were sterilizing more than a thousand individuals each week, all in the name of purifying the race and eliminating undesirables.

Skinner's emphasis on personal liberty and reproductive freedom has had a far-reaching impact. It has been stressed in landmark personal-liberty decisions on issues ranging from abortion rights and birth control to interracial marriage and marriage equality. "The 1942 case of a one-footed chicken thief," *Slate* magazine summarized after the *Obergefell v. Hodges* decision in 2015, "laid the foundation for marriage equality." In a powerful defense of reproductive rights, Justice John Paul Stevens once explained that "our cases represent a consistent view that the individual is primarily responsible for reproductive decisions, whether the State seeks to prohibit reproduction, *Skinner v. Oklahoma*, or to require it, *Roe v. Wade*."

Critics of such constitutional protections, in turn, have attacked and demonized *Skinner*. Conservative hero (and failed Supreme Court nominee) Robert Bork, for example, blasted *Skinner* as "improper" and "intellectually empty." His criticisms exemplify the enduring hostility by some on the right to the Roosevelt Justices and the jurisprudential world they established.

When the Supreme Court overruled *Roe v. Wade* in *Dobbs v. Jackson Women's Health Organization* in 2022, Justice Samuel Alito's opinion for the majority noted that a key abortion precedent reaffirming *Roe* had relied on *Skinner v. Oklahoma*. His *Dobbs* opinion did not expressly address the validity of *Skinner* or other non-abortion personal-liberty precedents; it stated that nothing in the decision "should be understood to cast doubt on precedents that do not concern abortion." But Justice Clarence Thomas, while not mentioning *Skinner*, called for a wholesale reconsideration of many of the Court's personal liberty decisions. And the *Dobbs* dissenters ominously warned that, "if the majority is right in its legal analysis"—that there is no constitutionally protected liberty interest in reproductive decisions—then *Skinner* and other personal-liberty "decisions were wrong, and all those matters properly belong to the States too."

In 1942, with the nation newly at war against a vicious regime embracing sterilization for race purification, the Supreme Court saw clearly that Oklahoma's asserted power over reproductive choices violated the US Constitution and the freedom guaranteed to every American, including reviled criminals.

As if to put an exclamation point on the War Court's protection of civil liberties and rights in *Skinner* and the contrast with the Nazis, on the same day that *Skinner* was decided, the Supreme Court issued two decisions vindicating rights of Black defendants. In *Hill v. Texas*, a unanimous opinion by Chief Justice Stone reversed an African American's rape conviction because Dallas County officials had deliberately excluded African Americans from the grand jury that charged the defendant. And in *Ward v. Texas*, the Court unanimously threw out a confession obtained by police after shuttling a beleaguered and terrified Black suspect from town to town over a three-day period. "The effect of moving an ignorant negro," wrote Byrnes, "by night and day to strange towns, telling him of threats of mob violence, and questioning him continuously" required setting aside his conviction because his confession was not voluntary and violated due process. While Byrnes's reference to "an ignorant negro" sounds jarring to today's ears, it again was notable that former Senator Jimmy Byrnes of South Carolina had written an opinion granting relief to an African American defendant.

DAYS AFTER THE *SKINNER* decision, the United States won a pivotal victory of World War II—the Battle of Midway, which took place from June

4 to June 7, 1942. While the Doolittle raid in April had provided enormous psychological and symbolic gratification, the Battle of Midway
was a victory with considerable military significance, establishing American naval power in the Pacific. For the first time, the United States had
won a decisive victory over Japan in a key strategic battle.

THROUGHOUT THE SPRING OF 1942, the Justices maintained their close
relationships with the President and continued to express explicit support for the war effort. Douglas had meetings with the President, including lunches, on at least five occasions between April and June 1942, and
he worked with a small group of other presidential advisers to create a
manpower mobilization board. Jackson traveled with the President and
an intimate party of a few other guests in April 1942 for a weekend in
Charlottesville, Virginia, during which they discussed matters of state
ranging from the postwar future of Germany to whether FDR should
establish a new position of White House Counsel. (Former Attorney
General Jackson opposed this new legal post.) Jackson also again raised
the issue whether he could be more useful to FDR in the war effort
off the Court, and FDR again demurred. Stone was with FDR as part of
the White House's official delegation to greet the King of Greece, who
had been forced to flee his war-torn country.

In May, Black addressed a record crowd of more than one million
in Central Park in New York at a patriotic "I Am an American" rally,
accompanied by the former heavyweight boxing champion, Army Private Joe Louis. Charles de Gaulle, the leader of the French government
in exile, broadcast a live message to the assembled multitude from his
London headquarters. That same month, Frank Murphy headlined a
war bond rally before fifteen thousand people at Olympia Stadium in
Detroit sponsored by the Colored Citizens Committee of Michigan.
The program included Louis, actress Olivia de Havilland, and singers
Marian Anderson and Paul Robeson.

Frankfurter continued to send FDR a steady stream of often-
oleaginous telegrams and letters. He praised the President's State of the

Union address; congratulated him on publicly releasing the Roberts Commission's Pearl Harbor report; sent a birthday message proclaiming FDR "a model to us all"; commended Roosevelt's statement that net income during war should be limited to $25,000 per year; transmitted information on the Zionist movement; conveyed thoughts on Australia and its ambassador; provided advice about organized labor during the war; and recommended that FDR appoint Byrnes to be head of naval affairs.

FDR enjoyed the missives and liked to banter with Frankfurter. On May 1, 1942, Roosevelt wrote Frankfurter that the Supreme Court needed to make its opinions more dramatic and suggested that his speechwriter, acclaimed playwright and screenwriter Robert Sherwood, could liven them up. Frankfurter responded a few weeks later by sending a just-released, exceedingly complex tax opinion and inviting the President to work his magic by "putting Supreme Court jargon into FDRese." On another occasion, FDR teased Frankfurter, "As your Commander-in-Chief I want you to know that I believe you would look awfully well in uniform, for you have retained a remarkable figure considering your age.... Incidentally, I need a Judge Advocate at Samoa. If you act fast you may get there just ahead of its capture by the Japs. Or, as an alternative, I will appoint you as a parachutist to drop in on Wake Island from the sky and recapture it singlehanded. Then, you could be buried in Arlington—the ultimate goal of every good soldier."

But even while the Justices were united in their love of Roosevelt and their support for his war effort, they became increasingly fractious and divided within the Court. While the new Roosevelt Court could come together unanimously on cases like *Taylor v. Georgia* (the peonage case), *Chaplinsky v. New Hampshire* (the fighting words case), and *Skinner v. Oklahoma* (the forced sterilization case), the Court, with its seven Roosevelt appointees and its FDR-appointed Chief, began to show signs of fracturing on other issues and cases, as it had on the *Bridges* First Amendment case, issued the day after the Pearl Harbor attack.

Two decisions in the final week of the Supreme Court term reflected this growing internal divide. First, in *Betts v. Brady*, the Court grappled with a fundamental question. The issue was whether, as Hugo Black had begun to argue forcefully, the Constitution's Bill of Rights applied directly to state governments as well as to the federal government. At that time, Supreme Court precedent held, and Felix Frankfurter fervently believed, that the Bill of Rights generally did not apply directly to the states (with limited exceptions, such as the First Amendment). Instead, individuals asserting the kinds of claims *against states* that could be brought against the federal government under the Bill of Rights (such as claims under the Fourth, Fifth, and Sixth Amendments) generally had to frame their claims as more general and amorphous violations of the Fourteenth Amendment's due process clause, rather than the specific protections of the Bill of Rights.

In *Betts v. Brady*, an individual named Smith Betts was convicted of robbery in state court without the assistance of counsel. He could not afford a lawyer, and the State of Maryland refused to provide one for him. In an opinion for six Justices, Owen Roberts reaffirmed that the Sixth Amendment, which guarantees "the assistance of counsel" to a criminal defendant, "applies only to trials in federal courts," not state courts. While due process may require counsel in particular cases, it is "a concept less rigid and more fluid" than the Sixth Amendment, and the lack of counsel in Betts's case did not violate this "fluid" due process protection.

In dissent, Black, writing for himself, Douglas, and Murphy, emphatically stated that the Fourteenth Amendment did not merely provide general due process protections: it also "made the Sixth applicable to the states," and Betts should prevail because he was denied the assistance of counsel.

The battle over whether the Fourteenth Amendment "incorporated" the Bill of Rights and made them directly applicable against state governments would rage on the Supreme Court for many years. Black and Frankfurter were the principal antagonists. Today, with very rare exceptions, the protections of the Bill of Rights apply directly to the states in the same way that they apply to the federal government. In fact, twenty-one years after the *Betts v. Brady* decision, in *Gideon v. Wainwright*, Black would write a landmark decision overruling *Betts* and holding that the Constitution requires a state to provide counsel for indigent defendants in criminal cases. But in 1942, *Betts* highlighted emerging splits among the Justices.

Divisions on the Court also surfaced in a decision issued on the last day of the term, June 8. *Jones v. City of Opelika* involved Jehovah's Witnesses—a religious minority at the center of numerous civil liberties controversies in the 1930s and '40s (as in the *Chaplinsky* case earlier that term). In the *Opelika* decision, which consolidated and decided three separate cases, a narrowly divided 5–4 Supreme Court upheld convictions of Jehovah's Witnesses in Alabama, Arkansas, and Arizona for failing to pay license taxes before distributing their religious leaflets. The majority opinion by Justice Stanley Reed found the towns' licensing requirements reasonable.

But four Justices dissented—the three who had also dissented in *Betts* (Black, Douglas, and Murphy), now joined by Stone. They viewed the Jehovah's Witnesses' leafleting as protected by the First Amendment. In addition to dissents by Stone and Murphy, three of the dissenters— Black, Douglas, and Murphy—fired an extraordinary salvo. In a joint additional statement, they noted that they had voted with the majority in an 8–1 decision by Frankfurter in 1940 upholding a Pennsylvania law requiring all schoolchildren, including objecting Jehovah's Witnesses, to salute the flag; Stone had been the lone dissenter. In the wake of that opinion, violence against Jehovah's Witnesses had escalated dramatically throughout the country. Now the three dissenting Justices put the Court—and the public—on notice that they regretted their votes and disagreed with Frankfurter's decision: "This is but another step in the direction which *Minersville School District v. Gobitis* [the Frankfurter decision] took against the same religious minority, and is a logical extension of the principles upon which that decision rested. Since we joined in the opinion in the *Gobitis* case, we think this an appropriate occasion to state that we now believe that it also was wrongly decided. Certainly our democratic form of government, functioning under the historic Bill of Rights, has a high responsibility to accommodate itself to the religious views of minorities, however unpopular and unorthodox those views may be." It was a bold and unusual statement, taking direct aim at a recent Frankfurter decision for the Court which they had joined.

❧ ❧ ❧

CLOSE DIVISIONS ON THE Court were part of an emerging pattern. The Court in the 1941 term (from October 1941 to June 1942) experienced a substantial jump in 5–4 decisions—sixteen 5–4 decisions in the 1941 term compared with far fewer 5–4 decisions in the preceding four terms (three in the 1937 term, six in the 1938 term, two in the 1939 term, and three in the 1940 term). The number of nonunanimous opinions rose to fifty-nine, or 36 percent of the Court's 162 opinions.

As in *Betts v. Brady* and *Jones v. City of Opelika*, disagreements focused on the merits of the cases. But personal dynamics and considerations also undoubtedly played a part.

One factor involved the unfortunate reality that Harlan Fiske Stone, in his first term as Chief, was proving to be an exceptionally weak Chief Justice. Any new Chief Justice would have had a difficult time succeeding the universally esteemed Charles Evans Hughes. But Stone proved to be particularly ill-suited to the task. Discussions at the Justices' conferences, which took place on Saturdays, now droned on endlessly. Stone seemed unable to set a crisp, orderly pace. He personally filed dissenting opinions in twenty-two cases, a practice that some thought encouraged others to disagree rather than to search for common ground.

The Court also now contained a striking mix of strong personalities, including Felix Frankfurter, Hugo Black, and William Douglas. Many of the Justices enjoyed a prominent public profile. And almost all of them reveled in their own special relationships with the much-loved President, who had dominated the country for a decade and who enjoyed a distinctive role with each of them. Unimpeded by a weak Chief, the Justices' powerful personalities, contentious tendencies, and personal rivalries, along with genuine differences on issues, bubbled in a toxic brew.

The press noticed the emerging divisions on the Court. "If President Roosevelt expected peace and unity of thought to flow from a Supreme Court of his making," wrote one columnist, "he must be profoundly disappointed with the result of the first year in which his appointees have had unchallenged sway in that tribunal.... Never has any Supreme Court produced more divided opinions in a single term than this one, and rarely has there been so much evidence of personal feuding.... Two justices who don't hit it off at all, as judged by their conflicting opinions, are Hugo Black of Alabama and Felix Frankfurter of Massachusetts.... Bitter antagonism between Justices Frank Murphy and Robert H. Jackson, begun when they served together in the Department of Justice, also is reflected in the court divisions.... Black more and more has been receiving the support of Justices Douglas and Murphy."

Some Court watchers thought the disagreements among the Roosevelt-appointed Justices healthy because their failure to march in lockstep demonstrated "the independence of the judiciary," according to one article. But many observers were astounded at the occasional signs of emerging enmity on the Court.

Frankfurter became increasingly livid at the three Justices—Black, Douglas, and Murphy—he perceived as opposing him and obstructing what he viewed as his natural destiny to be the leader on the Court. He began privately to refer to the three as "the Axis"—the most baleful term that could be used in America at that time, a widely used phrase for the alliance among Germany, Italy, and Japan. In another context, they might even be termed "fighting words."

In its first term during World War II, the Court had issued a pathbreaking decision on civil liberties that marked a clear and obvious contrast with the Nazis—and, at the same time, deep personal and jurisprudential divides had emerged among the Justices. Both patterns would continue throughout the war years, along with an unwillingness to cross or confront FDR on the issues he cared about.

As the Court adjourned for the summer on June 8, 1942, many of the Justices undoubtedly were relieved to be getting away from Washington, and away from their fellow Justices, until the start of the next term in October. Little did they know they would be called back soon, in the middle of the summer, for an explosive and consequential case at the very heart of the war on the home front.

· chapter five ·

SUMMER SESSION

COLONEL KENNETH ROYALL HAD A PROBLEM. ROYALL WAS THE lead counsel for seven of eight Germans who were accused of being Nazi saboteurs. They had entered the United States after crossing the Atlantic on German submarines. When FBI Director J. Edgar Hoover announced their arrest in a dramatic Saturday evening press conference on June 27, 1942, it created a national furor.

Nearly a month later, the defendants were being tried in a secret military commission personally ordered and convened by the President. They faced likely convictions and death sentences. Their trial had just a few days to go.

Royall thought he had good grounds for a challenge to the legality and constitutionality of the military commission. He wanted to take his challenge to the Supreme Court, but he worried that if he waited until the trial finished, the defendants would be immediately executed. There had been a public clamor for swift justice and retribution. In Royall's view, the meritorious claims of the Germans would not be heard, a grave injustice would be done, and the case would be moot because the defendants would be dead.

Royall needed the Supreme Court to agree to take the case. But the Court had adjourned for the summer and would not be in session again until the first Monday in October. So on Wednesday, July 22, Royall brooded about the possibilities.

Royall already had reached out to Hugo Black, one of the only Justices still in the DC area during the oppressive summer heat, to see if he would be of assistance. Each Justice had the authority to issue a stay until the Court could hear the case. A North Carolina native, Royall knew that Black was a fellow southerner. He also knew that Black, at times, had emerged as a civil liberties champion on the Court. With high hopes, Royall had gone to see Black a couple of days earlier at Black's home in Alexandria, Virginia, where he made his case for Supreme Court review. Black responded that he wanted nothing to do with the case. "Mr. Justice," Royall told him, "you shock me. That's all I can say to you."

After Royall tried and failed to reach his former Harvard Law School professor, Felix Frankfurter, who was spending the summer in New Milford, Connecticut, he was at a loss. Then he saw a report in a Washington newspaper that Owen Roberts was in town that day for the funeral of retired Justice George Sutherland. Royall went to Roberts's chambers at the Supreme Court and waited for him to return. When Roberts arrived, Royall explained his dilemma and said that he needed the Supreme Court to consider the legality of the military tribunal before it was too late.

Roberts was intrigued. He advised Royall, "I think you've got something here that ought to be reviewed." He invited Royall to come to his Pennsylvania farm the next day to discuss the matter further. He also told Royall to bring Attorney General Francis Biddle, who was personally heading the prosecution team in the military commission. Roberts assured Royall that, despite Black's rebuff, he would have Black with him at the farm as well.

Royall conferred with Biddle. The patrician Attorney General favored a Supreme Court resolution; he wanted no cloud over the conviction and execution of the saboteurs. After consulting with the White House, Biddle agreed to accompany Royall and support Supreme Court review.

The next day, Thursday, July 23, Royall and Biddle took an Army plane to Philadelphia. They were accompanied by Royall's co-counsel, Colonel Cassius Dowell, and Biddle's co-counsel, Judge Advocate General Myron Cramer. An FBI car met the lawyers at the Philadelphia airport and whisked them to Roberts's farm in eastern Pennsylvania.

There, they met with Roberts and Black. Roberts, the genial host, served fresh milk from his farm, along with crackers and cheese. Black and his wife had arrived the previous day as guests, and Black now was in a much friendlier mood.

Royall laid out his case for prompt Supreme Court review, with Biddle indicating his agreement. When Royall finished, Roberts told the lawyers to take a stroll around the farm so the Justices could confer.

Roberts and Black spoke by phone to Chief Justice Stone, who had decamped for the summer to Peckett's on Sugar Hill, New Hampshire, nestled in the White Mountains. Stone agreed that the Supreme Court should call an extraordinary summer session to consider the saboteurs' petitions for writs of habeas corpus (legal requests that they be freed because they were being held unlawfully). The Court would hear the claims the following Wednesday, July 29. It would be the Court's first summer session in twenty-two years. When the lawyers returned from their walk, Roberts and Black told them the news.

Roberts and Black called their fellow Justices to let them know about the special summer sitting. They reached all but two—Douglas and Murphy. As was his custom when the term ended, Douglas had driven across the country, with his wife and two young children, to a remote summer cabin in the mountains of Oregon, and it was difficult to get through. Frank Murphy posed a different challenge. He was spending his summer in the United States military.

Immediately after the Supreme Court had finished its term and recessed for the summer, Murphy had begun a special four-month assignment in the Army. He had been pressing FDR for an opportunity to join the war effort; this was the result. Murphy did not consult his fellow Justices before announcing his enlistment—a sore point that Chief Justice Stone emphasized in private communications.

The Army gave Murphy the rank of lieutenant colonel and immediately sent him to an officer training program at Fort Benning, Georgia. Murphy was fifty-two years old, a bachelor, and a World War I veteran. Newspapers across the country displayed photos of the newly uniformed Justice arriving at Fort Benning, the first of several stops in his military summer. Newsreels in movie theaters included stories about Lieutenant Colonel Murphy performing his Army duties. Murphy made a point of declining to stay in the comparative comfort of the officers' quarters at Fort Benning, living instead in the barracks. But gossip columnist Walter Winchell reported that "a swank tailor," Nesbitt in New York, had made his Army uniforms.

The press chronicled Murphy's activities. His military day began at 5:30 a.m. In the evening, after completing his military activities, he sat in the barracks reviewing Supreme Court filings.

Many hailed Murphy's wartime patriotism. "Associate Justice Frank Murphy sets a splendid example for men in all walks of life," proclaimed a North Carolina newspaper, "as he leaves the United States Supreme Court for active military duty." But others criticized him. A Kentucky newspaper, in an editorial headlined "Justice Murphy Ought to Have Resigned," observed that "the fact that no Justice before him has done such a thing speaks strongly against this leave, for the court, composed of men of high quality, has served through all our other wars after the Revolution. Justice Roberts' service in the Pearl Harbor inquiry was an entirely different thing, well justified by special circumstances."

Drew Pearson and Robert Allen, in their syndicated Washington Merry-Go-Round column, sought to defuse criticism of Murphy: "Only insiders at the war department know it, but Justice Frank Murphy offered to resign from the supreme court altogether if the army would definitely give him combat service abroad. However, word came back, first, that the army could make no promises as to where any officer would serve; second that he was too valuable in the supreme court. So Murphy will go back to the bench when the summer recess is over."

In late July, finally reached on a field telephone hanging from a tree at a military base in Dilworth, North Carolina, Lieutenant Colonel Murphy was informed that he had to return to Washington, in the midst of the summer, to hear a case about the President's powers during the war.

While other Justices did not join Murphy in military service, they had been actively supporting the war effort in the weeks since the Court began its summer recess. In June, at FDR's request, Hugo Black undertook a covert fact-finding mission for the President in Birmingham, Alabama, to investigate slowdowns in war production resulting from racial strife. On July 14, again at the personal request of President Roosevelt, Black spoke at a "Win the War" rally in Raleigh, North Carolina, where he issued a sharp warning that dissatisfied Americans who were "sniping at our allies" were "playing Hitler's game and…giving aid and moral comfort to the enemy." On July 17, Felix Frankfurter publicly escorted FDR's White House aide Lauchlin Currie to his Pan-American Clipper airplane in New York as Currie departed for a special mission to war-torn China. Frankfurter buoyantly put his arm around the envoy as he left, a moment captured, as the Justice surely knew it would be, in news photos throughout the country.

Stanley Reed spoke at a massive Russian war-relief rally at Madison Square Garden on June 22 and at a "Victory Rally" at the University of Wisconsin field house on June 30. At the former, he lauded the Soviet Union's role in "tearing the mask of invincibility from Axis might"; at the latter, he told the cheering crowd that "war work is the people's work" and "the chain of captive nations, toiling under the lash of Axis taskmasters," has "dramatized too well the frightful penalties of disunity."

Jimmy Byrnes warned against public comments that provided fodder to the enemy. "Whenever an American utters or prints a statement that is used successfully by the axis propagandists to promote the cause of our enemies," Byrnes declared in a speech to the Illinois Bar Association in June, "he is responsible for prolonging the war and shedding the blood of American boys." He followed up with a Fourth of July speech to thousands at a municipal stadium in his hometown of Spartanburg, South Carolina, proclaiming, "God and time and Russia are on our side."

The speeches continued all summer. In a CBS radio address on July 5, Owen Roberts called for unity in supporting Britain, the Soviet Union, and China in their battle against the "personification of evil." "Once let the tide of nationalistic prejudice and suspicion sweep over us," he told the national radio audience, "and we are lost to the enemy." Robert Jackson announced to a Dallas Bar Association audience in early July that "there must be no half victory. We must win so that we will be able to write the peace, not trade out on any basis of compromise."

As with other Americans, the war dominated the lives and thoughts of the Justices in the summer of 1942, the first summer of the war for Americans, as the case of the accused Nazi saboteurs landed in their stately, white-columned building.

IN LATE MAY, TWO German submarines had departed from occupied France, bound for the United States. Each carried a team of four saboteurs. After Germany had declared war on the United States the previous December, Hitler had personally ordered a mission to disrupt the US industrial war machine. The eight saboteurs were recruited based on their familiarity with American culture. All had lived in the United States for a period of time in the 1920s and '30s. All spoke English.

The saboteurs were not the German equivalent of James Bond or George Smiley. Rather than covert operatives or sophisticated spies, they had been workaday laborers in the United States struggling to get by—a machinist, a waiter, a driver, factory workers. The Nazis trained them at a special sabotage school on a lake forty miles from Berlin. They were instructed to settle in the United States for a brief period and then blow up industrial targets: aluminum plants in Tennessee, Illinois, and

New York; a light-metals manufacturing plant in Philadelphia; an electric plant at Niagara Falls; a railroad terminal in Newark; bridges in New York; railroad sites in several states. They also were directed to set off explosives in department stores and retail establishments.

One group of four arrived in Amagansett, New York, on June 13. The other arrived in Ponte Vedra, Florida, a beach near Jacksonville, on June 20. The Amagansett group wore German uniforms when they landed; the Ponte Vedra group wore German naval uniform hats with bathing trunks. They had been instructed that, if apprehended during landing, their uniforms would give them prisoner-of-war status and protection. Both groups immediately changed into civilian clothes and buried their uniforms on the beaches. They also buried explosives, bomb kits, and detonators disguised as pen sets.

During the Amagansett landing, a twenty-one-year-old US Coast Guardsman stumbled upon two of the Germans—the group leader, George Dasch, and his colleague, Ernest Peter Burger. Dasch claimed to be a fisherman, told the Coast Guardsman he did not want to kill him, gave him $260, and told him to keep quiet and leave. The Coast Guardsman raced back to his station for additional support. But the four Germans managed to evade detection and made their way, wet and dirty, to Manhattan.

Dasch then decided that he wanted to report the sabotage plan to US government authorities and become a hero to the Americans by exposing the plot. He may have been prompted at least in part by fear of discovery after the encounter with the Coast Guard. Dasch had a complicated and contradictory personality, and his motivations have never been completely clear.

In their New York hotel room, Dasch confided his plan to Burger, who had his own deep grievances against the Gestapo, including a seventeen-month imprisonment he bitterly resented and abusive Gestapo treatment of his wife. He readily agreed to Dasch's disclosure plan.

On Sunday, June 14, Dasch called the FBI office in New York and said that he had important information. The FBI treated it as a crank call and did nothing. A few days later, Dasch traveled to Washington

and called a general government number to ask where to report information "of military as well as political value." The government operator
told him to call Military Intelligence. Dasch dutifully called and left a
message, and then tried to call J. Edgar Hoover directly. He eventually
reached an FBI agent who had heard about the Amagansett incident
with the Coast Guard; the agent dispatched an FBI car to the Mayflower Hotel to bring Dasch to the Bureau. Dasch spent five days telling
the FBI everything he knew about the plan and his seven colleagues.

Acting on Dasch's information, the FBI arrested the members of the
Long Island team, including Burger and Dasch himself. Days later, the
Bureau arrested the four members of the Florida team, who had made
their way to Chicago and New York. All acknowledged they had arrived
with instructions to commit sabotage.

On Saturday, June 27, at 8:30 p.m., J. Edgar Hoover summoned the
press to FBI headquarters in New York. He announced the sabotage plot—
the first public revelation of the sensational news. Hoover emphasized the
FBI's masterful work in capturing the culprits and averting catastrophe.

Hoover's public account was deeply misleading. He omitted Dasch's
crucial role in telling the FBI about the plans and the saboteurs. He likewise did not mention the Coast Guard's role in detecting the Amagansett landing. Hoover may have been, at least in part, trying to keep the
Nazi government guessing about how and why the saboteurs' plot had
unraveled. But he also clearly saw an opportunity for the FBI to steal the
limelight.

It worked. The press hailed the FBI's achievement. Walter Winchell
proclaimed the capture "the most exciting achievement yet of John Edgar Hoover's G-men." "Almost from the moment the first group set foot
on United States soil," reported a St. Louis newspaper, "the FBI was on
the trail."

Attorney General Biddle reveled in the public deception. Twenty
years later, he exulted, "Nothing was said about Dasch's long, minute
rambling signed confession. The country went wild.... It was generally
concluded that a particularly brilliant FBI agent, probably attending the

school in sabotage where the eight had been trained, had been able to get on the inside, and make regular reports to America."

The evening before Hoover's press conference, Attorney General Biddle called President Roosevelt to tell him about the arrests. Relaxing at Hyde Park while he entertained the exiled King of Greece and Princess Martha of Sweden, FDR was ebullient on hearing the news. When Biddle told him that the FBI had recovered $175,000 in cash from the saboteurs, the President responded with glee, "Not enough, Francis. Let's make real money out of them. Sell the rights to Barnum and Bailey for a million and a half—the rights to take them around the country in lion cages at so much a head."

The issue now was how to proceed. Should the captives be charged with crimes and tried in the ordinary civilian courts? Or was there a better alternative?

Secretary of War Stimson and Attorney General Biddle agreed that federal criminal charges in the civilian courts presented a troubling problem. The penalties for violations of the applicable laws in civilian court might be relatively light because the accused saboteurs had taken almost no actions in the United States; charges might lead to sentences of perhaps two or three years. Stimson and Biddle thought that most— and perhaps all—of the saboteurs should receive the death penalty. Together, they came up with a solution: Charge the Germans in a special military tribunal as unlawful enemy belligerents. Rather than the federal criminal statutes, they would be charged in the military proceeding under the general "law of war" and under specific "Articles of War" (provisions adopted by Congress to govern military matters in the early days of the country and later revised).

American precedent existed for the use of military tribunals. Shortly after the Civil War, a military tribunal had convicted Mary Surratt and three associates of conspiring with John Wilkes Booth in the Lincoln assassination and had ordered their execution. But the use of such special military commissions had been sparse and infrequent in the years since.

President Roosevelt had his own strong views. He wanted the Germans tried, convicted, and executed, and he wanted a swift military trial. On June 30, FDR sent Biddle a memo detailing his thoughts. He first noted that two of the accused saboteurs were thought to be naturalized American citizens; they should be tried for "high treason" by court-martial. "Surely they are as guilty as it is possible to be," the President observed, "and it seems to me that the death penalty is almost obligatory." As for the other six, FDR noted that, although they had arrived in uniform, they "were apprehended in civilian clothes." The President, a history buff, found it "an absolute parallel of the case of Major Andre"—a British spy in the American Revolution working with Benedict Arnold—"and Nathan Hale," the American hero and spy captured by the British. "Both of them were hanged. Here again it is my inclination that they can be tried by court martial as were Andre and Hale. Without splitting hairs, I can see no difference."

With the preferred presidential path now clear—a military trial, with military charges—one major question remained: Who would handle the prosecution for the government?

Biddle wanted to head the team himself. Stimson was surprised—and miffed. He thought that Biddle had caught "the bug of publicity" and that it would be peculiar to have the Attorney General of the United States personally handling the prosecution in a military proceeding of low-level failed saboteurs.

Biddle insisted that he was the man for the job. The case might go to the Supreme Court, he argued, and he was best positioned to represent the government. Biddle implored the President, "We have to win in the Supreme Court, or there will be a hell of a mess." FDR immediately replied, "You're damned right there will be, Mr. Attorney General." And FDR warned Biddle, "I want one thing clearly understood, Francis: I won't give them up. . . . I won't hand them over to any United States marshal armed with a writ of *habeas corpus*. Understand?"

ON THURSDAY, JULY 2, FDR signed two official documents formalizing his position. The first was a general proclamation stating that all federal and state courts would be unavailable to enemies who entered the country with a goal of "sabotage, espionage, hostile or warlike acts, or violations of the law of war." They would be tried instead in "military tribunals" under "the law of war."

The second was an order regarding the eight captured Germans. They would be tried by a military commission. The commission would be led by retired Major General Frank R. McCoy, one of Justice Owen Roberts's colleagues on the Pearl Harbor Commission; he would be joined by three Major Generals and three Brigadier Generals.

FDR's order also named the lawyers on both sides for the military commission proceeding. The prosecution would be headed by Attorney General Biddle and Judge Advocate General Myron Cramer, the defense by Colonel Kenneth Royall and Colonel Cassius Dowell. The commission would begin on July 8, 1942, less than a week following the issuance of the order. The eight saboteurs would be tried under "the law of war and the Articles of War." They were charged with four violations—one violation of the law of war, two violations of the Articles of War, and conspiracy to commit the other three offenses.

The President signed the proclamation and order, along with other paperwork, while still in his bed in Hyde Park, as he chatted with his secretary, William Hassett. "Hanging would afford an efficacious example to others of like kidney," Hassett wrote in his diary after his session with "the Boss." "There's no doubt of their guilt, but we are always too soft in dealing with spies and traitors."

When the military trial began on Wednesday, July 8, Royall already had the possibility of Supreme Court review in mind. He and others on the defense team believed they had substantial challenges on at least three grounds.

First, an 1866 Supreme Court decision, *Ex parte Milligan*, had held that a military commission generally lacks jurisdiction in a geographic area where the regular civilian courts are open and functioning; the courts in New York and Florida, where the saboteurs landed, surely were open and functioning, as were the courts in the District of Columbia, where they were being held.

Second, Royall and his associates believed that the four charges were fundamentally flawed. The asserted violation of the general "law of war"—based on acting with hostile intentions while out of uniform—was vague and unsupported. The Articles of War charges—"relieving" the enemy under Article 81 and espionage under Article 82—could not be sustained because the defendants had done too little and because they were not in a war zone. And the charge of conspiracy to commit the other three offenses depended on the validity of those other charges.

And finally, the procedures in the President's order conflicted with statutory provisions applicable to military trial. Under this new military commission's procedures, a death sentence for the saboteurs would require only a two-thirds vote rather than a unanimous vote; review would go directly to the President rather than receiving an intermediate review before transmittal to the President; and the standard for admissibility of evidence was simply "probative value to a reasonable man," as determined by the head of the commission, rather than the established rules of evidence, with their traditional safeguards.

On the first day of the military trial, Royall, a buoyant six-foot-five trial lawyer who had excelled at Harvard Law School and had recently joined the military after leaving his North Carolina law practice, raised the defendants' legal objections to the commission. Royall was conscious of the military chain of command. As a colonel attacking the legality of his Commander in Chief's proclamation and order, Royall had cautiously requested White House approval for his challenge. FDR had instructed presidential assistant Marvin McIntyre to tell Royall simply to use his best judgment. Taking it as a green light, Royall presented his objections to the Commission.

The Commissioners listened to Royall's challenge and took a break. They stayed out long enough for "a good cigar," according to Lloyd Cutler, then a young lawyer on the prosecution team and later the White House Counsel to two Presidents. They returned and denied the challenge.

The trial proceeded on the fifth floor of the Justice Department, in a crowded room previously used for training FBI agents that had been quickly converted for the purpose. The proceedings were secret. Nobody from the press or the public was allowed to witness the trial, and no information was released other than brief status reports. The doors of the converted FBI room were locked, the windows blacked out.

The proceedings took several days. Royall and Dowell represented seven of the eight defendants. Dasch, the man who had gone to the FBI and revealed the plot, had his own military defense lawyer, Colonel Carl Ristine. Dasch was outraged that, far from the hero's treatment he had expected from the Americans, he had been charged with exactly the same offenses as the others.

A mélange of witnesses testified in the secret room, ranging from the Coast Guardsman who encountered Dasch and Burger to a Chicago girlfriend of one accused saboteur. All eight defendants testified. All agreed about what had happened; most denied that they had actually planned to follow through with the sabotage.

The defense rested on Monday, July 20. It was at this point that Royall began reaching out urgently to Supreme Court Justices to try to obtain review. On Wednesday, he visited Owen Roberts in his Supreme Court chambers, and the day after that, he and Biddle made their trip to Roberts's farm.

On Monday, July 27, at 5:45 p.m., Supreme Court Clerk Charles Elmore Cropley summoned the press and released a brief statement from the Chief Justice. The Supreme Court would "convene a special term of the court on Wednesday, July 29 at noon" to receive petitions for writ of habeas corpus "on behalf of certain persons now being tried by a military commission appointed by the President."

The news was a bombshell. The *New York Times* reported that "the astonishing announcement that the court would meet in special session came without the slightest advance indication"; it was "a startling move." The *New York Daily News* observed that the "historical significance is that it pits the authority of the Supreme Court directly against that of the President."

Many denounced the Court's decision to hear the case. The *Los Angeles Times* objected that "the Supreme Court should never have been dragged into this wartime military matter." The *Detroit Free Press* was scornful: "Realism calls for a stone wall and a firing squad, and not a lot of silly holier-than-thou eyewash about extending the protection of civil rights to a group that came among us to blast, burn, and kill."

But others saw the Court's action as a sign of strength, a testament to the rule of law in the midst of war. The *Washington Post* defended the Court and commented that the case involved "not their liberties ... but ours. . . . In a time when, in so many parts of the world, law has become a mockery and justice an obscenity, it will cheer the free men everywhere that here in this citadel of liberty, law and justice still function—even for the benefit of those who surreptitiously invaded our land to do us injury."

The Supreme Court would hear the case, but the procedural path for getting there on a dramatically accelerated timetable was not entirely clear. Initially, Royall thought he could simply file his papers directly in the Supreme Court; he would ask the Justices to issue writs of habeas corpus and decree the military commission unlawful. On Monday, July 27, however, the same day that the Court announced the special summer session, Justice Owen Roberts, who had played the pivotal role in orchestrating the special summer sitting, left Royall a troubling phone message. He pointedly referred him to *Marbury v. Madison*, the landmark opinion striking down as unconstitutional a law that allowed individuals to file cases in the Supreme Court without bringing them to lower courts first. Roberts's implication was clear. Royall should not rely on filing original papers in the Supreme Court without first going to a lower court.

Justice Roberts's preargument outreach to Royall about the pending case was extraordinary. To be sure, Roberts had been deeply involved with Royall and Biddle in discussions about the Court taking the case; under the norms at the time, lawyers' personal outreach to Justices in the context of requesting a stay was not unusual. But this new private communication by a Justice to the lawyer for one party in a case that was about to be briefed and argued—about how to frame the case for the Court after the Court had decided to take it—was altogether different.

Boris Bittker, then a young lawyer working for Royall (and later a preeminent tax law professor and scholar), did not learn about Roberts's call to Royall for many years. "Colonel Royall did not entrust me with the secret of this phone call, an *ex parte* conversation on a matter that was about to come before the Court," he reflected decades later. "Such an event would have astonished me, despite my total immersion in legal realism at the Yale Law School."

In response to Roberts's message, the next day, Tuesday, Royall filed a legal pleading attacking the military tribunal in the federal district court in the District of Columbia, knowing that it would be denied. Within hours, at eight that evening, Judge James W. Morris issued a terse two-paragraph opinion rejecting Royall's petition on behalf of the seven defendants (all except Dasch, who continued to separate himself from the others and declined to join the legal challenge to the commission). One of the saboteurs' names was Richard Quirin, and the case now acquired the name by which it would be known: *Ex parte Quirin*.

The stage was set for the extraordinary summer session.

THE JUSTICES RETURNED TO Washington—Stone from New Hampshire; Roberts from his Pennsylvania farm; Reed from a summer home in Tuxedo Park, New York; Frankfurter from New Milford, Connecticut; Jackson from his home in Jamestown, New York. Douglas, traveling from a remote corner of the Oregon wilderness, would not arrive at the Court until Thursday, July 30, missing the first day of the special proceedings.

The eight Justices gathered in the Justices' conference room at 10:30 a.m. on Wednesday to prepare for the session that would convene at noon. Frank Murphy showed up in his military uniform from his base in North Carolina, planning to participate. Frankfurter immediately objected to Murphy's involvement. Murphy was now a member of the military, Frankfurter complained. It would be inappropriate for him to sit in judgment on the propriety of a military tribunal.

Murphy grudgingly agreed and recused himself. The *New York Times* already had raised the question whether Murphy would disqualify himself; it quoted an unnamed Supreme Court "attaché" that "a Supreme Court justice is the keeper of his own conscience regarding his eligibility." But Murphy insisted he would stay and listen to the argument, even while not sitting on the bench or participating in the case.

Although he successfully argued for Murphy's recusal, Frankfurter was conspicuously silent about a fact he did not disclose that should have led to his own recusal. Frankfurter had directly advised Stimson on the composition of the military commission. On the evening of June 29, just two days after J. Edgar Hoover's press conference and three days before FDR's order establishing the military commission, Stimson and Frankfurter had dinner. Stimson told Frankfurter he had wanted Under Secretary of War Robert Patterson to chair the military commission. Patterson was a respected former US Court of Appeals judge who had resigned from the bench to join Stimson at the War Department. But Patterson objected, reasoning that all members of the saboteurs' commission should be military men. Stimson recorded in his diary that Frankfurter "shared Patterson's view the court should be entirely composed of soldiers," and that view carried the day. Frankfurter thus had advised the Secretary of War on the creation of the military commission whose legality was now before the Court.

Nor was that the only pertinent conversation between Stimson and Frankfurter. On July 8, the first day of the highly secret military tribunal, Stimson noted that "Frankfurter asked me about the situation in the saboteur trial, and I told him what happened. He is not an admirer of Biddle and admiration was not kindled by what he heard from me."

None of this was revealed. Frankfurter, having engineered Murphy's recusal, continued to participate in the case.

Justice Byrnes also did not recuse himself despite his extensive involvement with the President and the Administration on war efforts. Since shortly after Pearl Harbor, Byrnes had worked closely with the Executive Branch, including Attorney General Biddle, crafting war legislation and steering it through Congress. But Byrnes also continued to sit in the case.

Chief Justice Stone advised his colleagues about a possible disqualification issue of his own. Stone's son Lauson had enlisted in the Army after Pearl Harbor and was now a major. He had been assigned to work with Royall on the defense team, and he had been active in the military commission proceedings. Royall deliberately had kept Lauson away from the federal court challenge in light of Stone's potential participation in a Supreme Court proceeding. Stone told the other Justices at the morning meeting that he would announce the situation in open court and that, if any party objected, he would recuse himself.

Roberts shared with the Justices a troubling report. Biddle had told him that FDR would order the saboteurs shot after the military tribunal no matter what the Supreme Court decided. "That would be a dreadful thing," replied the Chief Justice.

It is difficult to say which was more egregiously improper: the President's determination to flout the Supreme Court if it did not give him what he wanted or the Attorney General's conveying to the Justices the President's explicit threat about the pending case.

While the Justices conferred before the formal start of the proceedings, the audience in the courtroom buzzed with excitement. FBI Director J. Edgar Hoover was there. So were other luminaries. A line snaked around the Court building in the morning hours before the hearing, with onlookers eager to watch the spectacle. In the words of Michael Dobbs, a leading chronicler of the saboteurs saga, the Supreme Court hearing was the "event of the season" for the wartime capital. Public interest was so great that the Court suspended its usual rule against standing; when all the seats were filled, it permitted spectators to stand within the colonnades around the room.

Even though the accused saboteurs remained far from the Court in the DC jail, security at the Court was extremely tight. Armed guards roamed the corridors. With far more press interest than the ordinary case, reporters were given seats in alcoves on the southern wall of the courtroom in addition to the usual three tables for the regular Court reporters. The FBI agent in charge instructed an agent assigned to monitor the journalists, "You can see them all from here and if anybody moves, you can crack 'em."

Promptly at noon, the seven Justices—all except Douglas and Murphy—emerged from the heavy red curtain behind the Supreme Court bench and took their seats. The recused Murphy sat just behind the curtain, positioned to hear every word.

That morning, the lawyers for both sides had filed their briefs, which totaled close to two hundred pages. Royall's written argument stated that, under *Ex parte Milligan*, the civilian courts, rather than military courts, should be used when the civilian courts are open and the geographic area is not subject to martial law. In *Milligan*, decided a year after the end of the Civil War, the Supreme Court had rejected a military commission for a Confederate sympathizer in Indiana accused of plotting against the Union. Royall emphasized that the difference between a military court and a civilian court for the saboteurs was profound. For example, civilian courts would provide certain constitutional rights, such as the right to a jury trial, that the military commission would not. Royall further challenged the four charges against the defendants. The vague "law of war" charge reflected an effort to make up an offense after the fact; the "relieving the enemy" and "espionage" charges were not supported and would be better addressed under federal criminal statutes; none of the charges were in a "theater of operations"—a site of military conflict—a consideration emphasized by the *Milligan* Court. And, in any event, the procedures for this military commission flouted those required by the law governing military proceedings. Royall concluded with a flourish, proclaiming that "the soundness of a system of government proves itself in the hard cases where there is an element of public clamor."

Biddle's brief counterattacked on every point. The President's proclamation precluded judicial consideration of the defendants' challenge. *Milligan* could be easily distinguished: Milligan was a resident of Indiana and had never been to any Confederate state, in contrast to the enemy saboteurs who had landed on American soil. Congress had provided for trial of enemy belligerents in military tribunals by enacting the Articles of War. The military charges were well founded; it did not matter whether there were analogous federal statutes for the civil courts. The statutory procedures for courts-martial did not bind the President, and, in any event, Royall's claims of conflict with the procedures were overstated. Biddle vehemently challenged the defense claim that the offenses occurred outside a theater of military operations. "In the year 1942, we have had concrete experience with the swiftness of modern warfare.... The time may now have come when the exigencies of a total and a global war must force a recognition that every foot of this country is within the 'theatre of operations.'"

With the lawyers' written submissions in hand, Chief Justice Stone called the session to order. He began by announcing that Douglas was "in the West and on his way" but would subsequently participate in the case. He then addressed his own situation. "I am informed," he announced, "that my son, who is an officer in the Army, was assigned to participate in the defense." He asked whether either party objected to his participation. Biddle replied that lawyers for both sides agreed that "your son, Major Lauson H. Stone, did not in any way participate in these habeas corpus proceedings" and had worked only on the military commission matter; both Biddle and Royall requested that the Chief Justice sit in the pending case. Stone acquiesced and remained.

Almost immediately, Royall received a barrage of jurisdictional questions, particularly from his former professor Frankfurter, about his decision to skip the Court of Appeals after the DC court's decision and go directly to the Supreme Court. Jackson suggested to Royall that he could easily remedy the situation by "filing an additional piece of paper" in the Court of Appeals. Royall readily agreed.

Dressed in his full military uniform, Royall reprised his primary arguments. The military tribunal could not proceed in this context, with the civilian courts open and functioning. The military charges could not be sustained. The military commission violated existing requirements and procedures.

The hastily called proceeding had a pell-mell quality. The briefs had been filed that very morning; most of the Justices had hurried back to Washington. Early in the argument, Frankfurter candidly admitted, "I have not read any of the papers, Colonel Royall."

Some Justices expressed concern about the reach of Royall's argument. Byrnes asked whether, if Hitler and seven of his generals secretly landed and discarded their uniforms, they would have to be indicted and tried in the civilian courts. Royall did not flinch. He responded, "My argument would have to carry that fact, and does."

As in his brief, Royall emphasized that neither Amagansett nor Ponte Vedra was "a theater of operations"—a site of military conflict. Frankfurter pressed him with an example that struck close to home: "If a parachutist should come into this building or near this building, would this not be a theater of operations?" Royall acknowledged that it would be.

Royall emphasized that the defendants had taken no concrete steps toward sabotage, and he maintained that all simply had wanted to escape from Nazi Germany. The secrecy regarding the testimony before the military commission—and, in particular, the secrecy about Dasch's and Burger's roles in disclosing the plot to the US government—at times lent an air of unreality to the discussion. At one point, Jackson chided Royall, "They did not go to any agency and say, 'We got away from the Germans. Thank God we are free, and we will tell you where we buried [the explosives].'" Royall replied, "No, sir. If they had done that, there would not have been this litigation." But of course, that was exactly what Dasch had done, with Burger's explicit agreement.

While legal historian David Danelski has suggested that Royall's answer was "technically correct" because Dasch had chosen not to be a party to this legal challenge, Burger certainly was one of the parties before the Court, and he had been a participant in Dasch's disclosure plan. Perhaps Royall's response was influenced by the fact that six of his seven clients (all except Burger) had not gone to the US authorities and had not known of Dasch's disclosures; perhaps it was influenced by the strict confidentiality of the testimony before the military commission (including the secrecy regarding Dasch's still-confidential role in informing the US government); perhaps Royall did not know all of the underlying facts. But whatever the reason, Royall's answer was, at the very least, unfortunately misleading on an important point.

After two hours, the Court took a thirty-minute lunch recess and then resumed with Royall's argument. In concluding, Royall returned to the *Milligan* precedent: "The *Milligan* case, which has been law seventy-five years, is still law today, and...these petitioners are entitled to trial before a criminal court just as the court in the *Milligan* case granted." As the argument progressed, the air-conditioning in the Supreme Court chamber, not yet a standard feature in government buildings in Washington, failed. "The justices sweltered in their robes," observed a reporter, "and the closely packed rows of soldiers and civilians stifled."

At 4 p.m., Biddle, dressed in a white linen suit, strode to the podium to present the government's case. "The United States and the German Reich are now at war," he began. The defendants "are enemies of the United States who have invaded this country." They engaged in "warlike acts calculated to destroy the country under whose constitution they are now claiming these rights." The military commission to try them was lawful and proper.

Some of the Justices were troubled by the breadth of his position. Suppose, Black asked him, "there had been some trouble in a plant and a man had been accused of trying to interfere with work in a defense plant, and it was said that in some way he had received instructions from a foreign country. Under the order would he still be tried by a court-martial?" Biddle hedged: "It is right on the edge."

Jackson raised similar questions. He asked Biddle about workers involved in an illegal strike that hindered production in a plant related to war production. "Would you say that they would be tried by a military tribunal?" Biddle now limited his position: "I do not think they could." When Biddle emphasized that his position applied only to "enemies," Frankfurter suggested that a better formulation would be "enemies who are engaged in combat or in preparation for combat." At 6 p.m., the Court adjourned and said it would return for further argument.

The next day, Thursday, July 30, the Court again convened at noon. Douglas had arrived from Oregon and now joined the seven other Justices on the Court, all except Murphy. That morning, Royall and Dowell had filed the "piece of paper" suggested by Jackson—an appeal in the Court of Appeals, which would allow the Supreme Court to use a technical procedure to decide the case before the Court of Appeals. But in the second day of arguments, they still had not filed a petition for review in the Supreme Court.

Biddle began his argument by taking direct aim at *Milligan*. "The case of *Ex parte Milligan*," he announced, "is very bad law and...its effect not only on courts but the Army is harmful." He asked the Court to "overrule that portion" of the decision "which says that where civil courts are sitting under the circumstances in the *Milligan* case, there can be no trial by military commission."

Jackson pressed him on this point. In Biddle's brief, he had said that *Milligan* was vastly different in the facts, which would mean that the case could be distinguished rather than disavowed. Biddle agreed that "you can satisfy all the requirements of this case without touching a hair of the *Milligan* case." Frankfurter interjected, "You want to touch the head as well as the hair?" Biddle said, "Yes," and then conspicuously invoked President Roosevelt: "The President is interested in this Court sustaining to the limit the power of the President in court."

After the Court's thirty-minute lunch break, Royall rose for rebuttal. He emphasized again that, when arrested, the petitioners had not undertaken any actions against the United States. He implored the Court to protect the rights of these reviled defendants.

At 3:55 p.m., after close to nine hours of argument over two days, the lawyers were done. The case was submitted. Stone announced that the Court would reconvene at noon the following day, Friday, July 31.

The Justices decided that they would issue a brief order rejecting the defendants' claims, with an opinion explaining their reasoning to be issued at some unspecified date in the future. This was a highly unusual procedure—decision now (permitting the military commission trials and the expected executions to proceed), reasoning to follow. It came close to echoing the famous line by the Queen of Hearts in *Alice's Adventures in Wonderland*: "Sentence first—verdict afterwards."

One point troubled the Chief Justice. He was concerned about Royall's claim that FDR would not follow the laws governing military trial procedures, which, Royall had argued, would require a layer of review by senior military officials before the verdicts and sentences reached the President. Stone circulated a brief proposed order rejecting the defendants' claims and stating that an opinion with reasoning would follow; he included a paragraph pointedly noting that, with regard to a layer of review before the President's decision, the Court would not "assume in advance that the President would fail" to follow the law. This would put the President on notice about the Court's expectations. But four Justices—Frankfurter, Douglas, Byrnes, and Jackson (perhaps not coincidentally, the four who were personally closest to FDR)—objected. Stone deleted the paragraph.

At 11:59 a.m. on Friday, the saboteurs' lawyers finally filed a petition for Supreme Court review based on their filing in the court of appeals the previous day. One minute later, the Court granted review in the case it had been hearing for two days. As one contemporaneous commentator noted, "The Court's jurisdiction caught up with the Court just at the finish line."

At noon, in a brief session, Chief Justice Stone read the Court's unusual order, with its decision-now-and-explanation-to-follow approach. After reciting the procedural history, the Court summarily announced that the charges allege "an offense or offenses which the President is authorized to order tried before a military commission." The order further stated, without explanation, that the military commission was "lawfully constituted" and that the petitioners were "in lawful custody."

The Court's ruling would take effect "forthwith"—immediately.

The military commission trial wound to its conclusion. At 10 a.m. on the morning of Friday, July 31, knowing that the Supreme Court would issue its ruling at noon, Royall and Biddle began their closing arguments to the seven Commissioners in the sealed confines of Room 5235 in the Justice Department. Biddle emphasized that, to the extent any of the saboteurs were entitled to favorable consideration (an obvious reference to Dasch and Burger), leniency should come from executive clemency, not from the commission.

The lawyers took a brief break at 11:45 to rush to the Supreme Court and hear the ruling rejecting the challenge. Then they headed back to resume their arguments. They concluded in the early afternoon of Saturday, August 1.

On Monday, the tribunal reached its verdict. The Commissioners found all eight defendants guilty and imposed death sentences. They also recommended commuting the sentences of Dasch and Burger to life imprisonment. The Commissioners sent the verdict, the death sentences, and the three-thousand-page record directly to the White House for the President's review. The verdicts and sentences were secret. It was publicly announced only that they had reached a decision, not what the decision was.

An Army major ferried the package to FDR at Hyde Park by military plane, arriving with a thick pile of papers from the Commission at 3:50 p.m. on the same day the military tribunal ruled.

The President reviewed the record over the next several days and agreed with the guilty verdicts. He also upheld the death sentences of six of the saboteurs and, on Biddle's recommendation, commuted Dasch's sentence to thirty years at hard labor and Burger's to life imprisonment at hard labor.

FDR had been keenly interested in the method of execution throughout the proceedings. On July 12, just a few days after the secret tribunal began, he asked his secretary William Hassett, "What should be done with them? Should they be shot or hanged?" "Hanged, by all means," replied Hassett. "What about pictures?" Roosevelt continued. "By all means," Hassett repeated. He then reminded the President that "anyone who had ever looked at the photographs in old Ford's Theater of the hanging of the Lincoln conspirators was not likely to forget it—Mrs.

Surratt and the rest of them swinging in air under the hot July sun." On the weekend after the Supreme Court order, before the military commission reached its verdict and sentence, FDR again confided to Hassett that he hoped the commission would recommend death by hanging (and also that he was "not surprised" by the Supreme Court decision rejecting the saboteurs' claims).

On Saturday morning, August 8, the six condemned saboteurs were escorted, not to a hangman's noose, but to "Sparky," the District of Columbia's electric chair. They proceeded, one by one, in alphabetical order. The first, Herbert Haupt, was killed by electrocution at one minute past noon. The last, Werner Thiel, was killed an hour later, at four minutes past one. They were secretly buried in unmarked graves in Blue Plains, a potter's field in Washington, DC. Dasch and Burger, meanwhile, were sent to federal prison.

After the executions, the White House announced that all eight had been convicted; that six had been executed; and that the President had commuted the death penalties of Dasch and Burger to prison sentences. It was the first official confirmation of the military tribunal's judgments and the President's decisions.

The evening of the executions, Saturday, August 8, the President relaxed at Shangri-La (the presidential retreat now known as Camp David) with some of his closest companions: Judge Samuel Rosenman and his wife Dorothy, Librarian of Congress Archibald MacLeish and his wife Ada, FDR's cousin Margaret "Daisy" Suckley, and FDR's secretary Grace Tully.

Just hours after the public announcement of the executions, FDR was in high spirits. He and Rosenman reminisced about clemency requests they had worked on in Albany when FDR was Governor. That evening and the next morning, the President—"inspired," Dorothy Rosenman recalled, "by the fact that six German saboteurs had been put to death that noon"—regaled his guests with tales of murder and cannibalism. He told of a barber during the siege of Paris in 1870 who provided delicious "veal" to the butcher, a delicacy that locals greatly enjoyed until they realized that many of the barber's customers had mysteriously disappeared. And the President shared the tale of a slain British general after the Battle of New Orleans in the War of 1812. His body was stored in a barrel of rum on a ship bound for England, a circumstance that did not prevent the thirsty British sailors from imbibing the liquor.

While Roosevelt entertained his guests with macabre stories, the Supreme Court now had a problem. It had to give the reasons explaining why it had allowed the convictions and executions to proceed.

chapter six

A MORTIFICATION OF THE FLESH

ACK AT HIS SUMMER RESORT IN NEW HAMPSHIRE, THE CHIEF Justice was in pain. He had a severe case of lumbago, an excruciating back condition that had developed, he explained to former Chief Justice Charles Evans Hughes, from "an extremely cold Pullman car on the way back from Washington to Sugar Hill, after the strenuous days...during the Saboteur trials" and subsequent "climbing over mountain trails."

But it was not just the lumbago that afflicted Stone. Exercising the Chief Justice's prerogative, he had assigned himself the opinion in the saboteurs' case. Now he was finding the process of writing it, and supplying the reasons for the already-announced decision, agonizing. The experience, he confided, was a "mortification of the flesh."

Stone was not happy with the lawyers. "Both briefs have done their best to create a sort of a legal chaos," he groused to his clerk. "I sincerely hope the military is better equipped to fight the war than it is to fight its legal battles." And he was irritated by the press coverage. Somehow, he noted, the *New York Times* had printed a draft of the July 31 per curiam decision (the unsigned brief opinion for the Court) rather than the final version. The draft included his paragraph, which the Court had deleted, saying that the Court would not assume that the President would violate the statutory review requirement. The development perturbed the Chief, leading him to confirm with his clerk that the paragraph actually had been deleted from the official version. Shortly after the issuance of the per curiam opinion, moreover, Attorney General Biddle declared a sweeping victory. He told the *New York Times* that the opinion would permit military commissions as a "routine" matter during the war without judicial review. The statement greatly annoyed Stone. It was "most unfortunate," he grumbled.

Stone's crankiness was understandable. It was clear that the Court's opinion, in this closely watched case involving the President's power, would be a defining test of his tenure as Chief Justice.

❖ ❖ ❖

HARLAN FISKE STONE DID not always seem destined for the pinnacle of the legal profession. When he was seventeen and attending a farming school, his rowdy behavior led to his expulsion. But he would make a career out of surprising people.

Stone was born in 1872, in Chesterfield, New Hampshire. His father was a farmer; the family's New England roots dated back to 1635. At the age of two, Stone moved with his family to a farm in western Massachusetts. When he was fifteen, he enrolled at Massachusetts Agricultural College, but, in his sophomore year, he was kicked out after a melee in which he grabbed and shook a professor, not realizing the identity of his combatant. It was not a promising start.

Regrouping, Stone managed to gain admittance to Amherst. Heavyset and jowly-jawed, he became a star football player. In later years, he enjoyed reminiscing about the glories of the gridiron in the "bone-crushing" era. He also emerged as a popular campus leader—president of his class three times, Phi Beta Kappa honors, voted "most likely to succeed." One of his more reticent Amherst friends, Calvin Coolidge, a year behind Stone, would play a significant role in his future.

After college, Stone began teaching science and coaching football at a high school in Newburyport, Massachusetts. He became interested in the local courts and regularly attended sessions, striking up a close relationship with the local District Attorney, William H. Moody, who himself later became a Supreme Court Justice, appointed by Theodore Roosevelt. Stone decided to attend Columbia Law School. Again he excelled, thriving as a law student while teaching history to support himself.

After graduating in 1898, Stone went to the prestigious Wall Street law firm Sullivan and Cromwell and began teaching at Columbia Law School. He eventually became dean, with occasional stints at leading corporate law firms. In 1899, Stone married his childhood friend Agnes Harvey. They had two sons: Marshall, who would become a world-renowned mathematician, and Lauson, who would become a prominent lawyer (and would serve on Kenneth Royall's defense team in the saboteurs' case).

In 1924, Stone's college pal Calvin Coolidge, now President, summoned him to be Attorney General. The Department of Justice was plagued with scandal. The previous Attorney General, Harry Daugherty, was Warren Harding's crony, corrupt and deeply enmeshed in the Teapot Dome scandal. Coolidge appointed Stone to revitalize the Justice Department. Stone promptly instituted reforms, including the appointment of a serious young civil servant named J. Edgar Hoover to head the problem-ridden agency then known as the Bureau of Investigation.

Less than a year later, in January 1925, Coolidge had another post for Stone—Supreme Court Justice, replacing Justice Joseph McKenna. Stone's nomination initially met resistance in the Senate. As Attorney General, Stone had refused to drop the Department's prosecution of Montana Senator Burton K. Wheeler; many in the Senate believed the prosecution had been brought, before Stone's tenure, as retaliation by Daugherty and his loyalists against Wheeler for leading the Senate's Teapot Dome investigation. To quell the controversy, Stone appeared personally before the Senate Judiciary Committee in a public hearing and addressed the issue—the first Supreme Court nominee to make

such an appearance. His vigorous defense of the Department's handling
of the Wheeler case mollified most critics, winning him confirmation
in a 71–6 vote.

Stone's handful of remaining opponents, led by progressive Republican Senator George Norris of Nebraska, stressed a different point. They
charged that Stone, with his corporate law background and clients,
would be too protective of Wall Street interests and "a tool of the House
of Morgan."

On the Court, Stone quickly proved them wrong. He joined Justices
Brandeis and Holmes (and Holmes's successor, Benjamin Cardozo) in
opposing the Four Horsemen's rejection of federal and state laws that
regulated business and working conditions. Stone wrote much-heralded
dissents protesting the Supreme Court's anti–New Deal decisions. In
one, he admonished his archconservative colleagues that "courts are not
the only agency of government that must be assumed to have capacity
to govern." Eventually, after Owen Roberts's "switch" in 1937, Stone's
deferential view on economic legislation carried the day and became
the majority view. Stone famously articulated, in his *Carolene Products*
footnote 4 in 1938, the influential principle that, unlike economic laws
and regulations (which should receive great judicial deference), searching judicial review is appropriate when legislation targets "discrete and
insular minorities" or obstructs the opportunity for meaningful political
participation.

Over the years, Stone's rugged football physique faded into paunch
and flabby folds, but he remained physically active. Stone was a proud
member of President Herbert Hoover's medicine ball group—a group of
Hoover intimates who threw a weighted ball with the President on the
South Lawn of the White House every morning at 6:30 a.m. He regularly walked a brisk two miles daily, often with his wife or a breathless
law clerk at his side.

Stone put others at ease with his self-deprecating humor. After the
Supreme Court moved from its cramped Capitol quarters to its new
"marble palace" in 1935, Stone suggested that the Justices should enter

their new home riding on elephants. His journey to the Supreme Court resulted, he would observe, not from careful career planning but rather "as the dog went to Dover, leg by leg." And he liked to tell the story of how, when he learned about his Amherst admission, he was shoveling horse manure with a pitchfork on the family farm. Hearing the news, he howled with joy and threw it aside—but, Stone always added, if he had known what he would be doing later in life, he would have kept the tool handy.

Although Roosevelt's elevation of Stone to Chief Justice in 1941 generated public praise and acclaim, with very few people doubting Stone's fairness and ability, one who did was Stone's Supreme Court colleague Hugo Black. Black resented Stone for what he viewed as Stone's condescending treatment when Black had joined the Court, and he unsuccessfully tried to block Stone's promotion to Chief Justice. But Black was an outlier. Even Senator George Norris, who had led the opposition to Stone's confirmation in 1925, announced that he had been wrong in thinking Stone would be too partial to Wall Street.

The Senate confirmed Stone unanimously. He remains the only Justice to have served in every position on the Court—from most junior Associate Justice to most senior Associate Justice, as well as Chief Justice.

But the skills that made Stone an impressive Associate Justice did not easily translate into the administrative skills and consensus-building required of a Chief Justice. In 1929, when Hoover was rumored to be considering elevating Stone if William Howard Taft retired as Chief, Taft was concerned that Stone would have difficulty in the crucial responsibility of "massing the Court."

Stone had reservations about the close relationships between many of the Justices and FDR. Stone himself had been publicly embarrassed by Roosevelt's wiles in 1939. After FDR hosted Frankfurter and Stone on a Potomac River cruise aboard the presidential yacht, the President announced at a press conference that he and the two Justices had discussed his plan to incur deficits for needed military barracks without

congressional approval, thereby suggesting that the Justices already had
blessed the legality of his Executive Branch gambit. Stone quickly sent a
denial to an outraged Republican Congressman.

Although he had participated in FDR's Fourth of July national ex-
travaganza in 1941, Stone uneasily observed the activities of his fellow
Justices: Byrnes worked extensively for the White House on legislative assignments; Roberts took a leave from the Court to head FDR's
Pearl Harbor Commission; Frankfurter conspicuously advised the
President; Douglas and Jackson were in close touch with FDR. Stone
became self-conscious about his own past White House contacts.
After a law clerk pointed to the prominently displayed medicine ball
Stone had used with Hoover in their early-morning sessions, Stone removed it from his office. As the clerk later recounted, "The press at the
time was full of stories about Justice Douglas and Justice Frankfurter
going over to the White House to see F.D.R. and advise him," and "occasionally Stone would grumble about the Court participating in such
affairs."

On July 17, 1942, FDR asked Stone to head an urgent study of rubber production while remaining Chief Justice. The issue of adequate
rubber supplies was paramount to the war effort—and deeply controversial. At an Alfalfa Club dinner in the spring of 1942, with Justices
Reed and Byrnes in attendance, Commerce Secretary Jesse Jones and
Washington Post publisher Eugene Meyer burst into a fistfight over a
Post editorial criticizing Jones for rubber shortages. The capital reveled
in the fracas featuring the sixty-eight-year-old cabinet secretary and the
sixty-six-year-old publisher—with the secretary five inches taller and
thirty-four pounds heavier than the diminutive publisher.

Now FDR wanted Chief Justice Stone to tackle this vexing problem. On July 20, Stone sent a letter declining FDR's entreaty. He stated
that the President's proposed rubber assignment would be inconsistent
with his judicial role and duties. In a letter on July 30 (the second day of
the Supreme Court's argument in the saboteurs' case), FDR told Stone
he understood. And in a reply letter, Stone expressed his gratitude, telling the President, "I cannot tell you the sense of relief I feel at your

assurance that you do understand my scruples." Stone sent his appreciative reply on August 1, the day after he announced the Court's per curiam decision allowing FDR's military commission to proceed.

❧ ❧ ❧

As the summer of 1942 drew to a close, Stone battled his lumbago, struggled with the lack of a law library at his New Hampshire resort, and began drafting the opinion. He faced a welter of issues that the lawyers had not clearly delineated or crisply organized, perhaps the result of their hasty dash to the Supreme Court.

The arguments and counterarguments boiled down to six major questions. First, could the Supreme Court hear the saboteurs' claims at all in light of FDR's Proclamation that federal courts could not hear such cases? Second, as a general matter, was this kind of military commission authorized and lawful for individuals who had not been captured on a battlefield? Third, assuming that Congress generally had authorized military tribunals for unlawful combatants, was a military tribunal appropriate for *these* charges against *these* individuals? Fourth, did *Milligan*, with its broad language about the inapplicability of martial law when the federal courts are open and functioning, mean that any trial of the saboteurs had to be in a federal civilian court? Fifth, did it matter that one of the accused saboteurs (Haupt) maintained that he was an American citizen (a claim disputed by the federal government)?

And sixth, did the procedures mandated by the Articles of War for military trials apply to this military commission? FDR's procedures, set forth in his order of July 2, 1942, contained apparent conflicts with the procedures in the Articles of War, including the conspicuous lack of intermediate review before the case reached the President.

Stone grappled unhappily with all of the issues, finding problems everywhere he turned. But it was the last question, about the inconsistency between the President's order and congressionally specified procedures, that most troubled him, and it came close to fracturing the Court.

Stone rued the deletion from the per curiam opinion of his proposed paragraph on the procedural issue, with its message to FDR about the Court's expectation that the President would comply with required procedures. "I think it would not have been" taken out, he told his law clerk, "if we had had a little more time to consider it." Many aspects of the procedural issue worried Stone. He was concerned that, because of the secrecy of the military commission and the fact that the commission transcript remained sealed, the Court did not even know how the military commission had resolved some of the disputed procedural points. Most alarmingly, Stone was distressed by the possibility that the accused saboteurs might well have been correct in their legal challenge to the procedures—and now six of them were dead.

Stone believed the Court had two options to justify its previous action. It could say that the issue of compliance with required procedures had been raised prematurely: the military commission trials had not yet been completed when the Court considered the case. But this was problematic. It would be awkward, to say the least, to hold out the possibility that the defendants—including the six who had been executed—might have had meritorious claims that the Court had not considered as a matter of timing. Alternatively, the Court could conclude that the statutory procedural requirements simply did not apply to the President when he personally convened a military commission. But Stone found this option intellectually troubling. His subsequent research, he told his clerk, fortified "the conclusion which I reached in Washington that the President's order probably conflicts with the Articles of War."

Stone decided to engage Frankfurter on this vexing problem. It "seems almost brutal," he confided, "to announce this ground of decision [that the issue had been raised prematurely] for the first time after six of the petitioners have been executed and it is too late for them to raise the question if in fact the articles as they construe them have been violated." The two surviving saboteurs, moreover, could now raise the claim after the war and after the transcripts became public; if they were successful, it "would not place the present Court in a very happy light."

Frankfurter tried to reassure Stone that the statutory procedures simply did not apply to the President and that the Court should rest on that ground. Characteristically, Frankfurter also launched a separate campaign to rally allies on the Court. He wrote to Roberts, Reed, and Byrnes explaining his recommended approach. In a cover memo to Reed, he included a dig at the Chief: "I spelled it out in case the C.J. should continue in the fog of pedantic unreality on this phase of the case.... I have *not* sent him this memo—in the hope that he will discover the plain meaning & common sense of it (with Boskey's help) and then tell us all about it." Bennett Boskey was Stone's law clerk; he previously had clerked for Reed and had been a Frankfurter protégé at Harvard Law School.

On Friday, September 25, almost two months after the per curiam decision, Stone sent his draft opinion to his colleagues with an accompanying memo. He'd decided that he would leave the issue about compliance with Articles of War procedures temporarily unresolved. His draft included options A and B. Under option A, the Court would say that the issue had been raised prematurely. Under option B, the Court would say that the Articles did not apply to the President. Stone highlighted his uncertainty, noting that he had "expounded the matter in both aspects as fully as possible."

Frankfurter continued to believe that the Court should interpret the Articles of War as not binding the President. Reed advised him privately that he did not agree, but he also thought that procedural violations would not necessarily justify relief for the defendants. Frankfurter now undoubtedly looked to Roberts and Byrnes, the other two recipients of his previous memo, and probably to Jackson as well. He likely did not turn to Black and Douglas, two leaders of "the Axis," as he had described them; their Axis ally Murphy, whom Frankfurter would not have relied on in any event, was recused. Stone, for his part, seemed hopelessly indecisive.

Just a few days after Stone circulated his opinion with option A and option B, Frankfurter faced another problem in rallying his closest allies on the Court in defense of the government's position. Byrnes was resigning in order to join FDR at the White House.

❖ ❖ ❖

ON FRIDAY, OCTOBER 2, President Roosevelt triumphantly signed the Stabilization Act, legislation he had championed that gave him sweeping powers to control wages and prices in the wartime economy.

The next morning, he met with Byrnes at the White House, again in the presidential bedroom, leaning against pillows, his breakfast tray cast aside and newspapers and documents strewn on the bed. He wanted Byrnes to be the new Director of Economic Stabilization. Even more broadly, he wanted Byrnes to manage the nation's economy while he focused on the war. "For all practical purposes," the President told the Justice, "you will be assistant President."

Byrnes jumped at the chance. He had chafed at life in the Supreme Court, finding it quiet and dull. One day at the Court, he had told an old friend, journalist Turner Catledge, "I get so damn lonely here." Byrnes immediately told FDR he would resign from the Court, rather than take a leave of absence, and accept the post. His tenure on the Supreme Court—fifteen months—was one of the shortest of any Justice in history, a record of brevity rivaled only by Justice Thomas Johnson in George Washington's first term.

Frankfurter wrote FDR about his mixed feelings on Byrnes's imminent departure from the Court: "Let me tell you what I said to Jimmie—for the first time in my life something *very* good for my country is very bad for me?! You will know best of all how deeply accurate I am in saying that I am sadly happy that you have put Jim Byrnes where you and the war should have him. . . . And so—my gratitude to you for depriving me of my most congenial pal."

The press reaction was generally favorable, praising Byrnes's suitability for the new post. But some criticized FDR's raid on the Supreme Court. They likened it to FDR's appointment of Roberts to the Pearl Harbor Commission, his effort to get Stone to head the rubber survey, and his close relationships with various Justices. One Senator acidly noted, "Maybe we ought to pass another stabilization act—to stabilize the Supreme Court." Merlo Pusey, a *Washington Post* columnist, wrote that FDR's record "strongly suggests that the President regards the

Supreme Court as a part of his own Administration. That attitude un-avoidably detracts from the prestige of the court."

Chief Justice Stone was relieved that Byrnes no longer would be torn between the Court and White House assignments. He told Byrnes he was sorry to lose him but pointedly noted that he was "glad [they] had one member of the Court who could make up his mind about his own career."

While the other Justices remained on the Court, they continued their ardent public support for the war effort. At a war bonds dinner in September 1942, Douglas decried war profiteering: "This is no time for haggling over profits, conspiring for juicy profits, jockeying for personal advantage. We survive as a nation or the Japanese and Germans dictate the peace in Washington." Jackson, speaking to a glittering group gath-ered at a Washington estate to honor visiting Russians, told the crowd that the "greatest encouragement we get these days comes from soviet Russia.... I am sure that you, like myself, find your greatest inspiration these days in the headline, 'Stalingrad Holds.'" Roberts told federal judges in Hershey, Pennsylvania, "The Japanese attack on Pearl Har-bor...failed to jolt [the American people] out of the 'it can't happen here' spirit that will destroy our country if we don't wake up.... What in God's name will it take to put the American people behind this effort for the salvation of our people and our country?"

The Justices did not limit their war support to speeches. One news photo featured Roberts proudly gathering scrap metal for the war drive at his Pennsylvania farm; it was a time when newspapers implored Americans to collect scrap metal for their country, even running ads ex-horting, "Bring in Scrap to Kill a Jap!" And, in a period of gas rationing and tire shortages, another news photo showed Jackson engaging in a "gasless" ride near his Virginia home (Hickory Hill, later famous as the home of Robert and Ethel Kennedy and their brood) by driving a horse and buggy.

Frankfurter, meanwhile, remained a lightning rod for publicity, pos-itive and negative, often contradictory. *Forbes* named him one of FDR's "five most important inside advisers on national policy," a select list that included Harry Hopkins and Samuel Rosenman. *Talk of the Town*, a popular Hollywood movie that opened in the fall of 1942, featured a courageous law professor nominated to the Supreme Court, a likable character said to be inspired by Frankfurter. But a national columnist claimed that Frankfurter was now "in the bad graces of the White House" because he had grown increasingly conservative and was too intrusive on foreign policy. And columnist Drew Pearson admonished Frankfurter to stop interfering in the Executive Branch: "Busybody Justice Felix Frankfurter...ought to stick to his job on the Supreme Court."

Frank Murphy, recused from the saboteurs' case and fresh from his summer Army stint, looked exceptionally fit after his military service—fifteen pounds lighter and, according to the *Chicago Tribune*, "seemingly harder than some of the rocks he tramped across in maneuvers this summer." Rumored to be a candidate to succeed the seventy-five-year-old Secretary of War Stimson, he publicly praised American weapons as the best in the world and eagerly anticipated seeing "tanks made in Detroit" rolling through the streets of Tokyo. With the Japanese-occupied Philippines close to his heart, he told a reporter, "I understand some cousin of Hirohito's is staying in my bed in Manila now. If I have my way, it's one person who is going to be very roughly shoved out of bed some day."

Murphy seemed to be everywhere. He admonished business and labor to work together in the war effort. He told unions that the American Federation of Labor and the Congress of Industrial Organizations likewise should cooperate for the common good. Most dramatically, Murphy undertook a public mission in late September—at FDR's personal request—to inspect war production plants in Michigan. He reported his findings in a nationally broadcast evening radio address on NBC's *March of Time* program, grimly warning that "outside our armed forces, this nation is not mobilized to win this kind of war."

On Tuesday, October 13, 1942, the eight Justices arrived at the White House for their annual start-of-term meeting with the President.

They met with FDR in the Red Room for an hour. According to the official schedule, it was for "tea"; since it was at 5:30 p.m., it's likely the cocktail-hour-loving FDR offered stronger libations. The Justices were joined by their former colleague, now Director of Economic Stabilization, Jimmy Byrnes, along with Attorney General Francis Biddle and Solicitor General Charles Fahy, both prominently mentioned for Byrnes's Court seat. This time, the relaxed dress of the Justices, who were in their business suits, did not even merit press comment. The eight Justices, along with Biddle and Fahy, posed for photos in front of the White House. Douglas leaned forward in his western-style white hat; Black laughed with Roberts and Stone; Stanley Reed gently smiled. "Jovial Justices," the *Des Moines Register* captioned its photo. They beamed like a happy team—the eight Justices and the President's two senior Justice Department officials.

WITHIN THE COURT, THE process of hammering out the saboteurs' opinion continued. On most points, Stone ultimately was able to achieve consensus.

First, on the question of whether the Supreme Court should have heard the saboteurs' claims at all, Biddle had argued that, pursuant to the court-closing language in FDR's Proclamation, the federal courts, including the Supreme Court, could not even consider the validity of the military tribunal. Stone stated that nothing in the President's Proclamation precluded access to the courts for determining whether the Proclamation was applicable and whether it violated the Constitution or a statute.

Second, on the lawfulness of the military commission, Stone acknowledged the enormous stakes. Core constitutional rights, such as the right to a jury trial, applied in civilian courts but not in military commissions. After reviewing the constitutional authority of Congress and the President, Stone concluded that the long-standing congressionally enacted Articles of War authorized the President to create military commissions for unlawful combatants violating the law of war and that this statutory authority was constitutionally permissible. Accordingly, the Court did not need to consider the explosive question of whether the President could have proceeded without congressional authorization to create the military commission—a proposition vigorously advocated by Biddle. Distinguished military law historians later savaged this interpretation, arguing that Stone had mangled the history and purpose of the Articles of War.

Third, on the question of whether a military tribunal was appropriate for *these charges* against these individuals in this context, Royall and the defense team had challenged all four counts as legally flawed. Stone maintained that it was necessary to find only one of the four charges valid and that the other three could simply be ignored in the analysis. He never explained why it was not necessary for the Court to consider the validity of all four charges; each had a different possible impact on the proof and on the sentences. Stone found that one "specification" in the first charge—entering the country in civilian dress, rather than a military uniform, on behalf of a belligerent enemy nation for the purpose of "sabotage, espionage, and other hostile acts"—was sufficient to establish a violation of the law of war by an unlawful enemy combatant. Stone confided to his law clerk that the precedent for this civilian-dress principle was thinner than he had supposed: "I am troubled some by the statement from [a treatise writer] as to the use of the uniform. I have written the opinion on the assumption that the law is the other way as I think it ought to be." Stone plowed ahead, emphasizing historical examples that he cited as purported support.

Fourth, regarding the Civil War–era *Milligan* opinion, with its broad language about the inapplicability of martial law and military courts when the ordinary federal courts are open and functioning, Stone sought to distinguish it. He said that Milligan "was not an enemy belligerent"—a peculiar statement in light of the fact that Milligan had been convicted of a "violation of the law of war" in plotting against the Union. And he asserted that Milligan was not "associated with the armed forces of the enemy"—also a questionable statement in light of the fact that Milligan had been convicted of, among other things, "holding communication with the enemy" and giving aid and comfort to the "rebels against the authority of the United States."

Fifth, on the significance of the claim by one accused saboteur (Haupt) that he was an American citizen, Stone stated that it did not matter. Citizens, just like noncitizens, could be treated as unlawful combatants (a conclusion fiercely contested within the Supreme Court in a 2004 case about an American citizen initially held at Guantanamo).

Some Justices had reservations and suggestions. Black, reflecting the concern he and Jackson had expressed at oral argument about a broad theory that would permit a military trial for striking workers at a defense plant, insisted that Stone limit the decision to "entry into this country as part of the enemy's war forces." Stone obliged. Douglas objected to a sentence stating that a trial of some kind for the apprehended saboteurs was required; while they had received one, he did not want to suggest it was constitutionally required. Stone again acquiesced and deleted the sentence. Frankfurter disagreed on the scope of the President's military powers; he thought explicit discussion of this issue would open a "Pandora's box" and suggested language papering over it. The final version explained that, since the Court had concluded that "the Commission has jurisdiction to try the charges," the Court need not consider "contentions of the parties unrelated to this issue."

The Court stumbled toward agreement on most issues. But the simmering procedural question—whether the President could create procedures that conflicted with the Articles of War enacted by Congress—now erupted.

ONE POINT OF CONSENSUS among the Justices had been that the Court should speak with one voice on this high-profile case, with its explosive combination of already-executed saboteurs, the President's personal actions, a highly sensitive wartime issue, and a per curiam opinion allowing the presidentially ordered executions to proceed. Robert Jackson, however, was threatening to blow up the Court's unanimity.

Jackson believed that the President's inherent authority in this enemy-belligerent context could not be limited by Congress or the courts. Jackson had been a strong proponent of executive powers in his position as Attorney General and in other Executive Branch posts. Barely more than a year into his service on the Court, he bridled at the suggestion that the President's authority could be constrained by judicial review of the propriety of his actions in this context, even if the Court ruled for the President.

On October 23, Jackson circulated a ten-page draft concurrence (which he labeled a "memo"). He argued that, as a constitutional matter, the President had inherent authority over prisoners who were invaders from a hostile enemy. "This whole business of reviewing the President's Order as being governed by this Act of Congress," he wrote, "seems to me unauthorized and possibly mischievous."

Other Justices were horrified by Jackson's proposed separate opinion, which would prevent the Court from speaking unanimously. Frankfurter quickly circulated a memo he titled "F.F.'s Soliloquy"—what has been called "one of the most unusual documents" in Supreme Court history. Frankfurter emphasized that, "after listening as hard as I could to the views expressed by the Chief Justice and Jackson about the *Saboteur* case problems at the last Conference, and thinking over what they said as intelligently as I could, I could not for the life of me find enough room in the legal differences between them to insert a razor blade. And now comes Jackson's memorandum." He then presented an imaginary dialogue between himself and the accused saboteurs (six of whom were now dead).

Frankfurter told the saboteurs they were "damned scoundrels" with "a helluva cheek to ask for a writ that would take you out of the hands of the Military Commission and give you the right to be tried, if at all, in a federal district court....You've done enough mischief already without leaving the seeds of a bitter conflict involving the President, the courts and Congress after your bodies will be rotting in lime." They should be grateful because they had been "humanely ordered to be tried by a military tribunal convoked by the Commander-in-Chief himself." He continued with a direct plea to his fellow Justices, invoking his close relationships with talented young lawyers in military service: "They would say something like this but in language hardly becoming a judge's tongue: 'What in hell do you fellows think you are doing? Haven't we got enough of a job trying to lick the Japs and the Nazis without having you fellows on the Supreme Court dissipate the thoughts and feelings and energies of the folks at home by stirring up a nice row as to who has what power?' "

Frankfurter's bizarre document—presenting his imagined dialogue with dead men and invoking his personal connections with those in battle—had the desired effect. Roberts told Frankfurter he and Black favored addressing the issue "in as brief a form as possible." Stone undertook what he later described as "patient negotiations," and the Court agreed on a minimalist approach. Jackson agreed to withdraw his concurrence.

Stone glossed over the differences, but he did so at the cost of clarity, transparency, and reasoned explanation. He wrote in the opinion that some unspecified number of unnamed Justices thought that the Articles of War did not apply to the President at all and others thought that the Articles applied but had not been violated: "A majority of the full Court are not agreed on the appropriate grounds for decision." But the Court was "unanimous" that the saboteurs could not obtain relief and thus it was not necessary to "inquire whether Congress may restrict the power of the Commander in Chief to deal with enemy belligerents"—one of Jackson's core concerns.

Finally, the opinion was ready. On Thursday, October 29, 1942, nearly three months after the executions of six of the petitioners, the Court released its opinion. The Court did not announce its ruling from the bench, as was customary. It simply had the clerk's office distribute it to reporters.

❖ ❖ ❖

MEMBERS OF THE EXECUTIVE Branch were elated. Biddle excitedly reported the news to Roosevelt, proclaiming, "The *Milligan* case is out of the way and should not plague us again."

Oscar Cox, a senior government lawyer and Biddle's deputy in the military commission proceedings, wrote Stone an appreciative letter: "To those of us who worked on the brief, your opinion in the Saboteur case is more than excellent." In an unusual missive to the lawyer for a litigant in a decided case, Stone replied with an apology for the limits of his decision: "I am sorry that the exigencies of the case precluded my saying more as to the construction of the Articles of War."

The initial press reaction was muted. After the per curiam opinion on July 31, editorials generally had praised the Court, saying it had upheld justice even in the midst of war. Norman Cousins of the *Saturday Review of Literature* was an exception. With the outcome foreordained, he objected, there was "no need to make a farce out of justice." When the Court's full opinion was released on October 29, the bottom line—victory for the government—had long been known. The only suspense was whether the Court would endorse Biddle's sweeping claims of executive authority, which might have implications for other presidential war powers. Reporters found it anticlimactic that the Court's finding of congressional authorization made such a determination unnecessary.

But soon after the decision, Frankfurter asked his former student Frederick Bernays Wiener, a military law expert, to evaluate *Quirin*. Wiener reported that Stone's opinion was deeply flawed. He was one of the first, but not the last, to take this view. He stated that the conclusion that the Articles of War authorized military commissions in any instance of a claimed law-of-war violation badly distorted the history and text of that Article, and that the Commission's procedures clearly conflicted with controlling statutory requirements. Only five years after the *Quirin* decision, constitutional historian Edward Corwin derided it as "a ceremonious detour to a predetermined goal."

Withering criticism continued. Stone's generally admiring biographer Alpheus Thomas Mason observed that the Justices' "own involvement in the trial through their decision in the July hearing practically compelled them to cover up or excuse the President's departures from customary procedures." Professor Amanda Tyler recently summarized that "the foundations of the Court's holding in *Quirin* do not hold up under scrutiny."

Some of the Justices themselves came to regret the Court's actions. Frankfurter observed that *Quirin* was "not a happy precedent." Douglas told an interviewer in 1962 that *Quirin* shows "it is extremely undesirable to announce a decision on the merits without an opinion accompanying it. Because once the search for the grounds, the examination of the grounds that had been advanced is made, sometimes those grounds crumble." And he later elaborated, "While it was easy to agree on the original per curiam, we almost fell apart when it came time to write out the views." Black's law clerk during the *Quirin* case, John Frank, recalled that the Court acted in "haste" and "allowed itself to be stampeded." He continued, "If the judges are to run a court of law and not a butcher shop, the reasons for killing a man should be expressed before he is dead."

This is not to say that *Quirin* has had no effects or staying power. It has never been overruled or formally disavowed, even though Justices Antonin Scalia and John Paul Stevens caustically noted in a 2004 dissent that *Quirin* was "not the Court's finest hour." Justice Sandra Day O'Connor invoked *Quirin* about the military detention of an American citizen deemed an enemy combatant; Stevens cited it in a majority opinion as support for the Court's authority to consider Guantanamo detainees' challenges to their detention over the vehement objections of the Bush Administration.

But it remains a decision rife with errors and sloppy reasoning. In addition to those emphasized by commentators, other problems abound. As noted, for example, the Court never explained why consideration of one specification in one charge was all that was necessary to sustain military-commission jurisdiction in a four-charge case, when the other charges potentially would have an impact on the proof and the sentences. And the Court's terse explanation for omitting a rationale on its conflict-with-procedures point—that it lacked a majority, with "some members of the Court" of one view and "others" holding

a different view—is sophistry. Seven Justices were participating, with
Murphy recused and Byrnes resigned. Four favored one rationale and
three another—a numerical fact deliberately not disclosed in the final
opinion; nor were the respective Justices identified. (A draft of the opinion had noted that four Justices believed that the Articles applied and
that the saboteurs' claims failed, while three believed that the Articles
did not apply, but the final version omitted this information.) With a
seven-Justice Court, a majority of four typically decides the case, as had
happened in one case in May 1942 and would happen again in another
case in December 1942. But in *Quirin*, the Court simply said there was
not "a majority of the full Court" on the issue and thus it would say no
more—an explanation that makes no sense (despite the coy reference
to the "full court") and that has led otherwise-thoughtful observers to
erroneously suggest the Court was evenly divided and could not reach
a decision.

The *Quirin* case stands as an object lesson of the harm that results
from a Court that is too close to the President. Here, in addition to the
reluctance to challenge the revered President's powers in a time of war,
the case reveals glaring problems—Frankfurter's secret advice on the
composition of the tribunals; FDR's private threat, communicated to
the Court, that he would defy an adverse judgment; the Court's rush
to hear and decide the case so that the military-commission trial and
executions could speedily proceed. The danger, as Alpheus Mason expressed it, was that the Court had become "part of an executive juggernaut." In the words of constitutional expert Louis Fisher, "the Court
carried water for the Administration.... Instead of functioning as an independent institution, it served more as a wing of the White House."
And, as David Danelski has summarized, "For the executive branch, the
Saboteurs' Case was a constitutional and propaganda victory.... For the
Supreme Court, it was an institutional defeat. If there is any lesson to be
learned from the case, it is that the Court should be wary of departing
from its established rules and practices, even in times of national crisis,
for at such times the Court is especially susceptible to co-optation by the
executive."

Perhaps the most telling coda is a plaintive comment by Stone to a friend a few weeks after the decision. He lamented that the Court had not received sufficient credit for reviewing the accused saboteurs' challenge, the only point on which it had gone, ever so mildly, against the President and his lawyers, who had argued against any judicial review. "I hope you noticed that the opinion flatly rejected (as unobtrusively as possible) the President's comment that no court should hear the plea of the saboteurs. That, I thought, was going pretty far." That the Chief Justice felt such trepidation about even this limited and tepid challenge to the President's position speaks volumes about the Court's excessive timidity in the case, and its excessive closeness to the President.

• chapter seven •

A BAREFOOT LAWYER

D AYS AFTER THE SUPREME COURT ISSUED ITS OPINION IN THE
saboteurs' case, the Court's ornate chamber hummed with anticipation. "The courtroom was full," reported the Associated Press, "and a
double line waited hopefully outside."

As the session began on Monday, November 9, 1942, a buzz ran
through the hushed crowd. A heavyset lawyer in a three-piece suit
strode to the lectern to argue for William Schneiderman. The secretary of the California Communist Party, Schneiderman had come to
the United States from the Soviet Union at the age of three and had
become a naturalized citizen in 1927, when he was twenty-one. The
US government now sought to strip him of his American citizenship
because of his Communist Party membership; the asserted ground was
that Schneiderman's Communist Party activities proved he had been
deceitful when he had stated in his citizenship application that he was
committed to the US Constitution.

Schneiderman's lawyer—and the cause of the crowd's excitement—
was Wendell Willkie. The Republican presidential candidate against

Franklin D. Roosevelt in the 1940 election, Willkie was appearing for the first time before the Supreme Court. As he vigorously argued for the Communist, a reporter noted, the "familiar lock of hair fell over his forehead," as it had when he had barnstormed the country running for President.

AT FIRST BLUSH, SCHNEIDERMAN seemed an odd client for Willkie. The fifty-year-old Willkie was a prominent corporate lawyer who had been a pro-business president of a major utility. Schneiderman, in contrast, was a proud and defiant Communist, scathingly critical of capitalism and captains of industry.

But Willkie was an atypical Republican. The Republican Party had turned to him in 1940 as a breath of fresh air after two landslide drubbings by Roosevelt (against incumbent President Herbert Hoover in 1932 and Kansas Governor Alf Landon in 1936). Parting company with his party's isolationists, Willkie had called for strong actions supporting Britain. Despite his career in corporate boardrooms and councils, Willkie projected a down-home, regular-guy, aw-shucks manner, speaking plainly, throwing his jacket aside, waving his hands as his untamable hair cascaded downward. FDR's Interior Secretary, Harold Ickes, mocked the Indiana-born candidate as the "simple, barefoot Wall Street lawyer." Although Willkie lost the 1940 election, he received almost 45 percent of the popular vote—a better showing than Hoover and Landon, neither of whom had topped 40 percent against Roosevelt. (Willkie also won ten states in the electoral college, compared with six for Hoover and two for Landon.)

Willkie's incongruous role defending a prominent Communist was not entirely surprising. Alongside his Wall Street roots and Republican candidacy, Willkie had displayed a strong civil libertarian streak. He had spoken out in favor of First Amendment protections for unpopular speech. In March 1940, he had written a much-discussed *New Republic* article called "Fair Trial," in which he criticized the prosecutions of both an American Nazi and an American Communist.

In June 1939, the federal government began a denaturalization proceeding to strip Schneiderman of his citizenship. The government won in the trial court and in the San Francisco–based US Court of Appeals for the Ninth Circuit.

Schneiderman's lawyer was Carol King, a leading civil liberties lawyer at a time when few women were members of the bar. In October 1941, she succeeded in obtaining Supreme Court review of Schneiderman's case.

On impulse, she sent Willkie her Supreme Court filing and asked him to become involved on Schneiderman's behalf. He was intrigued, and appalled by the possibility that the government would deprive an American of citizenship based solely on organizational membership and affiliation.

Willkie and Schneiderman met, coincidentally, on December 8, 1941, the day after the Pearl Harbor attack, in Willkie's law office on 15 Broad Street, just steps from Wall Street. As Schneiderman later recalled, "A more incongruous meeting would be hard to imagine: A Communist faced with the loss of his citizenship and deportation, and a Wall Street lawyer who only the year before had been the Republican candidate for president." They discussed his case, as well as the shocking attack and the war ahead.

Willkie agreed to represent Schneiderman in the Supreme Court without charge. Operating as lead counsel, he filed the opening brief in January 1942. Willkie worked on the draft extensively, emphasizing that he would not be a mere "shirt front" who let others do the work. King recalled that "the brief had to be completely his, a part of his very being, his own expression of the political injustice he had agreed to combat." In a clear invocation of the global struggle, he argued that stripping Schneiderman of citizenship for membership in an organization would be a "totalitarian" action.

The geopolitical situation threatened to upend orderly consideration of the case. American relations with the Soviet Union had taken a circuitous path. In August 1939, Germany and the Soviet Union signed their nonaggression pact, making Russia an ally of the hated Axis nations.

But then, in June 1941, Germany invaded Russia. US support for the Soviet Union became an important issue; one prominent American initiative was the inclusion of the Soviet Union in the Lend-Lease program in November 1941.

When Willkie filed his opening brief in January 1942, the United States was less than two months into the war, and the Soviet Union was a vital and essential ally on the eastern front. Schneiderman's case presented a sensitive dilemma for the Roosevelt Administration. The Justice Department had initiated the denaturalization proceeding and was committed to it; red-baiters in Congress, meanwhile, were always on the prowl for perceived softness toward Communists. But the Soviet Union now was an important wartime partner, and this punitive action against a Soviet-born American citizen, stripping him of his citizenship and deporting him, threatened to be a provocation.

Under Secretary of State Sumner Welles, a close friend of FDR, advised Chief Justice Stone, through an informal letter by government attorneys, that the United States wanted an indefinite postponement. He asked for the case to be put on hold in light of the war. As the *New York Times* later reported, "It was an open secret that the government wished to have the issue delayed because of possible friction with Russia."

Stone consulted his colleagues. "The Government," he wrote them on April 18, "for reasons which are obvious, has found it embarrassing to proceed with this case at the present juncture and has secured several postponements, the last one on consent of Mr. Willkie. While I should be glad to have the case postponed by agreement of counsel, my own view is that the Court cannot rightly force its postponement over Mr. Willkie's objections."

The issue generated a contentious discussion in the Court's private conference on April 22. Stone objected to the foreign policy ground for Welles's suggested indefinite postponement. "I feel embarrassed," he declared, "by that kind of request...for nonjudicial consideration....If we yield, we might be criticized as determining policy here as adjunct to diplomatic policy, and we ought not to do that....The only thing that keeps this Court alive and gives it...influence is that we are not influenced by things extrinsic to our job." Three Justices—Roberts, Douglas, and Murphy—leaned toward Stone's view. But others disagreed. Black said that the nation was "in…desperate danger," *Schneiderman* was not "a run of the mine case," and the Court should grant the government's request. Reed similarly emphasized that the Court was not "separate and apart from the rest of government" and that the foreign policy concerns should be taken into account. Frankfurter believed that, with regard to this timing issue, the Court could take into account "extra-legal considerations." When a Justice mentioned Willkie's view that foreign policy concerns should not enter the case, Frankfurter exploded: "I will take this policy from [the] State Department, not Willkie."

Eventually Byrnes, still on the Court at that point and experienced in steering legislation through congressional logjams, suggested a compromise, which all found satisfactory. The Court would give the government the opportunity to formally express its views favoring postponement on the record, and Willkie could respond.

But the government declined the invitation, not wanting to explain its position publicly and engage with Willkie. The government's machinations nevertheless had succeeded in delaying the case and putting it over until the following Supreme Court term.

WHEN WILLKIE MARCHED TO the podium on November 9, 1942, only seven Justices were on the bench. Byrnes was now gone from the Court and ensconced in the White House. His replacement had not been named, much less confirmed. Jackson, meanwhile, had recused himself because the case against Schneiderman had been pending in the lower courts while he was Attorney General. In contrast, Murphy, who had been Attorney General when Schneiderman's denaturalization proceeding began, continued to participate—a point that irked Jackson.

Willkie's argument was riveting for those in attendance. He began by pointedly noting that Schneiderman was born "near Stalingrad." At the time, the siege of Stalingrad dominated American headlines. Willkie's reference also was particularly striking because, just six weeks earlier, on September 27, Willkie had met with Stalin in Moscow amid great hoopla and public attention as part of a high-profile worldwide diplomatic mission approved by FDR.

Emphasizing Schneiderman's impeccable record of compliance with all US laws, Willkie said that Schneiderman could not be held responsible, by imputation or association, for every position of other Communist Party members or every tenet of Communist Party philosophy. "Why, you might just as well impute to me beliefs in Ham Fish's statements because we belong to the same political party," he told the Justices, who laughed with the audience at his reference to Hamilton Fish, the senior House Republican from New York with whom Willkie vigorously disagreed on many issues, including Fish's strident isolationism before the war.

Willkie also dismissed the suggestion that Karl Marx's advocacy of revolution justified punitive action against party member Schneiderman. He quoted statements from Abraham Lincoln, "the founder of my party," and Thomas Jefferson, "the founder of the Democratic Party," on their views that revolution sometimes is necessary to uphold democratic ideals. "Both the Lincoln and Jefferson statements are stronger than that of Marx," he told the Court.

Throughout his argument, the Associated Press noted, Willkie "[whacked] the lectern with the flat of his fingers." Commenting on Schneiderman's testimony that he had not read the acceptance speech of the Communist Party's presidential candidate, Willkie observed, to knowing chuckles from the Justices, "I doubt that any Presidential candidate's acceptance speeches are ever read." The *Baltimore Sun* reported that the Justices "found the session with the Hoosier-New Yorker an enjoyable and interesting experience."

Solicitor General Fahy, rising to answer Willkie, quickly shot back. "Jefferson strove to establish and Lincoln to preserve the form of government that petitioner would destroy. Let us not make a shambles of citizenship." Fahy continued that, when Schneiderman applied for and received his naturalization, he did not hold "true faith and adherence" to the principles of the US Constitution, and his allegiance lay "elsewhere."

At its conference on Saturday, November 14, the Court considered the case but could reach no resolution. It took up the case again at its conference three weeks later. Four Justices favored Schneiderman (Black, Reed, Douglas, and Murphy), and three supported the government's citizenship stripping (Stone, Roberts, and Frankfurter). Some Justices were irritated about having to decide the explosive case at all. Roberts, while voting for the government, complained, "It is very unfortunate that law officials have put up this case at this time. But that is for them and not for us."

According to a memo Frankfurter wrote for his files, when his turn came in the Justices' conference, he "spoke rather at length." He reminded his colleagues that he had wanted to put the case on hold, as the government had requested: "Last spring it seemed very important to me that the case should not be heard because of the posture of things in the world. For myself, I cannot understand why the government did not confess error in this particular case and let it go at that." (Since Frankfurter agreed with the government's legal position, it is curious he thought the government should "confess error"—formally deem its legal position erroneous—although perhaps he meant some other kind of government retreat on the denaturalization proceeding.) "But," he continued, "that is their concern and not ours. The case is now here for adjudication."

With the case now before them for decision, Frankfurter, who was perhaps the Justice most involved in foreign affairs and military matters through his ubiquitous network of relationships and protégés, proclaimed that the Court must ignore the geopolitical implications: "This case has nothing to do with the second front or the fifth front or Russia or our relations with Russia or with what will or won't be the possible consequences of deciding one way or another." Invoking his experience as the only naturalized Justice, the Vienna-born Frankfurter explained why he supported canceling Schneiderman's citizenship: "None of you has had the experience that I have had with reference to American citizenship.... American citizenship implies entering upon a fellowship which binds people together by devotion to certain feelings and ideas and ideals summarized as a requirement that they be attached to the principles of the Constitution." Frankfurter drew on his experience with the "Schneidermans" he had known, the Communists of his youth: "I have known the Schneidermans and a good many of them well since my college days, and I have admired, and still do admire, their devotion to their ideals. They are the salt of the earth so far as character and self-lessness go. But they are devoted to a wholly different scheme of things from that to which this country, through its Constitution is committed."

Uncomfortable with moving ahead, Douglas suggested putting the case off until a new Justice (Byrnes's replacement) was in place and allowing the Court to decide the case with eight Justices rather than seven. Murphy agreed. Reed then requested deferring consideration of the case for another week. Stone acquiesced.

The following week, on Saturday, December 12, the Justices conferred again. Black now again pushed for delaying the case until the conclusion of the war. "I would hold it for the duration because of the misuse that would be made by our enemies," he argued. Reed joined him, saying, "I would hold the case, if necessary, until after the war because of the risks of the war situation." Douglas renewed his suggestion to have the case reargued when a new Justice was in place. When Murphy again agreed with Douglas about deferring until a new Justice was confirmed, Stone noted that an eight-Justice Court might lead to a 4–4 tie, leaving the ruling against Schneiderman in place with no Supreme Court opinion—a result that some Justices thought would be "just right," a low-key way to resolve the highly charged case.

The Court decided to put the case over for reargument.

IN THE FALL OF 1942, the question of Jimmy Byrnes's successor on the Court loomed large. "Each time a justice joins the Court," explained Justice John Paul Stevens decades later, "it creates a new dynamic and a different institution—in effect, a new court."

Public speculation focused on Attorney General Francis Biddle or Solicitor General Charles Fahy to fill the vacancy. Felix Frankfurter, however, saw an opportunity to promote a candidate who would be closely aligned with him on the increasingly fractious Court and who was deeply respected and admired: Judge Learned Hand of the New York–based US Court of Appeals for the Second Circuit. Hand was legendary, perhaps the most esteemed lower-court judge in the country. Taft had appointed him to the federal district court, Coolidge to the appellate court. But there was a problem. Hand was seventy years old, and in 1937 FDR had emphasized the age of the Justices as his primary Court-packing justification.

Frankfurter was undeterred. He wrote at least three letters to FDR urging Hand's selection and met with the President personally to plead his case. Frankfurter suggested that Roosevelt explain the appointment of the septuagenarian Hand by invoking the extraordinary circumstance of the war. He even sent FDR his draft of a presidential statement announcing the Hand appointment: "In time of national emergency when each must serve where he can be most useful, it is fitting that in replacing a member of the Court who has been drafted into the war effort, considerations of age and geography—which in normal days might well be controlling—should yield to the paramount considerations of national need.... Judge Learned Hand enjoys a place of pre-eminence in our federal judiciary.... He will bring to the Court a youthful vigor of mind and a tested understanding of the national needs within the general framework of the Constitution." Frankfurter simultaneously enlisted allies to barrage the President with pro-Hand messages.

FDR responded cautiously. He determined that he did not want to make the nomination before the 1942 midterm elections—elections that turned out poorly for the Democrats, with Republican gains of forty-seven seats in the House and ten seats in the Senate (still leaving Democrats with comfortable majorities in both chambers). Turnout was exceptionally low—33.6 percent in House elections and only 29.6 percent in Senate races. Democrats tried to spin their disappointing results by saying that several million pro-FDR members of the armed forces were too preoccupied by the war to vote and that millions of other Democrats on the home front were too busy working for a living and supporting the war effort to vote.

After the election, FDR became irritated by Frankfurter's incessant pressure. During a poker game at the home of Treasury Secretary Henry Morgenthau Jr., the President told Douglas, "This time Felix overplayed his hand. Do you know how many people today asked me to name Learned Hand? Twenty, and every one a messenger from Felix Frankfurter. And by golly, I won't do it." FDR advised Frankfurter he could not contradict his previous statements on age. "Sometimes a fellow gets estopped by his own words and his own deeds," the President diplomatically wrote his longtime adviser, "and it is no fun for the fellow himself when that happens."

FDR settled on Wiley Rutledge for Byrnes's seat. Rutledge touched many bases for FDR—geography, youth, judicial experience (a rarity for FDR's Supreme Court appointments), and, not least, a demonstrated pro-Roosevelt record.

FDR loved the fact that Rutledge had spent his professional life west of the Mississippi and had lived in many places. At the time, Douglas was the only Justice who had any claim to being from the West, with his Washington State upbringing—and Douglas had spent his professional career in the East. Rutledge had enjoyed a peripatetic academic career at the University of Colorado Law School, Washington University Law School in St. Louis, and the University of Iowa Law School (where he was dean). He also had been born in Kentucky and raised in Tennessee. When FDR met Rutledge to discuss the Supreme Court nomination, the President gleefully proclaimed, "Wiley, you have geography!"

Rutledge was universally regarded as a kind, good-hearted, amiable person—in Douglas's words, "a quiet, dignified man with the presence of a parish priest." In obvious contrast to Learned Hand, he also was young—only forty-eight.

Rutledge's views were very much in sync with FDR's. During the 1930s, Rutledge had publicly criticized the Supreme Court's invalidation of New Deal legislation. While he was at the University of Iowa

Law School, he attracted notice from the President and his circle as one of the few prominent legal voices endorsing FDR's Court-packing plan. Influential editorial writer Irving Brant of the *St. Louis Star-Times* recommended Rutledge to the President and his advisers for the vacancies that went to Frankfurter and Douglas. FDR considered him for both and, in 1939, named Rutledge to the Court of Appeals in Washington, DC. As a judge, Rutledge strongly supported judicial deference to government programs and regulation.

Rutledge was the lone FDR appointee with previous experience as a federal judge. The only other Supreme Court appointees who had served as judges, Hugo Black and Frank Murphy, had been, respectively, a police court judge and municipal court judge, both for relatively short periods before they launched their political careers. Rutledge also was the only one of FDR's eight Associate Justice appointees with whom the President had no prior personal relationship, a fact that may have been appealing in light of the criticism he had begun to receive for placing allies and cronies on the Court (and continuing to use them for various tasks).

Attorney General Francis Biddle was active in the search for the new Justice. Biddle consulted Stone, Black, and Douglas about possible nominees. All were enthusiastic about Rutledge, a consensus Biddle reported to FDR. Stone also privately advised Biddle against another public front-runner, Solicitor General Charles Fahy. According to Biddle's memoir, Stone counseled against selecting Fahy because the Court should not have a second Catholic (in addition to Murphy). In a statement shocking to today's ears (particularly from a Chief Justice who often was sensitive to claims of religious discrimination in his time on the bench), Stone warned Biddle that, if Fahy were appointed, "the Church might feel it was always regularly entitled to two." Stone emphasized that he hoped for a Justice who would "stick"—a Justice who would stay on the Court and be devoted to its work.

Roosevelt nominated Rutledge on January 11, 1943. Confirmed by voice vote on February 8, he took his seat on February 15. On his inaugural day at the Court, Rutledge wrote the President a letter of appreciation, telling FDR that he was "very much in [Rutledge's] thoughts" and that Rutledge hoped his service might "help to establish more firmly the democratic institutions which you fight to keep, and to create throughout the world."

WITH A NEW JUSTICE in place and Jackson still recused, the Supreme Court held reargument in the *Schneiderman* case on Friday, March 12, 1943. Just weeks previously, the Soviet Union had won the brutal Battle of Stalingrad.

Once again, Willkie put on a show. Gesticulating energetically, he dropped his eyeglasses on the floor in excitement and left it to an associate to pick them up. Willkie emphasized his own experience reading *The Communist Manifesto* before he turned twenty-one, calling it "one of the great historical documents of all time." At the time, newspapers still ranked Willkie as a top candidate for the Republican presidential nomination in 1944 with Governors Tom Dewey of New York and Harold Stassen of Minnesota, but that did not dim his ardor in the Court on behalf of his client. "Willkie in Fiery Plea—Vehement Argument Presented for Communist Party Man," declared the headline in the *Kansas City Times*.

Once again, Solicitor Fahy forcefully responded. "This man was a Communist," Fahy declared. "His beliefs were contrary to the principles of the United States Constitution."

Newly ensconced at the end of the bench, Rutledge was active in the argument and appeared skeptical of the government's position. Rutledge emphasized that stripping a person's citizenship was the "most tremendous penalty that could be imposed short of capital punishment." Picking up on Willkie's point, he stressed that, in the Declaration of Independence, Jefferson had advocated the necessity for revolution under certain circumstances.

The case had become a sore point for the Justices. When Black elicited a concession from Fahy that Schneiderman had engaged only in "general political talk," Frankfurter asked, "Is it suggested that the

Communist Party has no principles?" He sought to frame Communist Party membership as adherence to an anti-American creed rather than membership in a debating society. According to Frankfurter's diary entry, Black turned to him "with blazing eyes and ferocity in his voice" and seethed, "The Hearst press will love that question" (referring to the conservative newspaper chain owned by William Randolph Hearst). Frankfurter shot back, "I don't give a damn whether the Hearst press or any other press likes or dislikes any question that seems to me relevant to the argument. I am a judge and not a politician." Black replied, "Of course, you, unlike the rest of us, live in the stratosphere." Frankfurter noted in his diary that Jackson remarked to him later that day, "It is an awful thing at this time of the Court's and country's history, with the very difficult and important questions coming before this Court, to have one man, Black, practically control three others, for I am afraid Rutledge will join the Axis." Jackson and Frankfurter feared that Rutledge, the new Justice, would be with Douglas and Murphy under the sway of what they perceived as Black's influence.

In conference, Black was emphatic. He no longer wanted to delay a decision. "The doctrine of imputed guilt is offensive to me," he declared in expressing his support for Schneiderman and Willkie—and, although it was unspoken, for a position that would not alienate the Soviet Union. Reed, Douglas, and Murphy agreed with Black that Schneiderman should prevail, as they had previously indicated, and Rutledge now joined them. Stone, Roberts, and Frankfurter, in contrast, held firm on supporting the US government's stripping of citizenship from Schneiderman and would dissent. As the senior Justice in the 5–3 majority, Black assigned the opinion to Murphy.

Murphy circulated his draft opinion on May 31. The core of his opinion was that taking away somebody's citizenship required "clear, unequivocal, and convincing" evidence; "rights once conferred should not be lightly revoked." The government's proof, Murphy concluded, fell short of that demanding standard.

Frankfurter's reaction, as recorded in his diary, was scathing. "The *Schneiderman* opinion," he wrote, "was circulated today after months of incubation. I know not in what incubators, except that it largely reflects cunning and disregard of legal principles to which Hugo Black gave expression from time to time in connection with this case. It is one of those extraordinarily shortsighted opinions which, to accomplish an immediate end, is quite oblivious of its implications for the future."

That same day, Frankfurter wrote Stone about Murphy's opinion. It was "plain as a pikestaff" that "the present war considerations—political considerations—are the driving force behind the result of this case." He thought it clear that, if the case involved a Bundist (a German organization favoring the Nazis) instead of a Communist, Murphy would have come to "the opposite result." Frankfurter also noted in his diary that Roberts, the third dissenter, "was deeply disheartened" by Murphy's draft and believed it "one more of these efforts to bring the Court into disrepute."

Never one to give up on all possible angles, Frankfurter tried various approaches to Murphy. "Thorough and comprehensive as your opinion is," Frankfurter needled his colleague, "you omitted one thing that, on reflection, you might have to add. I think it is only fair to state, in view of your general argument, that Uncle Joe Stalin was at least a spiritual co-author with Jefferson of the Virginia Statute for Religious Freedom." Shortly afterward, Frankfurter tried another clunky attempt at humor. He advised Murphy that the summary at the beginning of the opinion—known as the headnote—should read, "The American Constitution ain't got no principles. The Communist Party don't stand for nuthin'. The Soopreme Court don't mean nuthin'. Nuthin' means nuthin', and this country don't mean to us what Russia means to the Bolshies." Taking the high road and trying to reply in a light vein, Murphy responded that Frankfurter's draft headnote revealed "long and arduous preparation" as well as "commendable English understatement and New England reserve."

In Frankfurter's view, Murphy was uneasy because he knew the law commanded one result while his personal instincts drove him in another direction. He visited Murphy and told him, "I just know you cannot be happy about the result in the Schneiderman situation. I know it cannot really satisfy your conscience." According to Frankfurter, Murphy replied, "I think the Chief has the better of the law in this case but the faith of my whole life is wrapped up in support of Liberty." Frustrated, Frankfurter chided Murphy that the case was being decided on political grounds: "While it may not be true of us, you know very well, Frank, that it is true of some of the members of the Court that the dominating consideration in this case is thought of Russia and Russia's share in this war. And because of that legal principles are going to be twisted all out of shape. And when we get the case of the Bundists next year there will be some fine somersaulting."

Murphy, though troubled, would not move on his bottom line. Frankfurter likely failed to appreciate the entirety of Murphy's perspective. In a letter to his brother around this time, Murphy alluded to their Irish "forbears" who had immigrated to the United States. Murphy would not now force "the trek of exile back to the old world" without "clear and convincing" proof of wrongdoing.

Frankfurter also sought to pry Reed away from the majority. He told Reed that he understood Reed had voted for Schneiderman because the Soviets were in such dire circumstances at the time and "you, in your patriotic way, deemed yourself...a sort of liaison officer between hard-pressed Russia and this country." But, Frankfurter noted hopefully, Russian military fortunes had changed (with the victory over the Nazis at Stalingrad), and so Reed now should reverse himself as well, viewing the case as if it involved a Bundist. Reed, too, rejected Frankfurter's entreaties.

Stone's dissent, written for himself, Roberts, and Frankfurter, highlighted the US alliance with the Soviet Union—and said it was not at issue. "The case obviously has nothing to do with our relations with Russia, where petitioner was born," he proclaimed, "or with our past or present views of the Russian political or social system." Murphy quickly added a similar statement at the beginning of his opinion. "We agree with our brethren of the minority," he declared, "that our relations with Russia, as well as our views regarding its government and the merits of Communism, are immaterial to a decision of this case." Stone's dissent also decried the majority's reasoning. The factual findings about Schneiderman's Communist Party activities, he argued, amply demonstrated that he lacked the required "attachment" to the US Constitution at the time of his naturalization in 1927.

Conflicts among the Justices continued to emerge, not only between the opposing sides, but also within them. After leaving for a summer in Oregon, Douglas circulated a concurrence for publication—a concurrence that was final and would not be changed—emphasizing that Congress could prohibit membership in the Communist Party as a condition of citizenship but had not done so. Douglas's surprise separate opinion offended Murphy, who had been in discussions with Douglas and believed he could have accommodated Douglas in the majority opinion if Douglas had given him the chance. According to Frankfurter, Murphy was "greatly wounded by the Bill Douglas concurring opinion in the *Schneiderman* case and the circumstances attending it" and was "shocked" by Douglas's "skullduggery." Frankfurter wrote that he and Murphy suspected a political motivation: Douglas wanted his separate concurring opinion to protect his anti-Communist reputation while still allowing Schneiderman to retain his citizenship.

Rutledge also wrote a concurrence, emphasizing the potential impact on millions of naturalized citizens. Unlike Douglas's, Rutledge's concurrence was welcomed by Murphy as friendly and supportive. Only a few months on the Court, Rutledge wrote Murphy about his draft, "This is a magnificent opinion.... You will be proud of this opinion all your life."

Jackson explained in the Supreme Court opinion that he had recused himself because he had been Attorney General while the case was pending. He noted that the *Schneiderman* case "was instituted in June of 1939 and tried in December of that year," and that he became Attorney General in January 1940—a clear shot at the author of the opinion, Frank Murphy, who was Attorney General when the case was "instituted" and "tried" and yet declined to recuse himself.

The Court announced *Schneiderman* on Monday, June 21, the last day of the term and an exceptionally hot day in Washington. Many newspapers observed that the geopolitical issues played a central, if unspoken, role in the decision. The *Washington Post* editorialized, "Mr. Dooley's famous dictum that the Supreme Court follows the election returns may be given even wider application. Apparently the Court also follows the course of foreign affairs." The *Philadelphia Record* stated in its own editorial that "it is odd—and amusing—that both the majority and minority decisions hasten to say that the decision has 'nothing to do with our relations with Russia.' We all know, of course, that it has." The *Chicago Tribune* reported that "there was more than a suggestion in the opinions that the majority of the court may have been influenced by reference to our ally, soviet Russia, of which Schneiderman is a native, in giving the Communist a clean bill of health." And the *New York Times* observed that "the Schneiderman case attracted great attention in view of the issues involved and American relations with the Soviet."

Willkie took the opportunity to castigate the Roosevelt Administration, even though he generally had friendly relations with his 1940 electoral opponent and undertook foreign missions in coordination with him. "I have always felt confident as to how the Supreme Court would decide a case involving fundamental American rights," Willkie told reporters. "My bafflement has been as to why the Administration has started and prosecuted a case in which, if they had prevailed, a thoroughly illiberal precedent would have been established."

The standard announced by *Schneiderman*—the need for "clear, unequivocal, and convincing" evidence in denaturalization proceedings—would prove to be durable. And, contrary to Frankfurter's prediction that the Court would rule differently if it considered a case involving a Bundist, the following year the Court rejected the government's attempted denaturalization of a German American Bundist—in a unanimous opinion by Felix Frankfurter.

· chapter eight ·

"THE WHOLE SITUATION LOOKS MIGHTY BAD"

O N MAY 10, 1943, THURGOOD MARSHALL STOOD BEFORE THE Supreme Court for his maiden argument. A tall, svelte, charismatic man, he carried himself with a confidence bordering on swagger and an easy geniality punctuated by a raucous laugh.

Marshall was thirty-four years old, six foot one, 185 pounds, with a pencil mustache, long legs, and size 12 shoes. Born and raised in Baltimore, he had shortened his first name in grade school from Thoroughgood, which had been the name of his grandfather, a former slave. Marshall's mother was a schoolteacher who supervised his education, his father a railroad dining-car waiter and later a steward at an all-white club, who taught him to fight injustice.

As Marshall stood to face the Justices for the first time, he already was a prominent civil rights lawyer, a field he was creating with his colleagues and mentors. A 1933 graduate of Howard University School of Law, where he had been first in his class, Marshall joined the National

Association for the Advancement of Colored People as a staff lawyer in
1936. He had participated in briefing the landmark 1940 criminal case
Chambers v. Florida, which had led the Supreme Court to reject the
coerced confessions of four Black defendants who had been subjected to
incommunicado police questioning for five days.

Now the nationally renowned NAACP Special Counsel, Marshall had a high-profile docket of litigation in federal and state courts
throughout the country. His cases ranged from defending rural Black
defendants against rape and murder charges to representing African
American public school teachers seeking equal pay in the nation's cities. He also was active in policy campaigns, spearheading the push for
an antilynching bill in Congress. Many of Marshall's cases were in the
Deep South, but they also arose in states from New York to California;
from Connecticut to Oklahoma; from New Jersey to Minnesota; from
Massachusetts to Texas. Marshall estimated that he traveled thirty-five
thousand to fifty thousand miles each year.

Shrewd, strategic, and canny, Thurgood Marshall used his amiability to great effect with a wide range of individuals—from impoverished
defendants and their families to Justice Department lawyers, judges,
and courtroom personnel. "Thurgood Marshall is the amazing type of
man who is liked by other men and probably adored by women," gushed
the *Baltimore Afro-American* in an admiring wartime profile. "He carries himself with an inoffensive self confidence and seems to like the
life he lives. He wears and looks especially well in tweed suits." But Marshall's easy manner was accompanied by an instinct for the jugular and
a fierceness of purpose. Opponents underestimated him at their peril.

The case that led Marshall to the Supreme Court lectern for the
first time, in May 1943, was *Adams v. United States*. It involved an incident on an Army base. Federal civilian prosecutors charged three African American soldiers with raping a white woman on a military facility
in Alexandria, Louisiana, in May 1942. The mother of one defendant
had requested time to hire a lawyer. But the judge had refused and appointed reluctant local attorneys for the defendants. The jury promptly
returned convictions, and all three were sentenced to death.

African American newspapers highlighted the case, and individuals around the country beseeched the NAACP to become involved. With the soldiers facing imminent federal execution, Marshall took over the representation, along with two New Orleans lawyers working on his team. The convicted soldiers maintained that they had paid a white prostitute and that she falsely claimed rape.

Marshall vigorously proclaimed his clients' innocence. He emphasized that the accuser did not assert rape until after her roommate reported the soldiers' visits and she sought to justify herself. The soldiers' supposed confessions, moreover, had been obtained through beatings and threats of mob violence. "Although the NAACP did not get into the case until after the trial," Marshall announced, "we will stay in it until the men are released to fight Hitler."

DURING THE COURSE OF World War II, African American soldiers and sailors in the segregated military experienced abysmal mistreatment. As the poet Langston Hughes later summarized in a retrospective report, during the war, "the NAACP was called upon thousands of times regarding discrimination in recruitment, mistreatment because of race during military training, and failure to upgrade Negro service men because of color." As Hughes vividly described, "In the South, German prisoners of war were served promptly in railway station restaurants, whereas the Negro soldiers guarding them often had to go hungry." In the midst of the war, Army Lieutenant Jack Roosevelt Robinson—later known to the world as Jackie Robinson—refused a bus driver's order to move to the back of a military bus in Fort Hood, Texas. He was arrested and court-martialed but ultimately acquitted.

Following a visit to a military base regarding the *Adams* case, Marshall wrote a senior War Department aide that "the attitude of the Negro soldiers" at the base "is below bottom," permeated by "persecution because of race." He warned that "the whole situation looks mighty bad."

In December 1942, while the *Adams* case was pending in the Supreme Court, the NAACP issued a report coauthored by Marshall and civil rights pioneer William Henry Hastie documenting discrimination and violence against Black soldiers and sailors. Marshall told an NAACP student conference, "Negro boys are fighting and dying all over the world for democracy, and we want to see that they enjoy some of it when they return."

Marshall appealed the convictions and death sentences of his three soldier-clients—Privates Richard Adams, John Bordenave, and Lawrence Mitchell—to the New Orleans–based US Court of Appeals for the Fifth Circuit. In addition to the innocence claim, Marshall discovered an important technical issue. Under a federal law passed in 1940, the federal government could assert its ordinary civilian jurisdiction over newly acquired federal land only if it filed an official notice asserting such jurisdiction with the state's Governor. In 1940, the federal government had acquired the land for the Louisiana Army base, but it had never filed the required notice with Louisiana's Governor. Accordingly, Marshall argued, the Department of Justice—and the federal civilian court—lacked jurisdiction for the prosecution of the soldiers.

For Marshall, the issue highlighted a deeper problem. "It is another instance," he emphasized to the NAACP office, "of law enforcement officials rushing Negroes to trial and this time they rushed the trial so fast they did not take time to investigate whether or not they had jurisdiction and it turns out that they do not have jurisdiction."

When Marshall presented his technical objection to the US Court of Appeals in New Orleans, the judges were struck by the novelty of his jurisdictional claim. They certified the issue to the Supreme Court for resolution before their decision.

And then the case took an unusual turn. Solicitor General Charles Fahy was persuaded by Marshall's position. He filed a brief confessing error on behalf of the federal government. He conceded that Marshall was correct on the jurisdictional point. The convictions and death penalty should be vacated.

With the government's agreement in hand, Thurgood Marshall's first Supreme Court argument on Monday, May 10, 1943, carried the day. A mere two weeks after his appearance, on May 24, the Court issued a brief unanimous opinion by Justice Hugo Black ruling that, as Marshall had argued, the federal civilian courts lacked jurisdiction of the case because the federal government had not filed the necessary notice with Louisiana's Governor. The *Adams* case was not the last time that Marshall would argue before the Justices during the war. Just six months later, he would appear again in a major case freighted with meaning for civil rights in the political arena—and for America's wartime image.

But, for now, Marshall's initial Supreme Court argument—in a storied career that would see him argue a total of thirty-two cases there over the next twenty-four years—had been a rousing success, with his keen lawyer's eye for technical objections emerging as one of the many weapons in his formidable arsenal.

· *chapter nine* ·

"A FIXED STAR IN OUR CONSTITUTIONAL CONSTELLATION"

THROUGHOUT THE WAR YEARS, THE SUPREME COURT CON-
fronted cases involving a despised religious minority: Jehovah's
Witnesses. Founded in Pennsylvania in the late nineteenth century, the
sect believed in a coming Armageddon and in an individual's personal
relationship with God, including the responsibility to spread the word.
Jehovah's Witnesses opposed celebrations of birthdays, Christmas, and
Easter as pagan practices. They also fervently opposed war. During
World War I, Witness leader Joseph Rutherford and other sect officials
were prosecuted and imprisoned under the Espionage Act for their vehement opposition to the war; their convictions later were reversed on
appeal.

Jehovah's Witnesses aggressively proselytized—door to door, in
town centers, on public streets, anywhere they could find an audience.
They amplified their message with loudspeakers, frequently deriding

other religions as frauds and shams. Their activities sparked citizen complaints, encounters with police, criminal prosecutions, and other legal penalties.

In the eight years between 1938 and 1946, the Supreme Court decided twenty-three cases involving Jehovah's Witnesses. They raised novel issues about individual and religious rights. Harlan Fiske Stone once quipped that an endowment should be established for the Witnesses "in view of the aid they give in solving the legal problems of civil liberties."

The Witnesses' objections to military service incited public anger as war clouds gathered and even more so after the war began. Close to half of the men imprisoned for refusing military conscription during World War II—four thousand of the ten thousand—were Jehovah's Witnesses.

By the spring of 1943, the Supreme Court had already decided numerous important cases involving the Witnesses. On June 14, 1943, the Supreme Court protected the right of Jehovah's Witness schoolchildren to refuse to salute the American flag in public schools. The opinion, in *West Virginia State Board of Education v. Barnette*, decided at the height of World War II, ranks as one of the Supreme Court's greatest, most eloquent, and most inspiring on free speech and individual rights.

Justice Robert Jackson, on the Court not quite two years, wrote the landmark opinion. It featured the Court's ringing protection of civil liberties in the midst of a war for the country's survival.

ROBERT HOUGHWOUT JACKSON NEVER went to college. He attended only one year of law school. And yet he became one of the finest writers ever to grace the Supreme Court.

Born in northwestern Pennsylvania in 1892, Jackson moved with his family to a tiny town near Jamestown in western New York when he was six. His father had various jobs—logging and selling wood, raising and selling horses, running a hotel.

Jackson flourished in the small-town environment, graduated from high school as valedictorian, and spent a postgraduate year at another high school. Skipping college, he jumped into an apprenticeship in a Jamestown law office. He left his work to spend a year at Albany Law School, completing the requirements of a program for students with legal experience but never receiving his formal law degree; he then returned to his legal apprenticeship. He passed the New York bar when he was twenty-one, as soon as he became eligible. Along the way, he immersed himself in books—classics, literature, biographies. He had been inspired by two beloved high school teachers; even without the benefit of a college education, he became a deeply learned and well-read man.

Jackson quickly earned a dazzling legal reputation. He practiced briefly in Buffalo and then returned to Jamestown. He had a gift for language and an instinct for connecting with the common man and woman.

With his distinctive widow's peak and twinkling eyes, Jackson emerged as a popular leader of the bar, known and welcomed throughout the state. In 1916, he married Irene Gerhardt, a secretary in the state capitol whom he had met during his year at Albany Law School. They had a son in 1919 and a daughter in 1921.

Jackson had a keen interest in politics. Reflecting his family's affiliation since the era of Andrew Jackson, he was an ardent Democrat in an upstate Republican area. During his law office apprenticeship in 1911, he met a newly elected state senator with a famous last name: Franklin Roosevelt of Dutchess County. Jackson, eighteen years old, and FDR, twenty-eight years old, hit it off. During the Wilson Administration, when Roosevelt was Assistant Secretary of the Navy, Jackson visited him with a list of federal patronage appointment requests for supporters in New York. FDR happily obliged.

In 1920, when Roosevelt ran for Vice President on the Democratic ticket with presidential candidate James Cox, Jackson hosted him for a Jamestown campaign event. Jackson's political involvement, a hobby alongside his thriving legal practice, continued after Warren Harding and Calvin Coolidge trounced the Cox-Roosevelt ticket. In 1924, he saw FDR deliver his famous nominating speech at Madison Square Garden for New York Governor Al Smith's candidacy for the Democratic presidential nomination (a nomination that eluded Smith in 1924 but that he would gain in 1928). Roosevelt saluted Smith as the "Happy Warrior"; it marked FDR's dramatic return to politics following his devastating polio attack in 1921. Jackson supported FDR's gubernatorial campaigns in 1928 and 1930 and then worked on his presidential campaign in 1932. Jackson's role was not pivotal. He later reflected, "Nothing that I did was significant or worthy of political reward, nor was it done with that in mind."

In 1934, FDR brought Jackson to Washington as the top lawyer in the Bureau of Internal Revenue (now the Internal Revenue Service). Jackson pursued a civil tax fraud case against Andrew Mellon, the former Secretary of the Treasury in the Harding, Coolidge, and Hoover Administrations and one of the wealthiest men in the world. Jackson personally tried the hard-fought case against Mellon and his well-heeled lawyers, a proceeding capped by Jackson's dramatic cross-examination of Mellon. As part of Mellon's response to the pending tax case, the tycoon donated his enormous art collection to the nation, a contribution that directly led to creation of the National Gallery of Art in Washington. The federal government recovered more than $600,000 in back taxes from Mellon.

FDR was thrilled by Jackson's victory over Mellon, a man the President lambasted as "the mastermind among the malefactors of great wealth." And he delighted in joking that the new national art museum belonged to Jackson.

Roosevelt saw the savvy lawyer as a rising star. He dispatched Jackson to the Securities and Exchange Commission and then named him Assistant Attorney General, first for the Tax Division and then for the Antitrust Division, where Jackson excoriated predatory business practices. From there, it was on to the post of Solicitor General and crucial Supreme Court victories defending New Deal programs. Justice Louis Brandeis, not an easy man to impress, proclaimed that Jackson should be named "Solicitor General for life."

In 1940, FDR promoted Jackson to Attorney General after Frank Murphy left the post for the Supreme Court. Jackson promptly delivered a legendary speech to federal prosecutors about the need for prosecutorial restraint and careful judgment, admonishing Justice Department lawyers that the prosecutor has "more control over life, liberty, and reputation than any other person in America." As Attorney General, Jackson wrote the legal memo in September 1940 approving FDR's destroyers-for-bases deal. And while he was Attorney General, Jackson published *The Struggle for Judicial Supremacy*, a best-seller about the anti–New Deal Supreme Court.

Jackson was an ardent champion for the President. Perhaps the most effective advocate for FDR's ill-fated Court-packing plan in 1937, Jackson refused, in testimony before the Senate Judiciary Committee, to rely on FDR's pretense that Court-packing was necessary to address the Court's workload. Instead, he frankly stated that expansion was necessary because the Court had harmed the nation by overstepping its bounds. Jackson publicly argued for FDR to accept a third term and became one of the presidential advisers plotting a third-term election strategy.

FDR enjoyed Jackson's company, bringing him on cozy cruises with pals and cronies: a 1937 visit to Gulf of Mexico islands; a 1941 sail to the Bahamas (where Jackson earned good-natured ribbing for catching the biggest fish); jaunts on the Potomac. Jackson also joined the President's poker games, small-stakes contests in which FDR regularly fell behind and then came on strong through his trademark bluffing and guile.

Roosevelt even promoted Jackson as a possible political candidate. In 1938, FDR, concerned about the possibility that Democrats would lose the New York governorship if Herbert Lehman ran for the Senate, boosted Jackson as Lehman's replacement for Governor. (Lehman in fact ran for reelection.) In 1940, when it seemed that FDR might not run for a third term, the President suggested Jackson as a presidential candidate and his successor. But, with FDR, nothing ever was only one-dimensional. Even while touting Jackson for political posts, he occasionally expressed doubts. He confided to others that, while Jackson was "a marvelous speaker," he might be "too much of a gentleman" to succeed politically.

When Chief Justice Charles Evans Hughes retired in 1941, FDR initially wanted Jackson to replace Hughes as Chief before settling on the Republican Harlan Fiske Stone for national unity, with Jackson taking Stone's place as an Associate Justice. FDR signaled to Jackson that he would be Chief down the road, following the sixty-eight-year-old Stone's presumably brief tenure.

After Jackson joined the Court, he and the President remained close. Jackson stated that, once he became a Justice, FDR mentioned only one Supreme Court case to him. It was the Court's 5–4 decision in 1942 rejecting a decision by FDR's National Labor Relations Board that sailors on a commercial vessel who engaged in a strike at sea (a mutiny, in the eyes of the ship captain) could have their jobs back. Jackson had voted with the majority ruling against the NLRB position. After the decision was issued, FDR, a proud man of the sea with deep respect for a skipper's prerogatives, privately advised Jackson that he strongly supported the Court's opinion against the striking sailors even though it rejected his own Labor Board's ruling.

Now, in the spring of 1943 and in the midst of the war, Jackson faced the vexing issue, on an increasingly divided Court, about whether members of a reviled religious sect could have their children refuse to salute the American flag in public school.

ON JANUARY 9, 1942, barely a month after the Pearl Harbor attack, the West Virginia State Board of Education adopted a resolution imposing a mandatory flag salute in its public schools. The exercise required reciting the pledge of allegiance while saluting the flag with right hand raised and palm turned up. Two Jehovah's Witness schoolchildren—Gathie Barnette, twelve years old, and Marie Barnette, nine years old—refused, and the teacher promptly reported them to school administrators. When the principal questioned the girls, they said that "pledging allegiance to a flag was an act of worship, and [they] could not worship anyone or anything but [their] God Jehovah."

School officials sent the Barnette girls home. Every day they showed up at school, and every day they were sent home because they refused to salute the flag. It was not an isolated incident. Schools expelled Jehovah's Witness children for their defiance, threatened to send them to reformatories for "criminally inclined juveniles," and discussed prosecuting parents for causing delinquency.

The Barnettes' father, Walter Barnette, and the parents of other Witness children sued in federal court on behalf of themselves and all those in West Virginia who were similarly situated.

The Barnettes' case arose against the backdrop of a controversial Supreme Court decision, *Minersville School District v. Gobitis*, issued on June 3, 1940. In *Gobitis*, the Supreme Court upheld the expulsion of twelve-year-old Lillian and ten-year-old William Gobitis, Jehovah's Witnesses, for failing to join their public school's mandatory flag salute in Minersville, Pennsylvania. In an 8–1 opinion by Felix Frankfurter, the Court stated that it would defer to local governments on the wisdom of mandatory flag salutes; it would not become "a school board for the country."

But Frankfurter's opinion went beyond a studied neutrality. It stressed the patriotism, national unity, and beneficial purposes of the flag salute. The "ultimate foundation of a free society," Frankfurter emphasized, "is the binding tie of cohesive sentiment." The "flag is the symbol of our national unity, transcending all internal differences, however large, within the framework of the Constitution." A "society which is dedicated to the preservation of... ultimate values of civilization may in self-protection utilize the educational process for inculcating those almost unconscious feelings which bind men together in a comprehending loyalty, whatever may be their lesser differences and difficulties."

The four other Roosevelt appointees on the Court when *Gobitis* was announced—Hugo Black, Stanley Reed, William Douglas, and Frank Murphy—all joined Frankfurter. So, too, did three of the four pre-FDR appointees—Chief Justice Charles Evans Hughes and Justices Owen Roberts and James McReynolds. Only Harlan Fiske Stone dissented.

When *Gobitis* was before the Court, the desperate situation in Europe loomed large. The case was argued on April 25, 1940, and decided on June 3, 1940. On May 10, 1940, the Nazis invaded France and the Low Countries (Belgium, the Netherlands, and Luxembourg). Days after the invasion, the Netherlands surrendered, and the Germans continued to advance relentlessly in France, smashing through the vaunted French military and defenses.

Frankfurter, who had been deeply concerned about Hitler since Hitler's accession to power in 1933, was dismayed and alarmed. On May 26, 1940, Frankfurter wrote the President that "hardly anything else has been on my mind" except the war. On June 5, Secretary of the Interior Harold Ickes noted in his diary, "Felix... is really not rational these days on the European situation." On the day that *Gobitis* was announced, the last British troops evacuated Dunkirk, and just a few weeks later, the French government formally capitulated. Supreme Court law clerks called *Gobitis* "Felix's Fall-of-France Opinion."

But rather than fostering national unity, the *Gobitis* decision unleashed a wave of violence against Jehovah's Witnesses. While the sect already had been the target of hostility, *Gobitis* "helped to ignite some of the worst anti-Witness violence of the period." Within days of the decision, vigilantes attacked Witnesses across the nation—from Kennebunk, Maine, to Jackson, Mississippi; from Rockville, Maryland, to Litchfield, Illinois.

In one southern town, during a vigilante assault on seven Witnesses, a journalist asked the sheriff why he did not intervene. "Jehovah's Witnesses. They're running them out of here," he replied. "They're traitors—the Supreme Court says so. Ain't you heard?"

By the end of 1940, more than 1,500 Witnesses had been assaulted in 350 separate attacks. Some were especially sadistic. In Richwood, West Virginia, American Legion members and a deputy sheriff tied Witnesses together and forced them to drink large quantities of castor oil, resulting in the Witnesses urinating blood; they then marched the Witnesses in a raucous procession through jeering onlookers. And in

Nebraska, attackers led a Witness into the woods, assaulted him, and removed a testicle.

Many elites from the political, journalistic, and legal worlds were aghast at the *Gobitis* decision. Two days after the ruling, it sparked a major flare-up at the wedding of Frankfurter's former law clerk Philip Graham to Katharine Meyer, the daughter of *Washington Post* owner and publisher Eugene Meyer.

As Katharine Graham recounted decades later, at lunch just before their wedding, Phil Graham and two other former Frankfurter clerks "differed violently from Felix" as they discussed *Gobitis* with him. Other guests joined the fracas. Tempers flared, with "bitter passion," streaming tears, and "reddened cheeks." Frankfurter "broke up the argument by grabbing [the bride's] arm with his always iron hand and saying, 'Come along, Kay. We will go for a walk in the woods and calm down.'" After a stroll, they returned for the wedding ceremony.

More than 170 newspapers published editorials opposing the *Gobitis* decision. "To compel school children to salute the flag," objected the *New York Herald Tribune*, "is a step in the 'Heil Hitler' direction." Harold Ickes recorded his "utter astonishment and chagrin" at the opinion. "As if the country can be saved, or our institutions preserved, by forced salutes of our flag by these fanatics or even by conscientious objectors!"

Even the Roosevelt family became involved. During cocktails at Hyde Park a few weeks after the decision, Eleanor Roosevelt chided Frankfurter that "there seemed to be something wrong with an opinion that forced little children to salute a flag when such a ceremony was repugnant to their conscience." Frankfurter replied that liberals had long complained that "the Court had exceeded its powers.... It was not the business of the court to set itself up as a local school board or to overrule the judgment of the legislature."

FDR, mixing drinks and playing the genial host, mildly agreed with Frankfurter that religious practices sometimes had to yield to applicable law. "Suppose people desecrated the flag," the President asked, "or suppose religious custom involved being bit by rattlesnakes to obtain salvation, the local authorities would have to intervene." The mandatory flag salute, while "stupid, unnecessary, and offensive," was "within their legal power."

The First Lady continued to express concern. In her nationally syndicated My Day newspaper column on June 23, just a few weeks after the Gobitis opinion, she highlighted an attack on Jehovah's Witnesses in Wyoming: "Something curious is happening to us in this country and I think it is time we stopped and took stock of ourselves. Are we going to be swept away from our traditional attitude toward civil liberties by hysteria?"

Franklin and Eleanor's son Elliott Roosevelt joined the fray. In a radio address the day of the Gobitis opinion, he "greatly deplored" actions against Jehovah's Witnesses in Texas. "It is pitifully easy," he told his audience, "to crush out freedom in an overzealous attempt to preserve it."

As the Barnette case proceeded in the spring of 1943, the context for a constitutional challenge to compulsory flag salutes had changed dramatically since Gobitis in three respects.

First, three Justices from the Gobitis majority had announced a change of heart. In June 1942, in dissenting from a decision upholding leafleting restrictions against Jehovah's Witnesses (Jones v. City of Opelika), Black, Douglas, and Murphy announced that, even though they had joined the Gobitis opinion, they "now [believed]" it was "wrongly decided." Murphy had been dubious about Gobitis from the start; he had prepared a draft dissent, but, as a rookie Justice on the Court only a few months, he had refrained from circulating it and instead went along with the 8–1 majority. Now Black, Douglas, and Murphy jointly and publicly disavowed the precedent they had joined.

In his grievance-laden diary, Frankfurter noted a conversation with Douglas in the fall of 1942. According to Frankfurter, Douglas told him that Black had changed his mind on compulsory school flag salutes. Frankfurter asked if Black had reread the Constitution. Douglas replied, "No—he has read the papers." Douglas later maintained that, in Gobitis, the three Justices had mistakenly deferred to Frankfurter.

Second, there had been important personnel changes on the Supreme Court. Two other Justices from the *Gobitis* majority—Hughes and McReynolds—had retired in 1941. And the two newest Justices (Jackson and Rutledge) had sharply criticized *Gobitis*. At a Cabinet meeting days after the decision, Jackson decried "the hysteria…sweeping the country" and was "bitter" about *Gobitis*. Ickes exclaimed to FDR and the Cabinet, "And to think that Felix Frankfurter wrote that opinion!"

As for Rutledge, even though he was a lower-court judge when *Gobitis* was decided, he publicly objected to the decision soon after its announcement. "We forget," he said at a University of Colorado graduation, "that it is [in] the regimentation of children in the Fascist and Communist salutes that the very freedom for which Jehovah's Witnesses strive has been destroyed."

And third, the war context had changed. "Felix's Fall-of-France Opinion" was decided as darkness shrouded Europe. Almost three years later, glimmers of light shone through the gloom. In early 1943, FDR announced in a summit with Churchill in Casablanca that the Allies would settle for nothing less than "unconditional surrender"; the Soviet Union defeated the Nazis at Stalingrad; the Allies pushed Rommel's troops into retreat in Africa; and the United States drove Japan from Guadalcanal. The war's outcome was far from guaranteed. German and Japanese armies remained strong. Tough fighting and many casualties lay ahead. But there was a new hopeful, if guarded, spirit about the Allies' prospects.

When the Supreme Court heard *Barnette* on March 11, 1943, the Witnesses' lawyer was Hayden Covington. He was a top official in the sect and their chief legal counsel in courtroom battles around the country, including the Supreme Court.

On March 10 and 11, Covington gave five separate arguments on behalf of the Witnesses, with *Barnette* the fifth and final one. The other cases concerned fines and penalties levied against the Witnesses in various states for leafleting and sales solicitation. Two matters involved multiple consolidated proceedings—distinct cases combined for the Court's consideration because they raised similar issues. As a result, Covington actually gave arguments in fourteen cases over the two-day period, an astonishing feat and probably a Supreme Court record.

Though Covington previously had achieved some success before the Court, he was an unconventional advocate, sometimes bordering on the bizarre. As *Newsweek* reported in describing his arguments that week, Covington was "a tall, Texas tornado with sea-green eyes." He wore "a bright green suit with padded shoulders and red plaid tie." Just as the Witnesses frequently interrupted the quiet of small towns, Covington's style was unconventional in the placid confines of the Court: "Bending his body into a right angle, or tucking his thumbs into his green vest and lifting his head, he roared, first at the black-robed justices and then at the audience." He could be tart to the Justices, even disrespectful and offensive. In one reported exchange, he sharply told Frank Murphy, the Court's only Catholic, that Jehovah's Witnesses "don't preach in a dead language," a disparaging reference to the Catholic Church's use of Latin in religious ceremonies.

Covington turned to the *Barnette* case on the afternoon of Thursday, March 11. A three-judge district court had ruled for the *Barnette* plaintiffs and barred enforcement of the West Virginia law "as it applies to children having conscientious scruples against giving such salute." Ruling in the wake of the Black-Douglas-Murphy proclamation disavowing *Gobitis*, the lower-court judges had concluded that the three Justices had weakened *Gobitis* as a precedent and that it did not prevent deciding in favor of the children and their families.

Rising to argue after the state lawyer's defense of the mandatory flag salute, Covington blasted *Gobitis* as "one of the greatest mistakes that this Court has ever committed," a grievously flawed precedent that had precipitated a "civil war against Jehovah's Witnesses." In his brief to the Court, a scattershot submission that cited more than sixty separate biblical passages, Covington derided West Virginia's salute as "very much like that of the Nazi regime in Germany."

The American Legion's amicus brief supporting West Virginia invoked the war for the opposite point. In the Legion's view, the mandatory flag salute was essential to national cohesion. "An adequate national defense is not alone concerned with armies and navies and matters distinctly military in character, but includes as well, the moral strength or public opinion of its citizens. This is vital to the maintenance of national security. Government can be destroyed more quickly by assaults from within than by attack from without."

At the Justices' conference after the argument, Frankfurter strongly objected to the overruling of his *Gobitis* decision. But he had only two Justices with him—Roberts and Reed. The Court voted 6–3 in favor of the Barnettes. Chief Justice Stone, the lone dissenter in *Gobitis*, now was joined by the three Justices who had changed their position (Black, Douglas, and Murphy) and the two new Justices (Jackson and Rutledge).

Stone assigned the opinion to Jackson. It was an inspired choice. Jackson generally was unsympathetic to the Jehovah's Witnesses. He objected to their noisy disruptions, with their loudspeaker harangues and aggressive leafleting and solicitations. In each of the other cases argued on March 10 and 11, Jackson voted against the Witnesses. The Court ruled 5–4 for the Witnesses in all except one of the cases. (The lone exception was a unanimous decision against the Witnesses on a technical ground.) In all four of the 5–4 cases, Jackson joined the three dissenters in *Barnette* (Frankfurter, Roberts, and Reed). On the fundamental issue of compelling schoolchildren to express a message that they strongly opposed, however, Jackson parted company with his fellow dissenters. Stone's law clerk later confirmed that Stone assigned Jackson the *Barnette* opinion to entrench the shakiest vote for striking down the mandatory salute.

Over the next several weeks, Jackson circulated several drafts to the Court. Initially, he highlighted the widespread attacks on the Witnesses that had occurred since *Gobitis*. Stone thought these references "rather too journalistic." Invoking "the dignity which should characterize an opinion of the Supreme Court of the United States," he urged Jackson to take them out, and Jackson eventually did so.

Jackson also was keenly aware that FDR's Department of Justice had expressed concern about the mandatory flag salutes. Francis Biddle,

Solicitor General at the time of the *Gobitis* decision and now Attorney General, had condemned the violence against Jehovah's Witnesses. Just two weeks after the *Gobitis* decision, Biddle had criticized violence against Witnesses in a radio address and implored, "We shall not defeat the Nazi evil by emulating its methods." The Justice Department's new civil rights unit also had been investigating the attacks on the Witnesses. Two of the top officials in that section published an article in the *American Political Science Review* in December 1942 condemning the Witness assaults as an "ugly picture" and calling for *Gobitis* to be overturned.

On May 3, 1943, while Jackson and the other Justices continued to work on *Barnette*, the Court issued the four decisions in the other Witness cases—sweeping 5–4 victories for the Witnesses in three of the four (the exception was the one involving a technical jurisdictional issue).

Jackson blasted the majority opinions in his own separate writing. He detailed the Witnesses' disruptions and intrusions. In one case, more than one hundred Witnesses had flooded into tiny Jeannette, Pennsylvania, on Palm Sunday. They went door to door playing records on phonographs, flaunting literature attacking other religions as a "racket" and a "whore," expressing particular vituperation toward Catholics, denouncing "Jewish and Protestant clergy," and returning to the same homes repeatedly. Residents flooded the small-town police with complaints.

In searing personal terms, Jackson highlighted a class dimension about the Justices' rulings for the Witnesses—and against the towns seeking to preserve their peace and quiet. "We work in offices affording ample shelter from such importunities and live in homes where we do not personally answer such calls and bear the burden of turning away the unwelcome," he chided his brethren. "But these observations do not hold true for all." In the industrial communities invaded by the Witnesses, "the householder himself drops whatever he may be doing to answer the summons to the door.... Many men must work nights and rest by day."

As Jackson listened to Douglas and Black announce their majority opinions vindicating the Witnesses, he seethed. On the spot, he decided to read his searing dissent. Both Roberts and Frankfurter sent him appreciative notes on the bench. "You gave 'em hell!" wrote Roberts. "As my God is my witness," Frankfurter exclaimed, "these Jehovah cases were of that importance which called for 'testifying.'"

But even while castigating the other decisions, Jackson continued to craft his *Barnette* opinion upholding the rights of Jehovah's Witness schoolchildren. Jackson grounded his decision not in free-exercise-of-religion precepts protecting the sect's religious practices but rather in generally applicable free-speech principles. That choice gave the opinion, and the ground for decision, the majesty of broad applicability.

In one of the most eloquent passages ever included in a Supreme Court decision, Jackson proclaimed, "If there is any fixed star in our constitutional constellation, it is that no official, high or petty, can prescribe what shall be orthodox in politics, nationalism, religion, or other matters of opinion or force citizens to confess by word or act their faith therein. If there are any circumstances which permit an exception, they do not now occur to us.... The very purpose of a Bill of Rights was to withdraw certain subjects from the vicissitudes of political controversy, to place them beyond the reach of majorities and officials and to establish them as legal principles to be applied by the Courts."

Jackson made clear that he saw these principles of liberty as a rebuke to the totalitarian regimes the Allies were fighting in the war and their tyrannical historical predecessors. "As governmental pressure toward unity becomes greater," he wrote, "so strife becomes more bitter as to whose unity it shall be.... Ultimate futility of such attempts to compel coherence is the lesson of every such effort from the Roman drive to stamp out Christianity as a disturber of its pagan unity... down to the fast failing efforts of our present totalitarian enemies." And Jackson noted early in his opinion that "the extension of the right arm in this salute to the flag is not the Nazi-Fascist salute, although quite similar to it."

"Those who begin coercive elimination of dissent," Jackson continued, "soon find themselves exterminating dissenters. Compulsory unification of opinion achieves only the unanimity of the graveyard."

The Court issued Jackson's *Barnette* decision on Flag Day—June 14, 1943. It has never been confirmed that the Court's timing was intentional. The release of the flag salute opinion on that day was either a stroke of strategic genius or a glorious coincidence.

The decision represented a striking repudiation of *Gobitis*, decided only three years previously. Jackson methodically demolished the recent precedent point by point, including a forthright rejection of what he called "the very heart of the *Gobitis* opinion": its premise that government authorities may compel "national unity" as "the basis of national security." As Judge Jeffrey Sutton has observed, "No issue of federal constitutional law...has seen a greater shift of votes in a shorter period of time."

The trio from the *Gobitis* majority who now agreed with jettisoning the precedent they had supported—Black, Douglas, and Murphy—filed concurrences. Black and Douglas jointly explained that, in *Gobitis*, they had been motivated by "reluctance to make the Federal Constitution a rigid bar against state regulation of conduct thought inimical to the public welfare." But "long reflection" had made them realize that, "although the principle is sound, its application in the particular case was wrong." And in a separate concurrence, Murphy stressed the religious liberty principles that Jackson avoided in his broadly applicable free-speech opinion.

Roberts, Reed, and Frankfurter dissented. Roberts and Reed opted for a low-profile response, publishing only a single sentence stating that they "[adhered] to the views expressed by the Court" in *Gobitis*.

But Frankfurter, the author of *Gobitis*, was outraged. He began his dissent by invoking his own religion, as a Jew, and his background as a civil libertarian. (He had been a founder of the American Civil Liberties Union and an activist on celebrated cases such as the defense of accused anarchists Sacco and Vanzetti.) "One who belongs to the most vilified and persecuted minority in history," he said in his opening sentences, "is not likely to be insensible to the freedoms guaranteed by our Constitution. Were my purely personal attitude relevant I should wholeheartedly associate myself with the general libertarian views in the Court's opinion, representing as they do the thought and action of a lifetime. But as judges we are neither Jew nor Gentile, neither Catholic nor agnostic." He proceeded with a paean to judicial restraint and legislative discretion. "If the function of this Court is to be essentially no different from that of a legislature, if the considerations governing constitutional construction are to be substantially those that underlie legislation, then indeed judges should not have life tenure and they should be made directly responsible to the electorate."

Frankfurter's fellow Justices were appalled by his reference to his religion. Roberts told him the first two sentences were "a mistake." Frankfurter replied he had received criticism that, as a Jew, he should be sensitive to the claims of religious minorities. He "thought for once and for all [he] ought to put on record that in relation to our work on this Court, all considerations of race, religion, or antecedence of citizenship, are wholly irrelevant." Frankfurter noted in his diary that he had "good reason for believing that Roberts spoke to [him] at the instigation of Black. . . . [Black] is a great fellow for keeping things under cover."

Murphy likewise approached Frankfurter and told him, "as a friend," the opening sentences of his dissent should be deleted. He advised Frankfurter they were "too personal" and would be "catapulting a personal issue into the arena." Frankfurter answered that he did not "see what is 'personal' about referring to the fact that although a Jew, and therefore naturally eager for the protection of minorities, on the Court it is not my business to yield to such considerations." And, "in any event," Frankfurter continued, "the sentences will stay in because they are not the product of a moment's or an hour's or a day's or a week's thought—I had thought about the matter for months and I deem it necessary to say and put into print what I conceive to be basic to the function of this Court and the duty of the Justices of this Court."

Jackson's opinion was a masterpiece—the rare masterpiece appreciated both contemporaneously and over the long sweep of history. "Blot removed," proclaimed *Time*. The *Barnette* opinion, wrote a *New York*

Times columnist, marked "a clear contradiction of the Hitler method—
that every child, indeed every grown-up, must learn to click his heels,
salute and shout 'Heil Hitler.'"

Legal scholars and commentators continue to praise Jackson's opinion as "a gem" and "majestic." "Justice Jackson was the single finest
writer in the Court's history," wrote Professor Justin Driver in 2019, "and
Barnette finds him at the apex of his authorial powers. Indeed, whatever
Supreme Court majority opinion might claim the runner-up spot in el-
oquence lags so far behind *Barnette* as to render the event no contest at
all." Frankfurter's plea for judicial restraint may have been rooted in his
past opposition to the Supreme Court's overreach in striking down New
Deal and progressive laws. But it also revealed a massive blind spot on
the compelling constitutional case for a persecuted minority's unwillingness to engage in government-compelled public school speech with
which it vehemently disagreed.

What accounts for Jackson's simultaneous castigation of the Witnesses in the leafleting and solicitation cases and his protection of the
Witnesses in *Barnette*? It was an idiosyncratic combination joined by
none of the other eight Justices. Jackson biographer John Q. Barrett
emphasizes the difference, for Jackson, between the Witnesses' harass-
ment of ordinary working-class families in the leafleting and solicitation
cases and the Witnesses' quiet fidelity to conscience in the government-
mandated public school environment.

As Barrett relates, Jackson often shared a telling anecdote. When
Jackson was a boy, he was home on one occasion with his grandfather
and baby sister. A door-to-door preacher rang the bell and asked Jackson's
grandfather if he could pray for his soul. "The old man, not much of a
believer, said yes, but he also asked the preacher to keep it down, so as
not to wake the baby." Jackson had no patience for the Witnesses' noisy,
baby-waking intrusions. But he saw their freedom to refuse a government command to salute a flag as an essential liberty, especially while
the nation fought odious totalitarian regimes forcing similar obeisance.

Jackson's *Barnette* opinion itself has become a fixed star in the US
constitutional constellation. The Supreme Court has invoked it as a

guiding principle on liberty issues ranging from marriage equality to free speech rights. Forged in the midst of the war, *Barnette* stands as an expression of our loftiest and most important constitutional values.

The high-mindedness of Barnette was, however, almost immediately eclipsed: Just a week after the decision, the Supreme Court issued a vastly different one. It addressed the treatment of Japanese Americans.

· chapter ten ·

"JUST A SCRAP OF PAPER"

S HORTLY AFTER NOON ON WEDNESDAY, MAY 19, 1943, THE SU-preme Court Justices gathered in the House of Representatives chamber.

Once again the speaker was Winston Churchill, delivering his first speech to Congress since his stirring address after Pearl Harbor. The expectant audience included Senators, Representatives, Cabinet Secretaries, and assorted Washington paladins. Behind the Justices sat an array of leaders from Great Britain's military and foreign policy establishment.

Rapturous applause greeted Edward, the former King of England and now the Governor of the Bahamas, as he and his wife made their way to the diplomatic gallery. The man who had abdicated the throne to marry his American lover, divorcée Wallis Simpson, continued to enchant the American public. His friendly visit to Hitler in 1937 and what some suspected to be his pro-German sympathies apparently did not dim his luster. The couple, reported the *Chicago Tribune*, "received an ovation equaling the greeting of the prime minister by American officialdom."

The war outlook was much brighter than the last time Churchill addressed Congress. In January 1943, FDR, traveling on the first official airplane trip by an American President, had joined Churchill in their dramatic meeting in Casablanca, Morocco. The high-profile summit, which had not been publicly revealed before the leaders' arrival, came just two weeks after FDR hosted a New Year's Eve screening of the new Hollywood movie *Casablanca* at the White House.

The meeting was a buoyant occasion. The President's announcement that the Allies would demand "unconditional surrender" surprised and delighted Churchill. The bond between the two had grown strong and intimate. They happily ascended a tower in Marrakech to take in the magnificent view, with FDR carried up the sixty steps by military aides.

Then in May, days before the Prime Minister's speech to the joint session of Congress, FDR and Churchill learned that the Allies had triumphed in Tunisia, giving them decisive control of North Africa. As the two leaders met in Washington and at the presidential retreat in Maryland, they discussed possible aggressive new actions, including a major offensive in Italy to topple Mussolini.

But irritation at Britain was surfacing in Congress. Some believed that Churchill focused excessively on the European front and left the Americans to bear the burden in the Pacific. Just two days before Churchill's appearance in Congress, on Monday, May 17, Senator A. B. "Happy" Chandler of Kentucky slammed Great Britain on the floor of the Senate for making "no determined effort" to drive the Japanese from Burma. "I do not see," said Chandler acidly, "how Great Britain could render greater aid to Japan than doing what she is now doing."

Churchill, on the podium, sporting a dark-blue polka-dot tie to complement his black business suit, gazed out at the assembled audience, including the Justices in the center front row. The Justices sat in their ordinary business suits rather than judicial robes and in order of seniority, from Chief Justice Stone at the right end of their row to the most junior Justice, Wiley Rutledge, at the left end. Just a bit behind the

Justices, in the third row, Senator Chandler sat prominently, peering at Churchill.

Churchill immediately blasted Japan. Invoking "the treacherous attack upon Pearl Harbor by Japan," he proclaimed, "Let no one suggest that we British have not at least as great an interest as the United States in the unstinting and relentless waging of the war against Japan. And I am here to tell you that we will wage that war side by side with you in accordance with the best strategic employment of our forces, while there is breath in our bodies and while blood flows through our veins." Churchill even cast the Allies' effort against Hitler in an anti-Japanese frame: "While the defeat of Japan would not mean the defeat of Germany, the defeat of Germany would infallibly mean the ruin of Japan."

The Prime Minister was just warming up. He praised the "notable part in the war against Japan... by the large armies and by the air and naval forces now marshaled by Great Britain on the eastern frontiers of India" and scorched what he mockingly called the land of "the Rising Sun." "The cold-blooded execution of United States airmen by the Japanese government," Churchill told his rapt audience, "is a proof... of their barbarism." "It is the duty of those who are charged with the direction of the war to... begin the process so necessary of laying the cities and other munitions centers of Japan in ashes." And, in the most quoted line of his speech, Churchill thundered, "For in ashes they must surely lie before peace comes back to the world."

While Churchill went on to discuss the war's progress on all fronts, his antagonism to Japan was clear. "Pulverize Japs After Hitler: Churchill Vow" ran the headline in the *Chicago Tribune*. "There was widespread impression through the Capitol," wrote *New York Times* reporter C. P. Trussell, "that the Prime Minister had directed much of his speech to that Senate episode and, more particularly, to Senator Chandler.... Heads turned in his direction in the big House chamber midway in Mr. Churchill's address."

The crowd reacted enthusiastically. "It was one of Mr. Churchill's greatest parliamentary efforts in a long parliamentary career," noted one journalist, and "widely regarded here as one of his greatest successes." Churchill had shown that the United Kingdom stood shoulder to shoulder with the United States in the war against Japan, the hated perpetrator of Pearl Harbor. Like the others, the Justices cheered lustily during Churchill's fifty-minute speech. One wire service reported that, "in Mr. Justice Felix Frankfurter of the supreme court, the Prime Minster had an auditor who could scarcely contain his enthusiasm."

Even skeptics acknowledged the stirring speech and called for deeds to match it. "Mr. Churchill talks a good Jap war," said Senator Edwin Johnson of Colorado. "I hope that action will follow his words."

After the speech, the Justices headed back to their Court chambers across the street. With Churchill's rousing condemnation of Japan fresh in their ears, they resumed work on a pair of cases argued the previous week. The cases involved two American citizens of Japanese descent, Gordon Hirabayashi of Seattle and Minoru Yasui of Portland. They had been prosecuted and convicted for violating military curfews on the West Coast.

The curfews applied to those who were from Japan or whose parents or ancestors were from Japan. According to the Roosevelt Administration, individuals of Japanese descent in the western states, including American-born US citizens, posed a grave security threat to the nation. Their rights and liberties, said the government, needed to be sharply curtailed.

The post–Pearl Harbor frenzy against Japanese Americans on the West Coast did not emerge immediately. The *Los Angeles Times* initially called for calm. In an editorial the day after the attack, it called the Pearl Harbor assault "the act of a mad dog." But the conservative newspaper pleaded for tolerance of blameless Japanese Americans: "We have thousands of Japanese here and in other Coast cities. Some, perhaps many, are loyal Nisei [Japanese American citizens born in the United States]....Let there be no precipitation, no riots, no mob law. Panic and confusion...serve the enemy." Congressman John M. Coffee, a Democrat from Tacoma, Washington, stated that "residents of the United States of Japanese extraction" should not "be made the victim[s] of pogroms directed by self-proclaimed patriots and by hysterical self-anointed heroes." Attorney General Biddle assured the nation that "every effort will be made to protect [noncitizens] from discrimination and abuse." When the FBI swiftly arrested more than two thousand Japanese, German, and Italian suspects in the United States (1,291 Japanese, 857 Germans, and 147 Italians), FBI Director J. Edgar Hoover concluded that the Bureau had nabbed "practically all" of those who needed to be apprehended.

But then hysteria took hold. It would lead to President Roosevelt's signing an infamous executive order just ten weeks after Pearl Harbor, on February 19, 1942, and to a cascading series of events, including Supreme Court decisions, that remain deeply shameful.

Three separate accelerants fueled the fire. The first was longstanding anti-Japanese racism on the West Coast, where many Japanese immigrants had arrived and settled. Congress drastically limited immigration from Japan in 1908 and completely prohibited it in 1924. (Congress had previously adopted similar restrictions and exclusions against Chinese immigrants.) Congress also categorically excluded Japanese immigrants from American citizenship. But it could do nothing about the children of Japanese immigrants born in the United States, who automatically became American citizens under the Fourteenth Amendment based on their "birthright citizenship." The Japanese success in West Coast agriculture—by Japanese noncitizens and citizens alike—rankled American farmers and agricultural interests. California and other western states even prohibited land ownership by Japanese immigrants.

The second was a public statement by Navy Secretary Frank Knox. A week after Pearl Harbor, Knox returned from a hasty trip to Hawaii to inspect the damage. Eager to shift blame away from the Navy, the Secretary proclaimed, "I think the most effective Fifth Column work of the entire war was done in Hawaii with the possible exception of Norway." ("Fifth column" was a term newly popularized in the Spanish Civil War to refer to the effort of secret agents within a country to undermine the government.) Knox was insinuating that covert activity by Japanese or

Japanese Americans was a major contributing cause to the devastating Pearl Harbor attack. His statement was contrary to J. Edgar Hoover's conclusion and FBI reporting and was not based on fact. But West Coast newspapers, citing Knox's statement, ran lurid headlines claiming "fifth column treachery" in Hawaii.

The third was the report by Justice Owen Roberts's Pearl Harbor Commission. A statement in the report (but not in its formal conclusions) about Japanese espionage in Hawaii before the Pearl Harbor attack had an explosive effect. According to the Roberts Commission report, released on January 23, 1942, "There were, prior to December 7, 1941, Japanese spies on the island of Oahu. Some were Japanese consular agents and [others] were persons having no open relations with the Japanese foreign service. These spies collected and, through various channels transmitted, information to the Japanese Empire respecting the military and naval establishments and dispositions on the islands.... The center of Japanese espionage in Hawaii was the Japanese consulate at Honolulu." The Roberts Commission's statement, which included no documentation, was selective and misleading. It failed to mention important secret testimony from the FBI, Military Intelligence, and Naval Intelligence that the agencies had found no evidence of sabotage—none—by any Japanese or Japanese Americans in Hawaii. Nor did the report include the fact that more than two hundred Japanese consular representatives in Hawaii had been arrested immediately after Pearl Harbor and were already in custody. And it did not address what a later report called "conflicting opinions from the intelligence services about the security danger, if any, posed by the ethnic Japanese on the islands."

The Roberts Commission's report had an immediate impact. A few days after its publication, Los Angeles County Manager Wayne R. Allen said the report established that the Pearl Harbor "debacle had been facilitated by wide-spread espionage and fifth column work." He now was convinced that it was "difficult if not impossible to distinguish between loyal and disloyal Japanese."

Anti-Japanese groups on the West Coast demanded the removal of all Japanese and Japanese Americans. The organizations included the xenophobic Joint Immigration Committee and the Native Sons and Daughters of the Golden West. The American Legion post in Portland, Oregon, called for "the removal from the Pacific Coast areas of all Japanese, both alien and native-born, to points at least 300 miles inland.... This is no time for namby-pamby pussyfooting, fear of hurting the feelings of our enemies... [no] time for consideration of minute constitutional rights of those enemies." More than three dozen American Legion posts in Washington State adopted resolutions advocating expulsion. The California American Legion branch stated that Japanese with dual citizenship—which they viewed as the status of any Japanese American with parents from Japan—should be placed in "concentration camps."

Elected officials took up the cause. On January 16, 1942, California Congressman Leland Ford wrote Administration officials that "all Japanese, whether citizens or not" should "be placed in inland concentration camps." He said that loyal Japanese American citizens should not object to their internment: "If an American born Japanese, who is a citizen, is really patriotic and wishes to make his contribution to the safety and welfare of this country, right here is his opportunity to do so, namely, that by permitting himself to be placed in a concentration camp, he would be making his sacrifice and he should be willing to do it if he is patriotic and is working for us."

On February 13, congressional delegations from California, Oregon, and Washington sent FDR a letter that "all persons of Japanese lineage" should be excluded from "all strategic areas." They defined "strategic areas" as "the states of California, Oregon, and Washington, and Territory of Alaska."

In California, Earl Warren, the Attorney General and the Republican candidate for Governor, advocated removing Japanese residents and Japanese American citizens from the state. Incumbent Governor Culbert Olson, whom Warren would defeat in November, likewise supported mass expulsion.

In addition to post–Pearl Harbor security concerns, some explicitly expressed an economic motivation. Japanese farmers had achieved substantial success. According to one estimate, the Japanese share in California's agriculture was 40 percent of commercial agricultural truck crops and 90 percent of strawberry acreage. "We're charged with wanting to get rid of the Japs for selfish reasons," acknowledged the Grower-Shipper Vegetable Association. "We might as well be honest. We do. It's a question of whether the white man lives on the Pacific Coast or the brown man. They came into this valley to work, and they stayed to take over.... If all the Japs were removed tomorrow, we'd never miss them in two weeks, because the white farmers can take over and produce everything the Jap grows. And we don't want them back when the war ends, either."

WITHIN THE FEDERAL GOVERNMENT, a sharp disagreement emerged about the mass removal of Japanese Americans and Japanese noncitizens from the West Coast. It pitted Justice Department officials against War Department officials.

Attorney General Biddle tentatively opposed mass expulsion. Two of his aides—James Rowe Jr. and Edward Ennis—fought heroically and persistently against the plan. Rowe, thirty-two years old and a likeable Montana native, had been a Frankfurter protégé at Harvard Law School. He had clerked for retired Justice Oliver Wendell Holmes, serving from 1934 until Holmes's death on March 6, 1935. Rowe then immersed himself in the New Deal, becoming an FDR favorite and working at the President's side in the White House until early 1942. Soon after Pearl Harbor, with FDR's blessing, he moved to the Justice Department as one of Biddle's top aides. Ennis, thirty-four, was an energetic former prosecutor and alumnus of the Solicitor General's office. In December 1941, Biddle appointed Ennis to serve as Director of the Justice Department's "alien enemy control unit."

At the War Department, it was a different story. Stimson assigned the matter to Assistant Secretary of War John J. McCloy. McCloy had been at Harvard Law in Frankfurter's early days as a professor and graduated in 1921. Recruited by Stimson to the War Department from a prestigious Wall Street law firm, McCloy arrived brimming with confidence and self-importance. Beginning in 1941, he served as Assistant Secretary of War. McCloy quickly became a formidable Washington presence, cultivating relationships and fortifying his standing in the capital.

One of McCloy's relationships was with Frankfurter, who relished his network of contacts throughout the government. McCloy and Frankfurter spoke by phone every day, took evening walks together, and socialized at their around-the-corner Georgetown homes.

McCloy, a luminary of the legal establishment, overcame his initial reservations about the mass expulsion and possible incarceration of individuals of Japanese descent. Army Provost Marshal General Allen Gullion and his aide Karl Bendetsen strongly supported the expulsion policy and pushed it aggressively.

And then there was Lieutenant General John L. DeWitt, a career Army official. DeWitt, the commanding general of the Western Defense Command at his headquarters at the Presidio in San Francisco, oversaw US military activities on the West Coast. While he was at first uncertain about removal and incarceration, he became a fervent champion of the idea, imbued with racism and undeterred by facts. DeWitt had seen what happened to Admiral Husband Kimmel and General Walter Short, the Navy and Army commanders in Hawaii. They had been relieved of command nine days after Pearl Harbor. DeWitt vowed that he would not be "a second General Short."

The patrician Stimson, an esteemed lawyer, had his own conflicting feelings about expulsion and internment. He recorded in his diary that "we cannot discriminate among our citizens on the ground of racial origin." But Stimson was deferential to McCloy and other aides as they proceeded with their evaluation.

A few days before public release of the Roberts Commission's report, Stimson spent a long evening with Justice Owen Roberts. Roberts told Stimson that the "great mass of Japanese [in Hawaii], both aliens and Americanized," presented "a great potential danger" and a "menace."

Roberts's admonition made a deep impression on Stimson. He noted it in his diary as he continued to wrestle with the issue.

The Roberts Commission's report triggered new urgency from the War Department's expulsion advocates. DeWitt advised Bendetsen that, "since the publication of the Roberts report," the "best people of California feel that they are living in the midst of a lot of enemies. They don't trust the Japanese, none of them." The *Los Angeles Times* now proclaimed that "the rigors of war demand proper detention of Japanese and their immediate removal from the most acute danger spots."

THE ISSUE NOW BECAME SO pressing that Justice Department and War Department officials gathered in Biddle's office for a Sunday meeting on February 1. Joining Biddle were Rowe, Ennis, and J. Edgar Hoover. McCloy represented the War Department, accompanied by Gullion and Bendetsen.

Biddle tried to lay down a marker. The Justice Department would have "nothing whatsoever to do with any interference with citizens, whether they are Japanese or not." Biddle also produced a draft press release stating that the Justice Department and the War Department agreed that "the present military situation does not at this time require the removal of American citizens of the Japanese race."

According to Gullion's contemporaneous account, McCloy erupted at Biddle. "You are putting a Wall Street lawyer in a helluva box," he told the Attorney General. "But if it [is] a question of safety of the country, the Constitution of the United States, why the Constitution of the United States is just a scrap of paper to me."

As the meeting progressed, McCloy, a cagey operator, gauged Biddle's opposition and suggested they put off the discussion until they obtained a written analysis and recommendation from DeWitt. Biddle agreed.

BIDDLE DECIDED TO RAISE his concerns directly with the President. On Saturday, February 7, 1942, Biddle joined FDR for a White House

lunch. As on many issues, FDR had a complex record on the subject
of the Japanese in America. As early as 1936, five years before the Pearl
Harbor attack, in response to reports from Hawaii about possible suspicious meetings with Japanese ship crews, FDR had advocated possible
future incarceration. "One obvious thought occurs to me," he wrote the
Chief of Naval Operations, "that every Japanese citizen or non-citizen
on the island of Oahu who meets these Japanese ships or has any connection with their officers or men should be secretly but definitely identified and his or her name placed on a special list of those who would be
the first to be placed in a concentration camp in the event of trouble."
But, in early January 1942, less than a month after the Pearl Harbor attack, FDR publicly stated that the firing of workers "who happen to be
aliens or even foreign-born citizens" was "as stupid as it is unjust" and
"plays into the hands of the enemies of American democracy."

Now, on February 7, Biddle advised Roosevelt that "there were no
reasons for mass evacuation." The Attorney General told the President
of his concern regarding "the danger of the hysteria." When he finished,
Biddle recorded in his diary, FDR stated that "generally he approved being fully aware of the dreadful risk of Fifth Column retaliation in case
of a raid."

It was a classic example of Roosevelt's talent for deflection. While
Biddle opposed mass expulsion and possible incarceration, moreover,
the Attorney General did not advise the President that such an action
would be unconstitutional or beyond lawful authority. Even though he
was concerned, Biddle was unwilling to stake out a position that might
be seen as too aggressive on this sensitive wartime issue. In fact, when
Rowe and Ennis objected to Biddle that the expulsion and possible
incarceration of American citizens would be unconstitutional, the Attorney General solicited additional advice on the issue from three government lawyers outside the Justice Department: New Deal prodigy
Ben Cohen, former Frankfurter clerk Joe Rauh, and Office of Emergency Management General Counsel Oscar Cox. Their memo stated
that expulsion and broader measures would be a constitutional exercise
of the President's powers but that, as a policy matter, they should be

undertaken sparingly; voluntary efforts should be pursued first. Biddle embraced this view, which allowed him to avoid telling the President that the policy would be unconstitutional.

As late as February 10, Secretary of War Stimson had recorded his fear that the evacuation and incarceration of Japanese American citizens would "make a tremendous hole in our constitutional system."

The next morning, Stimson met with McCloy and an Army general who had just returned from the West Coast. They told him that De-Witt planned to seek permission for the mandatory removal of 120,000 individuals of Japanese descent—citizens and noncitizens alike—from the West Coast. Stimson viewed DeWitt's request as "a stiff proposition" requiring "very drastic steps." But he also was impressed that the formal recommendation had come from the military commander in charge of defending the West Coast. The Secretary now believed he needed direction from the President.

Stimson tried to set up an in-person meeting with FDR, but he had to settle for a telephone conversation. At 1:30 p.m. on February 11, they had a fateful discussion. Japan had invaded the British possession of Singapore a few days previously and would complete a stunning victory over the Allies later that week. As Stimson related in his diary, "I took up with him the west coast matter... and told him the situation." The President "was very vigorous about it and told me to go ahead on the line that I had myself thought the best." While the President's language was not explicit, Stimson thought the presidential message unmistakable. He hung up with the understanding that FDR wanted a prompt resolution of this festering issue—and that the President had just authorized a mass removal plan targeted at all those of Japanese descent on the West Coast, including American citizens.

Stimson's pro-expulsion aides were gleeful. While they did not initially advise their Justice Department counterparts about the presidential decision, they aggressively moved forward with their planning. McCloy called Bendetsen, who was with DeWitt in San Francisco, and told him, "We have carte blanche to do what we want to as far as the President's concerned." He continued that, according to FDR, if the

Army's plan could "involve citizens, we will take care of them too. He states there will probably be some repercussions, but it has got to be dictated by military necessity [and] as he puts it, 'Be as reasonable as you can.'"

Powerful media voices added to the clamor. On February 12, syndicated columnist Walter Lippmann wrote that "the Pacific Coast is in imminent danger of a combined attack from within and without.... There is the assumption that it is a problem of 'enemy aliens.' As a matter of fact, it is certainly also a problem of native-born American citizens.... Nobody's constitutional rights include the right to reside and do business on a battlefield."

Others chimed in with a harder and nastier edge. Hearst newspaper columnist Henry McLemore proclaimed, "I am for immediate removal of every Japanese on the West Coast to a point deep in the interior. I don't mean a nice part of the interior either. Herd 'em up, pack 'em off and give 'em the inside room in the badlands. Let 'em be pinched, hurt, hungry and dead up against it.... Personally, I hate the Japanese. And that goes for all of them." Right-wing columnist Westbrook Pegler exclaimed, "Do you get what [Lippmann] says?... We are so damned dumb and considerate of the minute constitutional rights and even of the political feelings and influence of people whom we have every reason to anticipate with preventive action!... The Japanese in California should be under armed guard to the last man and woman right now and to hell with habeas corpus until the danger is over."

On February 17, Biddle sent a last-ditch memo to FDR, drafted by Rowe, expressing concern about the mass expulsion of American citizens. They were apparently unaware of the conversation between FDR and Stimson a few days earlier. The memo was blunt. "For several weeks, there have been increasing demands for evacuation of all Japanese, aliens and citizens alike, from the West Coast states. A great many of the West Coast people distrust the Japanese, various special interests would welcome their removal from good farm land and the elimination of their competition, some of the local California radio and press have demanded evacuation, the West Coast Congressional Delegation are asking the same thing and finally, Walter Lippman[n] and Westbrook Pegler recently have taken up the evacuation cry on the ground that attack on the West Coast and widespread sabotage is imminent. My last advice from the War Department is that there is no evidence of imminent attack and from the F.B.I. that there is no evidence of planned sabotage.... It is extremely dangerous for the columnists, acting as 'Armchair Strategists and Junior G-Men,' to suggest that an attack on the West Coast and planned sabotage is imminent when the military authorities and the F.B.I. have indicated that this is not the fact."

Once again, however, Biddle did not rule out such a course of action as unconstitutional or beyond the President's authority. Instead, Biddle carefully distanced the Justice Department from the plan, confirming that, if it went forward, it would be a military responsibility. The "hurried evacuation" of the Japanese from California, including sixty thousand "American citizens," would "require thousands of troops.... The practical and legal limits of this Department's authority which is restricted to alien enemies are clearly understood. The Army is considering what further steps it wishes to recommend." Even while objecting to the removal of citizens, Biddle was kicking responsibility for such a plan to the military.

Congressional pressure on Biddle, meanwhile, was mounting. California Congressman Leland Ford boasted that he "phoned the Attorney General's office and told them to stop fucking around. I gave them twenty-four hours notice that unless they would issue a mass evacuation notice I would drag the whole matter out on the floor of the House and of the Senate and give the bastards everything we could with both barrels."

With FDR's "carte blanche" to Stimson, military aides Bendetsen and Gullion urged General DeWitt, the West Coast commander, to submit his formal recommendation. On February 14, 1942, DeWitt wrote Stimson proposing the removal from the West Coast of all individuals of Japanese descent, including American citizens. "In the war in which we are now engaged," he maintained, "racial affinities are not severed by migration. The Japanese race is an enemy race and while many second and third generation Japanese born on United States soil, possessed of United States citizenship, have become 'Americanized,' the racial strains are undiluted.... It, therefore, follows that along the vital Pacific Coast over 112,000 potential enemies, of Japanese extraction, are at large today." In a conversation with McCloy a couple of weeks before submission of his proposal, DeWitt explained his position succinctly. For people on the West Coast, he said, "a Jap is a Jap."

DeWitt's formal submission acknowledged that there had been no sabotage by Japanese American citizens, or even by Japanese noncitizens. But, with an Orwellian twist, DeWitt pointed to that gaping hole as proof of dangerousness: "The very fact that no sabotage has taken place to date is a disturbing and confirming indication that such action will be taken."

Stimson approved DeWitt's formal proposal, which he viewed as having been already blessed by the President. On February 17, the same day as Biddle's memo to FDR attacking the "Armchair Strategists and Junior G-Men," Stimson met with War Department officials. He instructed them to "fill in the application of this presidential order"— placing responsibility squarely on FDR—and prepare a presidential document embodying the mass evacuation policy.

That evening, Biddle hosted a meeting in the living room of his comfortable Georgetown home. Prepared for pitched battle, Rowe and Ennis attended, along with McCloy, Gullion, and Bendetsen from the War Department. Rowe and Ennis pressed their constitutional objections to the forced expulsion of American citizens.

Gullion reached in his pocket and pulled out a draft presidential order permitting the compulsory removal of citizens and noncitizens. Rowe scoffed. And then, to Rowe's astonishment and horror, Biddle acquiesced. Although Rowe and Ennis did not know it, Biddle had called FDR before the meeting to discuss the issue. The Attorney General had advised the President he would not oppose the War Department's proposal. As Biddle later explained in his memoir, "The decision had been made by the President. It was, he said, a matter of military judgment. I did not think I should oppose it any further. The Department of Justice, as I had made it clear to him from the beginning, was opposed to and would have nothing to do with the evacuation."

According to Rowe, "Ennis almost wept. I was so mad that I could not speak at all myself and the meeting soon broke up."

The next morning, in Stimson's office, Biddle, Rowe, and Ennis met with Stimson and other War Department officials to finalize the document for the President's signature. Stimson recorded that Biddle, McCloy, and Gullion "had done a good piece of work in breaking down the issues between the Departments the night before." With a few tweaks, Stimson approved the draft.

For Rowe and Ennis, it was a heartbreaking day. In the taxi back to the Justice Department, Rowe later recalled, he "had to convince Ennis that it was not important enough to make him quit his job." Amid James Rowe's principled courage on this defining issue, this comment shows a rare questionable judgment. How could the forced removal of tens of thousands of American citizens, for whom there was no individualized suspicion, not be "important enough" for a resignation? And in fact, might a public resignation made in protest have affected the subsequent course of events? But the mindset of Administration officials at the time was that a presidential decision had been made and the war required their unstinting efforts. Rowe and Ennis also may well have thought that it was better to stay in government than to abandon the field.

In a cruel twist, it was left to Rowe to obtain the presidential signature formalizing the action. On February 19, 1942, Rowe took the executive order to Budget Director Harold Smith, who controlled the flow of presidential orders to the President. Smith knew nothing about the document. As Smith reviewed it, Rowe told him, "It's all been cleared, Harold. Justice has cleared it, and the Secretary of War has cleared it. Now take it to the President." Smith complied—in Rowe's view, "reluctantly."

FDR signed the order—Executive Order 9066—without comment. The deed was done.

The President's private thoughts on this hugely consequential measure are unknown—whether he thought wartime security required it; whether he believed he was simply deferring to the War Department's military judgment; whether he was concerned about the political controversy on the West Coast and the coming midterm elections; or some combination of these factors. Rowe later reflected on the man he revered who bitterly disappointed him in this instance: "I don't think he spent much time [on the matter].... It's a terrible thing to say, but it was a minor problem with the President." Biddle similarly observed, "I do not think he was much concerned with the gravity or implications of this step. He was never theoretical about it. What must be done to defend the country must be done. The decision was for his Secretary of War.... Nor do I think that the constitutional difficulty plagued him— the Constitution has never greatly bothered any wartime President. That was a question of law, which ultimately the Supreme Court must decide. And meanwhile—probably a long meanwhile—we must get on with the war." Biddle's speculation conspicuously omits his own failure as Attorney General to press the "constitutional difficulty" arising from an official government policy of persecuting blameless American citizens, despite the urging of his top aides Rowe and Ennis that he do so.

FDR's Executive Order 9066 gave the Secretary of War, and military commanders designated by the Secretary, sweeping authority to delineate military zones. Within these zones, they could impose any restrictions on the entry, presence, or departure of "any or all persons" the military deemed appropriate. The order also authorized "such other steps as [the Secretary of War] or the appropriate Military Commander may deem advisable to enforce compliance with the restrictions applicable to each Military area."

The order never mentioned "Japan," "Japanese," or "Japanese American citizens." But it didn't have to. Everybody understood that it authorized the forced removal of American citizens of Japanese descent and Japanese noncitizens from the West Coast. That was the clear origin and purpose of the order.

The following morning, February 20, Biddle, now fully on board, sent FDR a memo approving his executive order as legal and constitutional. "The President is authorized in acting under his general war powers without further legislation," wrote the Attorney General. "The exercise of the power can meet the specific situation and, of course, cannot be considered as any punitive measure against any particular nationalities. It is rather a precautionary measure to protect the national safety.... These disturbances cannot be controlled by police protection and the threat of injury to our war effort. A condition and not a theory confronts the nation."

The War Department moved promptly. With authority delegated from Stimson, DeWitt issued a blizzard of orders, some 108 edicts over the next several months. After designating military zones on the entire West Coast, he progressively ordered, first, "voluntary" evacuation of all those of Japanese descent, including American citizens; mandatory curfews for all those of Japanese descent; mandatory expulsion of those of Japanese descent; a requirement that all who had been expelled file change of address cards with the federal government if they were moving to a different location; and, finally, incarceration in "assembly centers" and then what were euphemistically labeled "relocation centers" in remote areas of inland western states—under military guard, in squalid conditions, surrounded by barbed wire fences. In all, approximately 120,000 men, women, and children of Japanese descent were imprisoned in American incarceration camps based solely on their racial lineage, nearly two-thirds of them American citizens.

Congress also moved quickly. The War Department wanted legislative ratification of the executive order, and it wanted criminal penalties for violations of military edicts issued under the order. DeWitt was eager for the penalty to be a felony so that he could use deadly force: "You can shoot a man to prevent the commission of a felony." But McCloy and others in the Administration asked Congress to make violations misdemeanors, punishable by up to a year in jail and a fine of up to $5,000.

Only four weeks after FDR signed the executive order, Congress took up terse legislation imposing the requested criminal penalties for violations. On March 19, both houses adopted it with little discussion. Republican Senator Robert Taft of Ohio, an experienced lawyer and the son of former Supreme Court Chief Justice and former President William Howard Taft, said with disgust on the Senate floor, "I think this is probably the sloppiest criminal law I have ever read or seen anywhere. I certainly think the Senate should not pass it." But in the post–Pearl

Harbor environment, not even Taft voted to oppose the bill. FDR signed it on March 21.

One poll in the spring of 1942 showed Americans strongly favoring the removal from the coast of both Japanese noncitizens and Japanese American citizens. Isolated objectors raised lonely voices of protest. Monroe Deutsch, Provost of the University of California, pleaded in a telegram to Frankfurter that individuals should not be forced to leave their homes on the basis of their group identity, calling it "an unprecedented blow at all our American principles."

Frankfurter forwarded the telegram to McCloy. McCloy responded that "the President knows of the program and has approved it." He also asserted that they were proceeding in "as humane and intelligent a manner as possible" and plaintively asked, "Since when has war distinguished between the innocent and the guilty?" Frankfurter praised his friend and former student for his deft handling of the issue.

The Executive and Legislative Branches had spoken. The President had issued the executive order. On the West Coast, pursuant to delegated authority from the President and the Secretary of War, Lieutenant General DeWitt had issued orders establishing a harsh and oppressive regime for anybody of Japanese descent, including American citizens. Congress had passed a law criminalizing the violation of any measures issued under authority of the executive order.

The only opportunity to block this blatant racial persecution now lay in the courts. Two American citizens in the designated "military zones"—Gordon Hirabayashi and Minoru Yasui—bravely challenged General DeWitt's curfews. The Supreme Court heard their cases on May 10 and 11, 1943, shortly before the Justices cheered Churchill's vow to reduce the Land of the Rising Sun to "ashes."

chapter eleven

AN ODIOUS CLASSIFICATION

GORDON HIRABAYASHI, A COLLEGE STUDENT IN SEATTLE, KNEW about General DeWitt's curfew. It applied to Japanese American citizens like him and to others of Japanese descent. From the night the curfew took effect, on March 28, 1942, he raced home every evening shortly before 8 p.m. and stayed home until the curfew ended the next morning at 6 a.m.

After five weeks of punctilious compliance, on the night of Monday, May 4, something changed. As Hirabayashi started his dash home shortly before the 8 p.m. deadline, he paused. "I stopped and said, 'Why the hell am I running back? Am I an American or not? Why am I running back and nobody else is?'" Instead of heading home at the curfew witching hour, he walked his friend Helen Blom back to her apartment and only then returned to his own residence in a YMCA dormitory.

"I received a lift—perhaps it is a release—when I consciously break the silly old curfew," wrote Hirabayashi in his diary.

❖ ❖ ❖

BORN IN 1918, GORDON Hirabayashi grew up twenty miles south of Seattle in Auburn, Washington. His parents were from Japan, pacifists
who belonged to a religious group known as Friends of the World. His
father operated a roadside fruit market. In high school, Hirabayashi
was president of the Christian Fellowship organization and then, at the
University of Washington, he became involved in the University Quak-
ers, the YMCA, and the Japanese Students' Club. In the summer of
1940, he participated in a program in New York on social activism and
pacifism hosted by Columbia University and Union Theological Sem-
inary. When he returned, he applied for conscientious objector status
with the local draft board and was quickly approved. He had never traveled to Japan and had never attended a Japanese-language or Japanese-
affiliated school.

Hirabayashi began regularly breaking the curfew and recording his
violations in a diary. On May 10, General DeWitt issued Civilian Exclusion Order Number 57, which required the expulsion from Hirabayashi's
neighborhood of "all persons of Japanese ancestry, alien or non-alien."
The order mandated that all covered individuals report to a government
center within the following two days, where they would receive instructions about a forced move to a government assembly center and then be
shipped to an internment camp, where they would be imprisoned.

Hirabayashi consulted Arthur Barnett, a Seattle lawyer he knew
through Quaker circles, about a possible court challenge. On the deadline
of the expulsion requirement, May 16, Hirabayashi, accompanied by Barnett, arrived at the FBI office in Seattle. He announced that he refused to
comply with the expulsion order and wanted to challenge its legality. The
FBI promptly arrested him and confiscated his briefcase. It contained his
diary recording his curfew violations, a subject he had not planned to raise.

Within days, a federal grand jury returned a two-count indictment
charging Hirabayashi with two crimes: being a person of Japanese ancestry who had failed to report for evacuation and being a person of
Japanese ancestry who had violated the curfew. The judge rejected his
legal challenge with a tirade. "It must not for an instant be forgotten
that since Pearl Harbor last December we have been engaged in a total

war with enemies unbelievably treacherous and wholly ruthless, who intend to totally destroy this nation, its Constitution, our way of life, and trample all liberty and freedom everywhere from this earth." At Hirabayashi's trial, the jury convicted him on both counts after deliberating for only ten minutes. The judge sentenced him to two concurrent ninety-day sentences—and then Hirabayashi would face the expulsion-and-incarceration regime created by General DeWitt's orders.

MINORU "MIN" YASUI ALSO decided to mount a legal challenge. His Japanese parents had settled in Hood River, Oregon, where his father became a prominent apple orchard owner. Born in 1916, Yasui was raised as a Methodist, attended public schools, and proceeded to the University of Oregon. He spent a summer in Japan when he was eight years old and attended a Japanese language school in Oregon for three years. While in college, he received four years of American military training, obtaining a commission as an Army Second Lieutenant in the Infantry Reserve. He then studied at the University of Oregon School of Law under the acclaimed young dean Wayne Morse, who would be elected to the Senate in 1944. Morse had "a relatively high opinion" of Yasui. But after graduating in 1939, Yasui found it difficult to land a legal job. Through his father's connections, he was hired as an attaché at the Japanese consulate in Chicago. Complying with legal requirements, he registered with the State Department as a foreign agent.

When Japan attacked Pearl Harbor, Yasui immediately quit his consulate job. He rushed to take a train home to Oregon and join the US military active forces. At the Chicago train station on the day after the Pearl Harbor attack, railroad agents refused to sell him a ticket because of his Asian appearance. He tried again a few days later and succeeded. Yasui showed up at a fort to assume command of his platoon. But the Army now did not want him. He returned eight more times and was rejected each time.

Yasui opened a law office in Portland, but as a Japanese American on the West Coast in early 1942, he attracted little business. He became incensed at General DeWitt's curfew order. When Yasui saw that it applied to "all persons of Japanese ancestry," he explained, "I said, 'There the general is wrong, because it makes distinctions between citizens on the basis of ancestry.' That order infringed on my rights as a citizen." He decided to fight it.

On the first night of the curfew, Saturday, March 28, 1942, Yasui strolled the streets of Portland. Nothing happened. He had his secretary call the police and report a Japanese man walking outside after curfew, but to no avail. At 11 p.m., Yasui tried to turn himself in to a police officer on the street. The officer told him to go home. Yasui finally went to a police station and explained his situation to the police sergeant on duty, who responded, "Sure, we'll oblige you." The police arrested him and put him in the drunk tank at the jail for a couple of days, until a lawyer he knew bailed him out. After his case was transferred to the US Attorney's office, he was charged with one count of violating the curfew.

Yasui launched his legal challenge. Unlike the judge in Hirabayashi's case, Yasui's trial judge agreed that the curfew was a violation of the Constitution's "guarantees of individual liberties" with regard to Japanese American citizens (but not Japanese noncitizens). But the judge withheld any relief. In his view, Yasui could not benefit from his ruling because Yasui had forfeited his American citizenship by working for the Japanese consulate. The judge sentenced him to a year in prison and fined him $5,000.

Now it was on to higher courts for Hirabayashi and Yasui. While they fought in the courts, thousands of Japanese Americans and Japanese noncitizens complied with military orders, forced to abandon their homes and possessions and suffer incarceration in bleak and crowded internment camps.

The US Court of Appeals for the Ninth Circuit gathered in San Francisco to hear the appeals of Gordon Hirabayashi and Min Yasui on February 19, 1943—coincidentally, the first anniversary of FDR's Executive Order 9066. "The courtroom was packed with spectators," one wire service reported. "The court itself indicated the importance of the case by sitting en banc"—the full seven-member court rather than a three-judge panel—"a most unusual procedure."

A little more than a month later, the Ninth Circuit issued a surprising announcement: It would not decide the cases. Instead, the court certified questions to the Supreme Court concerning the constitutionality of FDR's executive order, DeWitt's orders, and Congress's action criminalizing violations. The cases raised "novel constitutional questions." The lone dissenter, Judge William Denman, was furious; he thought that, in light of the "threat of penitentiary sentences" to the "70,000 American citizens" whom the government "was driving from their homes to internment camps," the Court of Appeals should decide the cases immediately.

The certification order had an unusual origin. Attorney General Biddle had secretly suggested it to the appeals court because he wanted a fast track to the Supreme Court. Even more remarkably, the Ninth Circuit's certification order was drafted, at Biddle's direction, by Edward Ennis, the Justice Department lawyer who had vigorously fought to prevent the anti-Japanese orders from taking effect and who now was one of the lawyers representing the government on legal challenges to the De-Witt orders. (Ennis's colleague James Rowe had left the Justice Department to join the Navy.) Ennis later told legal historian Peter Irons that he deliberately phrased the certification order to try to help the Japanese American defendants while also remaining faithful to his government duties.

THE SUPREME COURT AGREED to review the Hirabayashi and Yasui cases and set them for oral argument in May. The briefs for the Japanese American men painted a dire picture. Yasui's lawyer described the "disgraceful situation where American citizens are staring through barbed wire barricades on this land of freedom." Lawyers for both men highlighted the racism of the policy. They emphasized DeWitt's public comments that he didn't "want any Jap back on the Coast," that "a Jap is a Jap," and that "it makes no difference whether the Japanese is theoretically a citizen—he is still a Japanese."

The defendants' focus on DeWitt may have had a drawback. Black and his wife were longtime friends of DeWitt and his wife; Douglas also knew and liked the General.

The Solicitor General's brief emphasized the Pearl Harbor attack and the sizable Japanese and Japanese American communities on the West Coast. It also stressed that "an unknown number of the Japanese" may have "a heightened sense of racial solidarity" and a "feeling of racial pride in Japan's achievements." The government highlighted characteristics of Japanese culture, such as religion and education, as facts that "should be considered in determining the constitutionality" of the anti-Japanese policy. It acknowledged that "the majority" of the 112,000 people of Japanese descent in the western states—two-thirds of whom were American citizens—"might be regarded as loyal to the United States." But "a disloyal minority, if only a few hundreds or thousands, strategically placed, might spell the difference between the success or failure of any attempted invasion" by Japan. "The operative fact on which the classification was made was the danger arising from the existence of a group of over 100,000 persons of Japanese descent on the West Coast and the virtually impossible task of promptly segregating the potentially disloyal from the loyal."

THE GOVERNMENT'S BRIEF OMITTED a crucial fact. The Justice Department had received a confidential memo from a Naval Intelligence official explaining that it was entirely feasible to separate the loyal from the disloyal and that wholesale restrictions against those of Japanese descent were neither appropriate nor justified.

The memo was written by Lieutenant Commander Kenneth Ringle of Naval Intelligence, an official who had served in Japan, was fluent in Japanese, and had extensive knowledge of Japanese American organizations and individuals. In 1940, Ringle had led a secret "black bag" break-in of the Los Angeles Japanese consulate. He and others had rifled through consulate files to learn the identity of Japanese sympathizers. For Ringle, the mission confirmed that Naval Intelligence already knew the likely suspects in the Japanese American community.

In early 1942, Ringle wrote memos emphasizing the government's capacity to distinguish between loyal and disloyal Japanese American citizens. Ringle argued that "the entire 'Japanese Problem' has been magnified out of its true proportion, largely because of the physical characteristics of the people." The removal and internment of every person of Japanese descent would be "not only unwarranted but very unwise"; "the most dangerous" individuals of Japanese descent "are either already in custodial detention or are members of" organizations whose "membership...is already fairly well known to the Naval Intelligence service or the Federal Bureau of Investigation." Ringle emphasized that he "firmly [believed] that the potentially dangerous can be rather readily sifted out."

Ringle obtained permission from Naval Intelligence to publish a condensed anonymous version in *Harper's Magazine* in October 1942— "The Japanese in America: The Problem and the Solution" by "An Intelligence Officer." The magazine's editor noted that the author was "an intelligence officer who for a number of years was stationed on the West Coast and who...had made a particular study of the Japanese population"; it was "made public with government assent." Ringle's anonymous article concluded that the " 'Japanese Problem'... should be handled on the basis of the *individual*, regardless of citizenship, and *not* on a racial basis."

On April 30, eight days before the government's Supreme Court brief was due, Ennis wrote Solicitor General Fahy with concerns. He noted that, while he had previously read the *Harper's* article, he had just reviewed an actual memo by Ringle. He found it enormously significant. Ringle had credibility as a well-respected Naval Intelligence official on the West Coast. His memo reflected "the views," Ennis understood, "if not of the Navy, at least of those Naval Intelligence officers

in charge of Japanese counter-intelligence work." And the analysis reflected "the most reasonable and objective discussion of the security
problem presented by the presence of the Japanese minority."

Most fundamentally, Ringle's memo contradicted the Solicitor General's proposed position in the Supreme Court. "In one of the crucial
points of the case," Ennis stressed, "the Government is forced to argue
that individual, selective evacuation would have been impractical and
insufficient when we have positive knowledge that the only Intelligence
agency responsible for advising Gen. DeWitt gave him advice directly
to the contrary." The Ringle analysis showed that an individual, "selective evacuation" was "not only sufficient, but preferable." Ennis then
sounded the alarm. "In view of this fact, I think we should consider very
carefully whether we do not have a duty to advise the Court of the existence of the Ringle memorandum and of the fact that this represents the
view of the Office of Naval Intelligence. It occurs to me that any other
course of conduct might approximate the suppression of evidence."

This was an extraordinary statement. A high-ranking government
lawyer was suggesting that failure to inform the Court of Ringle's analysis might be "suppression of evidence," a very grave charge. Every lawyer
has a duty of candor to a court. And the Solicitor General's responsibility for accuracy in the government's representations to the Supreme
Court is especially important.

In response to Ennis's break-the-glass memo, Solicitor General
Fahy apparently did nothing, or at least there is no record of him doing
anything. When the issue became a subject of public controversy more
than seven decades later in 2014, Fahy's grandson Charles Sheehan vigorously defended his grandfather. Sheehan's arguments included that
Ringle did not speak for Naval Intelligence; that Ringle's perspective
was not the official view of the Navy or the War Department; that Ennis's presentation was flawed and confused; that the government's brief
included a footnote cite to the *Harper's* article and so Ringle's views were
not hidden by the government; and that Fahy's brief carefully referred to
possible dangers rather than *definite* dangers.

But these arguments fall short. Ringle's analysis was unrefuted. With its focus on the feasibility and benefit of individualized determinations, it was clearly material to the government's submission. Ringle's undisclosed identity and position were significant. The government's reference in its brief to the *Harper's* article—for the proposition that some Japanese Americans educated in Japan were loyal to Japan—was an out-of-context citation invoked for the *opposite* point of the *Harper's* article's conclusion. In any event, the citation to the *Harper's* article hardly substituted for disclosure of the Ringle memo (or its substance). And the fact that the Solicitor General's brief was equivocal rather than certain about the possible dangers actually made the Ringle analysis more important, not less.

Quite simply, the Solicitor General failed to advise the Supreme Court of an important government military analysis directly refuting an essential element of the government's legal justification for the harsh and discriminatory orders directed against Japanese American citizens.

On May 8, Solicitor General Fahy submitted the government's brief unchanged. And in the continuing saga of Edward Ennis, despite his private warning about possible "suppression of evidence," he signed the government's brief with Fahy, in silent acquiescence.

THE FAILURE TO MENTION the Ringle analysis was not the only significant omission by the US government. The other concealment was by the War Department, and it concerned the reasons for General DeWitt's decisions. At the time of the *Hirabayashi* and *Yasui* cases, the Justice Department did not know of this information and evidence. But the US government—through the War Department—clearly did.

On April 15, three weeks before the Solicitor General's brief was due in the Supreme Court, DeWitt formally transmitted to the War Department printed copies of his *Final Report: Japanese Evacuation from the West Coast 1942*. It was his official explanation of the basis for his orders regarding mandatory evacuation. In conflict with the Justice

Department's explanation to the Court that mass evacuation was required because timing did not permit a loyalty determination, DeWitt unequivocally stated that timing had nothing to do with his decision. The exclusion of Japanese, he emphasized, must continue "for the duration of the present war." In DeWitt's view, the necessity for mandatory evacuation lay in the racial characteristics of those of Japanese descent, including American citizens: "Because of the ties of race, the intense feeling of filial piety and the strong bonds of common tradition, culture and customs, this population presented a tightly-knit racial group.... It was not that there was insufficient time in which to make such a determination; it was simply a matter of facing the realities that a positive determination could not be made, that an exact separation of the 'sheep from the goats' was unfeasible."

Assistant Secretary of War John J. McCloy was agitated by DeWitt's explanation, which contradicted the government's proposed position in the Supreme Court about the basis for the policy, and he made that clear to the General. DeWitt initially bristled at changing his explanation. But he eventually stated in a letter to the War Department on May 5—three days before the Justice Department's Supreme Court brief was due—that he did not "desire to compromise in any way govt case in Supreme Court." He heeded McCloy's request to delete from his *Final Report* his explanation that it was impossible to make loyalty determinations among Japanese Americans and that their expulsion must last for the entire duration of the war. On June 5, DeWitt submitted a revised report, with a revised statement of his reasons for issuing the orders.

Military aide Karl Bendetsen ordered the destruction of all versions of DeWitt's April 15 report. One copy survived, however. It was discovered decades later in the National Archives by researcher Aiko Herzig-Yoshinaga, a Japanese American citizen who had been imprisoned during the war as the result of DeWitt's orders. In the spring of 1943, Solicitor General Fahy, Edward Ennis, and the others were unaware of DeWitt's formal expression of his actual reasons for the expulsion— reasons that contradicted the core of the US government's position in the Supreme Court.

❧ ❧ ❧

AT ORAL ARGUMENT, THE Justices' questions seemed to express great deference to the President and the military determinations. Responding to Hirabayashi's lawyer about the lack of justification for DeWitt's orders, Douglas asked, "Isn't that within the exercise of military judgment?" Jackson, a recent Attorney General and Solicitor General for the Roosevelt Administration, pressed him, "Can't the President anticipate that certain areas are open to attack and act accordingly?" And, responding to an argument by Yasui's lawyer that DeWitt's order exceeded the scope of the President's executive order, Jackson continued, "Can we review the question as to whether DeWitt followed the orders of his Commander-in-Chief?"

Yasui's lawyer emphasized the racial animus underlying the orders and DeWitt's statement that "a Jap is a Jap." Black challenged him: "Suppose the General decided that the orders were necessary for military reasons. To what extent can we review the military decision of a general selected to make those decisions?" Douglas mused that "it is to be expected that some individuals among those evacuated are loyal Americans, but that does not affect the soundness of the military judgment."

Then it was the government's turn. Known as "Whispering Charlie" for his soft pitch and hushed voice, Solicitor General Fahy emphasized broad executive authority in wartime. Jackson raised the discrimination issue. "We all agree that the Government may not say in peacetime that it is a crime for a descendant of an Irishman to do what would not be a crime if committed by a descendant of another national," Jackson said. "The basis of the discrimination is therefore in the war powers." Fahy readily agreed, eager to emphasize the war context. "Certainly this could not be done in peacetime," he replied. "What makes it reasonable now is the war power and the circumstances of war." And then he made an extraordinary assertion: "We do not admit, however, that there is any discrimination involved." Fahy closed by suggesting that American citizens of Japanese descent should embrace the expulsion and curfew imposed on them as their patriotic duty. American citizens, including

Japanese American citizens, should shed an attitude of "I am a citizen and I have rights." Instead, Fahy told the Court, American citizens should live by the creed "I am a citizen and I have obligations."

❖ ❖ ❖

ON MAY 17, JUST two days before Churchill's reduce-them-to-ashes speech at the Capitol, the Justices met in their ornate private conference room to decide on the criminal convictions of American citizens Gordon Hirabayashi and Min Yasui.

Chief Justice Stone sought to limit the case to the curfew order. He wanted to put off the more troubling issue of the mandatory expulsion and accompanying detention in incarceration camps. Stone stressed that there "may be [a] difference between [a] curfew of this kind and going to [a] concentration camp"; he acknowledged that it was "jarring" that "U.S. citizens were subjected to this treatment." But Stone thought he had found a path forward. If the Court upheld Hirabayashi's curfew conviction, his sentence would be the same regardless of the exclusion order violation in light of the fact that his concurrent sentences (for the curfew violation and the expulsion violation) ran simultaneously. Thus the Court could duck the legality of the expulsion order and decide only the curfew order.

Stone urged upholding DeWitt's curfew. While "no one doubts that many Japs are loyal," there were "earmarks of treachery" at Pearl Harbor and a "grave danger that these people would create damage," which justified the curfew. Yasui, meanwhile, had been convicted only of a curfew violation, and so his case also did not impede this curfew-only resolution. The other Justices agreed.

But there was one exception. Frank Murphy was troubled. He announced that he would reserve his vote. In doing so, Murphy threatened a lack of unanimity regarding the lawfulness of a major wartime initiative—an action taken in the name of national security by President Roosevelt and his War Department.

❖ ❖ ❖

A FEW YEARS AFTER Frank Murphy joined the Court, a saying gained currency: "The Supreme Court tempers justice with Murphy." The quip had a dual meaning, either mocking or admiring depending on one's point of view. It reflected the duality that characterized Murphy's life and career.

William Francis Murphy—known as Frank from an early age—was born in 1890, the third of four children of John Murphy and Mary Brennan Murphy of Sand Beach, Michigan, 120 miles north of Detroit. Frank Murphy attended public schools and then college and law school at the University of Michigan. His father was a lawyer and active in Democratic politics.

After a few years of private practice, Frank enlisted in the military during World War I and served brief stints in France and Germany. Back in Michigan, he worked as an Assistant US Attorney and then as an elected judge on Detroit's criminal court. Murphy's handling of the highly publicized, racially charged Sweet trials in 1925 and 1926 resulted in freedom for Dr. Ossian Sweet and other African American defendants who had fought off a white mob attacking Sweet's home after he moved into a white neighborhood. Legendary trial lawyer Clarence Darrow represented the defendants and remarked that Murphy was "the kindliest and most understanding man I have ever happened to meet on the bench."

A devout Catholic, Murphy became friendly with Father Charles Coughlin, a young priest in Detroit who later became a national radio host and a well-known demagogue, bigot, and antisemite. While Murphy condemned Coughlin's noxious views, they remained cordial—a surprising relationship for a man of Murphy's sensibilities.

In 1930, in the midst of the Depression, Murphy was elected Mayor of Detroit. The humanistic, social-minded Murphy vowed that nobody would starve in Detroit. He began vegetable gardens to feed the poor. Murphy became an enthusiastic supporter of Franklin Roosevelt's 1932 presidential campaign, touring the country on FDR's behalf. Murphy's support was especially important because he was a prominent Catholic, and Al Smith (FDR's predecessor as Governor and the 1928 Democratic candidate for President) loomed large on the political landscape. The leading Catholic politician on the national stage, Smith had turned on Roosevelt, his former protégé, with a vengeance. Murphy's reputation as a reform-minded, good-government Mayor also helped insulate FDR from the charge that he was the candidate of corrupt big-city bosses.

After his election victory, FDR rewarded Murphy with the post of Governor General of the Philippines (and then High Commissioner of the Philippines). Murphy found it a deeply moving experience as he led the US protectorate on its path to independence. At FDR's urging, Murphy came home to run successfully for Governor of Michigan in 1936. His refusal as Governor to have the National Guard remove auto workers from their sit-down strike at the General Motors plant in Flint, Michigan, was a principled stand that earned him wide respect from labor. But it also contributed to his reelection defeat in 1938 when he was attacked for being too weak on lawbreakers.

The following year, Roosevelt named Murphy his Attorney General. In a legacy-defining move, Murphy established the Department's first civil rights unit, an office that became the storied Civil Rights Division. He also oversaw federal corruption prosecutions of big-city bosses, including Kansas City's Tom Pendergast. But Murphy was a poor leader, failing to project strong leadership or a consistent vision. Douglas noted in his diary that "department heads at Justice" viewed Murphy as "a lousy administrator & a loose witted fellow, full of indiscretions...irresponsible & a publicity hound." Murphy's successor as Attorney General, Robert Jackson, restored vigor, morale, confidence, and focus to the Department.

In January 1940, following the death of Justice Pierce Butler, one of the archconservative "Four Horsemen," Roosevelt tapped Murphy for what was then known as "the Catholic seat." After a prompt confirmation, Murphy took his seat on February 5, 1940.

Murphy was a bachelor. He dated Hollywood actresses, and gossip columnists delighted in reporting on his social life. One called him "the Irishman of strawberry-colored eyebrows" and the "answer to ladies' prayers." When FDR received a letter from a Tennessee widow expressing her desire to meet and marry Murphy, FDR merrily threw himself into the matchmaker role, offering in jest to represent Murphy and promising he would be "highly discreet" and charge "reasonable" fees. Joe Kennedy, an avid connoisseur of starlets, wrote the Justice that he had "yet to meet a girl in New York or Washington who doesn't know Frank Murphy." Murphy had wavy, receding red hair and bushy eyebrows. When Charles Evans Hughes retired in 1941, one columnist noted that "there isn't a whisker left on the United States Supreme Court—only Associate Justice Frank Murphy's eyebrows."

But Murphy's public life dating starlets may have masked a different reality. From the time he was in college until his death, Murphy was very close to a male companion, Edward Kemp, who had attended college and law school with Murphy. They lived and traveled together for decades. Kemp also served as a legal adviser to Murphy in the Philippines and in other government positions. In their book on the history of gay and lesbian rights at the Supreme Court, Joyce Murdoch and Deb Price review Murphy's relationship with Kemp and other evidence and conclude that, "with modern-day gay eyes, it's easy to read Murphy" as gay. Private rumors about Murphy's sexuality circulated in Washington, including among FDR Administration insiders, at a time when disclosure would have been a death knell to a public career. Murphy biographers are more equivocal than Murdoch and Price and view the issue as unresolved.

Far more consequential than the question of Murphy's sexual orientation is the fact that Murphy shared confidential Supreme Court information with Kemp. Murphy even had his trusted companion draft opinions and provide him with analysis. Then, as now, such sharing of the Court's internal information—and such a role for a Court outsider—was highly improper.

Murphy is often viewed as one of the less impressive Justices of the period. He lacked the brilliance of former law professors like Stone, Frankfurter, and Douglas; the dazzling lawyer skills of Robert Jackson; the self-taught erudition and confidence of Hugo Black. Murphy's law clerk during 1941 and 1942, John Pickering, recalled that Murphy "readily admitted that he was not a great legal scholar." After Murphy joined the Court, Frankfurter cruelly mocked him behind his back, even while currying Murphy's favor and seeking his support. Douglas recorded that Frankfurter began a "poisonous whispering campaign on Frank's incompetence & stupidity."

But Murphy had a strong personal compass, a moral sensibility, a commitment to liberty, compassion, and empathy. And unlike his lustrous brethren, Murphy at least knew enough to be the Justice most troubled by the Roosevelt Administration's persecution of Japanese American citizens.

AT THE END OF May, Stone circulated his majority opinion. It recounted the grave military threat to the United States in the wake of the Pearl Harbor attack and the early Japanese victories in the Pacific; it also emphasized cultural characteristics that purportedly "prevented [the] assimilation" of those of Japanese ancestry "as an integral part of the white population." The opinion stressed the deference due the military judgments of other branches, especially on the lack of time to make the necessary distinctions. The undisclosed Ringle analysis, of course, undermined this very point, as did DeWitt's undisclosed explanation.

Nor did a curfew crime for citizens of Japanese descent reflect unconstitutional discrimination. To be sure, it was an "odious" classification. But "we cannot close our eyes to the fact, demonstrated by experience, that in time of war residents having ethnic affiliations with an invading enemy may be a greater source of danger than those of a different ancestry." Stone cited the Roberts Commission report for the proposition that "espionage by persons in sympathy with Japanese Government had been found to have been particularly effective in the surprise attack on Pearl Harbor."

Douglas promptly circulated a draft concurrence. It was an odd document. The first part sounded a war cry justifying the curfew; the second part suggested that individualized legal review at some point must be available to the affected individuals. Douglas's law clerk Vern

Countryman thought he knew the basis of Douglas's confidence in the military's determination: "Douglas encountered DeWitt on the West Coast the previous summer, and [DeWitt] filled him with horrible stories about Japanese submarines lurking off the coast.... DeWitt sold him a bill of goods."

Frankfurter, meanwhile, erupted at Douglas's suggestion that at some point individuals must be able to file legal challenges. He rushed to see Black, Douglas's close ally on most matters. While Frankfurter had a stormy relationship with Black, they shared a sweeping deference to FDR and his War Department on the Japanese American orders. As Frankfurter's law clerk that term, Philip Elman, recalled, "Frankfurter was not only very close and devoted to Roosevelt.... He was even more devoted to Henry Stimson. There was also Jack McCloy, a close friend who owed his job to Frankfurter." Nobody in the senior ranks at the War Department had been more responsible for FDR's Executive Order 9066, and for the military's curfew, expulsion, and detention orders, than John J. McCloy. In a revealing comment about a Justice he revered, Elman summarized that Frankfurter "saw himself as a member of the President's war team." Just days before the fracas over Douglas's draft, Frankfurter recorded in his diary that he had met at length with McCloy and, separately, with Stimson to discuss pressing War Department issues, ranging from the military strategy in the Pacific to the new Office of War Mobilization and discussions with Churchill about tactical matters.

Frankfurter warned Stone that Douglas's concurrence would lead to "a thousand *habeas corpus* suits." Black told Frankfurter that, "if he were the Commanding General he would not allow [the Japanese Americans] to go back even if the Court should establish their loyalty"—a shocking statement that Frankfurter relayed to Stone with evident approval. The next day, Black repeated his comment in the Justices' conference, adding that, "in time of war, somebody has to exercise authority and he did not think that the courts could review anything that the military does." Frankfurter implored Stone to muscle Douglas into compliance: "Overcome your natural hesitation and send for Brother Douglas and talk him

out of his opinion by making him see the dangers that he is inviting."
Frankfurter also recorded that Murphy told him that Douglas's rhetoric
was "the most shocking thing that has ever been written by a member of
this Court" and "a regular soap-box speech."

After a back-and-forth between Douglas and Stone, the Chief
tweaked his draft and Douglas toned down both sections of his concurrence. Rutledge added a brief concurrence stating that, in his view, the
Court's decision did not preclude judicial review in future cases.

That left only Murphy. Murphy was deeply troubled by Stone's draft
opinion. He jotted question marks in the margins, and, when Stone
referred to the dangerous nonassimilationist role of Japanese-language
schools on the West Coast, Murphy wrote, "Catholic and other church
schools." He decided that he would dissent.

Alarmed and desperate for unanimity on this defining decision
about the President's wartime authority, Frankfurter deployed a range of
efforts to persuade Murphy. He clumsily tried humor, writing Murphy
about his pending opinion upholding the rights of Native Americans:
"Are you writing Indian cases on the assumption that rights depend on
ancestry? If so—I cannot give my imprimatur to such racial discrimination!" Murphy carefully replied, "Felix, I would protect rights on the
basis of ancestry—But I would never deny them." Frankfurter appealed
to Murphy's institutional loyalty: "Please, Frank—with your eagerness
for the austere functions of the Court and your desire to maintain and
enhance the *corporate* reputation of the Court, why don't you take the
initiative with the Chief in getting him to take out everything that either
offends you or that you would want to express more irenically."

But Murphy persisted and circulated a vigorous dissent. He objected
that the "round-up" and deprivation of liberty for "no less than 70,000
American citizens…because of a particular racial inheritance" is "so
utterly inconsistent with our ideals and traditions, and in my judgment
so contrary to constitutional sanctions, that I cannot lend my assent."

Frankfurter redoubled his efforts. "Of course, I shan't try to dissuade
you from filing a dissent," he began with disingenuous self-deprecation,
"not because I do not think it highly unwise but because I think you

are immovable." He asked whether "it is conducive to the things you care about, including the great reputation of this Court, to suggest that everybody is out of step except Johnny, and more particularly that the Chief Justice and seven other Justices of this Court are behaving like the enemy and thereby playing into the hands of the enemy?"

Rutledge expressed support for Murphy but refused to join him in dissent. "I have strong sympathy with Mr. Justice Murphy's views," Rutledge advised the Court. DeWitt's order "approaches the ultimate stain on democratic institutions constitutionally established." But the urgency of war permitted the curfew order as "a racial discrimination only war's highest emergency could sustain."

Murphy began to have doubts about being the lone dissenter. He eventually folded, changing his bottom line from a dissent to a concurrence. His law clerk John Pickering observed that Murphy expressed "unhappiness that he had not persisted in a dissent. If he'd gotten any adherents to that circulated dissent, I don't think he would have changed."

Even while changing his vote, Murphy maintained the core of his criticism. "Under the curfew order here challenged no less than 70,000 American citizens have been placed under a special ban and deprived of their liberty because of their particular racial inheritance. In this sense it bears a melancholy resemblance to the treatment accorded to members of the Jewish race in Germany and in other parts of Europe." But, even while finding it at "the very brink of constitutional power," he reluctantly voted to uphold the anti-Japanese curfew because of "the critical military situation which prevailed on the Pacific Coast area in the spring of 1942." He closed with a warning: "Whether such a restriction is valid today is another matter."

To Frankfurter's delight, the Court had achieved unanimity in upholding the government's curfew order. He congratulated Murphy on "the wisdom of having been able to reach a concurrence" and praised Stone for an opinion "worthy of the Torah."

With regard to Min Yasui, Stone, in a brief unanimous decision, reiterated the curfew's constitutionality as applied to citizens like Yasui. But Stone rejected the district court's holding that Yasui had renounced his citizenship by working at the Japanese consulate; even the Justice Department had not defended that position. He remanded Yasui's case for resentencing.

In ruling only on the curfew, the Court put off the more difficult issues of mandatory expulsion and incarceration. A year later, a case involving a Japanese American citizen named Fred Korematsu would bring the expulsion and detention issues back to the Court. But for now, the Court had resoundingly upheld the Roosevelt Administration.

The Court announced *Hirabayashi* seven days after it decided *West Virginia State Board of Education v. Barnette.* In the course of one week in the midst of the war, the Roosevelt Court issued one of the Court's staunchest defenses of civil liberties—and one of its greatest betrayals of civil liberties. The Constitution protected American schoolchildren from being forced to salute the flag. But it did not protect American citizens from mandatory home confinement, enforced by criminal penalties, for ten hours of every day, solely on the basis of the country that their parents had come from.

To protect the rights of the American schoolchildren in the flag salute case, the Justices had no need to confront the President who had appointed nearly all of them. To protect the rights of American citizens of Japanese descent, however, would have required directly challenging Franklin D. Roosevelt and his Administration on a sweeping action that they claimed was anchored in national security and the needs of war. Not one Justice was ready to take that step, even for a classification that the Court itself recognized as "odious."

The Justices and top Department of Justice officials assemble after an informal visit with FDR at the White House in October 1942. *Left to right*: Solicitor General Charles Fahy, Attorney General Francis Biddle, Justice Robert Jackson, Justice Frank Murphy, Justice William O. Douglas (in hat), Justice Felix Frankfurter, Justice Stanley Reed, Justice Hugo Black, Justice Owen Roberts, and Chief Justice Harlan Fiske Stone. *Credit: ACME*

A *Washington Star* cartoon shows FDR presenting William O. Douglas to the Supreme Court in 1939. *Credit: Granger*

In July 1941, FDR swore in Attorney General Robert Jackson to the Supreme Court at a joyful ceremony in the President's office attended by the New Deal's top officials. *Credit: Library of Congress, Prints and Photographs Division, photograph by Harris & Ewing*

The Japanese attack on Pearl Harbor on December 7, 1941, shocked the Justices, like all Americans. *Credit: Library of Congress*

Justice Owen Roberts leaves the White House, surrounded by reporters, after delivering his Pearl Harbor Commission's report to FDR in January 1942.

Justice Frank Murphy (manning the weapon) served in the Army on a special assignment during the Supreme Court's summer recess in 1942. Murphy's military service led to his recusal from the Court's consideration of pleas from accused Nazi saboteurs that summer. *Credit: AP Photo*

Soldiers stand guard in August 1942 as ambulances transport the bodies of six Nazi saboteurs who had been executed in the District of Columbia jail's electric chair. *Credit: Photo © Hulton-Deutsch Collection / CORBIS / Corbis via Getty Images*

Schoolchildren begin their day with a flag salute in Rochester, New York, in March 1943. Three months later, in *West Virginia Board of Education v. Barnette*, the Supreme Court ruled that students could not be compelled to engage in the flag salute. *Credit: Library of Congress, Prints and Photographs Division, Farm Security Administration / Office of War Information Black-and-White Negatives.*

Wendell Willkie, FDR's Republican opponent in the 1940 election, won a Supreme Court case in 1943 for William Schneiderman, a Soviet-born California Communist whom the Roosevelt Administration sought to strip of his citizenship. *Credit: AP Photo*

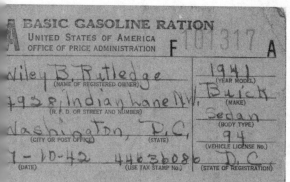

The Justices lived under the same wartime rationing and price controls as other Americans. The photo displays Justice Wiley Rutledge's gasoline ration card. The Supreme Court gave sweeping approval to the Roosevelt Administration's economic programs in *Yakus v. United States*. *Credit: Collection of the Supreme Court of the United States*

Thurgood Marshall (*far right*) is shown with NAACP leaders Roy Wilkins and Walter White in the 1940s. Marshall argued his first Supreme Court cases in the war years and won a landmark victory striking down Texas's "white primary" in *Smith v. Allwright*. *Credit: Library of Congress / Corbis / VCG via Getty Images*

Lonnie Smith, the Houston dentist who challenged Texas's discriminatory elections, votes for the first time in a primary in July 1944. *Credit: Life magazine, August 7, 1944*

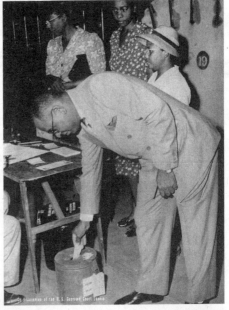

Civil rights demonstrators support the right of African Americans to drive trolleys in Philadelphia. *Credit: Courtesy of John W. Mosley Collection, Temple University Libraries*

Fred Korematsu and Mitsuye Endo challenged the US government's incarceration of Japanese Americans in the Supreme Court. Korematsu had been a shipyard welder and Endo a typist for the California Department of Motor Vehicles. *Credit: Left, National Portrait Gallery, Smithsonian Institution, gift of the Fred T. Korematsu Family; right, National Archives*

Heavily guarded by US soldiers, people of Japanese ancestry arrive for incarceration at the Santa Anita Assembly Center, a converted racetrack. *Credit: Clem Albers / National Archives*

A *Washington Star* cartoon in January 1944 shows Justices Hugo Black and Felix Frankfurter heatedly disagreeing while former Chief Justice Charles Evans Hughes asks his successor, Chief Justice Harlan Fiske Stone, how he is getting along "without the old fogies on the bench." Sharp divisions among the Roosevelt Justices attracted public attention. *Credit: Reprinted with permission of the DC Public Library, Star Collection © Washington Post*

On April 14, 1945, the funeral procession in Washington, DC, carries FDR's body while crowds line the streets. *Credit: Pictorial Press Ltd / Alamy Stock Photo*

• chapter twelve •

"I AM UNABLE TO BELIEVE YOU"

B EYOND THE SUPREME COURT'S DOCKET OF WAR-RELATED
cases, every Justice felt intimately connected to the nation's exis-
tential fight against the Nazis and the Japanese Empire. Even among
his deeply concerned colleagues, however, Felix Frankfurter stood out.
Since Hitler's earliest days in power, he had energetically sought to
rally support against the brutal fascist regime and to open doors for its
victims. And yet, in the summer of 1943, when Frankfurter personally
heard an eyewitness account about the worst of Nazi atrocities, it overwhelmed him.

WHEN THE SUPREME COURT adjourned on the day that Stone announced the *Hirabayashi* and *Yasui* decisions (June 21, 1943), it concluded a difficult term for Frankfurter. The departure of Jimmy Byrnes
for the White House at the beginning of the term meant the loss of an
ally. Byrnes's replacement, Wiley Rutledge, quickly bolstered the Court's
Black-Douglas wing. Frankfurter's invocation of his Jewish identity in

his flag salute dissent, bristling with resentment at the overruling of his
Gobitis decision, was a rare personal-identity judicial statement by the
Vienna-born Justice—a sign of his deep distress. Frankfurter carefully
recorded his brooding resentments in a journal during the 1942 term, a
sign of his inner turmoil as he found himself unable to lead the Court in
the way that he had always imagined.

Frankfurter was not without successes and satisfaction in the 1942
term. He had labored mightily and successfully to keep the Court uni-
fied on the cases of greatest importance to FDR and his war leadership
(the Nazi saboteur and Japanese curfew cases). He continued to bask in
the glory of his relationship with his beloved Roosevelt, and was cited in
the press that summer as one of the President's trusted "idea men." He
reveled in his closeness with other top officials, including Stimson as
he oversaw the war effort. And Frankfurter cherished the "Happy Hot
Dogs," his strategically placed network of acolytes and former students
in key positions throughout the federal government.

One prominent issue in Frankfurter's policy portfolio was the fate
of European Jews. Frankfurter, the only Jewish Justice and one of the
highest-ranking Jews in the federal government, had been an ardent advocate on this matter. He also had undertaken his own successful initiative, working through Lady Nancy Astor in England and the State
Department, to secure the release of his uncle Salomon Frankfurter
from a Nazi prison in Vienna. For Frankfurter, his biographer Brad Snyder explains, "the threat of Nazi Germany was political and personal."

And so it came to be that, two weeks after the Supreme Court recessed for the summer in 1943, Felix Frankfurter met with Jan Karski,
a leading figure in the Polish underground who had secretly infiltrated
and personally witnessed the horrors of both the Warsaw ghetto and a
Nazi concentration camp.

❖ ❖ ❖

IN ORDER TO UNDERSTAND the significance of Frankfurter's meeting, it
is necessary to understand Jan Karski and what he had experienced.

Karski was born in Lodz, Poland, to a religious Roman Catholic family in 1914, the youngest of eight children. After studying law and diplomacy, he entered the Polish Foreign Service. Shortly before the Nazis invaded Poland on September 1, 1939, as German military maneuvers triggered concern, he was ordered into army service as part of a general mobilization. Karski shared the general Polish overconfidence that Poland's prowess would quickly rebuff Hitler. Instead, Karski and his fellow soldiers had to flee the invading Nazi army and retreated eastward until they encountered the Soviet army. The Soviets, in their new nonaggression pact with the Nazis, captured and imprisoned Karski and his unit.

Desperate to leave the harsh Soviet incarceration, Karski secured a place in a prisoner transfer to German custody because of his heritage as a native of Lodz, which had historic ties to Germany. On the train to the German prison, Karski arranged for other prisoners to throw him through a ventilation slit at the top of the crowded cattle car, and then he escaped into the woods.

Karski promptly joined the Polish underground. With a photographic memory, mastery of several languages, and diplomatic manner, he quickly became a valued courier. But in June 1940, on a mission to the Polish government-in-exile in France, he was forced to take a circuitous route through the Slovakian countryside. At a supposedly safe farmhouse, he was betrayed by the farmer and captured by the Nazis. The Germans savagely tortured Karski, seeking information about the Polish Resistance. But he again escaped, this time jumping from a hospital window.

Undeterred, Karski resumed his Resistance activities, earning respect from all sides of the fractious underground movement. In August 1942, Jewish leaders approached him. They implored him to witness what was going on in the Warsaw Ghetto so that he could let the world know. The ghetto had been cut off from the outside world by the Nazis in 1940. The Nazis had herded 460,000 Jews into a narrow, confined area of the city with very little food and rations. They regularly seized Jews from the ghetto and shipped them to concentration camps.

With the approval of Resistance leaders, Karski agreed. Just outside the enclosed ghetto, he met a youth from a Jewish underground organization, who led Karski and a Jewish leader, both wearing ragged clothes and Star of David armbands, through a hidden tunnel into the streets of the ghetto. Karski was shocked. He saw naked bodies in the streets, emaciated and starving people, teenagers in Hitler Youth uniforms gleefully shooting Jews for sport. After secretly leaving, Karski repeated the appalling tour two days later. But the ghetto was only part of the horrors being inflicted by the Nazis. The Jewish leader now urged him to infiltrate a concentration camp as well. Again, Karski agreed.

Karski and a member of the Jewish Resistance took a train to a small town in Poland. A Polish underground member gave Karski the uniform of a Ukranian guard working at the camp under German command; the guard had been bribed to take the day off. Another Ukrainian guard, also bribed by the Resistance, accompanied Karski into a concentration camp where Jews were imprisoned and abused before being shipped to long-term camps such as Belzec. (Karski mistakenly thought he was at Belzec itself.)

A scene from hell unfolded in the camp. Karski heard people crying and smelled burning flesh. He saw Jews beaten and kicked, Jews herded into boxcars sealed with toxic quicklime, Jews struck by rifles and clubs if they did not move into the boxcars quickly enough, Jews shot and bayoneted if they were too infirm, Jews screaming and moaning from the burn of the quicklime. Overwhelmed, Karski began to weep and lose control. The Ukrainian guard roughly grabbed him, led him away, and scolded, "You endanger people! You've got no business being here!" After leaving the camp and shedding his guard's uniform, Karski vomited violently and repeatedly.

Desperate Jewish leaders beseeched Karski to tell the world what he had seen and seek aggressive actions by the Allied government. They sought a public declaration that preventing the extermination of the Jews was an official war goal of the Allies; an announcement that, unless the German people immediately acted to stop the genocide, they would be held collectively liable for the massacre; the destruction of important

German cultural sites; and the execution of Germans in Allied custody. They pleaded with Karski to let the Allies know that millions of Polish Jews would be murdered without immediate, dramatic intervention by the Allies.

Karski became fiercely determined to convey the enormity of the unfolding crimes. In November 1942, Karski secretly traveled to London, the location of the Polish government-in-exile after the fall of France, on an official Resistance mission to smuggle documents and report on developments in the country. But conveying the shocking plight of the Jews figured prominently in his plans. Karski stayed in London for eight months, meeting with a wide range of British leaders. He was disappointed in the British response. Foreign Secretary Anthony Eden was abrupt and unwilling to hear the plight of the Jews; other British leaders were similarly lukewarm and uninterested. Karski suspected that the British leaders thought he was exaggerating or even making up stories. He was told that Churchill could not find time to meet with him.

The Polish government-in-exile decided to send Karski to the United States. The Poles had increasing concerns about Soviet ambitions in Poland after the war. The USSR was now an important American and British ally against the Nazis, following the German invasion of the Soviet Union in June 1941. The Polish government-in-exile hoped that Karski's account of Soviet activities on the ground would strengthen Allied resolve to preserve an independent postwar Poland.

Karski arrived in the United States in June 1943. Poland's Ambassador to the United States, Jan Ciechanowski, promptly arranged meetings with high-level US officials to hear Karski's report on the situation in Poland. Karski's very first meeting in Washington, on the evening of July 5, was with a small group that included Justice Felix Frankfurter.

BY THE TIME OF his appointment to the Supreme Court in 1939, Felix Frankfurter had made an astonishing impact on the country he entered as a boy—a leading public intellectual, a skilled warrior in public controversies, a close adviser to the President and other top officials, the sponsor and guide to many protégés in key governmental positions.

The third of six children, Felix was born in Vienna, Austria, on November 15, 1882, ten months after the birth of Franklin D. Roosevelt in Hyde Park, New York. When he was eleven, the Frankfurter family left the Old World for New York and arrived at Ellis Island. His father, Leopold, the descendant of a long line of rabbis, had decided not to join the rabbinate; he became a linen salesman in New York. Although young Felix arrived not knowing a word of English, he thrived. He participated in debating societies and excelled at the City College of New York, graduating in 1902. After working for a year to earn money, Frankfurter went on to Harvard Law School, where he compiled an extraordinary record. He was first in his class all three years. He then briefly worked at a top Wall Street firm, a rarity for a Jew at the time.

In 1906, during President Theodore Roosevelt's Administration, Henry Stimson, the patrician US Attorney in New York, recruited Frankfurter to join his office, and the two became close. In 1909, Stimson unsuccessfully ran for Governor of New York, with Frankfurter as one of his top campaign aides. Just two years later, in 1911, Stimson returned to government, moving to Washington as President William Howard Taft's Secretary of War, and he took Frankfurter with him. Frankfurter's prosaic title—law officer in the Bureau of Insular Affairs at the War Department—masked his wide range of activities on Stimson's behalf.

Washington was a whirlwind for the young lawyer. He stayed in a townhouse in Dupont Circle at 1727 19th Street with other young ambitious officials and intellectuals committed to a new liberalism. This "House of Truth," the name its inhabitants proudly adopted, teemed with intellectual energy and brilliant socializing. Frankfurter's housemates included journalist Walter Lippmann; their roster of regular guests featured Supreme Court Justices Oliver Wendell Holmes and Louis Brandeis, as well as artist Gutzon Borglum, who would sculpt Mount Rushmore. Frankfurter later reflected that "almost everybody who was interesting in Washington sooner or later passed through that house."

In the 1912 presidential election, Frankfurter, disillusioned with Taft, embraced Theodore Roosevelt's campaign for a presidential comeback through his third-party bid in the Bull Moose Party. After Woodrow Wilson defeated both Roosevelt and Taft, Stimson left government and returned to private practice. But Frankfurter stayed in the Wilson Administration until 1914. That year, he joined with Lippmann and others in founding the *New Republic*, a journal of cutting-edge ideas.

When he left the Wilson Administration, Frankfurter moved to Harvard Law School as a professor. Holmes advised him against it. "Academic life is but half life," the Justice instructed. "It is withdrawal from the fight in order to utter smart things that cost you nothing except the thinking them from a cloister." But Holmes underestimated Frankfurter. He quickly threw himself into "real world" activities—writing regularly for the *New Republic*; joining the American Civil Liberties Union at its creation in 1920; emerging as a leading defender of Nicola Sacco and Bartolomeo Vanzetti, immigrants and anarchists charged with murder who, despite Frankfurter's passionate public advocacy, were executed in 1929; and developing law school classes focused on practical issues of governance and social policy, such as the regulation of utilities. Frankfurter also became active in the National Consumers League, an organization that Brandeis had represented, leading him to argue before the conservative Supreme Court in important cases defending the constitutionality of minimum-wage and maximum-hours laws.

After the US entry into World War I in 1917, Frankfurter returned to government, serving as a special assistant to Secretary of War Newton Baker and then as counsel to the President's Mediation Commission on labor problems. Back in his Harvard Law School position after the war, Frankfurter went to Paris for the postwar peace conference as an American Zionist representative, energized by Britain's commitment in the Balfour Declaration to a Jewish homeland in Palestine.

Throughout this period, Frankfurter maintained close relationships with Justices Holmes and Brandeis, regularly sending them law clerks. The wealthy Brandeis even covertly subsidized many of the less-flush Frankfurter's public-interest activities, a fact not known at the time.

Frankfurter's renown as a scholar of the Constitution and the Supreme Court grew rapidly. He became one of the nation's leading legal academics—and a trenchant critic of the conservative activist Supreme Court, which struck down federal and state economic legislation. Frankfurter prided himself on his attention to nuance and practicalities rather than adherence to rigid ideology. Asked why he was not a socialist, Frankfurter replied, "Because I cannot compress life into a formula."

Frankfurter fell in love with Marion Denman, a graduate of Smith College whom he courted from his first glimpse of her. They married in 1919 in a ceremony presided over by then New York Court of Appeals Judge Benjamin Cardozo. Twenty years later, Frankfurter would take Cardozo's seat on the Supreme Court. Marion was not merely a non-Jew; she was the daughter of a Congregational minister. Their interfaith marriage was a bold move for both, unusual at the time and subject to hostility and skepticism from Jews and Christians alike. Frankfurter was not a religious or practicing Jew, but his Jewish identity was important to him. Frankfurter's mother, Emma, bitterly opposed the marriage; Marion confided to a friend that she endured difficult social pressures from marrying a Jew.

They were a complicated couple. Frankfurter's energy, activities, and ego knew no bounds. Marion was brilliant and captivating but troubled. She suffered bouts of anxiety and depression, along with physical maladies, and was frequently bedridden during their marriage. She viewed her husband's hyperactivity and volubility with bemused skepticism, once commenting that "there are only two things wrong with Felix's speeches: He digresses and he returns to the subject." They never had children. Frankfurter's close relationships with his protégés sometimes seemed a replacement for them.

Frankfurter developed a warm and enduring relationship with Franklin Roosevelt. They got to know each other in the Wilson Administration, when FDR was serving as Assistant Secretary of the Navy. Meeting Frankfurter for the first time, Eleanor Roosevelt, who had not yet shed the prejudices of her upbringing, found him "an interesting little man but very Jew." When FDR became Governor of New York after his 1928 election, Frankfurter regularly advised him.

After FDR was elected President, he asked Frankfurter to become Solicitor General in his new Administration. Frankfurter declined, but he remained one of FDR's trusted counselors. "Felix has more ideas per minute than any man of my acquaintance," FDR once observed. "He has a brilliant mind but it clicks so fast it makes my head fairly spin. I find him tremendously interesting and stimulating."

In 1938, after the death of Justice Cardozo, FDR asked Frankfurter to prepare an evaluation of the top candidates for the vacant Court seat. For political reasons, the President stressed, he wanted a westerner. Frankfurter provided the requested analysis.

In January 1939, as Frankfurter stood in his underwear while dressing for a dinner party, a call came from the President. "I told you I can't name you," the familiar voice boomed, "but wherever I turn and to whomever I talk that matters to me, I am made to realize that you're the only person fit to succeed Holmes and Cardozo. Unless you can give me an unanswerable objection, I'm going to send your name in for the Court tomorrow at twelve o'clock." Frankfurter, the man who had come to the country as an eleven-year-old immigrant boy, softly replied, "I only wish that my mother were here for this moment."

That night, Frankfurter wrote FDR, "And now I have the highest authority in the land to prove that those much malign me [who] say that I'm a talker. You will testify that you found me tongue-tied. How could I have responded to your gracious message other than to be moved to mumbling silence.... Believe me that I am humbly aware of the consecrated task that you have laid upon me. And to have it at your hands— with all that you signify for my most precious devotion to the country—is to sanctify Law with its humanest significance." Frankfurter closed the letter, "With the affectionate devotion of old friendship."

Frankfurter's nomination did not happen by accident. A group of well-connected FDR intimates, including Secretary of the Interior Harold Ickes, Solicitor General (and future Justice) Robert Jackson,

and presidential advisers Harry Hopkins and Tommy Corcoran (a former Frankfurter student), had launched an intense lobbying campaign
to put him on the Court. Despite Frankfurter's professions of humility
about the nomination, he knew about his boosters' efforts and had encouraged them.

The day that FDR announced the nomination, Ickes gathered
luminaries in his office to celebrate, including Hopkins, Attorney General (and future Justice) Frank Murphy, SEC Chair (and future Justice)
William Douglas, and presidential secretary Missy LeHand. Corcoran
came with two bottles of champagne. Ickes proclaimed, "All of us regard this as the most significant and worthwhile thing the President
has done."

Frankfurter's nomination received widespread but not universal
public acclaim. Some viewed him as a radical—the defender of Sacco
and Vanzetti, a founder of the American Civil Liberties Union. FBI Director J. Edgar Hoover once called him "the most dangerous man in the
United States." Decrying Frankfurter's Supreme Court nomination, Republican Congressman J. Parnell Thomas announced that he could not
"conceive of a worse appointment." According to Thomas, FDR "might
as well have appointed Earl Browder," the Secretary of the Communist
Party of the United States.

Frankfurter testified publicly before the Senate Judiciary Committee, the first Supreme Court nominee to give public testimony on
unrestricted topics. (Stone had publicly testified before the Judiciary
Committee in 1925, but his testimony, by agreement, was limited to
his handling of the Teapot Dome matter as Attorney General.) Testifying one week after his nomination, on January 12, 1939, Frankfurter
was grilled about whether he had belonged to the Communist Party.
"I have never been" a Communist, Frankfurter proclaimed, "and I am
not now." In response to continued questions, Frankfurter emphatically
declared, "That does not represent my view of life nor my view of government!...You will have to decide, in the light of my whole life, what
devotion I have to the American system of government." The contentious hearing was a glimpse of what confirmation proceedings would

become at the end of the twentieth century and the beginning of the twenty-first century. But the outcome was far different. The Senate confirmed him on January 17, a mere twelve days after FDR nominated him. It was a voice vote—not a single Senator voted against him.

On January 30, 1939, Frankfurter officially became a Supreme Court Justice, the sixth foreign-born Justice and the third Jewish Justice, following Brandeis and Cardozo. The top tier of the New Deal arrived at the Supreme Court for his official seat-taking—Ickes, Hopkins, Missy LeHand, Murphy, Jackson, and Corcoran among them.

As a close friend and confidant of Holmes and Brandeis, as a leading scholar of the Court, and as a man of enormous self-regard, Frankfurter assumed that he would naturally be the intellectual leader of the Court and the dominant Justice. He was sorely disappointed. Black (appointed before Frankfurter in 1937), Douglas (appointed a few months after Frankfurter in 1939), Murphy (appointed in 1940), and Rutledge (appointed in 1943) frequently challenged him. Rifts developed between Frankfurter and these other FDR-appointed Justices on the role of the Supreme Court in matters such as protecting civil liberties. In Frankfurter's view, particularly in light of the Supreme Court's all-too-recent record invalidating New Deal and other social reform legislation, the Court should be very deferential to government policies across the board.

To be sure, at times Frankfurter stood firmly for the enforcement of constitutional rights. But, broadly speaking, he viewed the "Axis" Justices—the scathing term he embraced—as far too willing to depart from what Frankfurter viewed as the proper judicial role. Frankfurter's journal is rife with his personal grievances. In caustic comments, he thought Black untrustworthy, Douglas unprincipled, Murphy superficial, Rutledge naive. And the contempt was not a one-way street. Murphy viewed Frankfurter's academic writings as "pure bunk" and saw Frankfurter as a hypocrite. Douglas called Frankfurter "the little bastard" and "Der Fuehrer" in notes to Murphy. Frankfurter's style could be overbearing. Potter Stewart, who served with Frankfurter after joining the Court in 1958, once said that Frankfurter often would speak in the Justices' conferences "for fifty minutes, no more or less, because that was the length of the lecture at the Harvard Law School." And even Frankfurter's occasional allies on the Court—such as Reed—did not seem to treat him with the reverence he believed he was due.

Frankfurter continued to advise Roosevelt and top government officials on a wide variety of issues. In contrast to his grievances about the Supreme Court, Frankfurter's diary from the 1942 term gleefully records policy conversations with decision-makers on a dizzying array of topics— the role of China, the future of postwar Europe, infighting at the War Production Board, policy decisions by the Office of Price Administration.

Paul Freund, a Frankfurter protégé and top New Deal lawyer (and later a distinguished constitutional scholar), compared being in Frankfurter's presence to "opening a bottle of champagne." The five-foot-four-inch Justice would grab the listener's arm, lean in close, punctuate his story with a roaring laugh, and finish with an affectionate punch to the shoulder and a buoyant "Wasn't that good? Wasn't that good?"

Frankfurter had long focused on the issue of Zionism and the future of Palestine as a home for the Jewish people. Frankfurter especially relished his discussions with Chaim Weizmann. Born in Russia, Weizmann, a distinguished chemist, was a leader of the Zionist movement during World War II, and he would go on to be the first President of Israel. Frankfurter had grown close to him at the Paris conference following World War I, and he delighted in their relationship.

And now, in the summer of 1943, Frankfurter was introduced to a man who had personally witnessed the horrors of the Warsaw Ghetto and the Nazi concentration camp.

❦ ❦ ❦

ON MONDAY, JULY 5, 1943, Ambassador Ciechanowski hosted an intimate dinner at the Polish embassy. It was Karski's first meeting with US government officials. Joining Ciechanowski and Karski were three influential Jewish Americans: presidential adviser Ben Cohen, Assistant Solicitor General Oscar Cox, and Justice Felix Frankfurter.

Over dinner, Karski discussed the operations of the Polish underground. Heeding his instructions from Polish government-in-exile leaders, he emphasized the aggressive and worrisome activities of Soviet partisans and agents within Poland. Karski also briefly outlined the plight of the Jews. It made an impression on his guests. Shortly after the dinner, Cox wrote acquaintances that Karski's experiences were "blood-curdling" and "make your hair stand on end."

Frankfurter wanted to hear more. Staying after the other guests departed, the Justice joined Karski and the Ambassador in an adjoining room. Frankfurter sat next to Ciechanowski and across from Karski. Frankfurter stared at the visitor and said, "Mr. Karski, do you know that I am a Jew?" Karski nodded. Frankfurter continued, "There are many conflicting reports about what is happening to the Jews in your country. Please tell me exactly what you have seen."

For the next hour, Karski described his covert visits to the Warsaw Ghetto and the concentration camp, relating in detail the horrors he had witnessed. Frankfurter interjected from time to time to ask logistical questions, including how Karski had managed to enter the ghetto and the camp. Finally, Karski finished.

Frankfurter stood up and paced for a few minutes, and then sat again. "Mr. Karski," the Justice said in a low voice, "a man like me talking to a man like you must be totally frank. So I must say: I am unable to believe you." Ciechanowski erupted. "Felix, you don't mean it," he exclaimed. "How can you call him a liar to his face! The authority of my government is behind him. You know who he is!"

"Mr. Ambassador," Frankfurter replied. "I did not say this young man is lying." He continued, "I said I am unable to believe him. There is a difference."

Frankfurter did not explain the difference or what he meant. Did he mean that he could not comprehend the enormity of the crimes described by Karski? Was it a recognition, perhaps implicit, that believing Karski would have required drastic action on his part? Frankfurter did not elaborate.

After perfunctory farewells, Frankfurter and Ciechanowski left the room. Karski remained, listening to the retreating footsteps of one of America's most powerful Jews.

There is no record of Felix Frankfurter, with his frequent communications with the President and his vast network at the highest echelons of the federal government, ever taking any action in response to Jan Karski's urgent personal testimony about the ongoing genocide of the Jews of Poland. Nor did Frankfurter, who just two and a half weeks previously had written the last of his more than one hundred journal entries for the 1942–43 term, refer to the Karski meeting in his diary or otherwise acknowledge the conversation. For whatever reason, at least so far as the surviving records reflect, Karski's graphic account proved too much for Frankfurter to process or act on.

Ciechanowski proceeded to arrange meetings for Karski with high-ranking officials from the State Department and War Department, as well as leading journalists. As he had been instructed, Karski stressed the Soviet threat and the harmful influence of Communist agents on the Polish underground. But he also took every opportunity to raise the plight of the Jews. In a session with officers from US military intelligence, a Polish attaché reported, Karski discussed "terrible, horrible things, things that cry out for God's punishment, about what the Germans were doing to the Polish Jews, about pogroms and massacres."

Karski's comments about Soviet aggressiveness greatly interested former US Ambassador to the Soviet Union William Bullitt, a leading voice urging FDR to take a hard line with the Soviets in eastern Europe. Bullitt quickly arranged a meeting between Karski and the President.

On Wednesday, July 28, at 10:50 a.m., Karski and Ciechanowski met at the White House with FDR for an hour, in which Karski provided an overview of Nazi and Soviet activities in Poland. The President asked him detailed questions about the Nazi occupation and the operations of the Polish underground.

Karski then brought up the mortal dangers and atrocities facing the Jews. Perhaps chastened by his session with Frankfurter, Karski did not describe his own personal experiences witnessing the horrors of the ghetto and the concentration camp. But he starkly described the desperate situation. He told the President, "I am sure that many people are unaware of just how horrible the situation of the Jewish population is." He explained, "More than 1,800,000 Jews have been murdered in my country." While the Germans "[wanted] to ruin the Polish state as a state," they "[wanted] to devastate the biological substance of the Jewish nation." Karski soberly advised the President, "If there is no effort at Allied intervention, whether through reprisals or other action," the "Jewish people of Poland...will cease to exist."

Roosevelt puffed on his cigarette. Always a master deflector, he grandly replied, "You will tell your leaders that we shall win this war! You will tell them that the guilty ones will be punished for their crimes. Justice, freedom will prevail!"

Karski was dazzled by Roosevelt, even walking backward out of the room rather than turn his back on the great leader of the West. But he also was crestfallen. Karski later reflected that FDR was "clever. About the dead Jews, Roosevelt said nothing. So I was disappointed after all."

Others painted a different picture about Karski's effect on the President. A few days later, Secretary of State Cordell Hull advised Ciechanowski, "The president seems so thrilled by his talk with your young man that he can talk of nothing else." And John Pehle, appointed by FDR to head the new War Refugee Board in January 1944, believed that Karski's meeting had a profound impact on FDR. In Pehle's view, after Karski's White House visit, American policy on war refugees changed "overnight" from "indifference at best to affirmative action." In Karski's view, however, the visit had been a tragic failure: it did not lead to immediate, urgent American action to stop the mass murder of millions of Polish Jews. Whether the US actually could—or should—have done more is a source of rich historical debate. But there is no question that Karski was deeply disappointed.

Karski returned to London, but the Polish government-in-exile almost immediately sent him back to the United States. To call attention to the problems in Poland, with his superiors' approval, he wrote *Story of a Secret State* in 1944, a book that quickly became a best-seller. Karski felt that he had to ensure that his book did not compromise sensitive secrets and that it came out quickly to publicize what was happening in Poland. Perhaps as a result, the book occasionally omits, disguises, and shades significant facts. But Karski devoted two chapters to his experiences in the Warsaw Ghetto and the concentration camp, and he did not hold back in describing the horrors. In the ghetto, "everywhere there was hunger, misery, the atrocious sense of decomposing bodies, the pitiful moans of dying children, the desperate cries and gasps of a people struggling for life against impossible odds." And in the camp, "the chaos, the squalor, the hideousness of it all was simply indescribable. There was a suffocating stench of sweat, filth, decay, damp straw, and excrement.... The two [railroad] cars were... crammed to bursting with tightly packed human flesh, completely, hermetically filled. All this while the entire camp... reverberated with a tremendous volume of sound in which the hideous groans and screams mingled weirdly with shots, curses, and bellowed commands."

After the Allied victory in 1945, the Soviet Union effectively took control of Poland with a puppet Communist government. Karski decided to stay in the United States. He became an American citizen in 1954 and was a beloved Georgetown University professor, living a life of relative anonymity until he was publicly rediscovered and then widely celebrated—lauded as one of the "righteous among the nations" by Yad Vashem in Israel in 1982; spotlighted in Claude Lanzmann's 1985 documentary *Shoah*; honored by Poland after the fall of the Soviet Union in 1989; venerated at the opening of the United States Holocaust Memorial Museum in 1993; featured in a definitive, admiring biography by E. Thomas Wood and Stanislaw Jankowski in 1994.

But Jan Karski, the man who personally experienced and witnessed the worst horrors of the twentieth century (savage viciousness by Nazis, sadistic genocide against Jews, oppressive abuse by Soviets), encountered yet another tragedy before his death in 2000. In 1992, Karski's wife, a Jewish Polish émigré and a noted dancer and choreographer, jumped from the eleventh-floor window of their Bethesda, Maryland, apartment and died at the age of eighty-one, tormented to the end by her memories.

IN THE END, 3 million of Poland's 3.3 million Jews were slaughtered in the Holocaust. The silence of Felix Frankfurter—so voluble on so many issues—about his conversation with Jan Karski is conspicuous and haunting. To his enormous credit, Frankfurter continued his energetic efforts on behalf of European Jews. But, apparently finding it too searing and too consequential, he never invoked Karski's powerful testimony.

chapter thirteen

THE WAR AT HOME

W HILE BATTLES RAGED OVERSEAS, THE HOME FRONT, FOR FDR and the country at large, was an actual front. The US economy was a pivotal battleground, and momentous legal issues emerged about the constitutionality of the domestic war program.

The Emergency Price Control Act of 1942 gave FDR and his Administration sweeping powers to impose price controls and rationing. The President hailed the law as "an important Weapon in our armory against the onslaught of the Axis powers." Soaring prices and war-fueled inflation would "serve the purposes of our enemies." Americans, moreover, had to limit their consumption of everyday goods, from nylon and metal to rubber and oil, to ensure adequate supplies for the soldiers, sailors, and airmen fighting in distant countries. "The total effort needed for victory," FDR emphasized, "means... increasing sacrifices from all of us."

The Supreme Court soon confronted a legal challenge to this expansive conferral of economic authority on the President and the Executive Branch. The case was brought by two meat wholesalers

convicted and sentenced for the crime of selling meat above the federal
price limit.

❧ ❧ ❧

THE OFFICE OF PRICE Administration became the lead federal agency
charged with overseeing the domestic economy program. The OPA
released a torrent of orders—setting prices, rationing goods, issuing
coupons required to buy various commodities, announcing an ever-
changing and ever-more-byzantine structure of geographic districts
and applicable controls. The agency mushroomed to almost sixty-five
thousand federal employees. Another three hundred thousand volun-
teers throughout the country monitored prices, reported violations, and
assisted consumers.

Tales of chaos and confusion were rampant. A shortage of nylon led
women to try stockings made of cotton; unhappy with the feel, some
began painting stockings on their legs instead. A federal ban on the sale
of sliced bread led to wails of outrage. Consumers rushed to buy new
bread-slicing knives for home slicing; the government reversed its ban.
Household thieves stole butter but left jewels untouched. A crackdown
on pleasure driving led to deserted highways. The government exhorted
Americans to carpool, warning that "the empty seat is a gift to Hitler."
And "every time you decide *not* to buy something," the government
urged, "you help to win the war." Hoarders were "on the same level
of spies." When the federal government led a drive for citizens to do-
nate rubber for the war effort, one Washington, DC, gas station posted
a sign proclaiming, "WE ACCEPT ANYTHING MADE OF RUBBER EXCEPT
CONDOMS."

Like all Americans, the Justices were plunged into this strange new
world. "The nine Justices," reported Newsweek in 1943, "like everyone
else, are tilting with rationing." Stone worked "close to a wood fire" in
his home office "to offset the rigors of fuel-oil rationing." Hugo Black
carpooled from Virginia with his neighbor, Librarian of Congress Archibald MacLeish, an FDR intimate. Reed and Murphy walked to the
Court from their downtown hotels. Frankfurter, who had never learned

to drive, used the trolley or received rides from a friend. Jackson worked from home as much as possible, going to the Court only two or three times during weeks when it was not sitting. Douglas had tried buses, streetcars, and the train but now drove most of the time. And Rutledge walked "uphill a mile to his bus stop several times a week to conserve gas." Stone wrote to a friend, "We...freeze occasionally for lack of fuel oil but it is all in a good cause."

ANOTHER FEATURE OF THE war economy had a direct impact on the Supreme Court: the mass entrance of women into the workforce. Around the time that the Court heard the meat wholesalers' case, Douglas hired the Court's first woman law clerk, Lucile Lomen. She would be the only one for decades.

Nearly seven million women flocked into the domestic workforce, some as office workers, some as industrial "Rosie the Riveters." When the dean of the University of Washington School of Law advised Douglas that, because of the war, he had no students to recommend for a clerkship, Douglas persisted. "When you say that you have 'no available graduates' whom you could recommend for appointment as my clerk, do you include women? It is possible that I may decide to take one if I can find one who is absolutely first-rate." The dean recommended Lomen, an outstanding student who had already written a pathbreaking article on constitutional law. She also had graduated from Whitman College, Douglas's alma mater. Douglas brought her on board.

Lomen arrived in a capital city still imbued with sexism and traditional gender stereotypes. The year that she was hired, the nationally syndicated column Wartime Washington reported on a German émigré author proclaiming at a posh Washington dinner that "the American woman does not give the man the impression that he is the 'be all' and 'end all' of her existence. By failing to do this, she fails to interest the man sufficiently to exert an important influence through him on politics or world affairs." The other Supreme Court clerks, while cordial, treated Lomen distantly. Lomen's social circle at the Court included the

Court's secretaries, women who welcomed and embraced her. Douglas found Lomen's work as a clerk outstanding. Known for his stinginess with praise, he lauded her "fine mind" and "firm foundation in the law."

Once the war ended, old patterns reappeared. The Supreme Court would not see another woman law clerk until 1966, when Black hired Tommy Corcoran's daughter, Margaret J. Corcoran. In 1958, Frankfurter refused to hire a law student named Ruth Bader Ginsburg even though she was recommended by a trusted law professor. And Douglas himself would not hire another woman law clerk until 1972—nearly three decades after domestic war exigencies led him to break, for one isolated moment, the clerk gender barrier at the Court.

THE CASE THAT WOULD become the Supreme Court's seminal decision on the government's sweeping wartime authority began in Boston. Albert Yakus was a wholesale meat dealer. Stringent OPA-imposed price controls capped the price that wholesalers could charge, and the squeeze for middlemen like Yakus was particularly acute because the farm lobby had successfully prevented restrictive limits on the cost of their sales to the wholesalers. Like some other meat dealers, Yakus began selling meat on the black market—covert sales at prices above OPA levels to retailers, who were eager to obtain meat for their stores in a time of shortage.

Yakus, then forty-three, had been born in Poland and had emigrated to the United States with his Jewish family. On February 12, 1943, a grand jury indicted Yakus and his company, the Brighton Packing Company, in federal court in Boston for violating OPA price limits in his sale of meat.

The Yakus indictment was part of a major government initiative to enforce the OPA regime. The US Attorney in Boston simultaneously announced criminal charges against a total of twelve meat industry wholesalers, individuals and companies alike, for similar black-market violations. Among them were Benjamin Rottenberg, whose case would become the lead OPA black-market case in the lower courts and then be subsumed into Yakus's case in the Supreme Court.

The judge presiding at Yakus's arraignment was well respected, with an impressive New Deal pedigree—Charles Wyzanski, a Frankfurter protégé who had taken his seat on the federal district court in Boston just nine days after the Pearl Harbor attack.

At the arraignment of the meat-dealing defendants, Wyzanski emphasized the gravity of the charges: profiteering in violation of wartime price controls. Vowing a prompt trial, he required defense motions to be filed in a mere seven days. The "guilty should be punished and the innocent cleared," he proclaimed, "as quickly as possible."

Yakus, Rottenberg, and the other defendants raised two principal challenges in arguing for the dismissal of their indictments. First, they contended that the Emergency Price Control Act unconstitutionally "delegated" legislative power to the OPA Administrator by its broad conferral of rule-making authority to set prices that would be "fair and equitable" and "effectuate the purposes" of the act. Second, the defendants objected that the Act unconstitutionally limited their criminal defense. It provided that challenges to OPA price control regulations could be brought only within sixty days of the adoption of the regulations at issue—and only in a specially created Emergency Price Control court. Here, the meat wholesalers had not filed a challenge within sixty days. They now wanted to raise their claim that the regulation was unlawful as a defense to their criminal prosecution, and they wanted to do so in the United States District Court in Boston rather than in a separate lawsuit in the special new Emergency Price Control court—a double problem under the act.

Wyzanski swatted away the constitutional challenges and ordered the cases to proceed. Rottenberg and Yakus were quickly tried and convicted.

Rottenberg's three-day trial was first. On March 10, less than a month after his indictment, he stood before Judge Wyzanski for sentencing. Wyzanski sharply noted that "the regulation of prices in time of war [preserves] morale on the home front by ensuring that available goods will be within the price range of all." He sentenced the meat executive to six months behind bars and fined him $1,000 for violating the government price limits.

Yakus's trial was next, before a different federal judge. Yakus also was convicted, sentenced to six months in prison, and fined $1,000 for selling above the government-mandated price. The two men immediately took their constitutional challenges to the Boston-based United States Court of Appeals for the First Circuit.

With the appeals pending, in May 1943, Judge Wyzanski met with his mentor, Justice Frankfurter, in Washington. As Frankfurter recorded in his diary, "Judge Wyzanski came to see me much disturbed about black market offenders in Boston. He wanted my general attitude in meting out sentences. The specified incident which came up was a sentence by him of a pretty bad offender whom he had given six months in jail." Wyzanski was upset that Attorney General Biddle "had called him by long distance to ask him whether he would not reconsider the sentence and make it lighter in view of representations that had been made to him. Wyzanski then called both the U.S. Attorney and the counsel for the prisoner before him,... told them of the communication that he had from the Attorney General, and then said he would not change the sentence."

Frankfurter reassured Wyzanski. "I told Charlie that he was absolutely right, that the Attorney General was absolutely wrong, and that it was a characteristic performance of irresponsibility on the part of Francis Biddle—that he was not a bad man or a wrong-doing man but a heedless fellow because he did not take things with sufficient seriousness. The fundamental fact about Francis Biddle is that he is an amateur in his view of life." Wyzanski reminded Frankfurter that the Justice had previously said, during a New Deal contretemps, that Biddle "was much too la-de-da." Frankfurter now told his protégé, "Did I say that? It is still my view. And la-de-da is not good enough in wartime."

Biddle's peculiar outreach to the sentencing judge should not obscure the extraordinary nature of the conversation between Wyzanski and Frankfurter. A federal judge had a private discussion with a Supreme Court Justice about a case pending on appeal that posed fundamental constitutional issues on a matter of great wartime importance. The judge whose decision was under review privately confided that the defendant was "a pretty bad offender" and obtained the Justice's reassurance about the correctness of the sentence he had meted out. Although he recounted the conversation in his journal, Frankfurter never publicly disclosed it, including during the period when Frankfurter actively participated in considering the legal correctness of this judge's rejection of the constitutional challenges and handling of the trial.

In August 1943, the US Court of Appeals affirmed the convictions of Yakus and Rottenberg. In its view, the OPA Administrator had been "conscientious and diligent in the fight that he has to lead on the home front." The court also relied on a new Supreme Court precedent, which the judges thought powerfully supported their conclusion: *Hirabayashi v. United States*, the Japanese American curfew case. "It is not amiss to note that in *Hirabayashi v. United States*," they observed, "under the war powers of the President and Congress, the Supreme Court upheld a military order which applied discriminatory treatment to citizens of the United States on the basis of their racial origin, a discrimination which would ordinarily be abhorrent to the Fifth Amendment. The Emergency Price Control Act discloses a much less striking exercise of the broad war power of Congress."

Yakus and Rottenberg had lost resoundingly in the Court of Appeals. Now it was on to the Supreme Court for their challenge to a pillar of the Roosevelt Administration's domestic war economy program.

When the Court heard arguments in the consolidated cases on January 7, 1944, the lawyers for Yakus and Rottenberg pressed their two primary arguments—the broad language of the Emergency Price Control Act was an unconstitutional delegation of legislative power to the OPA Administrator, and the prohibition against raising the regulation's illegality in the criminal case violated due process.

Solicitor General Fahy defended the OPA's authority. Emphasizing the difficulty of the OPA Administrator's task, he observed that the

OPA's two previous Administrators and General Counsel, who had left their posts amid public controversy, had been "casualties" in this difficult wartime struggle. Stone interjected that the Court was more interested in whether "they acted within the law and the constitution."

Just four days after the Supreme Court argument, on the evening of January 11, 1944, FDR gave his annual State of the Union address. Recovering from the flu, FDR spoke on the radio from the White House. He called for "a second Bill of Rights," with specified economic rights, including the right to "a useful and remunerative job" and to "adequate protection from the economic fears of old age, sickness, accident, and unemployment." "There are no two fronts for America in this war," he stressed in his familiar and soothing voice. "There is only one front... one line of unity which extends from the hearts of the people at home to the men of our attacking forces in our farthest outposts." Rising prices during the war, the President emphasized, would be "a particularly disastrous result on all fixed-income groups" and "fixed-income people"—"teachers, clergy, policemen, firemen, widows and minors on fixed incomes, wives and dependents of our soldiers and sailors, and old-age pensioners." In "a period of gross inflation, they would be the worst sufferers." He called on Congress to promptly extend the Emergency Price Control Act, scheduled to expire on June 30, 1944. Without the act and its extraordinary price control authority, he announced, "the country might just as well expect price chaos by summer."

That very week, the Justices considered the meat dealers' attacks on the lawfulness of the price control regime championed by the President and his Administration as indispensable to the nation's ability to wage war.

If there was one issue that frequently united the Roosevelt Justices, it was deference to economic legislation and regulation. Their stance stood in sharp contrast to the conservative activist Justices they had replaced. In one striking example, the Court unanimously upheld, in *Wickard v. Filburn* in 1942, federal wheat-growing quotas that prevented an Ohio farmer from growing grain above the limit for his own family's

consumption. The wartime context of the OPA's authority now amplified the grounds for deference.

Six Justices voted to uphold the OPA's sweeping authority in the
meat wholesalers' case. Stone again assigned the opinion to himself,
and in March 1944, the Court emphatically affirmed the OPA's powers.
Stone's opinion ruled that the Emergency Price Control Act, even with
its broad grant of authority, sufficiently constrained the OPA Administrator. It provided adequate specificity on the purposes (instructing the
agency "to stabilize prices" and "to eliminate and prevent profiteering");
the standard (setting "fair and equitable prices"); and the administrative
method (requiring the OPA Administrator to give "due consideration"
to factors such as prevailing prices during a designated base period).
Stone's opinion also rejected the defendants' constitutional objection to
their inability to challenge the meat price regulation in their criminal
trial: the price control act had been adopted "shortly after our declaration of war against Germany and Japan.... There was grave danger of
wartime inflation and the disorganization of our economy from excessive price rises."

The Supreme Court, like the Court of Appeals, explicitly relied on
its recent *Hirabayashi* precedent. "Even the personal liberty of the citizen may be temporarily restrained as a measure of public safety," Stone
explained with a cite to his curfew opinion. For the Supreme Court, as
for FDR, there seemed to be a single, continuous front, from the battles
in Italy and the Pacific to the curfew against Japanese Americans on the
West Coast and the prosecution of meat wholesalers in Boston.

This time, however, the Court's approval of sweeping wartime authority drew two dissenting opinions. Rutledge (joined by Murphy)
agreed that Congress had permissibly given the OPA Administrator
far-reaching price control authority but disagreed on the inability to
challenge the OPA regulation's illegality as a defense in a criminal prosecution. The second dissent—by Roberts—was more wide-ranging. In
his view, the Emergency Price Control Act's broad grant of price control
authority "unconstitutionally delegates legislative power to the [OPA]

Administrator." The Court's opinion, moreover, was not clear whether the extraordinary authority it sustained was lawfully conferred only because of the wartime emergency. "If the court puts its decision on the war power," he proclaimed, "I think it should say so. The citizens of this country will then know that in war the function of legislation may be surrendered to an autocrat whose 'judgment' will constitute the law.... If, on the contrary, such a delegation as is here disclosed is to be sustained even in peacetime, we should know it."

Albert Yakus and Benjamin Rottenberg would have to go to prison and serve their sentences for selling their meat above the OPA-specified prices.

The same day it announced the *Yakus* decision, the Supreme Court released a second opinion upholding broad OPA authority over the economy in a different context. Kate Willingham, a landlord in Macon, Georgia, had filed suit in a Georgia state court to block an OPA order requiring her to lower the rents she charged on three apartments in "defense rental areas." After the Georgia court ruled in her favor against the OPA, the US government sued in federal court for an injunction preventing her from violating the act. In an 8–1 decision by Douglas, the Supreme Court held that Willingham had to comply with the OPA orders limiting the rent she could charge. *Yakus* controlled the outcome. Douglas again highlighted the context: "Congress was dealing here with conditions created by activities resulting from a great war effort....A nation which can demand the lives of its men and women in the waging of that war is under no constitutional necessity of providing a system of price control on the domestic front which will assure each landlord a 'fair return' on his property."

Roberts was the lone dissenter—and an angry one. "It is plain," he thundered, "that this Act creates personal government by a petty tyrant instead of government by law." He continued, "War or no war, there exists no necessity, and no constitutional power, for Congress' abdication of its legislative power and remission to an executive official of the function of making and repealing laws."

The Roosevelt Administration's unprecedented administration of the wartime economy had prevailed. "Price-fixing and rent control regulations affecting virtually every person in the nation were upheld today by the Supreme Court," reported the Associated Press. The Court had sustained the foundation of FDR's economic program for the war at home.

❧ ❧ ❧

THE MEANING OF *YAKUS* would be debated in the following decades, and it continues to be debated today.

In 1970, Congress provided President Richard Nixon with price-control and wage-control authority. To the surprise of many, Nixon, who had been miserable as an OPA lawyer for eight months in 1942 before joining the Navy, decided to use the authority and set wage and price controls. Lower courts rejected constitutional challenges by relying on *Yakus*. The courts found that the war context of the *Yakus* decision was not determinative and that the decision supported upholding Nixon's wage and price controls. The Supreme Court never weighed in on the issue.

Yakus reflected broad deference to Congress's assignment of responsibilities to agencies, a cornerstone of Supreme Court decisions in this area since the New Deal. A number of conservative Justices on today's newly aggressive Court, led by Justice Neil Gorsuch, have called for a reinvigorated invocation of a constitutional "nondelegation" principle, with strict judicial limits on Congress's ability to confer broad authority on the Executive Branch. As part of this renewed interest in nondelegation, conservative scholars attack *Yakus* as an unconstitutional abdication to the administrative state. Other Justices, led by Justice Elena Kagan, continue to emphasize and apply the Court's decades-long deferential approach. They rely on *Yakus* and other precedents for the long-established principle that Congress, in its lawmaking discretion, may choose to give agencies authority as long as it sets forth an "intelligible principle" to guide that authority.

For the Justices considering the case in 1944, it was clear that, as a general matter, Congress was entitled under the Constitution to a wide berth in giving responsibility to agencies. It also was clear that the *Yakus* case, involving the criminal prosecution of meat sellers who violated government price orders, was intimately connected to the war. The Justices themselves daily grappled with the mystifying world of coupon books, rationing, price controls, and scarcity, as well as public exhortations to follow intricate and labyrinthine rules. For the Justices, the Emergency Price Control Act, with its sweeping conferral of authority on the OPA Administrator, was, as FDR had pronounced it, an indispensable weapon in the nation's global war for freedom and survival.

· chapter fourteen ·

THE DOUBLE V

T HURGOOD MARSHALL STOOD BEFORE THE JUSTICES FOR HIS second Supreme Court argument during the war in November 1943. The issue was far more consequential than the narrow technical jurisdictional issue in his case the previous year. Marshall was about to challenge the constitutionality of Texas's white primary for the Democratic Party at a time when the nation was at war with a murderous regime premised on the concept of racial purity and superiority. White primaries were a well-understood linchpin of white supremacy. The Supreme Court's decision on the white primary, forged in the crucible of the war, would be a milestone on the Court's path to condemning segregation.

THE CASE INVOLVED LONNIE Smith, a Houston dentist who tried to vote in the 1940 Democratic primary. Texas Democratic Party rules explicitly limited eligible voters to white people. Election officials barred Smith from voting because he was African American. Smith's lawyers, led by Marshall, filed suit claiming that the officials had violated Smith's constitutional rights.

Smith's team mounted the challenge in a daunting legal context. Just nine years earlier, in *Grovey v. Townsend*, the Supreme Court had unanimously upheld the white primary on the ground that, under Texas's law, the primary election was run by a private association (the Texas Democratic Party), not the State of Texas, and thus the Fifteenth Amendment's protection of the right to vote did not apply.

Despite this obstacle, Marshall sensed an opening for two reasons. First, when *Grovey* was decided, it had been a far different Supreme Court. Seven of the nine current Justices had joined the Court since that decision (all except Roberts, the author of *Grovey*, and Stone). By late 1943, the Supreme Court had started to show greater concern on some matters of civil liberties and civil rights—at least if they did not involve an issue that FDR and his Administration saw as crucial to the war effort.

And, second, Marshall thought he could deploy a new Supreme Court decision, *United States v. Classic*. That case, arising from a fight between warring wings of the Louisiana Democratic Party in the wake of Huey Long's 1935 assassination, involved a federal criminal prosecution for election fraud during a primary. In an opinion in 1941 by then Associate Justice Stone, the Court rejected the defendants' argument that a primary election was beyond the scope of federal power; it ruled that the Constitution authorized Congress to regulate primary elections as well as general elections in light of their close interrelationship. Marshall believed that *Classic* opened the way to repudiating *Grovey v. Townsend*.

Within months of the *Classic* decision, Marshall, along with three Texas lawyers, filed a complaint on behalf of Lonnie Smith against S. E. Allwright and James E. Luizza, the Election Judge and Associate Election Judge in the Forty-Eighth Precinct of Harris County. In the case titled *Smith v. Allwright*, Marshall's legal pleading recited that Smith met every requirement of voter eligibility, including his payment of a poll tax, but he had been prevented from voting in the Texas Democratic primary solely because of his race. Marshall's complaint prominently invoked the Supreme Court's recent *Classic* decision. Marshall also highlighted the decisive importance of the Democratic primary in Texas. "Since 1859," recited a joint stipulation of facts, "all Democratic nominees for Congress, Senate and Governor, have been elected in Texas with two exceptions." The Democratic Party primary was in fact the election to office; the subsequent general election was a formality with no practical consequence.

At a hearing in federal court in Houston, Marshall argued, with his trademark succinctness, that in light of the Supreme Court's recent decision regarding primary elections, "Grovey versus Townsend is out." In May 1942, however, the trial judge announced that he would "follow *Grovey v. Townsend* and render judgment for defendants."

Six months later, the New Orleans–based United States Court of Appeals for the Fifth Circuit agreed with the trial court in rebuffing Marshall's reliance on *Classic*. "The opinion of the court in [*Classic*] did not overrule or even mention *Grovey v. Townsend*. We may not overrule it. On its authority the judgment is affirmed."

Marshall's petition for Supreme Court review took direct aim at *Grovey v. Townsend*. "Conflicts between the theories of *United States v. Classic* and *Grovey v. Townsend*...should be resolved," he argued, and the resolution should be "in accordance with the sound theory in the *Classic* case."

Fortifying his legal team, Marshall had added the well-respected William Henry Hastie. Hastie was a prominent African American attorney, a mentor to Marshall, a former federal district judge in the Virgin Islands (the first African American federal judge), and a former high-ranking War Department official. He also had been a brilliant student at Harvard Law School, an editor of the *Harvard Law Review*, and a Frankfurter protégé. On June 7, 1943, the Court agreed to hear the case.

❖ ❖ ❖

As MARSHALL AND HIS team prepared their case for the Supreme Court in the summer of 1943, civil rights issues and racial tensions erupted throughout the country. African Americans reacted strongly to the paradox of fighting Hitler's racism abroad while suffering American racism at home. The *Pittsburgh Courier,* a leading African American newspaper, launched a "Double V" campaign calling for a double victory against fascism overseas and racial discrimination at home. The initiative caught fire in Black communities. With an emblem of one V superimposed over another and an eagle bestriding the double Vs, the campaign sparked giddy excitement—Double V gardens, Double V dances, Double V baseball games, Double V pins (one of which was proudly worn by Wendell Willkie), and even a Double V hairstyle ("the Doubler").

More than one million African American men and women served in the segregated armed forces during World War II, including the famed Tuskegee Airmen. The domestic war-production economy, meanwhile, opened opportunities for African Americans at home, permitting new entry to better-paying positions.

But the economic progress for Black workers frequently met a backlash from white workers, including racial resentments, race-based labor stoppages, and violence. In Detroit, beginning on June 20, 1943, whites and Blacks clashed, leading to the deaths of twenty-five African Americans and nine whites, hundreds of injuries, and the dispatch of federal troops to the Motor City (which had been dubbed the "Arsenal of Democracy" for its mass production of airplane engines, jeeps, and other machinery). At almost the same time, on June 15, in the war-boom industrial hub of Beaumont, Texas, white mobs terrorized Black neighborhoods with assaults and property destruction after false rumors of rape by an African American. In Los Angeles that summer, white vigilantes led the Zoot Suit Riots as they hunted and beat Latinos and African Americans. And other violent racial disturbances flared in Mobile, Newark, Harlem, and other cities.

Members of the Black community responded with anguish, fury, and determination. On July 3, through the Associated Negro Press, Langston Hughes published his poem "Beaumont to Detroit: 1943," in which he wrote,

You jim crowed me
Before hitler rose to power—
And you're STILL jim crowing me
Right now, this very hour.
Yet you say we're fighting
For democracy.
Then why don't democracy
include me?
I ask you this question
Cause I want to know
How long I got to fight
BOTH HITLER—AND JIM CROW.

Viewing the racial strife as a tinderbox that could inhibit the war effort, FDR weakly expressed "regret" over the violence. Civil rights pioneer Pauli Murray, later known for her pioneering legal strategy that inspired trailblazers from Thurgood Marshall to Ruth Bader Ginsburg, responded to FDR's expression of "regret" with a scathing poem, "Mr. Roosevelt Regrets (Detroit Riot, 1943)":

What'd you get, black boy,
When they knocked you down in the gutter,
And they kicked your teeth out,
And they broke your skull with clubs
And they bashed your stomach in?
. . . .
What'd the Top Man say, black boy?
"Mr. Roosevelt regrets. . . . . . ."

The NAACP quickly responded to the violence. In July 1943, Thurgood Marshall and NAACP President Walter White published a report, "What Caused the Detroit Riot?" They concluded that the "weak-kneed policy of the police commissioner coupled with the anti-Negro attitude of many members of the force helped to make a riot inevitable."

Some Roosevelt-appointed Justices had notable civil rights back-grounds. Before joining the Court, Frankfurter and Murphy both had been active in the NAACP. Frankfurter served on its legal committee and Murphy served on its board. During his tenure as Attorney General, Murphy had created the Civil Liberties Section at the Justice Department, soon renamed the Civil Rights Section. And in January 1941, while on the Supreme Court, both Frankfurter and Black attended an NAACP meeting at the Willard Hotel in Washington, DC, that had been convened to improve race relations.

At the same time, a number of Justices, even if receptive to legal claims about civil rights, occasionally displayed a striking personal insensitivity. Perhaps characteristic of the time, their actions are troubling and unsettling today. Liberal Justice Wiley Rutledge, for example, proudly attended a District of Columbia bar event in December 1943 in which four prominent white lawyers performed in blackface for laughs. Far from expressing discomfort, Rutledge kept the *Washington Post's* jocular coverage of the performance, complete with a photo of the lawyers in blackface and a reference to Rutledge's attendance, in his Supreme Court files. And while Lucile Lomen temporarily shattered the gender barrier among Supreme Court law clerks during the war, there would not be an African American law clerk until Frankfurter hired William Coleman for the 1948 term. As late as 1974, reporter Nina Totenberg described the Supreme Court as "the last plantation" because of its racially discriminatory workplace environment.

Despite these obstacles, with a Supreme Court that seemed at times increasingly receptive to claims of civil liberties and civil rights, Marshall pursued his assault on the white primary.

As Marshall prepared for the Supreme Court argument, he sought support from an important source. The Department of Justice had argued and won the *Classic* case. The Department's Office of the Solicitor General enjoyed considerable stature with the Court, which included two former Solicitors General (Reed and Jackson), three former Attorneys General (Stone, Murphy, and Jackson), and one Justice who had handpicked lawyers in the office (Frankfurter).

Marshall secured a meeting with Attorney General Francis Biddle and Assistant Attorney General Herbert Wechsler, later an eminent Columbia Law School professor identified with the legal process movement in 1950s, which emphasized sound procedure and "neutral principles." Taking the lead, Wechsler, who had argued for the government in *Classic* and who had previously served as a law clerk to Harlan Fiske Stone, politely explained that the Justice Department would not file a brief in the case. Marshall cheerfully stated that he understood.

But Marshall's bonhomie masked a fierce determination. The NAACP continued to lobby hard for the Administration's support. So much pressure was applied that FDR raised the issue with Biddle. "There is a good deal of howl because the Department of Justice has refused to participate as *amicus* in the Texas Primary case," the President wrote his Attorney General. "How about it?"

Biddle replied that the "howl" was coming from the NAACP's Walter White and that the Justice Department would not participate in the case. The Department had already "established the right to vote in primaries as a federal right enforceable in the federal courts in the *Classic* case." If they now filed a brief supporting Lonnie Smith's claim, "the South would not understand why we are taking sides." It was a remarkable, and clumsy, political justification by the patrician Philadelphian on a matter of fundamental civil rights.

Biddle's response echoed advice given him by the Solicitor General. Charles Fahy had written Biddle, "Although the legal questions have difficulties, whether or not to participate is essentially a policy question. We have already assisted the negroes by winning the *Classic* case which gives them their principal ammunition. Should we go further in their behalf and make a gesture which cannot fail to offend many others, in Texas and the South generally, in a case in which we are not a party? I think not." Biddle forwarded Fahy's memo to the President.

Despite the Biddle-Fahy position, an internal struggle emerged at Justice. The lawyers in the new Civil Rights Section wanted to support Marshall.

The combatants reached a compromise. Although the United States government would not file in the case, a top lawyer in the Civil Rights Section would publish a supportive legal analysis. Fred G. Folsom Jr., the assistant chief of Civil Rights, promptly wrote a *Columbia Law Review* article. Choosing his words with the prudence of a careful but determined government lawyer, Folsom concluded that, in light of *Classic* and other considerations, "probably *Grovey v. Townsend* should no longer be considered as an authority."

At the oral argument in November, Marshall and Hastie pressed their argument that the Court need not follow *Grovey v. Townsend*. They also maintained that the Court's opinion in *Grovey* had been mistaken and inaccurate about the nature of the Texas primary and its purported private character. "At this point in the argument," reported the newspaper *The Afro-American*, "the decorum of the nine Supreme Court justices was broken for the first time during the case as Chief Justice Stone and several others turned to Justice Roberts, author of the Grovey decision, and laughingly made remarks which caused him to redden."

Opposing Marshall and Hastie in the oral argument was...nobody. The defendants—the primary-election judges who had barred Lonnie Smith from voting—did not show up. They did not have a lawyer arguing for them. Nor had they filed a brief in the Supreme Court. Perhaps they were confident of victory based on *Grovey*. Perhaps they were treating the case with disdain. Or perhaps, once the case moved to Washington, war exigencies led them to view lawyers as a dispensable luxury.

In the wake of the argument by Marshall and Hastie, word apparently reached state officials that the white primary might be in trouble. The Texas Attorney General filed a motion requesting that the state be permitted to submit an amicus brief defending the primary and that the case be reargued with Texas actively participating.

The Court agreed. It announced that "the motion of the State of Texas for leave to file a brief to present oral argument as amicus curiae is granted and the case is restored to the docket and assigned for reargument."

Marshall and Hastie now had an active opponent. The Texas Attorney General filed an amicus brief vigorously defending the white primary. His lawyers carefully noted that, in light of the primary's supposed private and nongovernmental character, the Attorney General did not represent the party. "The Democratic Party in Texas is purely political, and...as Attorney General he is not authorized to represent the party as such." But, they continued, "the question involved in this litigation...is of such importance to the citizenship of Texas and to the preservation of the purity of the ballot in primary elections, that as Attorney General of Texas, he feels that it is his duty to file this brief." The "purity of the ballot," in their words, was under siege.

At the reargument on January 12, 1944, Texas Assistant Attorney General George W. Barcus adopted a comfortable, affable tone. Seeking to deflect Marshall's emphasis on the dominance of the Democratic Party in Texas, Barcus "enlivened the hearing," reported the Associated Press, "by saying, 'The only reason we have a Republican Party in Texas is so the members can get the plums when the party is in Washington.'" He added, "It's just like Democrats in Vermont and New Hampshire." Chief Justice Stone, a New England native, took the bait, replying, "They don't have many [Democrats] there." Barcus was trying to soften the sting of racism by connecting with the Justices on the realities of politics and patronage.

Barcus also suggested that voting-age "negroes" in Texas could form their own party and "whip us any time." Marshall replied, "We couldn't organize another Democratic Party in Texas, and, as you know, you don't just organize parties overnight." With the trial lawyer's eye for the telling point, Robert Jackson asked the young civil rights advocate, "If you formed a party of your own, could you exclude white persons?" Marshall emphatically answered, "We could not do that."

The Justices voted to overrule *Grovey*, strike down the white primary, and rule for Lonnie Smith, with only Roberts dissenting. Stone assigned the *Smith v. Allwright* opinion to Frankfurter.

Although, then as now, Justices rarely challenged opinion assignments by the Chief Justice, Jackson was troubled. As Frankfurter later recounted in a private memo to the file that he did not circulate, Jackson came to see him soon after the assignment. "He thought it was a very great mistake to have me write the *Allwright* opinion," wrote Frankfurter. He summarized Jackson's view: "For a good part of the country the subject—Negro disenfranchisement—was in the domain of the irrational and we have to take account of such facts. At best it will be very unpalatable to the South and should not be exacerbated by having the opinion written by a member of the Court who has, from the point of view of Southern prejudice, three disqualifications: 'You are a New Englander, you are a Jew and you are not a Democrat—at least not recognized as such.'"

Frankfurter replied that "all three accusations are true." Jackson told him that, unless he objected, Jackson would go to Stone and tell him that "of all the members of the Court," Frankfurter "was the last" who should "be asked to write this opinion.... It ought to be written either by the Chief or by a Southern member of the Court." Jackson said he was concerned about the Court, but also about Frankfurter: "A lot of people are bent on exploiting Anti-Semitism, as you well know, and I do not think they ought to be given needless materials."

Frankfurter must have been deeply injured. He saw himself as the most knowledgeable person in the country about the Supreme Court and as a respected and profoundly neutral jurist. Here he was being told that, in the eyes of the world, he was, first and foremost, a Jew, a Yankee, and a Teddy Roosevelt Republican—and that his interpretation of the Constitution would be seen through that lens. But Frankfurter stoically told Jackson, "I literally do not care what case is assigned to me. I can find interest in almost any case and, in any event, enough of them come around that are interesting." He even said that he saw "the force" of Jackson's "suggestion," and that "of course" Jackson was "free to put his views to the Chief."

Jackson wrote Stone expressing his concerns. He began by highlighting the sensitivity of the case. "It is a delicate matter," he explained. "We must reverse a recent, well-considered, and unanimous decision. We deny the entire South the right to a white primary, which is one of its most cherished rights." He then brought up Frankfurter. "It seems to me very important that the strength which an all but unanimous decision would have may be greatly weakened if the voice that utters it is one that may grate on Southern sensibilities. Mr. Justice Frankfurter unites in a rare degree factors which unhappily excite prejudice. In the first place, he is a Jew. In the second place, he is from New England, the seat of the abolition movement. In the third place, he has not been thought of as a person particularly sympathetic with the Democratic party in the past."

Jackson concluded with his request that the opinion be reassigned. "With all humility I suggest that the Court's decision, bound to arouse bitter resentment, will be much less apt to stir ugly reactions if the news that the white primary is dead, is broken to it, if possible, by a Southerner who has been a Democrat and is not a member of one of the minorities which stir prejudices kindred to those against the Negro. I have talked with some of [the other Justices] who are still in the building, and they feel as I do."

In Frankfurter's telling, Stone then met with him and "looked and talked like one under a heavy burden." He confided that an unnamed "member of the Court" had raised "the three reasons" Frankfurter should not write the opinion—"You are a New Englander, a Jew and not a Democrat." Frankfurter replied, "All three reasons are true.... The case is back on your desk as though it never had been assigned and you assign it to whomsoever in your wisdom you think should write the opinion." Stone seemed "as though a great weight had been lifted from his soul." Stone asked Frankfurter which southerner he thought should receive the assignment—Black or Reed. Not surprisingly, Frankfurter, already embroiled in his vitriolic battles with Black and his "Axis," told Stone that "the job required, of course, delicacy of treatment and absence of a raucous voice and that I thought of the Southerners Reed was the better of the two for the job."

Stone promptly reassigned the opinion to Reed.

❖ ❖ ❖

STANLEY FORMAN REED, ONE of the least known of FDR's Supreme Court appointees, was unabashedly loyal and devoted to the President he had served as Solicitor General.

Reed grew up in comfort. His lineage traced to pre-Revolutionary America, and his father was a prosperous physician. When he was ten, Stanley, an only child, and his parents moved to Maysville, Kentucky. Reed went to Yale, graduating with the class of 1906 and earning the Bennett Prize in American History. He attended law school for a year each at the University of Virginia School of Law and Columbia Law School but, unsure of his plans, never graduated from either.

In 1908, Reed married Winifred Elgin, and, the following year, they lived in Paris while Stanley studied law at the Sorbonne. After returning to Maysville and successfully reading for the bar with a local lawyer, Reed opened a law office. In 1911, at the age of twenty-six, he was elected to the Kentucky General Assembly as the Democratic candidate. He was reelected in 1913 but defeated for a third term by 153 votes in 1915. Throughout these years, he was active in a Kentucky organization for young Democrats.

When the United States entered World War I in 1917, Reed served as a lieutenant in the Army. At war's end, he returned to Maysville and joined a corporate law firm. Reed quickly established himself as a leading lawyer for Kentucky businesses, including a large agricultural cooperative and the Chesapeake and Ohio Railway. With their two sons, John and Stanley Jr., he and Winifred lived on a farm outside Maysville. The farm became known for its prizewinning cattle, even while Reed continued his practice as a prominent corporate lawyer.

When the stock market crashed in October 1929, the economic disaster exacerbated an agricultural crisis. Severe farm problems had led to creation of the Federal Farm Board. Despite Reed's identity as a Democrat, President Herbert Hoover named him to be the board's general counsel on the strength of his reputation in agricultural business circles. In December 1932, Hoover, now a defeated lame duck, appointed Reed general counsel of the Reconstruction Finance Corporation, an agency established to make loans to banks and businesses.

FDR was impressed by Reed. The new President liked the idea of continuity in the arcane world of the RFC. He also undoubtedly was reassured by Reed's status as a former Democratic elected official, including his role as a delegate at the 1920 Democratic convention, where FDR had been nominated for Vice President. Tall, bald, and courtly, Reed carried himself with a demeanor of seriousness and purpose.

Roosevelt kept Reed at the RFC. In the early years of the Administration, Reed's office became a launching pad for young New Deal legal stars, including Tommy Corcoran. In 1935, FDR named Reed to be his second Solicitor General. Frankfurter, still at Harvard Law School, had gotten to know Reed through his work at the RFC and strongly urged FDR to appoint him.

As Solicitor General, Reed encountered enormous challenges. Major New Deal laws faced a hostile Supreme Court in challenges brought by businesses. Reed led the charge for the government, overseeing the government's strategy and frequently arguing the marquee cases. But the government suffered devastating defeats in Reed's first few months, including "Black Monday" on May 27, 1935. On that gloomy day, the government lost a trio of much-watched contests: the Supreme Court found illegal the National Industrial Recovery Act, the Frazier-Lemke Bankruptcy Act for farmers, and even FDR's firing of a Hoover-appointed Federal Trade Commission member.

The pressures sometimes weighed on Reed. In the midst of a Supreme Court argument defending the Bankhead Cotton Control Act on December 10, 1935, he collapsed. As the *New York Times* reported, Reed was facing a barrage of withering questions from the Justices. Suddenly, he "paled," his "face was ashen," and he "showed signs of total exhaustion." Reed "said in a low voice, 'I must beg the Court's indulgence, but I am too ill to proceed further.'" Government lawyers helped him to his seat, and the Court adjourned for the day.

At the end of 1936, despondent over his failures, Reed offered FDR his resignation and rued that he had not had "very good luck with the Supreme Court in the solicitor generalship." "Oh, bosh, we'll get along all right," the President replied, and he summarily rejected Reed's resignation.

Reed's fortunes—and the fortunes of the Roosevelt Administration in the Supreme Court—dramatically turned in 1937 with the "switch in time." The federal government won sweeping decisions upholding landmark laws ranging from the Social Security Act to the National Labor Relations Act.

When, on January 5, 1938, Justice George Sutherland, one of the archconservative "Four Horsemen," announced his retirement at the age of seventy-five, Roosevelt named Reed to take his seat, the President's second Supreme Court appointment, four months after Hugo Black had joined the Court. In the wake of the national controversy over Black's past Klan membership, FDR wanted a smooth and uncontroversial confirmation. Reed seemed likely to receive widespread approval.

The strategy worked. Press accounts reported that "Mr. Reed, while having liberal views and defending scores of administration measures before the highest court, is universally regarded in Washington as realistic rather than radical.... He has a high reputation among lawyers and has won obvious respect from the justices by his forceful preparation and conscientious preparation of the issues." Only ten days after his nomination, on January 25, the Senate unanimously confirmed Reed by acclamation.

Reed did not have the type of well-publicized close relationship with FDR that Frankfurter, Douglas, and Jackson enjoyed. But he and the President were friendly. While serving as Solicitor General, Reed had sent FDR notes on political issues. In August 1935, for example, several months after becoming Solicitor General, he wrote FDR that the Young Democrats had responded to the President's talk with rapture. "As always [your] tone and reception were perfect." While Solicitor General, Reed served as a Kentucky delegate to the Democratic Convention in Philadelphia in 1936, where FDR was renominated for a second term. And, in coordination with the Democratic National Committee, Reed gave dozens of speeches around the country in the fall of 1936 to groups ranging from lawyers' associations to women's clubs.

After joining the Supreme Court, Reed continued to hail FDR's political triumphs, sending him a stream of notes filled with congratulations and flattery. In June 1942, with the war underway, Reed reminded the President, "If I can be of any service, of course, I am always at your command." After FDR's reelection in 1944, Reed wrote him, "Your election gratifies my every wish. Satisfaction over your continuance as President appears this morning among the people....Confidence in our future augurs for continued welfare at home and victory abroad." Throughout the war years, Reed plied FDR with carefully selected Christmas presents—"fine old Kentucky bourbon"; Haitian rum "from the last century"; a Kentucky ham; champagne; "pre-prohibition bourbons." FDR responded with delight, enjoying Reed's "most intriguing" bottles and his "most welcome Christmas gift of Kentucky sunshine."

Perhaps the most telling communication from Reed to FDR came at the beginning of Reed's first full term on the Supreme Court. "At a time least inconvenient to yourself," Reed wrote on October 26, 1938, "may I pay my respects? If it is not too much of an intrusion, this will help me to maintain, in some degree, my understanding of your objectives." Here was Reed—a Justice on the Supreme Court—asking for guidance in his new post on the President's "objectives." Less than a week later, the President and the Justice dined alone for a private hour-long lunch at the White House. While there is no record of the conversation, they undoubtedly discussed, as Reed had requested, FDR's "objectives."

Nearly six years later, Stanley Reed, a scion of distinguished Kentucky families and a former elected Democrat, found himself charged with writing the opinion striking down Texas's white primary.

REED'S OPINION HIGHLIGHTED A theme of overriding importance in the spring of 1944. "The United States is a constitutional democracy," he proclaimed, and "constitutional rights would be of little value if they could be thus indirectly denied." The ongoing world war against fascism, totalitarianism, and a regime rooted in racial supremacy and violence was not mentioned. But its significance as a framework for the decision was clear. As legal scholar Michael Klarman has emphasized, the war was of "fundamental importance" in *Smith v. Allwright*.

Reed made three points in concluding that the white primary violated the Fifteenth Amendment, which prohibits states from denying or abridging the right to vote "on account of race, color, or previous condition of servitude." First, although *Classic* had not mentioned *Grovey*, the *Classic* opinion had recognized the important "place of the primary in the electoral scheme." Second, contrary to the *Grovey* analysis, the primary election was an action of the state, not merely the private political organization, and it thus could be challenged under the Fifteenth Amendment. And, third, despite its recent vintage, *Grovey* must be overruled. "We are not unmindful of the desirability of continuity of decision in constitutional questions," Reed's opinion explained. "However, when convinced of former error, this Court has never felt constrained to follow precedent. In constitutional questions, where correction depends upon amendment and not upon legislative action this Court throughout its history has freely exercised its power to reexamine the basis of its constitutional decisions."

Seven Justices joined Reed's opinion. Frankfurter refused to join and merely published a terse sentence stating that he "concurred in the result." He had drafted a concurrence stating that the reason for the change from *Grovey* was simply that the current Justices viewed the issue differently from the previous Justices, not that *Classic* had changed the law—an explanation that he had unsuccessfully advocated as the ground for decision. But he had been persuaded by other Justices not to publish his separate opinion.

As in the OPA cases, Roberts vehemently dissented. He defended his unanimous decision in *Grovey v. Townsend*. "The opinion was written with care," he noted, and he listed every Justice on the Court who had joined it, including Holmes, Brandeis, and Stone, who now was a member of the majority overturning it. "The instant decision," he objected, "overruling that announced about nine years ago, tends to bring adjudications of this tribunal into the same class as a restricted railroad ticket, good for this day and train only"—a phrase that would become famous as a term of derision for Supreme Court decisions arbitrarily limited to their facts. Roberts closed with a blast, finding it "regrettable that in an era marked by doubt and confusion," the Supreme Court should "now itself become the breeder of fresh doubt and confusion in the public mind as to the stability of our institutions."

But Roberts's vote stood alone. In a momentous action, the Court had struck down the long-standing white primary in sweeping terms and by an 8–1 vote.

Commentators emphasized the war context of the opinion. A *Washington Post* editorial hailed the decision as "a bold stroke for democracy. It strikes down a form of discrimination that is a reproach to any freedom-loving people and is particularly anachronistic in a country fighting a world-wide war against tyranny and oppression." "The real reason for the overturn" of *Grovey*, stressed *New York Times* columnist Arthur Krock, "is that the common sacrifices of wartime have turned public opinion and the court against previously sustained devices to exclude minorities from any privilege of citizenship the majority enjoys." A letter in the *Pittsburgh Courier*, the African American newspaper leading the Double V campaign, applauded the Supreme Court's decision and pointedly inquired, "May I ask the white politician why should the Negro not vote? . . . They fight and die on the battlefield for their country."

Some southern states reacted with fury and dismay. A Florida Democratic Party official announced, "We'll certainly resist, if possible, any attempt to have Negroes vote in our primaries." A Mississippi official defiantly proclaimed, "The Supreme Court or no one else can control a Democratic primary in Mississippi." And South Carolina's Governor vowed, "White supremacy will be maintained in our primaries. Let the chips fall where they may!" Officials in other southern states were more guarded, expressing disappointment but declining to advocate noncompliance.

Smith v. Allwright signaled the demise of the white primary throughout the South, but it had some additional convulsions before the final death knell sounded. Just seventeen days after the decision, South Carolina removed all references to primaries from its laws in an effort to shield its system from the decision—a subterfuge that would be struck down as unconstitutional. Efforts at resistance in other states met the same fate.

For Thurgood Marshall, the announcement of the opinion brought both celebration and activity. At the NAACP headquarters in New York, the drinks flowed. The party was so boisterous that Marshall missed a congratulatory call from former NAACP board member Justice Frank Murphy—an eyebrow-raising communication by today's standards. Marshall and Murphy connected the next day, and Murphy invited Marshall to lunch. Marshall "apologized profusely" for missing Murphy's previous day's call. "Murphy agreed," Marshall recalled, "that a guy had a right to get drunk at a time like that."

While the case was pending, Marshall called it "one of the most important cases to Negroes that has ever been before the courts." Now he proclaimed it a "landmark.... The decision will be of tremendous benefit to the cause of the Negro voter in the South as well as to the cause of democracy in general."

Marshall also swung into action. It was his first major Supreme Court victory, and he was determined to use it swiftly and effectively. He fired off a letter to Attorney General Francis Biddle demanding that the Justice Department promptly enforce the decision throughout the South. "Although the Department of Justice did not deem it wise to intervene in this case as amicus curiae," he observed, "we are sure that the department will now recognize that criminal jurisdiction over interference with the right to vote because of color extends to primary elections.... We now urge the United States Department of Justice...to prosecute vigorously persons who deny to others rights under the Constitution and laws of the United States, especially the right to vote."

The decision did not guarantee victory in all cases involving civil rights, or in all cases argued by Thurgood Marshall. In fact, Marshall lost his next Supreme Court case two months after the *Smith v. Allwright* decision—his third appearance at the High Court during the war. It was a criminal case—*Lyons v. Oklahoma*, concerning the coerced confession of an African American defendant in a murder case. This time, on

June 5, 1944, Justice Stanley Reed wrote an opinion rejecting Marshall's argument—the first of only three losses Marshall would suffer as a Supreme Court advocate, compared with twenty-nine victories.

But *Smith v. Allwright* plainly had broad significance. Amid the Double V campaign, amid concern about racism at home while fighting fascism abroad, the Court took a giant stride. While it would take deeply courageous and determined citizen activism, culminating in the Voting Rights Act of 1965, to ensure the extension and protection of voting rights for African Americans, *Smith v. Allwright* was a crucial step on the journey. And even more broadly, as historian Darlene Clark Hine has emphasized, "*Smith* was the watershed in the struggle for black rights," setting in motion the trajectory of civil rights litigation and decisions that generated *Brown v. Board of Education* almost exactly ten years after the Court announced *Smith v. Allwright*.

On July 28, 1944, four years and one day after the election judges barred him from voting in the 1940 primary election, Houston dentist Lonnie Smith proudly cast his ballot. More than two thousand of his fellow African Americans in Houston joined him in voting for the first time in a Democratic primary.

· chapter fifteen ·

A NATIONAL TICKET

T HROUGHOUT THE WAR YEARS, FDR CONTINUED TO VIEW THE
Justices as members of his official family, trusted friends and allies.
Among the President's many interactions with them, one episode stands
out: the candidacy of William O. Douglas for the vice presidency in
1944. Like many political sagas, it is steeped in false starts, conniving,
and twists and turns. Its circuitous unfolding, however, does not obscure
the core fact: a sitting Justice possibly joining the President on the national political ticket.

AS THE SUPREME COURT ended its term in June 1944, an issue loomed
on the political horizon. Rumors spread that FDR would replace Vice
President Henry Wallace. Party leaders and insiders wanted to sack
him. They saw Wallace as a political liability—an erratic idealist with
a history of dabbling in mysticism, a starry-eyed liberal who would
alienate southerners and moderates. Adding to the importance of the
selection was the uncomfortable fact that the President seemed to be

259

ailing—increasingly pale and shrunken, though still with his irrepress-
ible buoyancy. Washington insiders whispered that the person chosen
to be Vice President would become President in the fourth term. But
Wallace retained strong support among labor and liberals.

As the time for the Democratic convention in Chicago approached,
FDR had an early favorite in mind: Douglas. FDR had long been captivated by Douglas's political appeal. In the summer of 1939, at a White
House lunch with Hugo Black, FDR told the former Alabama Senator
that Douglas "had vast potentialities as vice presidential timber and possibly later presidential material...but couldn't be developed by 1940."
Shortly before the 1940 Democratic convention, in a precursor to what
would happen in 1944, rumors circulated that Douglas would join FDR
on the national ticket. Vice President John Nance Garner would be replaced; he had served two terms and famously called the vice presidency
"a pitcher of warm spit" (or, in Garner's recollection, "a pitcher of warm
piss"). The *Washington Post* called Douglas the "favorite"; a columnist
cited him as "the New Dealers' first choice...young and tough, reasonably good on the platform, with a personality and personal history of
earned successes which are a fair match for Willkie's." FDR told aides
he was trying to decide between Douglas and Agriculture Secretary
Henry Wallace as his running mate. When party leaders objected that
Douglas was not well known, he settled on Wallace.

In what would become a pattern, Douglas claimed he had not been
interested. He told a friend, "I am delighted that I was passed by. I feared
for a period of two weeks that pressure might be put on me to go on the
ticket. So [as] far as I am personally concerned the result was most grati-
fying." Douglas also wrote Frankfurter that he had no interest in leaving
the Court and joining the ticket. But Douglas conspicuously did not
make any public statement to that effect—even though *New York Times*
columnist Arthur Krock had written that Douglas should make such an
explicit statement, for the good of the Court, when he was discussed for
the presidency before FDR clarified his third-term plans for the 1940
election. And, most tellingly, while the press touted his vice-presidential
candidacy, Douglas never communicated the slightest reluctance to

FDR. Far from it. During that very period, he wrote the President sharing his political observations.

❖ ❖ ❖

FROM HUMBLE BEGINNINGS IN the west, William Orville Douglas enjoyed a meteoric rise in academia and government, becoming FDR's youngest appointee to the Court at the age of forty.

Orville, as the future Justice was known in his youth, was the middle child of three, with an older sister and a younger brother. When he was not yet two, Orville nearly died from a serious and prolonged illness, generally thought to be polio. For months, his mother massaged his arms and legs for hours each day, even though the medical professionals were pessimistic about the boy's prospects. When he recovered, she viewed it as a miracle. From that point on, she showered him with unconditional love, affection, and support—and regularly told him that he would be President of the United States.

Orville's father, a Presbyterian minister, died when Orville was five; he had moved the family from Minnesota to California and then to Washington. Orville's mother settled the family, with little financial means, in Yakima, Washington.

Douglas flourished in Yakima. He graduated from high school as valedictorian and went on to Whitman College in Walla Walla, Washington, where he earned Phi Beta Kappa membership. After college, Douglas taught English at a local high school and became romantically involved with Mildred Riddle, a Latin teacher.

Bored with teaching, Douglas regularly visited the local courthouse. In 1922, he left for Columbia Law School, making his way east by herding sheep on a freight train in return for free passage, an experience he recounted with glee for decades.

Douglas excelled in law school, focusing on corporate law and immersing himself in the teachings of Justice Louis Brandeis. He married Mildred after his first year of law school, and she moved east to join him. In Douglas's first year at Columbia, Harlan Fiske Stone was the dean. When Stone became a Supreme Court Justice in 1925 after briefly

serving as Attorney General, Douglas hoped to become his law clerk; he
was bitterly disappointed when Stone selected a rival classmate.

After law school, Douglas was restless. He worked at the preeminent
Wall Street law firm Cravath, hated it, tried small-town practice back in
Yakima, quickly became bored, and left after a brief period. He jumped
at the opportunity to join the Columbia Law School faculty as a full-
time member in 1927, and then, a year later, in 1928, moved to Yale Law
School.

Douglas focused on financial law—including the laws governing
corporations, bankruptcies, and securities—and his specialty rocketed
to prominence after the stock market crash of 1929. Douglas quickly
gained renown as a young academic star with an important real-world
focus. When Joseph P. Kennedy became chair of the newly formed
Securities and Exchange Commission in 1934, he tapped Douglas to
head the SEC's Prospective Study Committee, a post in which Douglas launched aggressive investigations to protect small investors. In 1935,
FDR named Douglas to be an SEC Commissioner and then, in 1937,
to be chair of the Commission. Douglas attacked Wall Street titans with
relish and savvy, delighting the President.

By 1939, Douglas, always ambitious, was looking for new challenges.
He considered leaving government. And then, on February 13, 1939, eighty-
two-year-old Justice Louis Brandeis announced his retirement. Public
speculation focused on the need for a westerner on the Court, with the
retirements in 1937 and 1938 of the two Justices from western states
(Willis Van Devanter of Wyoming and George Sutherland of Utah).
The press heralded Senator Lewis Schwellenbach of Washington as the
leading candidate.

On Sunday, March 19, 1939, after playing a round of golf, Douglas received a message that the President wanted to see him. Hurrying
to the White House, he met Roosevelt in the President's study. FDR
mischievously told him that he had "a new job" for Douglas and that
it's "a mean job, a dirty job, a thankless job." The new assignment was
unnamed, but the implication was clear: the President wanted to move
Douglas to the troubled Federal Communications Commission, which

badly needed new leadership. "It's a job you'll detest," Roosevelt teased. "This job is something like being in jail." As Douglas stewed and fretted, FDR smiled. "Tomorrow I am sending your name to the Senate as Louis Brandeis's successor." On March 20, 1939, President Roosevelt officially named Douglas, forty years old, as his fourth Supreme Court appointment (after Black, Reed, and Frankfurter).

Although Douglas professed surprise at his nomination, he had been working with close Roosevelt associates, including Tommy Corcoran and Harold Ickes, in an aggressive effort to secure the appointment. He also had coordinated with prominent journalists like columnist Arthur Krock to publicize his credentials as a westerner.

On April 4, 1939, the Senate confirmed Douglas by a 62–4 vote, and he formally took his seat on April 17, 1939.

Douglas's wife and two children joined him at the official ceremony. Douglas would prove to have troubled and difficult family relationships, but these were not apparent during the war years. He and Mildred would divorce in 1953, and Douglas would go on to marry three other women and divorce two of them; his third and fourth marriages took place when he was in his sixties and his young wives were in their twenties, generating public mirth and derision.

But all of this was still in the future. In Douglas's first several years on the Court, he cultivated a public image as a family man, trotting Mildred and his children out for news photos of the active, youthful Justice.

The President and Douglas remained close. While Douglas could be unpleasant to those around him, he also could carry himself with wit and sparkle, particularly when seeking to impress, and Roosevelt delighted in his company. He became a regular at the President's poker parties and other social gatherings. "I saw FDR frequently at night," Douglas recalled in his memoir. "He maintained that I made the best dry martinis of anyone in town. He liked them dry—six to one—and very cold, with lemon peel."

While Douglas insisted that FDR never spoke to him about particular cases, they did talk in lighthearted terms about the Court. On one occasion, when FDR was talking at lunch about the crunch for office space in wartime Washington, Douglas playfully suggested moving the Supreme Court to Denver for the duration of the war and setting up "hundreds of tables in the hallways" and "a regular assembly line for memoranda and other paperwork" in the vacated Court building. FDR glanced at him and wryly replied, "How can I keep an eye on you all if you are way out there?"

In another conversation, FDR asked Douglas "why lawyers were so conservative, why they turned out to be stodgy judges." While FDR "mentioned no names," Douglas understood that the President "obviously had been disappointed at some of his own judicial appointees." Douglas told him that "there was nothing in the Constitution requiring him to appoint a lawyer to the Supreme Court." That got the President's attention. "'What?' he exclaimed. 'Are you serious?'" When Douglas confirmed it, Roosevelt "leaned back and after a moment's silence said, 'Let's find a good layman.'" Douglas suggested that a layman probably would need to be a Senator to be confirmed. With his usual brio, FDR plunged into considering possible candidates, ultimately announcing to Douglas that nonlawyer Wisconsin Senator Robert La Follette Jr. would be his next Justice. Whether FDR would have followed through will never be known. After that conversation, he never had another opportunity to fill a Supreme Court seat.

Even after joining the Court, Douglas discussed policy and political matters with the President. As war approached, Douglas recalled, "FDR would mull over his problems in the evening and he used me as a sounding board." And in June 1941, as Douglas made his annual cross-country drive to begin his summer sojourn in the Pacific Northwest, he stopped in Texas and sent FDR his view of the political situation there, including his account of a campaign rally for Congressman Lyndon Johnson in a Senate race and his discussion with Johnson about his chances.

Now it was Douglas's own political prospects that were front and center.

❧ ❧ ❧

IN THE SUMMER OF 1944, as the opening session of the Democratic National Convention in Chicago neared, party insiders were determined to keep Wallace off the ticket. And FDR appeared amenable to a new running mate.

At first, it seemed that Douglas had the inside track. On July 6, party leader Ed Flynn rushed to see former boxer and trainer Teddy Hayes, his close friend and political associate, in the apartment they shared in the Mayflower Hotel in DC. Flynn was one of the Democratic Party's most powerful leaders—the political boss in the Bronx, a Democratic National Committee member, and a former DNC chairman. He was coming from the White House, where he had seen FDR.

In the preceding weeks, Flynn and Hayes had discussed options to replace Wallace. Hayes strongly supported his friend Justice William O. Douglas, the crusader against Wall Street, a westerner with a modest and unassuming upbringing. Flynn favored Senator Harry Truman of Missouri, who had become prominent heading a Senate committee exposing war profiteering.

"Teddy," Flynn excitedly announced. "I think your man is in." He and the President had discussed the vice presidency, and FDR had expressed a preference for Douglas. Flynn told Hayes that, in light of the President's position, he had decided not to push for Truman. Flynn and Hayes called Bob Hannegan, the DNC chair. Like Flynn and Hayes, Hannegan was staying at the Mayflower. He immediately came to the Flynn-Hayes suite. Hannegan had been a party leader in St. Louis and had strong ties to Truman. Truman, in turn, had helped Hannegan get federal positions, including a local Internal Revenue Commission job and then, when Hannegan performed well, the position of Commissioner of Internal Revenue. In January 1944, Truman helped Hannegan become Democratic National Committee chairman.

Like other party leaders, Hannegan was determined to replace Wallace. In view of the President's declining health, they also knew the stakes. As DNC Treasurer and California oil executive Ed Pauley confided to political allies, "[We] are not nominating a Vice President of the United States, but a President."

When Hannegan arrived at their suite, Flynn reported on his conversation with the President and FDR's preference for Douglas as his Vice President. "The President wants to have a dinner...with the executive committee," Flynn said. "You're the chairman, Bob. You go and tell them." Hannegan arranged a July 11 dinner with FDR and the party leaders.

THE MORNING AFTER HEARING Flynn's account, Hayes excitedly called Douglas. He told the Justice that FDR had selected him for the ticket. The news would have to come from the President himself, and Douglas could not tell anybody. Two days later, Hayes called Douglas again to see if FDR had called. When Douglas responded that he had not, Hayes told him, "Don't worry about it. You're the choice."

But Bob Hannegan, the party chair from Missouri, had other ideas. He swung into action to try to secure the spot for Truman, his home-state patron and comrade, an experienced political pro, and a Senator from a border state with a reputation as a moderate. All of those qualities made him far more attractive than the Supreme Court Justice.

FDR DISCUSSED THE VICE-PRESIDENTIAL situation at a lunch with presidential adviser Sam Rosenman, Interior Secretary Harold Ickes, and FDR's daughter, Anna Roosevelt Boettiger. While the President was noncommittal about his running mate preference, he told them he had decided to move ahead without Wallace. Never one to enjoy delivering bad news, he instructed Rosenman to meet with Wallace and let him know that, even though Wallace was FDR's personal choice, unlike in 1940, FDR would not push the convention to nominate Wallace.

On Monday, July 10, Rosenman, accompanied by Ickes, had lunch with Wallace at Wallace's apartment in the Wardman Park. They tried to tell Wallace that, while the President had positive personal feelings for the Vice President, he had concluded that Wallace would hurt the ticket and hoped that Wallace would not seek renomination. Wallace stopped them and said he would discuss it with the President.

Wallace met with FDR later that day. According to Wallace, Roosevelt instructed him that, when he left the meeting, he should say that no politics were discussed. In what must have been a humiliating experience for Wallace as the President pretended not to talk to him, FDR announced, "I am now talking to the ceiling about political matters." The President then said he personally preferred Wallace. But some advisers had been reporting that Wallace would cost the ticket one to three million votes. Aides also were saying that Wallace could not be nominated unless FDR again demanded it. FDR and Wallace both agreed that, unlike in 1940, FDR should not force Wallace on the convention. Wallace asked if the President would issue a statement saying that, if he were a delegate, he would vote for Wallace. The President agreed.

FDR's lack of clarity was probably due to a number of reasons. He undoubtedly wanted to keep his options open as long as possible; he likely wanted to assess the reaction of Wallace's constituency of liberals and labor; and he certainly wished to avoid unpleasantness in a direct personal conversation, an experience the sunny President always hated.

Wallace joined the President again for lunch the next day and brought him an Uzbek robe from his foreign travels. His other gift was a political memo showing Wallace's strength in key states and a proposed draft statement in which the President would endorse Wallace as his running mate. FDR gently skirted around Wallace's draft statement; he said that he had "worked out another wording" and he would hold on to Wallace's draft.

Wallace came away believing that FDR had blessed his continuing effort to seek renomination. He sized up his competition. "The Hannegan game," Wallace recorded in his diary, "is to knock me at every possible turn in the hope that Truman will be the ultimate beneficiary. The Ickes game is to have Douglas as the beneficiary. . . . Word comes from several sources that Biddle, Tommy Corcoran's friend, is working very hard for Douglas and very strong against me."

ON THE DAY OF his lunch with Wallace, at one of his regular press conferences, FDR publicly announced for the first time that he would accept a fourth term. After ordering the doors blocked to prevent a mad dash of the reporters, he distributed a letter he had sent to Hannegan in his capacity as party chair. "If the convention should...nominate me for the presidency, I shall accept. If the people elect me, I will serve....If the people command me to continue in this office and in this war, I have as little right to withdraw as the soldier has to leave his post in the line....All that is within me cries out to go back to my home on the Hudson river, to avoid public responsibilities, and to avoid also the publicity which in our democracy follows every step of the nation's chief executive....Reluctantly, but as a good soldier, I repeat that I will accept and serve in this office if I am so ordered by the commander-in-chief of us all—the sovereign people of the United States."

FDR said nothing about his choice for Vice President. But the significance of his own announcement for the vice-presidential choice seemed clear. Unlike in 1940, when FDR had made running contingent on the selection of Wallace, he now was committing to run regardless of his running mate. The United Press thought the message so plain that it speculated Wallace might withdraw from consideration. And it highlighted an interesting new development: "Thomas G. Corcoran and other past and present White House advisers were booming Associate Justice William O. Douglas—a 100 per cent new dealer—for the vice presidential spot."

THE INCREASINGLY CROWDED FIELD for Vice President had another serious contender: Douglas's former Supreme Court colleague Jimmy Byrnes. In 1940, then Senator Byrnes had been a strong possibility for Vice President until FDR told him he wanted Wallace. Now, witnessing the general dissatisfaction with Wallace, the "Assistant President" saw himself as Wallace's logical successor. For months, FDR and Harry Hopkins had been making positive comments to Byrnes about his suitability for the vice presidency, including at a weekend at Shangri-La in June 1944. And Byrnes was interested.

On the evening of Tuesday, July 11, FDR hosted a dinner at the White House with Democratic Party leaders, including Hannegan and Flynn. Teddy Hayes, Douglas's friend and avid supporter, accompanied them on their short walk from the Mayflower Hotel to the White House. As they strolled, Hannegan brought up the number two slot on the ticket. "What about Truman?" he asked. Flynn expressed surprise. "I leaned toward Truman myself," he countered. "Why didn't you say something a week ago when I told you the President wanted Douglas?"

Hannegan casually inquired, "Do you think it is too late to raise the issue one more time?" Flynn was uncertain and asked if it had been raised with other members of the party's executive committee. Hannegan assured him it had, and they all were ready to support Truman. Flynn obliged. "Okay, I'll reopen the subject after dinner," he said. "You tell the President your thoughts. You can carry the ball. You're the chairman."

Teddy Hayes was alarmed. He returned to the Mayflower, called Douglas, and reported on the conversation. Douglas was unhappy. According to Hayes, he believed that Flynn, the man who had told Hayes only a week earlier that FDR had picked Douglas, had "double-crossed" him.

FDR heartily greeted the party leaders—Hannegan, Flynn, Postmaster General Frank Walker (another former DNC chair), Chicago Mayor Ed Kelly, DNC Secretary George Allen, and DNC Treasurer Ed Pauley. After martinis and dinner, they settled into the presidential study for a strategy session about the upcoming convention and election, with FDR now publicly a candidate. Presidential son-in-law John Boettiger joined them.

They discussed the vice-presidential slot. Everybody agreed that Wallace, eccentric and politically controversial, should not be renominated. A number of possible running mates, including Senate Majority Leader Alben Barkley and House Speaker Sam Rayburn, were discussed and quickly dismissed; they were not the right candidates at a time when fissures in the New Deal coalition were beginning to emerge. Jimmy Byrnes was the subject of extended conversation. FDR was concerned that Byrnes had two major political problems: the segregationist South Carolinian would hurt the ticket with African Americans in the North, and as a Catholic who became an Episcopalian when he married, Byrnes also would fare poorly with Catholic voters.

Roosevelt then raised two candidates for consideration: his Ambassador to Great Britain, John Winant, and Justice William O. Douglas. He was particularly enthusiastic about Douglas. FDR thought Douglas would keep Wallace's constituency in the fold. Douglas, he explained, enjoyed "the following of the liberal left wing of the American people, the same kind of people whom Wallace had." FDR also found Douglas's political profile attractive and engaging. He had "practical experience from the backwoods of the North West as a logger," said the President, and he looked and acted "like a Boy Scout." He would have "appeal at the polls." And then there was the clincher for the fun-loving President: Douglas "[played] an interesting game of poker." As Ed Pauley later recalled, "Roosevelt kept stressing Douglas."

The party leaders were not enthusiastic. According to George Allen, in their view, "Douglas had no visible followers, with the possible exception of Ickes, who also had no visible followers, with the possible exception of Ickes." In historian Robert Ferrell's telling, "When Roosevelt finished talking about Douglas there was dead silence on the part of everyone, for no one wanted Douglas—he was not as offbeat as Wallace but possessed the same amateur political status."

One of the guests brought up Truman. FDR replied that he did not know Truman well. He knew only that Truman had done "a good job" with the Senate committee, had "demonstrated his ability and loyalty," and had been "trained in politics." FDR asked about Truman's age, an obvious comparison to Douglas's youthfulness. (Douglas was then forty-five.) Just two weeks earlier, on June 28, the Republicans had nominated forty-two-year-old Governor Thomas Dewey (coincidentally a law school classmate of Douglas's).

Hannegan was well aware that Truman was sixty years old, but he feigned ignorance. He asked, "Does anyone know how old Truman really is?" and then, as he hoped, the conversation moved on. When Boettiger retrieved a congressional directory to determine Truman's age and handed it to Pauley, the DNC Treasurer kept the book in his lap and did not bring it up again.

Listening to the discussion, FDR tacked to the wind as he would have on one of his beloved ships at sea. He put a hand on Hannegan's knee and commented, "Bob, I think you and everyone else want Truman. . . . If that is the case, it is Truman."

That concluded the meeting. The party leaders filed out. Hannegan stayed behind. Frank Walker had quietly suggested that he get the President's agreement in writing. With the others gone, Hannegan now asked FDR for a note reflecting the conversation. FDR agreed and handwrote a message. He told Hannegan that he would date the missive July 19, the first day of the convention, so that it would appear he had sent it at that time.

Hannegan was delighted and put the note in his pocket without reading it. Ed Pauley returned to the room, having taken the wrong suit jacket in the hasty exit. FDR looked up and said, "I know that this makes you boys happy, and you are the ones I am counting on to win this election. I still think that Douglas would have the greater public appeal." They replied that, whatever "Truman might lack in this regard," the party leaders "would make up in enthusiasm." Then they shook hands and left before he could change his mind.

Gesturing to the note in his pocket, Hannegan excitedly told Walker, "I've got it." But Hannegan was surprised when he opened it: FDR had written that he would be happy to have either Truman or Douglas as his running mate.

❖ ❖ ❖

THE NEXT DAY, JULY 12, the party leaders decided they should break the news to Jimmy Byrnes. Hannegan, Walker, and Leo Crowley (the

well-connected head of the Foreign Economic Administration and a
Byrnes friend) met separately with Byrnes to tell him that, at a meeting
the previous night, opposition had emerged to his candidacy, and Truman and Douglas now were the leading candidates.

Upset, Byrnes called FDR. "You are the best qualified man in the
whole outfit," the President replied, "and you must not get out of the
race. If you stay in, you are sure to win." Byrnes hung up, reinvigorated
and still interested.

FDR's motives again are not entirely clear. He may have been the
master poker player letting the game unfold to maximize his own options. He may have been displaying his well-known penchant for playing advisers off one another and keeping them off balance. He may have
been keeping the most conservative candidate (Byrnes) and the most
liberal candidate (Wallace) in the mix so that the convention would settle on a compromise candidate (such as Truman) that both wings of the
party would find acceptable.

There also may have been other issues affecting FDR's attention
and judgment. A Navy physician had confidentially diagnosed him with
heart failure in March 1944, and it was clear to many that he was ailing.
He undoubtedly was preoccupied by the war. Throughout June and July
1944, FDR met regularly with top military officials to discuss the battles raging across the world, including the successful D-Day invasion
on June 6; indeed, at the very time of the vice-presidential sweepstakes,
from July 6 to July 8, he hosted French Resistance leader Charles de
Gaulle at White House events. And he was immersed in a secret personal life at this time, although there never has been a suggestion that
it distracted him from his duties. Unknown to Eleanor Roosevelt, who
remained at Hyde Park, FDR privately met repeatedly on July 7 through
July 9, for evenings at the White House and a day at Shangri-La, with
Lucy Mercer Rutherfurd, the woman FDR had promised Eleanor that
he would never see again after Eleanor had discovered romantic letters
between the two in 1918, an event that nearly destroyed their marriage.

Whatever the reasons, FDR's telephone conversation kept former
Justice Jimmy Byrnes an active contender for the vice presidency.

THE DOUGLAS TEAM, MEANWHILE, swung into action. It was headed by Tommy Corcoran, formerly one of FDR's closest aides, who had been disappointed by the President after FDR refused to name him Solicitor General in 1941. (Corcoran similarly resented his mentor, Frankfurter, for failing to back him.) Corcoran enlisted Ickes. The Interior Secretary, a former Republican who had been in the Cabinet and an FDR intimate since the first days of the Roosevelt Administration, sought to build support for Douglas. Corcoran recruited Ernie Cuneo, a well-connected DNC lawyer and former professional football player, to head to Chicago and act on Douglas's behalf at the convention. Corcoran also extensively coordinated with Eliot Janeway, a business editor at *Time* and a close friend and supporter of Douglas's.

Douglas joined Corcoran and Janeway in Corcoran's office. He listened as they discussed possible vice-presidential rivals, such as Speaker Sam Rayburn and Secretary of State Cordell Hull. Then Douglas gave his view. "Jimmy Byrnes," he said, "will be the man to beat, and he will be tough. As a South Carolinian, he can deliver a powerful coalition of southern states, every one of which FDR needs to be re-elected."

They agreed that Douglas could not be seen as campaigning for the job or be directly involved; that would be unseemly for a sitting Supreme Court Justice. But he could be drafted. And neither Corcoran nor Janeway had any doubts about Douglas's interest. Douglas "really wanted it," Eliot Janeway recalled, "because he knew the situation with Roosevelt's health. We all did." He "wanted the Presidency," Corcoran later wrote, "worse than Don Quixote wanted Dulcinea."

ON THURSDAY, FDR HAD a busy day on the vice-presidential front. At 11:30 a.m., he met with Byrnes. After discussing war-related matters, Byrnes brought up the vice presidency. FDR informed him that he would release a letter expressing his personal preference for Wallace but stating that the decision was up to the convention. The President also said that he would not support any other candidate; he did not mention the note he had given Hannegan stating that he would be pleased to run with either Truman or Douglas.

FDR remarked that some of his advisers believed that Byrnes, as a former Senator from segregated South Carolina, might cost the ticket African American votes in the North. Byrnes vowed that he would oppose the discriminatory poll tax and that, as a southerner who knew the Senate, he would be uniquely effective. "This is a serious problem," he told FDR, "but it will have to be solved by the white people of the South. If Mr. Wallace or Mr. Douglas says he is against the poll tax that is not news and they cannot change the views of southerners. But if I say I am against the poll tax, that means something." Telling the President that he was the most qualified, he also rejected the idea that his age (sixty-two) and religion would be political problems. Byrnes told the President that he probably would become a candidate. He came away believing that FDR had given a "green light" for his candidacy and that the contrast he had drawn with Wallace and Douglas had been effective.

The President then had lunch with his Vice President. FDR told Wallace about his dinner with party leaders earlier that week: they continued to believe that Wallace's renomination would jeopardize the ticket. Wallace offered to withdraw, but FDR declined, apparently wanting to keep candidates representing various constituencies in the hunt. Roosevelt also reviewed possible running mates if Wallace were not on the ticket. FDR observed that Douglas "was a picturesque figure because his hair got in his eyes and he had to sweep it out with a gesture of his hand" and noted that some of his advisers believed Douglas would help on the West Coast.

With words that cheered Wallace, FDR pulled him close and confided, "Of course I cannot say it publicly, but I do hope it will be the same old team." And then the President added a postscript that must have troubled Wallace because the President also was envisioning Wallace's defeat: if "they do beat you in Chicago, we will have a job for you in world economic affairs."

❖ ❖ ❖

FDR HAD OTHER POLITICAL meetings that day. He met with Democratic Party chairman Bob Hannegan and with Administration troubleshooter and Byrnes crony Leo Crowley. He told Crowley to make sure that Byrnes understood that, while FDR viewed Byrnes as a close friend, he had not endorsed him.

FDR also huddled with labor leader Sidney Hillman, a close political ally and the head of the Congress of Industrial Organizations' political action committee. The President showed Hillman the letter he would release stating his personal preference for Wallace, as well as a note stating that he would be happy to run with either Truman or Douglas. Hillman thought the message was clear: Wallace, the candidate supported by Hillman and labor, would not get the nod. Hillman suspected that FDR viewed Truman as the eventual nominee.

THAT EVENING, FDR BOARDED the presidential train for Hyde Park. He had decided he would not attend the Democratic convention, which would begin the following Wednesday. Instead, he would leave from Hyde Park for a cross-country train ride to visit military sites in California and then travel by ship to Hawaii. On the way, on Saturday, July 15, aboard his train in Chicago, he would meet with party leaders.

On Friday, Leo Crowley, along with Hannegan and Postmaster General Frank Walker, hosted a meeting at his apartment with Byrnes. Without mentioning the still-undisclosed note from FDR, Hannegan and Walker warned Byrnes that they would have to inform FDR's allies that the President favored Truman or Douglas as his running mate.

Concerned, Byrnes called the President. FDR denied that he had stated a preference. "We have to be damned careful about language," the President said. "They asked if I would object to Truman and Douglas and I said no. That is different from using the word 'prefer.' That is not expressing a preference because you know I told you I would have no preference." He again reassured Byrnes about his high regard for him. "After all, Jimmy, you are close to me personally, and Henry [Wallace] is close to me. I hardly know Truman. Douglas is a poker partner. He is good in a poker game and tells good stories."

In passing, FDR slipped into the conversation that "objection to you came from labor people, both Federation [the American Federation of Labor] and C.I.O." The party leaders thought that Truman or Douglas "would cost the ticket fewer votes" than Byrnes. But Byrnes took from the conversation the President's emphatic reassertion of his neutrality and his personal fondness for Byrnes.

Encouraged and again revitalized, Byrnes asked Truman, with whom he had a close relationship, to nominate him for Vice President at the convention. "Harry, the President has given me the go sign for the vice presidency," he declared, "and I am calling to ask if you will nominate me." Understanding Byrnes to be saying that FDR had made his decision, Truman agreed.

While some public speculation had included Truman as a possible running mate for FDR, Truman had publicly denied he would be a candidate. Though active behind the scenes in promoting Truman's candidacy, Hannegan apparently was not keeping his Missouri patron apprised of unfolding developments.

ERNIE CUNEO, THE DOUGLAS team's on-site organizer, arrived in Chicago on Friday to marshal forces for the Justice. As he talked to party leaders and foot soldiers swarming into Chicago, he kept hearing that Truman would get the nomination. He called Tommy Corcoran to report on the scuttlebutt. Corcoran said that he, too, was hearing rumors about Truman. But Corcoran also had big news. He had heard that Hannegan had received a letter from FDR expressing his choices for Vice President—Douglas and Truman, with Douglas listed first.

In Chicago, Cuneo discovered the difficulties of his position as the Douglas emissary. While Hannegan headed the Democratic National Committee, Cuneo was freelancing. Corcoran had arranged for him to have an assistant; the assistant was so frequently drunk that

Cuneo dismissed him. Cuneo sought out prominent individuals—Douglas-friendly Cabinet officials like Ickes and Biddle; party bosses like Jake Arvey of Illinois and Frank Hague of New Jersey. Nobody mentioned a Douglas groundswell.

Cuneo pressed Hannegan about FDR's letter. "What letter?" Hannegan coolly responded.

Corcoran reached out to California Attorney General Robert Kenny to nominate Douglas and head the Douglas effort on the floor. Kenny told Corcoran that he was committed to Wallace on the first ballot and that he had spoken to Truman backers about supporting him on subsequent ballots. But he would write a nominating speech for Douglas, and if it looked like the convention was deadlocked, he would start the break toward Douglas and deliver his nominating speech.

PRESS ACCOUNTS LEADING UP to the convention included Douglas as a prominent vice-presidential candidate, along with Wallace, Byrnes, Truman, and a smattering of other names.

Douglas departed for Oregon in mid-July. Even while Corcoran's efforts proceeded, Douglas wanted to create a record that he, as a sitting Justice, was not involved in them. On Wednesday, July 12, he wrote Chief Justice Stone that he was not a candidate and that the Court should not "be used as a stepping stone to any political office." And, on Friday, July 14, he wrote Connecticut Senator Francis Maloney that he had learned of public speculation regarding his candidacy; that he had "done all that is possible to discourage" it; that Maloney could let others know; and that he would be spending ten days in the remote mountains, where he would be unreachable.

Puzzled by the letter in light of the ongoing pro-Douglas activities, Maloney called Eliot Janeway. He asked whether he should release Douglas's letter. "Aw hell, just put the thing in your pocket and disregard it," Janeway replied. "Bill doesn't mean it. Douglas wrote this letter as a cover for what was really going on. So, just forget about it, and join forces with us in Chicago."

❦ ❦ ❦

ON SATURDAY, JULY 15, the presidential train rolled into Chicago. At 1:30 p.m., Chicago Mayor Ed Kelly, DNC Chairman Bob Hannegan, and DNC Treasurer Ed Pauley boarded and met with the President in the *Ferdinand Magellan*, his specially designed train. FDR asked about the convention. Hannegan said that none of the candidates for Vice President were withdrawing and that he'd like to get FDR's letter typed and then release it at some point. FDR approved, and Hannegan had the letter typed on White House stationery by presidential secretary Grace Tully.

The typed letter, addressed to Hannegan at the Blackstone Hotel and dated July 19, 1944, said in its entirety: "Dear Bob—You have written me about Harry Truman and Bill Douglas. I should, of course, be very glad to run with either of them and believe that either one of them would bring real strength to the ticket. Always sincerely, Franklin D. Roosevelt."

Hannegan previously had told Pauley that FDR had included Douglas in his letter, but Pauley now saw it for the first time. He later observed, "Here we were, then, with a letter we could not use, with Roosevelt on his way to the West Coast—and with that man, Douglas, confronting us again."

But Hannegan was not so sure they couldn't use it. The listing of Truman's name first, he could maintain, showed that Truman was FDR's preferred candidate.

FDR's longtime secretary and aide Grace Tully later insisted that Hannegan had switched the order of the names—that FDR's handwritten note had listed Douglas first and that Hannegan had told her to flip the names when he gave her the note to type up. According to Tully in her 1949 memoir, Hannegan "came directly to me. 'Grace, the President wants you to retype this letter and to switch these names so it will read 'Harry Truman or Bill Douglas!'" Tully continued, "The reason for the switch was obvious. By naming Truman first it was plainly implied by the letter that he was the preferred choice of the President."

Despite Tully's recollection, one Douglas biographer has concluded that FDR's original note actually listed Truman first and that Tully's assertion was erroneous. If he is correct, perhaps Tully simply was mistaken in her recollection. It is also possible that her memory was colored by her closeness to Douglas: when she published her 1949 book fondly reminiscing about working for "the Boss" from his time as the newly elected New York Governor in 1928 until his death, Douglas wrote the foreword.

Or perhaps there actually were more letters in play than we currently understand and somewhere there was an FDR letter listing Douglas first. As Truman biographer David McCullough has noted, "Grace Tully was not known for fabricating stories, nor was there any reason why she should have done so in this instance." And Tully's assistant Dorothy Brady, the person who actually typed the letter for Hannegan, corroborated Tully's account about Hannegan's order to flip the names.

EVEN WHILE GIVING HANNEGAN the letter saying that he would be glad to run with Truman or Douglas and that either would bring "real strength to the ticket," FDR continued to play a game of three-dimensional chess with various party factions. Aboard the train, the President told Hannegan to tell Byrnes that he had presidential backing and, at the same time, to sound out the CIO's Sidney Hillman and Philip Murray about Byrnes. In what became a famous FDR phrase, he told them, "Clear it with Sidney."

Hannegan and Kelly called Byrnes and delivered the good news. Byrnes excitedly took a train to Chicago.

On Sunday, July 16, Byrnes set up shop in Chicago in the Stevens Hotel (owned by the family of future Supreme Court Justice John Paul Stevens, who would be Douglas's eventual successor on the Court when Douglas retired in 1975). Byrnes had breakfast at Kelly's apartment with Kelly and Hannegan. They told Byrnes that FDR had been reassured by reports that, contrary to earlier concerns, Black voters would not be upset with Byrnes. Overwhelmingly Republican until the New Deal, African Americans now were a key Democratic constituency in large northern states like New York, Illinois, and Pennsylvania. Hannegan mentioned in passing that the President had told him to discuss the vice-presidential nomination with labor leaders Hillman and Murray. Byrnes viewed it as a formality.

Press accounts of the vice-presidential contest varied. On July 16, the International News Service reported that Byrnes had emerged as a "surprise" top contender for the vice presidency, along with Wallace, Douglas, and Senate Majority Leader Alben Barkley; the INS did not mention Truman. The Associated Press, meanwhile, reported that the vice-presidential race was "wide open" and might include a field of twelve to fifteen candidates.

That night, Sunday, July 16, Byrnes had dinner with party leaders, including Hannegan, Kelly, Walker, and Crowley. Hannegan continued to make supportive comments. Byrnes came away with the understanding that FDR's letter expressing his nonendorsement and personal support for Wallace would be released, and the party leaders then would announce their backing of Byrnes. On the way out, Hannegan again casually mentioned that he needed to run it by labor leaders Hillman and Murray—that the President wanted him to "clear it with Sidney."

On Monday morning, Byrnes met with the CIO's Murray and emphasized that, as a skilled former Senator who knew his way around the Hill, he would be able to accomplish far more for labor than Wallace.

Throughout the day, opposition to Byrnes snowballed. Hillman and Murray told Chicago Mayor Ed Kelly and Jersey City Mayor Frank Hague that labor would oppose Byrnes based on what they viewed as the antilabor positions he had taken on the wartime economy. Liberal leaders and activists likewise threatened to revolt against a Byrnes nomination. When Ed Flynn, a longtime Byrnes foe, arrived in Chicago and learned of Byrnes's rise, he undertook an aggressive effort to block him.

Flynn had long warned that Byrnes would severely hurt the ticket with Black voters in key states. Contrary to the earlier reassuring report from leaders of Chicago's African American community, Black leaders now expressed grave concern about a Byrnes nomination. Even though Byrnes had not been as extreme and demagogic on racial issues as some southern politicians, he was a segregationist steeped in South Carolina's regime of white supremacy. The previous day, NAACP President Walter White had told thousands of NAACP delegates, "Let me solemnly warn the Democratic convention that if it nominates a southerner as vice president it can kiss the Negro vote goodbye." And Representative William Dawson of Chicago, the lone African American in Congress, met with Byrnes on Sunday and told him flatly, "Mr. Justice, you cannot be my candidate." The significance of Dawson's statement somehow did not register with Byrnes and his aides, who obliviously continued to think that Byrnes could defuse African American opposition.

Hannegan and other party leaders called FDR on Monday evening and gave him an urgent update. FDR responded that Byrnes was a "political liability." He asked the leaders why they had not consolidated support for Truman, ignoring the fact that he had not urged them to take such an action.

Hannegan assigned Crowley the job of breaking the news to his friend Jimmy Byrnes. That evening, Crowley told Byrnes that FDR viewed him as a "political liability" and thought he should not run. "His face flushed," a Byrnes aide later recalled. It "cut him to the quick."

Surprised and injured, Byrnes called FDR early the next day, Tuesday, July 18. While denying that he had used the phrase "political liability," FDR explained that Byrnes's nomination might endanger the ticket in urban and industrialized states in the North, and that the South seemed secure. Roosevelt also now informed Byrnes that, in response to Hannegan's request, he had given the party chairman a letter saying he "would be happy with Truman or Douglas." This was a devastating blow to Byrnes. The President told him to talk to Hannegan about the letter.

Later that day, Byrnes met with Hannegan. The party chairman confirmed both Crowley's account of FDR's anti-Byrnes position and FDR's letter naming Truman and Douglas as candidates he could happily run with.

Dejected, Byrnes knew that, for him, the game was over. He wrote a letter, released the next day, to Senator Burnet Maybank, chairman of the South Carolina delegation, stating that, "in deference to the wishes of the President," he did not want to be nominated.

Byrnes was bitter. In the immediate aftermath, when press accounts mentioned he had left the Court at FDR's request, he sharply wrote a friend, "I got off the Supreme Court to serve my country—not Mr. Roosevelt. I owed a debt to the more than 15,000,000 men and women in the armed services." Soon after the convention, in a development that undoubtedly gratified Byrnes, the *New York Times* ran an explosive account of FDR's "Clear it with Sidney" instruction and Hillman's reputed veto power. Republicans jumped on the story—and the memorable quote— to charge throughout the campaign that labor bosses controlled Roosevelt and the Democratic Party. In his memoir, Byrnes acknowledged that he was "disappointed and felt hurt by President Roosevelt's action." And decades later, Byrnes ruefully observed to a fellow former Senator that, for FDR, "men were so many tools to be used for the accomplishment of what he believed to be a good purpose. Certainly he played upon the ambitions of men as an artist would play upon the strings of a musical instrument."

At 8:00 on Monday evening, July 17, Senator Samuel Jackson of Indiana, the convention chair, called a press conference in Chicago to release a letter from the President, dated July 14 from Hyde Park, expressing his views on the vice-presidential nomination. The letter began by praising Wallace. "I like him and I respect him and he is my personal friend. For these reasons, I personally would vote for his renomination if I were a delegate to the convention." But he then went on to make clear that he was leaving the question to the delegates. "At the same time, I do not wish to appear in any way as dictating to the convention. Obviously the convention must do the deciding. And it should—and I am sure it will—give great consideration to the pros and cons of its choices."

FDR's letter, the *New York Times* proclaimed, meant that "the choice of a Democratic candidate for Vice President was thrown wide open for the party's forthcoming national convention." "Associate Justice William O. Douglas," the *Times* explained, "is reported to be [the President's] second choice," behind only Wallace. But it cautioned that Wallace remained "a formidable aspirant"—with the President's "personal endorsement," the backing of "the more pronounced New Dealers, the CIO and many of the 'liberal' economic groups," and support from "the largest block of pledged delegates of any of the prospective candidates."

On Monday evening, after the conversation with FDR that eliminated Byrnes, Hannegan knew that his next goal was to undermine support for Wallace, the bête noire for Hannegan and other party professionals. Labor remained among Wallace's strongest supporters. That night, Hannegan met with Hillman and Murray over dinner. Instead of explaining that Byrnes had been eliminated, Hannegan made it sound like Byrnes was the likely nominee. When the labor leaders strongly objected, as Hannegan knew they would, he suggested that, if they would drop their backing for Wallace, or at least soften it, he would block Byrnes. The message was clear: If you don't want Byrnes, let's knock out Wallace as well and settle on a compromise candidate. They understood.

ON TUESDAY MORNING, ERNIE Cuneo, the Douglas team's man on the scene in Chicago, learned some disturbing news. Sidney Hillman was having breakfast with Harry Truman. Although Cuneo did not know exactly what was said, he was right to be concerned. Hillman told Truman at the breakfast that, if Wallace faltered, Truman was his first choice and Douglas his second choice. Truman, still believing that FDR wanted Byrnes, reasserted his commitment to Byrnes.

The bad news kept coming for Cuneo. Pennsylvania Senator Joe Guffey told Ickes that he could not deliver his delegation for Douglas unless Hillman approved.

Cuneo consulted with Corcoran. They agreed that FDR's letter naming Truman and Douglas, which they had heard about but which had not been released, needed to become public.

Cuneo continued actively courting state delegations for Douglas, including Michigan. Cuneo knew Michigan well. He had worked on labor issues there in 1938 for the man who was then Governor—Justice Frank Murphy. Swinging the California delegation—or at least a substantial chunk of it—to Douglas continued to be a prime possibility, particularly if it was clear that Wallace would lose.

Cuneo heard that Hannegan was meeting with the Missouri delegation in the Hotel Morrison. Though he was not invited, Cuneo decided to attend. He barged in and saw Hannegan, publicly neutral in his role as party chairman, haranguing his home state delegation to support their favorite son, Harry Truman. "Truman means everything to Missouri," Hannegan shouted. Hannegan saw Cuneo and froze as their eyes met. As Cuneo turned to leave, he announced, "Bob, you *are* a son-of-a-bitch." Cuneo was irate that the supposedly unaligned chairman was weighing in for Truman.

But Cuneo also was heartened. If Hannegan was working this hard with Truman's home-state delegation on Tuesday, the day before the opening of the convention, it meant that the fight was not yet over.

Later that day, Cuneo reached out to CIO President Philip Murray to strike a deal with labor. Wallace is going to lose, Cuneo told him. Could he—and labor—support Douglas when Wallace lost? Murray's response was disappointing. "I can't, Airnee," replied the Scottish-born Murray. "Wallace is in trouble, and if I admit I have a second choice it would break his line." Hillman's breakfast that morning with Truman was not mentioned.

THAT NIGHT, HANNEGAN AND Kelly gathered several Senators, including Florida's Claude Pepper and Pennsylvania's Joe Guffey. Hannegan confided the important news that FDR had sent him a letter endorsing

Truman as his running mate. Hannegan did not reveal that Douglas's name also appeared in FDR's letter. As Wallace later recorded in his diary, Guffey told him that "Hannegan worked one end of the table and Kelly the other, saying the President was for Truman but not saying a word about Douglas."

The convention opened on Wednesday, July 19. Hannegan asked Truman to join him in his seventh-floor suite in the Blackstone Hotel. Truman found the party's top brass assembled in the room. Ed Kelly and Ed Flynn were there; so were Frank Walker, Ed Pauley, and Frank Hague. Truman expressed reluctance about committing to be a candidate for the ticket, uncertain that FDR actually wanted him. Hannegan picked up the phone, called a number in San Diego, and held out the phone so that everybody could hear. A familiar patrician voice filled the room as the President joined the call. "Bob, have you got that fellow lined up yet?" he asked. Hannegan replied, "No. He is the contrariest goddamn mule I ever dealt with." "Well," said the President, "you tell the Senator that if he wants to break up the Democratic party in the middle of the war, that's his responsibility." He then promptly slammed the phone down. Truman turned to the room and said, "Well, if that's the situation, I have to say yes."

❖ ❖ ❖

THAT EVENING, UNAWARE OF FDR's call with Truman, Douglas's team huddled in Ickes's suite. Postmaster General Frank Walker sauntered into the room. "Hello, fellows," he greeted them. "I just dropped by to tell you it's Truman." Ickes was furious to learn the news from Walker.

For Cuneo, it seemed like there might still be one path forward: release of the FDR letter, which, he and Corcoran continued to believe, listed Douglas first.

❖ ❖ ❖

ON THURSDAY, JULY 20, the convention nominated FDR for a fourth term with overwhelming support. FDR delivered his acceptance speech remotely by radio hookup from a naval base on the Pacific. He promised that he would "win the war fast and ...win it overpoweringly," create "international organizations" to "make another war impossible within the foreseeable future," and "build an economy for our returning veterans and for all Americans which will provide employment and ...decent standards of living." (FDR's speech marked the last time a Democratic presidential candidate would accept a nomination remotely until Joe Biden's acceptance speech to a virtual convention during the COVID pandemic of 2020.)

On Thursday evening, at a press conference, Hannegan finally released FDR's letter naming Truman and Douglas as candidates with whom he would gladly run. "By that time," DNC Treasurer Ed Pauley later chortled, "it was too late for any Douglas forces to organize."

Reporters barraged Hannegan with questions, and he dissembled. When they asked him when he had received the presidential letter, he said simply, "It is dated July 19." When they asked why FDR's letter named only Truman and Douglas as acceptable running mates, Hannegan replied, "I had on other occasions discussed in general with the President a number of other possible candidates. A number of persons, some of them in Washington, had asked me about Justice Douglas." When they asked about the letter's origin, he asserted, "Some time ago, I received requests from Missouri delegates on how President Roosevelt looked upon the possible candidacy of Senator Truman and I also was asked about how he felt about the nomination of Justice Douglas."

CORCORAN HAD CONFIDENTLY STATED that FDR's letter would list Douglas first. He had been counting on that placement, and now the public letter listed Truman first. Cuneo was crestfallen. "Our throats were slit," he recalled. "The battle was over; you can't be deader than dead." Corcoran and Cuneo concluded that Hannegan had switched the order of the names.

The Douglas camp was desperate. At one point, Ickes said to Eliot Janeway, "Fuck 'em. What are they going to do if we just go on the floor and start voting for Bill?" Connecticut Senator Frank Maloney suggested reaching out to Joe Kennedy, who had always been close to Douglas. Never one to spend on futile causes, Kennedy, on the phone from Palm Beach, asked, "If I send you enough money to keep the floor fight going for a week, can you turn around enough votes to get it for Bill?" The Douglas forces had to decline. A weeklong fight would be bloody and self-destructive, particularly for a sitting Supreme Court Justice, and they were far from being able to guarantee they would have the votes.

Douglas's advisers concluded that their only hope lay in a direct conversation between them and the President. Not knowing how to call him on his train, they asked Hannegan. The party chairman responded, falsely, that FDR was sick and sedated and could not talk to them. In reality, Hannegan and Pauley had a direct line to FDR and spoke to him throughout the convention. "We brought Douglas to within a nickel's phone call of the vice presidency," Eliot Janeway later recalled. "But Hannegan was the only one who knew about Roosevelt's condition. Once the President left the station in Chicago, Hannegan was acting as the de facto acting president on election matters. What he said went because Roosevelt was totally out of touch."

EVEN WHILE RIDING A wave of momentum, the pro-Truman party leaders encountered an obstacle Thursday night. Vice President Henry Wallace delivered a rousing seconding speech for FDR, and the delegates seemed enthralled. The only people who hate Roosevelt, he thundered, are "Germans, Japanese, and certain American troglodytes." As the *New York Times* reported, "Whether or not Mr. Wallace wins renomination, he established himself as a convention favorite by his appearance. He was compelled to stand for some minutes before he could proceed amid the shouts and cheers of the crowd, especially that part in the galleries."

The scheduled activity for Thursday evening after FDR's nomination and acceptance was to proceed to the vice-presidential nominating speeches and votes. As excited demonstrations and chants for Wallace erupted throughout the convention, Hannegan, Kelly, and other leaders feared a spontaneous surge for Wallace; such sudden shifts had happened with other candidates at past conventions. As Ed Pauley recalled, "I had been greatly impressed by the way Wendell Willkie had stampeded the Republican convention in 1940, largely through demonstrations at the convention hall itself, and I certainly wasn't going to take a chance on Wallace followers wrapping him up as a little present from on high."

Seizing his prerogative as Mayor of Chicago, Ed Kelly quickly proclaimed the convention a fire hazard and announced that it needed to close for the night immediately. The proceedings would reconvene the following day.

Having doused the Wallace fire, the party leaders regrouped. At 11:30 a.m. the following day, Friday, July 21, the convention returned to business. Hannegan worked the floor, showing the delegates FDR's Truman-Douglas letter and emphasizing that Truman's name was listed first. Hannegan eventually ascended to the podium and read FDR's letter to the delegates, even though it already had been widely publicized.

Ickes sent FDR a lengthy, complaining telegram through FDR's press secretary, Steve Early. It included a reference to Hannegan's handling of the FDR letter naming Douglas as well as Truman. "Hannegan for several days circulated the report that he had a letter from you in which you had expressed preference for Truman as a candidate for Vice President," objected Ickes. "He refused to show the letter until yesterday after the demand had become so insistent that his hand was in effect forced. Then the letter appeared not only to be agreeable to Truman for the Vice Presidency but also to Douglas." Ickes complained that "city bosses" were dictating the selection. Early relayed a brief perfunctory summary to the President, stating he had received a "long telegram" from Ickes "[criticizing] Hannegan for not sooner releasing letter regarding Vice Presidential candidates"; Early did not mention Ickes's pointed objections regarding Hannegan's failure to mention Douglas.

The convention moved on to nominating speeches for Vice President. Twelve were given—for Wallace, Truman, Senate Majority Leader

Barkley, and nine favorite-son candidates. No nominating speech was made for William O. Douglas. California Attorney General Kenny kept his Douglas nominating speech in his pocket, promising to deliver it once Wallace faltered and the process opened up. Douglas's team also favored holding off on a formal nomination until victory seemed assured.

But there was one nominating speech for a Supreme Court Justice to be FDR's running mate. A Michigan delegate nominated Justice Frank Murphy, former Governor of Michigan and Mayor of Detroit. Detroit Congressman George O'Brien hailed Murphy as "an exemplar of the principles of justice among nations and individuals and a lover of his fellow man."

Late in the afternoon, voting began. The nomination required 589 votes. On the first ballot, Wallace received 429½ votes and Truman came in second with 319½. (Democratic Party rules at the time permitted delegates to split their votes into half votes.) More than a dozen other candidates received votes, including two from Michigan for Murphy. Douglas received zero votes.

Ickes cornered Frank Walker, hoping that he could swing a shift to Douglas. "It's going to be an impasse," Ickes implored. "We've got to do something, Frank. I'll see you after this ballot." Walker ignored him.

And then the convention broke for Truman on the second ballot—first Maryland and Oklahoma, and then a torrent of states. Ickes tried to get Robert Kenny, the designated nominator for Douglas, to quickly move for adjournment so that the Douglas forces could regroup. But Kenny, a savvy politician sensing Truman's inevitability, did not respond.

Truman ultimately coasted to the nomination on the second ballot with 1,031 votes. Wallace had only 105. A smattering of others received votes. And Douglas tallied a grand total of four votes.

❖ ❖ ❖

ACCORDING TO DOUGLAS, ON the day of the vice-presidential nomination, he was in the mountains on an extended expedition, unreachable by telephone or telegram. According to Douglas biographer and critic

Bruce Allen Murphy, however, Douglas actually was at the home of the Whitman College President on Friday, July 21, expecting the call that he had been nominated, and was crestfallen when Janeway called with the bad news. Regardless of whether Douglas was in the mountains or at his alma mater, it is clear that Douglas's close friends and advisers launched a fervent effort for his nomination and that Douglas never publicly disavowed the campaign or stopped it. As Douglas biographer James Simon concluded, he "never threw his hat in the political ring in 1944, but neither did he effectively take it out when it was thrown in by others."

After the convention, Douglas quickly moved to claim he had not been interested. Just days after the convention, on July 27, he wrote the President, "So it was only yesterday after my return to our summer place that I learned of your letter to Hannegan.... Some of the boys were whooping it up for me—much against my will. But I succeeded prior to the Convention in subduing that mild uprising."

Douglas expressed a very different view to Eliot Janeway—a pained and bitter perception of the prize he believed had been unfairly snatched from him: "All I needed to do to win," he ruefully told Janeway, "was get two cases of scotch and some girls and get a suite of rooms in the convention city and operate. But I have to get off of the Court to do it."

AT VARIOUS TIMES IN July 1944, FDR signaled, to different people and likely for his own complex reasons, that he favored Douglas, Truman, Byrnes, and Wallace for the vice presidency. Brenda Heaster has concluded that, because of the vice-presidential confusion, "the 1944 Democratic national convention stands as one of the most outwardly chaotic in American political history."

It is difficult to determine with precision FDR's actual preferences. In his memoir, Samuel Rosenman, who was with FDR throughout this period (including on the cross-country train during the convention), barely mentions Douglas as he describes FDR's path in jettisoning Wallace and elevating Truman. But FDR's son James Roosevelt, who also was with FDR at crucial times during the nomination process, recalled his "distinct impression" that his father "really preferred Justice William O. Douglas as the vice-presidential nominee." And it is undisputed that, when FDR met with the party leaders on July 11, he strongly praised Douglas as a possible running mate. He also persistently included Douglas's name on his letter mentioning Truman as an acceptable running mate.

IN OUR CONSTITUTIONAL STRUCTURE, the Supreme Court should stand apart from the political branches as an independent tribunal reaching its own conclusions on legality and constitutionality—a crucial role in our system of checks and balances. A Justice's candidacy for political office, even if unofficial and undertaken by others, undermines the institution. Though Douglas kept his distance from his supporters' efforts, the campaign to nominate him for the vice presidency was a problematic immersion in electoral politics for a sitting Justice.

This is not to suggest that no Justice previously had been entangled with electoral politics. In 1916, for example, the Republican Party nominated Associate Justice Charles Evans Hughes to be its presidential candidate against President Woodrow Wilson. Hughes sometimes is held out as an exemplar of proper conduct because he resigned from the Court promptly upon receiving the nomination on the Republican convention's third ballot (after being the highest vote-getter on the first two ballots as well). But the actual story is more complicated. Support for Hughes as a presidential candidate was a subject of extensive public attention and discussion throughout the election year. He actually had won two primaries and finished in the top three in two others while serving as a Justice. He had sought to maintain a semblance of propriety by refusing to comment on issues or speak on his own behalf; early in the campaign, he also had tried to keep his name off the ballot in one state, but then he had simply kept his silence. Most tellingly, he refused to state that he would not run if nominated.

There are other examples as well. The first Chief Justice, John Jay, twice ran for Governor of New York while sitting on the Court, losing one election and then winning another and resigning from the Court to assume the governorship. In one of the most conspicuous episodes of political entanglement, Justice Stephen Field actively sought the presidential nomination at the 1880 Democratic convention, receiving sixty-five votes from the delegates on the first ballot and ultimately losing to General Winfield Hancock.

In contrast, Chief Justice Morrison Waite modeled a very different approach in 1876 when he was discussed as a possible presidential candidate for the Republican nomination. He issued an explicit and unequivocal statement rejecting his candidacy and stating that Justices should keep far from the "political whirlpool."

As with Chief Justice Waite, Justices should definitively reject political activities on their behalf while they sit on the Court. In the end, Douglas's candidacy—and FDR's persistent promotion of him as a possible running mate—reflect an excessive closeness between the Justice and the man who appointed him.

• chapter sixteen •

KOREMATSU

RATHER THAN THE HUSTINGS OF A PRESIDENTIAL CAMPAIGN, Douglas now faced a return to the Court. And as the new term began in October 1944, one month before the presidential election, a major case loomed on the docket: a return to the issue of the incarceration of Japanese Americans on the West Coast.

Fred Toyosaburo Korematsu was an improbable constitutional crusader—an unassuming welder who was involved in a romantic relationship with a young Italian American woman and desperate to avoid detection of his Japanese ancestry. He was an American citizen, born in Oakland, California, in 1919. His parents had immigrated from Japan. The third of four sons, Fred graduated from Oakland High School. He worked at his parents' flower store during high school, competed on the high school's tennis and swimming teams, and attended Los Angeles City College. But financial straits forced him to leave school and return home after three months. After training as a welder, he secured a job in a shipyard.

Korematsu tried to enlist in the Navy in June 1941, but the Navy rejected him. The following month, his draft board ruled him ineligible for military service because he suffered from gastric ulcers. In the wake of the Pearl Harbor attack, his union expelled all members of Japanese descent, and Korematsu lost his job.

Korematsu was smitten with his girlfriend, Ida Boitano, a worker in a nearby San Leandro biscuit factory. Over the opposition of both families, they had been seeing each other since 1939. In March 1942, as conditions worsened for Japanese Americans, Fred decided to try to conceal his identity for two reasons. First, he wanted to evade the government's imminent anti-Japanese orders. And second, he and Ida encountered hostility as an interracial couple, especially one involving a person of Japanese descent on the West Coast in the weeks and months after Pearl Harbor. He hoped they could move to another part of the country, such as the Midwest, and start a new life. In the lexicon of Black Americans during that time, he wanted to "pass."

Korematsu began to use an alias, "Clyde Sarah." He altered a draft card to confirm his new identity. He even responded to a newspaper ad and visited a plastic surgeon in San Francisco. He wanted surgery to alter his appearance. The doctor, an elderly man with a shady background, happily obliged with operations on Korematsu's eyelids and nose, but he cautioned that he might not be able to make Fred "look like an American."

On May 3, 1942, General DeWitt issued Exclusion Order Number 34. The order and accompanying procedures forced all people of Japanese descent to leave their homes in the Oakland area, report to a "civil control station," and be transported to the Tanforan racetrack south of San Francisco. Formerly the site of galloping thoroughbreds and cheering crowds, Tanforan now housed more than one hundred dormitory-style barracks hastily constructed to imprison those of Japanese ancestry until they were transported to long-term incarceration camps. DeWitt's military order further provided that any person of Japanese descent in the prohibited Oakland area after noon on Saturday, May 9, would be "subject to immediate apprehension and internment."

Korematsu's parents and brothers dutifully reported and were imprisoned in the barbed-wire-enclosed, heavily guarded Tanforan racetrack. But Fred did not. Instead, he violated Order 34 and stayed in the prohibited area, continuing his life under his alias, picking up odd jobs as a welder, and preparing to move to another region with Ida.

Three weeks after the Order 34 ban took effect, on a Saturday afternoon, "Clyde" and Ida strolled down a street in San Leandro. Police approached. They suspected that Fred was of Japanese descent, and he was in an area now officially prohibited to Japanese Americans. Fred later concluded that a pharmacist probably recognized him in a local drugstore and called the police.

In questioning at the station house, Korematsu initially claimed that he was of Spanish and Hawaiian descent, not Japanese American, and that his name was Clyde Sarah. But the police quickly demolished his story. Korematsu did not know Spanish, and his "Clyde Sarah" draft card had been amateurishly modified with ink remover. Korematsu acknowledged his real identity. Arrested and sent to the San Francisco County Jail, he was held with two others who had violated the exclusion order.

An ACLU lawyer visited the jail and asked if the three imprisoned Japanese Americans wanted to challenge the legality of the new expulsion-and-detention orders. Only Korematsu volunteered. He had not been looking to champion a cause. But now he was ready to fight.

Ida, meanwhile, made her own decision after Korematsu's arrest. She cut off all contact and told the FBI that she regretted not immediately reporting him for his violation.

On September 8, 1942, the federal trial court in San Francisco heard the case of *United States v. Korematsu*. The defendant's crime, according to the official charging document, was that he was "a person of Japanese ancestry" and had been in a place from "which all persons of Japanese ancestry are excluded."

The one-day trial featured only two witnesses: an FBI agent for the government and Fred Korematsu for the defense. Korematsu had waived a jury trial. With the facts not in dispute and with the court's rejection of Korematsu's constitutional challenge, the judge promptly convicted him. But the judge apparently was impressed by his testimony, which included a description of his unsuccessful efforts to enlist. The judge sentenced him to five years of probation.

Korematsu and his lawyers thought that he now would be free while his appeal and constitutional challenge proceeded. But a court-room drama unfolded. A military policeman, with gun drawn, seized Korematsu and commanded him to remain in military custody. The flummoxed judge permitted the military policeman to take Korematsu. The soldier promptly delivered his prisoner to Tanforan to join the others imprisoned in the racetrack barracks.

Korematsu appealed his conviction. On December 2, 1943, after a delay while a preliminary procedural issue was resolved, the Ninth Circuit issued a brief opinion. It tersely held that the Supreme Court's *Hirabayashi* curfew decision controlled the outcome. Writing separately, Judge Denman, the dissenting judge in the Court of Appeals' *Hirabayashi* opinion, disagreed with the majority's reasoning (though not its bottom line) and objected that the imprisonment of Japanese Americans in "barbed wire stockades called Assembly Centers" and "in distant places under military guard" reflected "treatment... not unlike that of Hitler in so confining the Jews in his stockades."

Korematsu's lawyers turned to the Supreme Court, and on March 27, 1944, the Court agreed to hear the case. It initially scheduled the *Korematsu* argument for May 1944. But developments in another case led the Court to push the argument to the fall. The other case concerned a young Japanese American woman, Mitsuye Endo. She was imprisoned in a detention camp and had filed a habeas corpus suit seeking her freedom.

EVEN BEFORE FDR's EXECUTIVE Order 9066, the Japanese Americans Citizens League had contacted a San Francisco lawyer, James Purcell, to explore possible defenses to employment termination for state employees. As the expulsion and incarceration orders took hold, Purcell shifted his focus to a constitutional challenge against the new regime. He sent questionnaires to more than one hundred incarcerated Japanese

Americans. Sifting through the responses, he noticed Mitsuye Endo, who had been working as a typist for California's Department of Motor Vehicles in Sacramento when Pearl Harbor was attacked. Although her parents were from Japan, she had never been to the country; she did not know how to read or speak the Japanese language; she had worked for the State of California; and she had been raised as a churchgoing Methodist. And, perhaps most appealing, Endo's older brother served in the US Army.

Purcell reached out to her. Initially reluctant, the young typist, then twenty-two years old, agreed to challenge the government's Japanese American incarceration policy.

On July 13, 1942, Purcell filed a habeas corpus application on behalf of Mitsuye Endo, seeking her freedom on the ground that she was a loyal American citizen unjustly detained in a "concentration camp." A year later, on July 2, 1943, the district court rejected her claim. Purcell filed an appeal.

On April 22, 1944, the Ninth Circuit certified Endo's case to the Supreme Court. It listed four questions that focused on whether the government had legal authority for her continued confinement and, if so, whether such authority was constitutional. On May 8, the Supreme Court accepted the Ninth Circuit's certification.

Korematsu and *Endo* now would be heard together in the fall.

The federal government had instituted a cumbersome release policy in which Japanese American detainees could apply for release. It involved two stages: an application for general "leave clearance" and, if that was granted, an application for actual release. The application for actual release required that the detainee include a specific destination, a plan for financial self-sufficiency, and a commitment that he or she would not return to any area under exclusion orders. Though free from the incarceration camps, the released detainee remained under the close supervision of the federal government's War Relocation Authority.

Fred Korematsu went through the process, and in January 1944 the government granted him "indefinite leave" from his incarceration camp. He moved to Salt Lake City and then Detroit, where he worked in a machine shop. In addition to his War Relocation Authority supervision requirements, Korematsu had to report regularly to a federal probation officer as a continuing condition of his criminal sentence.

Mitsuye Endo received general leave clearance, the first step. But she balked at the second step, which required her commitment not to return to the excluded areas. She refused to swear she would not return to Sacramento, her home and the only place she had lived. In the summer of 1943, the government approached her with an offer of release if she would make the commitment not to return to an excluded area; the government wanted to avoid her legal challenge to incarceration. Knowing that accepting the conditions and gaining release would make her case moot, she felt a duty to proceed with her lawsuit. As she later told an interviewer, "I wanted to prove that we of Japanese ancestry were not guilty of any crime and that we were loyal Americans." That commitment, she continued, "kept me from abandoning the suit." She rejected the offer and remained imprisoned in the federal government's barbed-wire incarceration camp in Topaz, Utah.

IN JANUARY 1944, SHORTLY before Korematsu's lawyers filed their petition for Supreme Court review, the War Department publicly released a six-hundred-page report by General DeWitt. This was the final version of the report that Assistant Secretary of War John J. McCloy had suppressed and ordered to be edited during the Supreme Court's consideration of *Hirabayashi*. DeWitt had submitted the revised version on June 5, 1943, but the War Department had delayed its release for several months.

Dewitt's *Final Report: Japanese Evacuation from the West Coast* prominently asserted that West Coast collaborators gave the Japanese valuable intelligence to enable assaults on American targets. "The Pacific Coast had become exposed to attack by enemy successes in the Pacific," DeWitt announced. "There were hundreds of reports nightly of signal lights visible from the coast, and of intercepts of unidentified radio transmissions. Signaling was often observed at premises which could not be entered without a warrant because of mixed occupancy. The problem required immediate solution."

Justice Department lawyers Edward Ennis, who had pushed for greater transparency and accuracy in the *Hirabayashi* briefing, and John Burling read the DeWitt Report around the time that it was released. Immediately suspecting that DeWitt's claims were exaggerations and distortions, they convinced Attorney General Biddle to request evaluations by the FBI and by the Federal Communications Commission.

The FBI and the FCC shredded DeWitt's claims. On February 7, FBI Director J. Edgar Hoover wrote Biddle that "there is no information in the possession of this Bureau...which would indicate that the attacks made on ships or shores in the area immediately after Pearl Harbor have been associated with any espionage ashore or that there has been any illicit shore-to-ship signaling, either by radio or lights." FCC Chairman James Fly was just as emphatic. The FCC's "investigations of hundreds of reports, by the Army and others, of unlawful or unidentified radio signals showed that in each case there either was no radio transmission involved or...it was legitimate....There were no radio signals reported to the Commission which could not be identified, or which were un-lawful....The Commission knows of no evidence of any illicit radio sig-naling in this area during the period in question." And, in a devastating rebuke to DeWitt, Fly reported that the FCC had explicitly advised De-Witt of the actual facts belying his claims before he made his decisions about expulsion and incarceration, as well as in the immediate after-math of those decisions.

These unequivocal and authoritative rebuttals of the DeWitt Report— by the nation's leading law enforcement organization and by the expert federal agency on radio signals and transmissions—would ignite a con-troversy when the government's *Korematsu* brief was written and sub-mitted later that year.

❦ ❦ ❦

By the spring of 1944, at least two members of FDR's Cabinet had grown uncomfortable with the incarceration of thousands of American citizens based only on their ancestry. On December 30, 1943, Attorney General Biddle wrote the President that "the present practice of keeping loyal American citizens in concentration camps on the basis of race for longer than is absolutely necessary is dangerous and repugnant to the principles of our Government." Interior Secretary Ickes, whose department assumed jurisdiction over the War Relocation Authority in February 1944, similarly had sent Roosevelt a series of letters urging termination of Japanese American incarceration. But FDR dismissed both, failing even to respond to Biddle and sending Ickes pro forma acknowledgments.

At a Cabinet meeting on May 26, 1944, the incarceration issue was raised by an authority who could not be ignored—Secretary of War Henry Stimson. The Allies were advancing in the Pacific, launching attacks in the Marshall Islands, Burma, and New Guinea. Biddle had advised Stimson of "the likelihood of an adverse [court] decision on our power to hold" Japanese American detainees in a case to be heard in the fall. Stimson announced that the incarceration of Japanese Americans could now be terminated "without danger to defense considerations." The War Department supported "freeing those who had been screened and found loyal," while using "careful timing and methods" for their release. Stimson's only military concern had to do with possible Japanese retaliation against American prisoners: If Japanese Americans were released and then persecuted or harassed by other Americans, Japanese troops might abuse American prisoners in response. Stimson also noted that he "doubted the wisdom of doing it at this time before the election."

FDR responded that "the evacuees should be distributed in small numbers over the United States rather than dumped on California." His approach thus reinforced the status quo. Distribution of small numbers of detainees throughout the United States, rather than a return to their homes and communities in the areas of expulsion, was already being implemented in the government's cumbersome two-step leave process.

Ickes again wrote FDR urging an end to the entire regime. He emphasized Stimson's belief that "there is no longer any military necessity" for the policy. This time, FDR responded firmly in a memo to Ickes on

June 12. "The more I think of the problem of suddenly ending the orders excluding Japanese Americans, the more I think it would be a mistake to do anything drastic or sudden....As I said at Cabinet, I think the whole problem, for the sake of internal quiet, should be handled gradually." He reiterated the need to disperse incarcerated Japanese American citizens throughout the country—"one or two families to each county as a start," with perhaps a small number gradually returning to isolated areas in California.

DeWitt's successor, General Delos Emmons, had been working on a plan that would allow "a substantial number" of incarcerated Japanese American families to promptly return to their California homes, and word of Emmons's effort circulated in the government. The day after FDR's letter to Ickes, the President summoned John McCloy to the White House. FDR "was surrounded...by his political advisors," reported McCloy to War Department colleagues. "They were harping hard that this would stir up the boys in California, and California, I guess, is an important state." FDR firmly told McCloy he wanted no publicity about the return of Japanese Americans. "He doesn't want...to stir up the California situation," McCloy summarized, and he "put thumbs down" on Emmons's plan. If there were to be any West Coast returns, they had to be done "very gradually."

It was an election year, and for some in western states, the return of Japanese Americans was an explosive political issue. "Roosevelt's desire for partisan advantage in the 1944 elections," concluded historian Peter Irons, "provides the only explanation for the delay in ending internment."

THE GOVERNMENT'S SUPREME COURT brief in *Korematsu* was due on October 5. In light of the FBI and FCC reports to Biddle, Burling and Ennis sought to formally disavow DeWitt's misleading statements. Burling prepared a footnote on DeWitt's false claims. Burling's proposed footnote raised three important points. First, the Department of Justice relied on the DeWitt Report for "statistics and other details concerning the actual evacuation and the events that took place subsequent thereto." Second, the department had information "in conflict with" DeWitt's statements about "the circumstances justifying the evacuation as a matter of military necessity." And third, the subjects on which had the department had conflicting information included "the use of illegal radio transmitters" and "shore-to-ship signaling by persons of Japanese ancestry"; "in view of the contrariety of the reports," the department did not ask the Court to rely on ("take judicial notice of," in the legal parlance) the facts asserted in the DeWitt Report regarding those critical issues. Burling thus sought to highlight the Justice Department's knowledge that a cornerstone of DeWitt's justifications for his policies—supposed radio transmissions and shore-to-ship signals by disloyal Japanese collaborators—was contradicted by information known to the Department.

On Saturday morning, Captain Adrian Fisher, McCloy's legal deputy, called Ennis. McCloy had read the brief. He strongly objected to Burling's footnote. Ennis replied that it was too late. The government's brief was already at the printer. McCloy promptly called Fahy and complained, demanding the footnote's deletion. At noon that Saturday, in an archetypal "stop the presses" moment, Fahy ordered that the printer immediately cease printing the government brief.

Over the next forty-eight hours, an extensive back-and-forth ensued between the Justice and War Departments. A key official in the process was Assistant Attorney General Herbert Wechsler, a former (and future) Columbia Law professor and a former law clerk to then Associate Justice Harlan Fiske Stone in the 1932 Supreme Court term. As head of the War Division at the Justice Department, Wechsler shared responsibility for the *Korematsu* brief. He also was close to Attorney General Biddle and enjoyed a reputation for judgment and wisdom. Burling and Ennis urged Wechsler that the FBI and the FCC reports "establish clearly that the facts are not as General DeWitt states them in his report and also that General DeWitt knew them to be contrary to his report.... It is highly unfair to this racial minority that these lies, put out in an official publication, go uncorrected." The department had an "ethical obligation" to the Supreme Court.

Ultimately, with Fahy's approval and at his direction, Wechsler presented the War Department with two options: the Burling footnote and a footnote he had drafted, which he indicated was his preference. The Wechlser draft eliminated the second two points of the Burling footnote—no reference to "conflicting information," no reference to disputed facts about shore-to-ship signaling and radio transmissions, no reference to "the contrariety of reports," no statement that the Justice Department disclaimed reliance on the DeWitt Report for these purposes. All that remained was (1) Burling's statement about relying on the report for statistics and the like and (2) a general statement that "we have specifically recited in this brief the facts relating to the justification for the evacuation, of which we ask the Court to take judicial notice, and we rely upon the *Final Report* only to the extent that it relates to such facts."

The as-filed footnote is deeply problematic. While its inclusion certainly was better than no footnote at all, it avoided advising the Court—and the public—of material misstatements in the DeWitt Report. The footnote used language that was deliberately vague and opaque—language described by McCloy biographer Kai Bird as "almost nonsensical."

The government's brief, meanwhile, extensively relied on the DeWitt Report—citing the report no fewer than twenty times in a fifty-nine-page brief.

The government's *Korematsu* submission represents a historic and shameful failure by the best and brightest of the American legal establishment. John J. McCloy, who would reign at the pinnacle of American law and business for decades, orchestrated the withholding of critical information known to the government. Herbert Wechsler, who would become an esteemed leader of the American legal academy, drafted and engineered the deceptive footnote implementing the cover-up; Wechsler later told Peter Irons that he viewed the matter simply as a "public relations problem" for both the Justice Department and the War Department. The well-regarded Solicitor General Charles Fahy, who would soon become a respected judge on the US Court of Appeals for the District of Columbia Circuit, allowed the presentation to be submitted on his watch and under his authority. And Edward Ennis and John Burling, the committed, at-times heroic and valiant Justice Department lawyers, ultimately signed the Justice Department's brief (along with Fahy, Wechsler, and Ralph Fuchs, a lawyer in the Solicitor General's office), even though it lacked language they had identified as important in light of ethical obligations.

ON SEPTEMBER 16, 1944, Fred Korematsu's lawyer, Wayne Collins, filed his Supreme Court brief, a rambling and scattershot document. It invoked, among other grounds, Article III of the Constitution and the Fourth, Fifth, Sixth, Eighth, and Thirteenth Amendments; it attacked a "veritable reign of terror." Amid Collins's ricocheting theories and purple prose, he raised two important points. First, while Korematsu's conviction rested on his illegal presence in a prohibited area, the expulsion element of the military regime was inseparable from its incarceration element: "They are parts of one single program." Second, DeWitt's banishment-and-imprisonment program represented unconstitutional discrimination. DeWitt's public statements in 1943 confirmed his blatant anti-Japanese racism; DeWitt's "brutal evacuation program was the result of his personal prejudice."

In response, the Justice Department sought to emphasize, first, that Korematsu's case did not present the issue of *detention and incarceration*— it was simply a case of *exclusion* from a specified area—and second, that the exclusion policy was permissible based on military necessity. While nothing in the record called into question Fred Korematsu's personal loyalty, the government contended that the mandatory expulsion of all Japanese Americans was justified by the Japanese threat and the difficulty of separating loyal from disloyal Japanese American citizens. The government further argued that the *Hirabayashi* decision's ruling upholding the curfew established the legality of exclusion as well. Finally, if the Court did reach the incarceration question, detention was justified and lawful. In addition to the military exigency and the difficulty of screening for loyalty, the incarceration program, the government asserted, was actually an exercise in beneficent protection: Japanese American citizens and lawful Japanese residents on the West Coast had to be imprisoned because if they were permitted to go to other parts of the country after being expelled from their homes, they would be harassed and assaulted.

Shortly after the government filed its brief, the Supreme Court received three important amicus briefs. The first was from the American Civil Liberties Union. It had an unusual origin. In January 1944, Edward Ennis had met with ACLU Executive Director Roger Baldwin. Ennis had emphasized the need for the ACLU's active involvement in both *Korematsu* and *Endo*. Despite his role as a Justice Department lawyer, Ennis was sympathetic to the challenges. He worried about the quality of lawyering for both Korematsu and Endo, and he suggested possible arguments that could be made. Baldwin promptly enlisted Charles Horsky, a partner at the prominent Washington law firm Covington & Burling. Horsky and Ennis had served together in the Solicitor General's office in the 1930s; they were friends, and they now brainstormed about the cases.

Horsky's *Korematsu* brief for the ACLU crisply set forth the argument buried in Collins's brief: it was absurd to separate the issue of *exclusion* from the issue of *detention*. Korematsu had been ordered by the military to leave a specific area and to report for incarceration in an assembly center, and then he would have been sent to a long-term incarceration camp. Exclusion and imprisonment were inextricably interwoven. "The true issue posed by this case is whether or not a citizen of the United States may, because he is of Japanese ancestry, be confined in barbed wire stockades euphemistically termed Assembly Centers or Relocation Centers—actually concentration camps."

The second amicus brief was from the Japanese American Citizens League. It devoted two hundred pages to rebutting the harmful racial stereotypes in the DeWitt Report. "Americans of Japanese ancestry are well assimilated and loyal," the brief declared. "Abundant and reliable information was on hand to prove this at the time of evacuation."

The third brief, which opposed Korematsu, was from the states of California, Oregon, and Washington. Spearheading the states' brief was California Attorney General Robert Kenny—the designated floor leader at the 1944 Democratic convention floor for Douglas's vice-presidential campaign. The three states reported that, at the time of the Pearl Harbor attack, they had been home to 112,000 out of 126,000 people of Japanese ancestry in the United States. "The ethnic, educational, economic, political, language and family ties of this group with the enemy Japan," they proclaimed, generated grave concern. The Supreme Court should uphold DeWitt's exclusion orders "as a matter of military necessity to safeguard national security from enemy action, both from without and within." Having defended the forced expulsion from their states of tens of thousands of their residents, the states offered an empty rhetorical gesture: "The restrictions placed upon this group of our citizens must be removed as soon as the military authorities determine and the national security permits."

MEANWHILE, THE SUPREME COURT also received the briefs in *Endo*. Her case squarely presented the claim that the government was unlawfully incarcerating her and that she was entitled to her freedom. The Constitution, her lawyers argued, prohibited the continuing imprisonment of American citizens without charges and without individualized consideration of loyalty, especially when the sole basis of imprisonment was a person's ancestry.

In addition to constitutional grounds, Endo maintained that incarceration, as opposed to exclusion, was not authorized by FDR's executive order or the congressional statute. Executive Order 9066 authorized the military to "exclude" designated people from areas it specified and "to take such other steps" that the military thought "advisable to enforce" these "restrictions," but the order said nothing about detention. And the congressional statute simply added criminal penalties for the violation of military orders authorized by the executive order.

As in *Korematsu*, Charles Horsky filed a focused amicus brief for the ACLU in *Endo*. "The government has no power to detain a citizen against whom no criminal charges have been preferred," it said, and the "classification of citizens based solely on ancestry" was an unconstitutional basis for imprisonment.

The Justice Department lawyers had a problem. If the Supreme Court confronted the incarceration issue, they worried, the government might well lose. Mitsuye Endo presented a compelling case—a young typist for the motor vehicle department; a loyal American citizen who posed no threat to the nation's security. Yet she already had been imprisoned for two and a half years, without charges, without a determination of disloyalty, without an individualized justification related to military necessity.

Accordingly, the United States decided to emphasize a procedural issue. The government had established the two-step process for possible release from the incarceration camps. Endo had not completed the second step because she refused to be barred from returning to her Sacramento home. The Justice Department argued that only a narrow issue was before the Court: whether continued detention was permissible when the detainee could be released if she simply followed the government's procedure. Refusal to comply justified continued incarceration. Detention on that narrow ground, it claimed, was authorized by the executive order and by Congress's statute and was within the federal government's war powers under the Constitution.

The Justice Department's brief cited a September 1943 report by former Justice James Byrnes, in his role as Director of the Office of War Mobilization, that FDR had sent to the Senate. Byrnes's report expressed the government's position that expulsion and detention were justified by military necessity. But Byrnes's report also said that the government lacked authority under the executive order and the statute to detain loyal citizens for "longer than the minimum period necessary to screen the loyal from the disloyal, and to provide the necessary guidance for relocation"; such continued imprisonment "would be very hard to reconcile with the constitutional rights of citizens." The government's Supreme Court brief argued that Endo's detention was consistent with Byrnes's position. "The program which has been begun and carried forward has not been completed." In "light of the extraordinary powers invoked by reason of the war," the continued imprisonment of a detainee for refusing to comply with the government's release procedure was authorized and constitutional.

AT NOON ON WEDNESDAY, October 11, 1944, Chief Justice Harlan Fiske Stone gaveled the Supreme Court into session for the arguments in *Korematsu* and *Endo*. The arguments would proceed over two days, five hours in total.

As always, war news dominated national attention. That week, Winston Churchill, Joseph Stalin, and FDR envoy Averell Harriman met in Moscow to discuss postwar Europe. In the Pacific, American bombers strafed the Ryuku Islands in Japanese territory and shellacked Japanese strongholds in the Philippines and the island then known as Formosa. In Europe, Allied troops pressed pincer assaults—from the west, in Belgium and Germany itself; from the south, in Italy and Greece; from the east, in Latvia, Lithuania, and Hungary; and from the north, in Finland. At the Big 3 summit in Moscow, Churchill hailed Stalin's Red Army for "[clawing] the guts out of the filthy Nazis."

Amid the surging Allied advances, Wayne Collins rose at the Supreme Court to argue for Fred Korematsu. He blasted the incarceration policy. "There is no legal precedent for a mass imprisonment program of this nature," he asserted. "The only comparable program is that by Hitler where German citizens whose ancestors were Jewish were imprisoned." A "genuine military necessity did not exist for immediate internment of any citizens" unless an individualized hearing established the need. Congress and the President never intended "such mass imprisonment"; DeWitt's orders were based on "prejudice and suspicion."

Horsky then argued in support of Korematsu for the ACLU. Rejecting the Justice Department's effort to exclude the incarceration issue, he stressed that, in the relevant period, Korematsu was never "given a chance…to leave the Pacific Coast voluntarily." His only option was to evacuate and surrender to the United States for detention in an incarceration camp. Horsky also mocked the government's claim that it had engaged in beneficent "preventive detention" to protect Japanese Americans.

Arguing in turn for Endo, James Purcell emphasized her undisputed loyalty. "Once [the government] concedes her loyalty," it "has the duty to treat her…as it treats all other United States citizens." In response to the government's insistence that she agree to continued banishment from Sacramento for her release, he said simply that "she refuses to leave unless she can go to her home."

Throughout the arguments, reported the Associated Press, the Justices "fired pointed questions frequently." They queried Collins and Horsky about whether the Court had any business reviewing the military's determination of military necessity. "By what standard," asked Jackson, "are we better judges than [General] DeWitt?" Stone asked Purcell whether Endo's position that she wanted to return to her home in Sacramento in return, rather than be forced to another part of the country, meant that "she will be loyal in one place, and not loyal in another."

Solicitor General Fahy argued after Collins and Horsky in *Korematsu* and then after Purcell in *Endo*. In both cases, he sought to steer the Court to narrow grounds. *Korematsu* presented only the issue of exclusion from militarily sensitive areas, not incarceration; *Endo* presented only the issue of incarceration while the detainee had not agreed to the formal process for release, not broader issues of incarceration and exclusion. Fahy acknowledged that *Endo* was a more difficult case for the government than *Korematsu*.

Fahy's arguments were remarkable in at least three respects. First, despite the back-and-forth within the government over the wording of the disputed footnote in the weeks preceding the argument, Fahy defended the entire DeWitt Report in broad and sweeping terms. "The final report of General DeWitt was held up to Your Honors…as proving that he himself had no rational basis on which to make a military judgment," Fahy argued. "There is not a single line, a single word, or a single syllable in the report which in any way justifies the statement that General DeWitt did not believe he had, and did not have, a sufficient basis, in honesty and good faith, to believe that the measures which he took were required as a military necessity in protection of the West Coast." Fahy gave this wholesale endorsement without mentioning the FBI and FCC reports contradicting DeWitt's claims, including the FCC's representation that it had advised DeWitt of the actual facts before his report.

In the same vein, Fahy batted away the significance of the hotly contested footnote in his brief (the footnote that Wechsler had drafted). Picking up on a Horsky comment about the government's "extraordinary footnote," Fahy asserted that the footnote simply "[indicates] that we do not ask the Court to take judicial notice of the truth of every recitation or instance in the final report of General DeWitt"; any suggestion that the footnote undermined the military necessity justification was simply "a neat little piece of fancy dancing." When Jackson asked if the Court could take judicial notice of the facts in the report, Fahy replied, "Not all of them, your Honor. I think the Court is required to take judicial notice only of those facts which are of the character of public general knowledge"; Fahy did not specify which facts fell into which category. "Beyond that," he continued, "as to the details in the report, certainly the Court is entitled...to consider them in proving what the general was thinking, his motive, and what he had before him when he made the judgment he made." He then reasserted his embrace of DeWitt's document: "The report proves the basis for the exclusion orders. There is not a line in it that can be taken in any other way. It is a complete justification and explanation of the reasons which led to his judgment."

Second, Fahy emphasized that the entire federal government strongly backed Korematsu's conviction and the regime it reflected. "The Government stands four square and indivisible in support of this conviction and of the constitutionality of all issues which we believe are involved in this case." FDR had acted "in his capacity as President and Commander in Chief." It was "a program carried out not simply by the

General, but by the whole executive branch of the Government, with the full knowledge of everyone.... The whole matter was in the control of the Executive. The whole matter was known to Congress."

Third, Fahy vigorously proclaimed the humaneness of the government's actions in banishing and incarcerating its citizens. "Once the evacuation was decided upon," the fate of the evacuees was "one of the most difficult problems that the Government...has ever had to deal with." The incarceration without charges and without individualized suspicion reflected noble and exemplary conduct. "These citizens have been taken care of in the best manner, under the circumstances, that a fair and efficient government could possibly bring about." It was "a part of a necessary military measure to ward off, or assist in warding off, the threat caused by the eruption of the Japanese, in combination with Hitler, to destroy the very life of the nation." It had all been done as humanely as possible. The burdens on Japanese Americans were akin to burdens on other Americans. "These people suffered hardships and inconveniences, and temporary deprivation of their liberties and freedom; but it must be viewed in the perspective of this whole war. Many persons endure, and are required to endure, dislocations and changes in their lives and fortunes.... Those who have been injured...should be asked to view the situation along with the great injuries, losses, sufferings, and hardships of millions of our people in the fight of the nation for its life."

Like the lawyers arguing for Korematsu and Endo, Fahy faced a barrage of questions from the Justices. Roberts, Frankfurter, Douglas, Jackson, and Rutledge all sharply queried him about the basis for detaining American citizens whose loyalty had been established by government investigations.

When Fahy concluded his argument, the cases were submitted for decision. In *Hirabayashi* the previous year, the Supreme Court had carefully avoided addressing any issues about exclusion and detention. Now *Korematsu* and *Endo* squarely presented both questions.

• chapter seventeen •

"THE UGLY ABYSS"

O N MONDAY, OCTOBER 16, THE NINE JUSTICES GATHERED IN their private conference room at the Supreme Court. Then as now, only the Justices were permitted in the conference room where they discussed and decided the cases—no law clerks, no secretaries, no assistants of any kind. Justice Louis Brandeis once said of the Court that, uniquely among the branches of the government, "we do our own work."

The topic in the conference room on that brisk autumn day was the Japanese American expulsion and incarceration cases. First up was *Korematsu*. Chief Justice Stone suggested they decide only the legality of the expulsion order that Fred Korematsu was convicted of violating, not the legality of the incarceration that would have resulted from his compliance with the order. The Justices should uphold the military's expulsion order as lawful and constitutional, and Korematsu's criminal conviction should be affirmed.

Stone turned to his colleagues. Owen Roberts, the senior Associate Justice, spoke next. He had written the Pearl Harbor Commission report

in early 1942 and, at that time, had expressed concern about the possibility of Japanese sabotage. But Roberts also was the only Justice who
did not owe his Supreme Court position to FDR. He explained that, in
his view, the expulsion order was inextricably linked to detention. Korematsu had been given no choice other than (1) compliance with the
military order and its accompanying incarceration, or (2) violation of
the order. The military regime was unconstitutional, and Korematsu's
conviction should be reversed.

Proceeding in order of seniority, the next three—Black, Reed, and
Frankfurter—agreed with Stone in rejecting Korematsu's claim. But the
three Justices after them—Douglas, Murphy, and Jackson—lined up
with Roberts supporting Korematsu. Jackson emphasized that, for him,
the curfew sustained in *Hirabayashi* was the outer limit of constitutionality. "I stop with *Hirabayashi* and [go] no further."

With the Court split 4 to 4, it was up to the most junior Justice,
Wiley Rutledge. Rutledge explained that *Hirabayashi* had been a difficult vote for him, but he now reluctantly concluded that *Hirabayashi*
required upholding Korematsu's conviction. "I had to swallow *Hirabayashi*," he said. "I didn't like it. At that time I knew if I went along with
that order I had to go along with detention for [a] reasonably necessary
time. Nothing but necessity would justify it because of *Hirabayashi* and
so I vote to affirm."

Stone now had a 5–4 majority for his position upholding Korematsu's conviction. But his majority was shaky in light of Rutledge's wary
comments.

On *Endo*, in contrast, a consensus quickly emerged. The federal
government had conceded that Endo, imprisoned for more than two
years, was loyal. "Can a loyal citizen be held in a relocation center
under restraint with the privilege of release a condition," Stone asked,
simply because of "the presence of disloyal people among the mass of
Jap citizens?" He then summarized, "Once loyalty is shown the basis
for the military decision disappears. This woman is entitled to summary
release." The other Justice unanimously agreed. The result was that the
Court voted to reject Korematsu's challenge and to rule for Endo. In

both, it would, at least to some extent, be accepting the government's position—that the expulsion order for Korematsu had been valid and that Endo posed no current security risk (even though the government sought her continued incarceration).

Stone assigned the unanimous *Endo* opinion to Douglas. For the contentious, narrowly divided *Korematsu* opinion, he chose Hugo Black. A leader of the faction dubbed "the Axis" by Frankfurter, Black was the Justice perhaps most likely to keep the skeptical Rutledge on board with the majority.

THE WAR CONFRONTED HUGO Black on a deeply personal level. It had taken a severe toll on his wife Josephine.

Josephine had periodically experienced depression. Now, during the war, her affliction greatly worsened. With their two sons in the US military, she worried about them constantly. Both served in the United States because of health issues (Hugo Jr.'s asthma and Sterling's hearing problems), but their stateside service did not alleviate Josephine's anxiety. She had regular bouts of depression during the war, which she tried to conceal from visitors and friends. She suffered greatly, despondent and often sleepless. As for Black, even while maintaining his bonhomie and enjoying a social whirl with politically connected insiders, he agonized over Josephine's mental health struggles and tried to support her as she sought various treatments.

Black was not the only Justice with family members in the military. Three other Justices (Stone, Reed, and Jackson) had sons in the armed forces; a fourth (Roberts) had a son-in-law serving; and a fifth (Rutledge) had a son who would serve in 1945 as soon as he was of age. But the war's impact on Josephine made it distinctively painful for Black.

At the time he received the *Korematsu* assignment, Black, the former Klansman, had shown notable sensitivity as a Justice to claims involving civil liberties and civil rights. In 1940, Black had written *Chambers v. Florida* reversing the convictions of African Americans subjected to days-long incommunicado interrogation. In soaring words that would resonate for decades, he observed, "Under our constitutional system, courts stand against any winds that blow as havens of refuge for those who might otherwise suffer because they are helpless, weak, outnumbered, or because they are non-conforming victims of prejudice and public excitement."

But in the fall of 1944, Hugo Black, the Justice who had written so eloquently about the role of courts as a haven for the weak and victims of prejudice, prepared his opinion rejecting an American citizen's challenge to his forced banishment and incarceration based solely on his parents' birthplace.

BLACK CIRCULATED HIS DRAFT majority opinion in *Korematsu* on Wednesday, November 8, the day after FDR's fourth-term election victory over New York Governor Thomas E. Dewey. Black's opinion rested on three points. First, the anti-Japanese exclusion order that Korematsu violated was the only issue the Court would consider (and thus the Court would not address the incarceration that would have accompanied Korematsu's compliance). Second, General DeWitt had not exceeded the authority given him by the President and Congress; FDR's executive order and the subsequent statute authorized DeWitt's anti-Japanese expulsion order. And third, regarding the constitutionality of the forced expulsion, the Court would defer to the government's determination of military necessity. "In the light of the principles we announced in the *Hirabayashi* case," Black emphasized, "we are unable to conclude that it was beyond the war power of Congress and the Executive to exclude those of Japanese ancestry from the West Coast war area at the time they did."

Black dismissed the burdens imposed by the banishment order, likening them to other wartime sacrifices. "We are not unmindful of the hardships imposed by [the order] upon a large group of American citizens." He continued, "But hardships are part of war, and war is an aggregation of hardships. All citizens alike, both in and out of uniform, feel the impact of war in greater or lesser measure. Citizenship has its responsibilities as well as its privileges, and in time of war, the burden is always heavier."

Perhaps, when he referred to "the impact of war" on all citizens, Black was thinking, consciously or subconsciously, of his wife Josephine's wartime troubles or of his sons' service in the military. But to shrug and say that "hardships are part of war" in the context of the suffering inflicted on Japanese American citizens by the government's anti-Japanese expulsion and imprisonment was a stunning statement.

Reed and Rutledge quickly joined Black's opinion without comment. Frankfurter and Stone praised the opinion and made suggestions. Frankfurter wanted greater emphasis on the limited role played by courts; Stone sought to highlight further the expulsion-only nature of the decision. Black accommodated both concerns.

And then came the dissents. Douglas circulated an opinion that oddly sent mixed messages. He praised DeWitt's "good faith" and emphasized the military imperative for DeWitt's expulsion order. But he also opined that, in the initial expulsion stage when the military orders directed Korematsu to report to an assembly center, the expulsion could not be separated from the accompanying detention—a position contrary to the majority's approach. Douglas signaled to Black that he would abandon his dissent and join the majority if Black acknowledged that some Justices believed expulsion and detention were intertwined at the beginning of the process. Black obliged. Black's final opinion stated, "Some of the members of the Court are of the view that evacuation and detention in an Assembly Center were inseparable.... Whichever view is taken, it results in holding that the order under which petitioner was convicted was valid." That brought Douglas into the fold, enlarging the *Korematsu* majority to 6–3. But it had a considerable cost. With the language "whichever view is taken," the Court now was explicitly embracing the lawfulness of detention accompanying evacuation, at least in the initial assembly center stage.

Unlike Douglas, the three remaining dissenters—Roberts, Murphy, and Jackson—remained adamantly opposed to the majority opinion in *Korematsu*. Each wrote a separate opinion. For Roberts, "the indisputable facts exhibit a clear violation of Constitutional rights"; the indefinite detention was inseparable from the forced expulsion. Unlike *Hirabayashi*, the *Korematsu* case involved "convicting a citizen as a punishment for not submitting to imprisonment in a concentration camp, based on his ancestry, and solely because of his ancestry, without evidence or inquiry concerning his loyalty and disposition towards the United States."

Murphy, who had written a skeptical concurrence in *Hirabayashi*, now attacked the foundation of the government's forced-exclusion policy. "The exclusion of 'all persons of Japanese ancestry'...falls into the ugly abyss of racism....The exclusion, either temporarily or permanently, of all persons with Japanese blood in their veins has no...reasonable relation" to "the dangers of invasion, sabotage and espionage." Murphy excoriated the DeWitt Report. It was based, not on "bona fide military necessity," but on an "erroneous assumption of racial guilt." Murphy scathingly quoted DeWitt's racist anti-Japanese congressional testimony and carefully refuted the DeWitt Report's assertions about Japanese Americans as "misinformation, half-truths and insinuations that have for years been directed against Japanese Americans by people with racial and economic prejudices."

The third dissenter, Jackson, like Murphy, had been FDR's Attorney General; he also was one of the Justices closest to FDR personally. But that did not stop him from lacerating the Roosevelt Administration's anti-Japanese policy. "Korematsu was born on our soil, of parents born in Japan," he began. "The Constitution makes him a citizen of the United States by nativity and a citizen of California by residence. No claim is made that he is not loyal to this country....Korematsu, however, has been convicted of an act not commonly a crime. It consists merely of being present in the state whereof he is a citizen, near the place where he was born, and where all his life he has lived....Here is an attempt to make an otherwise innocent act a crime merely because the prisoner is the son of parents as to whom he had no choice and belongs to a race from which there is no way to resign." Jackson then crystallized the issue in a devastating and irrefutable example. "Had Korematsu been one of four—the others being, say, a German alien enemy, an Italian alien enemy, and a citizen of American-born ancestors, convicted of treason but out on parole—only Korematsu's presence would have violated the order." For Jackson, the stakes were enormous: "The principle of racial discrimination in criminal procedure and of transplanting American citizens... lies about like a loaded weapon ready for the hand of any authority that can bring forward a plausible claim of an urgent need."

Black was stung by the charge that his opinion sanctioned racism and permitted incarceration in what Roberts called "concentration camps." He added a passage rejecting the dissents. "Our task would be simple, our duty clear, were this a case involving the imprisonment of a loyal citizen in a concentration camp because of racial prejudice. Regardless of the true nature of the assembly and relocation centers—and we deem it unjustifiable to call them concentration camps with all the ugly connotations that term implies—we are dealing specifically with nothing but an exclusion order."

Black then doubled down on the proposition that Korematsu's race was not the issue. "To cast this case into outlines of racial prejudice, without reference to the real military dangers which were presented, merely confuses the issue. Korematsu was not excluded from the Military Area because of hostility to him or his race. He *was* excluded because we are at war with the Japanese Empire, because the properly constituted military authorities feared an invasion of our West Coast and felt constrained to take proper security measures, because they decided that the military urgency of the situation demanded that all citizens of Japanese ancestry be segregated from the West Coast temporarily, and finally because Congress, reposing its confidence in this time of war in our military leaders... determined that they should have the power to do just this. There was evidence of disloyalty on the part of some, the military authorities considered that the need for action was great, and time was short."

Black's desire to respond to the charge of racism is understandable. But his insistence that Korematsu was not penalized "because of hostility to him or his race" is simply not credible. Black's effort represented wordplay and sophistry, a flimsy and inadequate justification for a stark racial classification.

Black was not the only Justice stirred to respond to the dissents. Frankfurter, who saw himself as the guardian of judicial restraint, emphasized the importance of the constitutional war powers vested in the President and Congress. "The validity of action under the war power must be judged wholly in the context of war. That action is not to be stigmatized as lawless because like action in times of peace would be lawless.... To find that the Constitution does not forbid the military measures now complained of does not carry with it approval of that which Congress and the Executive did. That is their business, not ours."

One point overlooked by Frankfurter in his concurrence: it also was Fred Korematsu's "business," and the business of more than 110,000 other American citizens and lawful residents who had been forcibly expelled from their homes and imprisoned in detention camps.

DOUGLAS, MEANWHILE, WAS PREPARING his *Endo* majority opinion. The government's concessions greatly simplified the issue. In an opinion distributed on November 8, the same day that Black circulated his *Korematsu* majority opinion, Douglas explained that continued detention could not be justified now that Endo's loyalty had been established. In his reading, Roosevelt's executive order and Congress's statute—the applicable sources of authority—did not permit continued detention of a loyal American citizen at this point, long after her initial expulsion. Accordingly, "Mitsuye Endo is entitled to an unconditional release by the War Relocation Authority." Douglas was careful to stress that this conclusion rested on an interpretation of the executive order and the statute—*not* on a judgment that such a regime would violate the Constitution. He deliberately kept that question open.

Douglas also took pains to note that the government might well have had authority for initial incarceration as part of the expulsion program. "The fact that the Act and the orders are silent on detention does not of course mean that any power to detain is lacking. Some such power might indeed be necessary to the successful operation of the evacuation program.... We may assume for the purposes of this case that initial detention in Relocation Centers was authorized." In ruling against the Roosevelt Administration on an important war-related issue, Douglas crafted the opinion to be as narrow and as free of criticism of the Roosevelt Administration as possible.

All nine Justices agreed with Douglas's bottom-line conclusion that Endo must be given her freedom. Eight of them—all except Roberts—joined Douglas's opinion. Even while joining Douglas's majority opinion, Murphy added a concurrence emphasizing that, while he agreed that the executive order and statute did not authorize Endo's detention, the problem also was more fundamental: it was "another example of the unconstitutional resort to racism inherent in the entire evacuation program."

Roberts, meanwhile, refused to go along with Douglas's conclusion that FDR's executive order and Congress's statute did not allow continuing detention. In his view, they did provide such authorization—and that was the problem. Under the executive order and the enacted law, "an admittedly loyal citizen has been deprived of her liberty for a period of years," and her imprisonment violated the Constitution.

THERE HAD BEEN LESS back-and-forth, and less division, within the Court on *Endo* than on *Korematsu*. But now a timing issue emerged regarding the public release of the opinions. The circumstances were suspicious.

The Supreme Court issued the *Korematsu* and *Endo* opinions on Monday, December 18, 1944. The previous day, the War Department made a rare Sunday announcement. General DeWitt's exclusion orders were revoked, effective on January 2, 1945. The detainees would be released, without restriction, unless there was an individualized loyalty concern justifying continued incarceration. As a result of this unusual

Sunday announcement, when the Supreme Court announced the *Endo* decision the very next day, the Roosevelt Administration had already changed and ended the challenged policy.

The fortuitous timing was not a random development. The *Endo* opinion was ready for release by late November, but the Court continued to hold it back. On November 28, 1944, Douglas wrote Stone complaining that public release of the opinion "is at a standstill because officers of the government have indicated that some change in detention plans are under consideration." Douglas urged that "an opinion in the case should be announced on December 4, unless prior to that time Mitsuye Endo either has been released or has been promised her immediate and unqualified release." He wanted the Supreme Court to "act promptly and not lend our aid in compounding the wrong by keeping her in unlawful confinement through our inaction any longer than necessary to reach a decision." But the opinion was not released for an additional three weeks.

It is not clear where Douglas was getting his information about the government's imminent "change in detention plans" and the corresponding "standstill" at the Court. The United States had not filed anything on that subject. But Douglas was certainly correct that changes were under active consideration in the government.

THREE DAYS AFTER THE presidential election, at a Cabinet meeting on Friday, November 10, 1944, Attorney General Biddle raised the issue of Japanese American incarceration. He reported that he expected the Supreme Court to reject the government's position on forced exclusion and detention. Now that the election was over, he recommended allowing the detainees to leave the camps. Secretary of War Stimson supported him. Interior Secretary Ickes, who oversaw the Wartime Relocation Authority, also agreed.

With the election behind him, FDR acquiesced. He asked Stimson to provide an implementation plan. He also directed Stimson to include a letter confirming that there now was no military necessity for continued detention and to praise the "good war record" of a unit of Japanese American soldiers who had fought valiantly in Italy.

Over the next few weeks, Stimson, Biddle, Ickes, and their aides conferred on a plan. Word began to leak out. McCloy told Biddle he was getting calls asking about rumors. Within their departments, Biddle and Stimson emphasized the need for secrecy. In mid-November, California Governor Earl Warren publicly stated that California would not seek to prohibit the return of detainees and would protect their rights if they returned—an announcement that stoked further speculation.

On November 21, at one of FDR's regular meetings with the press, a *Los Angeles Times* reporter asked the President about "the matter of allowing the return of these Japanese who were evacuated in 1942." FDR replied with generalities about "scattering them throughout the country," a comment interpreted to mean no change in policy was imminent.

On Sunday, December 17, the day before the release of the *Endo* and *Korematsu* decisions, the War Department announced its policy change in Public Proclamation Number 21, issued by General H. C. Pratt (another of DeWitt's successors). The new proclamation formally stated that "the present military situation makes possible modification and relaxation of restrictions and the termination of the system of mass exclusion of persons of Japanese ancestry....Available information permits the determination of potential danger on an individual basis." DeWitt's orders accordingly were "rescinded" and "all persons of Japanese ancestry not designated by name for exclusion or other control" were exempt, effective January 2, 1945, from the previous orders. That afternoon, Pratt met with reporters—in what the *Oakland Tribune* called "an unusual Sunday press conference" by the military—at his Presidio headquarters in San Francisco to explain the policy change.

It now is generally believed that a Supreme Court Justice advised the Roosevelt Administration that *Endo* would be announced on December 18. This advance knowledge gave the government a chance to get ahead of the opinion. The understanding is so widespread that historian Greg Robinson, in his careful account of the Roosevelt Administration's record on Japanese American incarceration, states as fact,

"The government was tipped off in advance about the *Korematsu* and *Endo* rulings." Many observers think, moreover, that Frankfurter—who was personally close to both Stimson and McCloy, and who relished his insider role with the Roosevelt Administration—is the most likely source of the leak. According to historian Roger Daniels, a confidential source in McCloy's wartime office confirmed to him that Frankfurter advised McCloy about the date the Supreme Court would issue the *Endo* decision.

While there is no additional, definitive proof of a Supreme Court leak, the timing of the government's sudden announcement of its change of policy, on a Sunday the day before the opinions, seems too conspicuous to be coincidental. And Douglas's written complaint to Stone in late November that release of the *Endo* opinion was delayed because of statements by government officials about imminent policy changes lends further credence to that conclusion.

EDITORIAL REACTIONS TO THE *Korematsu* and *Endo* opinions varied. The *Los Angeles Times*, a fervent supporter of anti-Japanese banishment, objected to the *Endo* decision (as well as to General Pratt's order revoking the exclusion): "If Japs in large numbers on the Pacific Coast are dangerous under one set of wartime circumstances, they are dangerous under all sets of wartime circumstances." For the *Washington Post*, a severe critic of the expulsion-and-incarceration regime, it was *Korematsu*, not *Endo*, that was troubling: "We are inclined to take our stand with Mr. Justice Murphy's characterization of the majority opinion as a 'legalization of racism.' The whole history of the exclusion order gives color to his contention.... Much of General DeWitt's final report... reveals a marked bias, not to say bigotry, against all persons of Japanese ancestry."

Critical academic commentary emerged almost immediately. In March 1945, Nanette Dembitz, a cousin of Justice Louis Brandeis, published a disapproving article in the *Columbia Law Review*. She called *Korematsu* "an insidious precedent" and a failure of "judicial responsibility." Her denunciation was especially notable in light of her past employment. She had worked at the Justice Department—and had been one of the lawyers who signed the government's *Hirabayashi* brief in the Supreme Court and the government's *Korematsu* brief in the Ninth Circuit. Her article, she carefully noted, represented "the personal views of the author and in no way [represented] the official views of any government agency."

Eugene V. Rostow, a Yale Law professor who had worked for the State Department and the Lend-Lease Administration during World War II (and who later would be a leading hawk on the Vietnam War and on relations with the Soviet Union), similarly launched a broadside in June 1945. In a *Yale Law Journal* article titled "The Japanese American Cases—A Disaster," he pulled no punches: "The course of action which we undertook was in no way required or justified by the circumstances of the war.... All in all, the internment of the West Coast Japanese is the worst blow our liberties have suffered in many years.... We believe that the German people bear a common political responsibility for outrages secretly committed by the Gestapo and the SS. What are we to think of our own part in a program which violates every democratic social value, yet has been approved by the Congress, the President and the Supreme Court?"

The Justices in the *Korematsu* majority expressed different perspectives in succeeding decades. Black was unrepentant. Late in his life, in 1967, he told an interviewer, "I would do precisely the same thing today, in any part of the country. I would probably issue the same order were I President. We had a situation where we were at war. People were rightly fearful of the Japanese in Los Angeles, many loyal to the United States, many undoubtedly not, having dual citizenship—lots of them. They all look alike to a person not a Jap."

Justice Stanley Reed likewise defended his support for the majority opinion. He relied on DeWitt's claims that the policy was necessary to combat espionage—apparently unaware that internal government documents debunked fundamental elements of DeWitt's position.

In contrast to Black's continued defense of his opinion, Black's frequent ally Douglas expressed contrition. "My vote to affirm was one of

my mistakes," he rued in his memoir. "Grave injustices had been committed. Fine American citizens had been robbed of their properties by
racists—crimes that might not have happened if the Court had not followed the Pentagon so literally."

A future Chief Justice, Earl Warren, had been an enthusiastic advocate of the initial banishment as California Attorney General. He also
expressed remorse in his memoir: "I have since deeply regretted the removal order and my own testimony advocating it." Warren once wept
in an interview while discussing "the faces of children being separated
from their parents."

Two of the primary antagonists within the federal government had
conflicting reactions in later decades. Edward Ennis, the Justice Department lawyer who unsuccessfully fought for transparency regarding De-
Witt's misrepresentations, later worked for the ACLU. On behalf of the
ACLU, he said that "the mass evacuation and subsequent detention of the
entire Japanese-American population from the West Coast in 1942" was
"the greatest deprivation of civil liberties in this country since slavery."

But Ennis's opponent John J. McCloy remained a vehement defender to the end. Dismissive of critics, he said that the evacuation and
incarceration had not "adversely affected" Japanese Americans. McCloy
maintained that "the deconcentration of the Japanese population and
its redistribution throughout the country resulted in their finding a
healthier and more advantageous environment." McCloy derided Ennis as somebody who found "a civil liberties problem under every bed-
stead." In a telling and chilling comment, McCloy said that internment
was "in the way of retribution for the attack that was made on Pearl
Harbor." But he then caught himself and said that he did not "like the
word 'retribution.'"

ALTHOUGH IT WOULD TAKE decades, all three branches of the federal
government ultimately repudiated *Korematsu*. On February 19, 1976,
the thirty-fourth anniversary of FDR's Executive Order 9066, President
Gerald Ford officially terminated the order. Ford called the date "the

anniversary of a sad day in American history." The order had been a "setback to fundamental American principles."

In 1983, a bipartisan, congressionally created, blue-ribbon commission concluded that FDR's executive order "was not justified by military necessity, and the decisions which followed from it...were not driven by analysis of military conditions. The broad historical causes which shaped these decisions were race prejudice, war hysteria and a failure of political leadership....A grave injustice was done to American citizens and resident aliens of Japanese ancestry."

In 1988, Congress passed the Civil Liberties Act. It provided reparations of $20,000 to every former detainee or his or her survivors, and it formally apologized for the internment. Signing the legislation on August 10, President Ronald Reagan stated, "We gather here today to right a grave wrong."

In 1998, President Bill Clinton awarded Fred Korematsu the Presidential Medal of Freedom. Fourteen years later, in 2012, President Barack Obama awarded the same medal to Gordon Hirabayashi posthumously; then in 2015 he awarded it posthumously to Minoru Yasui. Of the four Supreme Court litigants, only Mitsuye Endo—the lone woman among the four Japanese American litigants and the person whose courageous and tenacious lawsuit actually brought an end to the incarceration camps for tens of thousands of detainees—never received the presidential honor, in her life or posthumously.

Disavowal of *Korematsu* also has come in the courts. In the 1980s, based on Peter Irons's discovery that the federal government had deceived the Supreme Court, Irons and other lawyers filed cases under the obscure writ of coram nobis, a legal mechanism designed to rectify fundamental errors, to set aside the convictions of Gordon Hirabayashi, Min Yasui, and Fred Korematsu. Korematsu and Hirabayashi won. Federal courts formally overturned their convictions in 1984 and 1987, four decades after the Supreme Court affirmed the convictions. Yasui's case became moot when he died in 1986.

In 2018, the Supreme Court upheld President Donald Trump's travel ban in a 5–4 opinion by Chief Justice John Roberts. The ban,

which had gone through various iterations, severely restricted immigration from seven countries. As a presidential candidate, Donald Trump
had called for a complete "shutdown" on Muslim immigration; he
claimed as a justification that his proposal was "the same thing" that
FDR had done with the incarceration of Japanese Americans. After becoming President and issuing the different versions of the ban, Trump
complained that it had been "watered down" by others in the government. As President, Trump continued to traffic in anti-Muslim invec-
tive, such as retweeting links to vicious anti-Muslim propaganda videos.

In upholding the ban, Chief Justice Roberts's opinion held that the
Trump Administration's claimed reason for the travel order was adequate. The government maintained that the policy rested on concerns
about vetting capabilities in the seven countries, two of which, the government emphasized, were not Muslim-majority nations. The Supreme
Court accepted the government's justification with great deference, noting that the Administration claimed it was a pressing matter of national
security. Since the Court found a valid "plausible" reason for the policy,
it would not view the anti-Muslim remarks of candidate Trump and of
President Trump as a basis for finding the ban unconstitutional.

Justice Sonia Sotomayor's dissent accused the majority of replicat-
ing the *Korematsu* injustice. "Today's holding," she objected, "is all
the more troubling given the stark parallels between the reasoning of
this case and that of *Korematsu v. United States*....In *Korematsu*, the
Court gave 'a pass [to] an odious, gravely injurious racial classification'
authorized by an executive order....As here, the Government invoked
an ill-defined national-security threat to justify an exclusionary policy
of sweeping proportion....As here, the exclusion order was rooted in
dangerous stereotypes about...a particular group's supposed inability to
assimilate and desire to harm the United States....As here, the Government was unwilling to reveal its own intelligence agencies' views of
the alleged security concerns to the very citizens it purported to protect....And as here, there was strong evidence that impermissible hostility and animus motivated the Government's policy."

In response, Chief Justice Roberts and the majority explicitly disavowed *Korematsu*. "Whatever rhetorical advantage the dissent may see...*Korematsu* has nothing to do with this case. The forcible relocation of U.S. citizens to concentration camps, solely and explicitly on the basis of race, is objectively unlawful and outside the scope of Presidential authority. But it is wholly inapt to liken that morally repugnant order to a facially neutral policy denying certain foreign nationals the privilege of admission." The Court then repudiated *Korematsu*: "*Korematsu* was gravely wrong the day it was decided, has been overruled in the court of history and—to be clear—'has no place in law under the Constitution.'" The final phrase was a quote from Justice Robert Jackson's *Korematsu* dissent, now enshrined seventy-four years later in a majority opinion.

While welcoming the majority's repudiation of *Korematsu*, Justice Sotomayor rejected the claimed distinction between *Korematsu* and the Court's new travel ban opinion. "By blindly accepting the Government's misguided invitation to sanction a discriminatory policy motivated by animosity toward a disfavored group, all in the name of a superficial claim of national security, the Court redeploys the same dangerous logic underlying *Korematsu* and merely replaces one 'gravely wrong' decision with another." In both situations, she objected, the Court wrongly deferred to the President's pronouncements on national security even though the assertions were belied by the facts and even though the actions wreaked harm on an identifiable and unpopular group.

IN DECEMBER 1944, THE Supreme Court refused to find unconstitutional the Roosevelt Administration's banishment-and-incarceration program. It refused to find unlawful a personal order of President Franklin D. Roosevelt regarding a measure he claimed necessary for fighting the war. The same Court that, during World War II, had invalidated forced sterilization, compulsory flag salutes, and white-only primaries—and that had reached those conclusions while explicitly comparing the challenged practices to those in the authoritarian regimes the Allies were fighting—now shamefully shirked its responsibility to protect the civil rights and civil liberties of Japanese American citizens and Japanese noncitizens.

The result was a decision—*Korematsu*—that is an indelible stain on American history and on the Supreme Court, a decision that sadly ranks with *Dred Scott* and *Plessy v. Ferguson* as among the worst ever issued.

• chapter eighteen •

THE END OF THE ROOSEVELT COURT

I T WAS A GRAY, OVERCAST DAY. THE EVENING'S INCH OF SNOW had turned to slush and ice. President Franklin Roosevelt stood in a dark blue suit, leaning on the arm of his uniformed eldest son, Marine Corps Colonel James Roosevelt, prepared to take the presidential oath for his fourth term on Saturday, January 20, 1945.

Facing him and ready to administer the oath in his black judicial robes was Chief Justice Harlan Fiske Stone. It was Stone's first time playing this role. Charles Evans Hughes had presided at FDR's three previous inaugurations.

In the midst of war, it was a very different ceremony—sparse, somber, and brief. In a deliberate show of restraint, FDR held it on the South Portico of the White House rather than at the usual location at the Capitol; it was the first inauguration at the White House since President Rutherford B. Hayes's 1877 ceremony after his tumultuous defeat of Samuel Tilden. There was no inaugural ball, no crowd-lined parade on

331

Pennsylvania Avenue from the Capitol to the White House. Congress had appropriated $25,000 for the inauguration; with an eye to wartime frugality, the President had spent only $2,500.

The White House limited the number of invited guests on the South Lawn to five thousand, in contrast to the twenty-five thousand guests at FDR's previous inaugurations. Fifty wounded veterans were among them, some without legs. The public gathered on the street near the fence, listening to the public address system and straining to catch a glimpse.

The sober ceremony and sleet-soaked weather could not entirely dampen spirits. FDR's grandchildren threw snowballs, chased by a harried housekeeper. The President joked with reporters that he looked forward to this inauguration because the first twelve years were always the hardest. And victory finally seemed within reach. Despite a brutal Nazi counteroffensive in the Battle of the Bulge at the end of 1944, Germany appeared to be reeling, under siege from Russia in the east and from advancing Allies in France, Belgium, and Italy. Allied attacks on Japan had escalated and intensified.

Sitting on the stage of the white-columned portico as Roosevelt prepared to take the oath was Washington's highest rung—the Cabinet, chiefs of the armed forces, Speaker of the House Sam Rayburn, the First Lady, other family members. The Supreme Court Justices were there too. Douglas looked "puckish" and motioned to a friend in the crowd. Frankfurter, milling about nervously, "shushed" a Spanish-language reporter describing the proceedings to Latin American audiences.

With the Chief Justice and the President at center stage, Stone administered the oath prescribed in Article II of the Constitution. Assisted by his son, with his hand on a Dutch Bible that had been in his family since 1686, FDR confidently repeated Stone's words and began his unprecedented fourth term.

The President turned to the crowd and delivered the second briefest inaugural address in history—558 words, taking barely more than five minutes. Only George Washington's second inaugural address was shorter. FDR stood bareheaded in the dreary winter weather, declining his much-loved naval cape when it was offered by aides. While rumors swirled about his health, the President's physician, Vice Admiral Ross McIntyre, told reporters that FDR was in fine shape—better than most sixty-three-year-olds, the age he would turn in ten days.

"Mr. Chief Justice, Mr. Vice President, and friends," the President began. The war costs had been high, but the country now could look forward to "total victory" and "a durable peace." As the war neared its successful conclusion, FDR hailed the Constitution as the enduring foundation of our democracy. "Our Constitution of 1787 was not a perfect instrument," he told the assembled crowd and the millions in the national radio audience. "It is not perfect yet. But it provided a firm base upon which all manner of men, of all races and colors and creeds, could build a solid structure of democracy."

The Justices charged with interpreting that Constitution joined in the celebration of the official start to the new term for the beloved President. But relations among the Justices had grown ever more contentious.

EVEN AS VICTORY IN the war approached, internal battles at the Supreme Court raged and intensified. "Petty Feuding Splits Personnel of Supreme Court," ran the headline of a syndicated columnist. Frankfurter, a frequent combatant, wrote Rutledge decrying the "increasing tendency on the part of members of this Court to behave like little school boys and throw spitballs at one another." Statistics confirmed the divisiveness. In the 1943 and 1944 terms, the Court experienced separate opinions and dissents at a higher rate than at any previous time: in both terms, a record-high 58 percent of the opinions were nonunanimous. And the dissents seemed especially barbed and personal.

The Justices shared one abiding passion: reverence for the President who had appointed eight of them. Douglas and Jackson regularly saw FDR, sharing poker games, inside jokes, and discussions about issues of the day. Frankfurter sent him a constant stream of ideas, compliments, and protégés, all welcomed by the man Frankfurter called "Frank." Black had been shoulder to shoulder with FDR in the political trenches. Reed sent the President admiring notes. Murphy reached out to him with messages and requests for meetings. Rutledge deeply respected FDR even though they did not have a close personal relationship. Stone tried to maintain a judicial distance but eagerly embraced the President's war leadership. Even Hoover appointee Roberts had an FDR connection, with his service chairing the President's Pearl Harbor Commission.

FDR, in turn, continued to see the Justices as his personal allies and the Court as a place he could wield influence, formal and informal. On March 16, 1945, FDR told Biddle he was concerned about yet another Supreme Court case involving the influential Australian-born labor leader Harry Bridges; the federal government had succeeded in obtaining a deportation order based on Bridges's radical activities, and the case was now before the Justices. In a reference to Frankfurter and Douglas, the President told his Attorney General, as Biddle recorded it that day, to "slip a word to Felix or Bill that he would just as leave if the Government got licked." While Biddle's mangled syntax leaves the exact meaning unclear, FDR's comfort with conveying a message to Justices about a pending case was clear.

❀ ❀ ❀

ON THURSDAY, APRIL 12, FDR was in his cottage in Warm Springs, Georgia, the "Little White House." He had been visiting since the 1920s; the natural spring waters were a relief to his polio. He had built a rehabilitation center and a foundation there, and he lovingly presided when he was in town. The President had been relaxing and working in Warm Springs since late March. Before the trip, he seemed wan, fatigued, and ailing. His aides hoped the visit would rejuvenate him. The presidential entourage included FDR's White House secretary Grace Tully, his top Secret Service agent Mike Reilly, a Navy physician, and FDR's cousins Daisy Suckley and Laura Delano.

Also present were Lucy Mercer Rutherfurd, FDR's former lover, and an artist Lucy had recruited to paint his portrait, Elizabeth Shoumatoff. Lucy's presence was a well-kept secret.

At 1 p.m. that Thursday, FDR worked at his desk, reviewing correspondence and preparing his speech for the launch in San Francisco on

April 25 of a new organization called the United Nations. Shoumatoff prepared her portrait as he worked; a few others lounged in the room. Suddenly, FDR began fluttering his right hand in front of his forehead. His cousin Daisy Suckley approached and asked if he had dropped his cigarette. FDR looked up and said, "I have a terrific pain in the back of my head." And then he collapsed. He had suffered a cerebral hemorrhage. Without regaining consciousness, Franklin Delano Roosevelt died at 3:30 p.m.

Rutherfurd and Shoumatoff, along with Shoumatoff's aide, fled. They hurriedly drove back to Rutherfurd's home in Aiken, South Carolina.

Back in Washington, Eleanor Roosevelt was summoned to the White House from an event at the Sulgrave Club. White House press secretary Steve Early quietly gave her the news. In Speaker of the House Sam Rayburn's office, Vice President Harry Truman received an urgent call to come to the White House. After hurrying up Pennsylvania Avenue, Truman met with Eleanor, who told him, "Harry, the President is dead." Stunned, he asked the First Lady if he could do anything for her. She responded, "Is there anything we can do for you? For you are the one in trouble now."

Truman ordered that a military plane fly Eleanor to Georgia so that she could accompany her husband's body back to Washington on the presidential train. It was in Warm Springs, as Eleanor prepared for the sad journey home, that she learned for the first time, from FDR cousin Laura Delano, that Lucy Mercer Rutherfurd—the woman who had nearly destroyed her marriage three decades previously—had been there with Franklin in his last waking moments. Eleanor also discovered that this was not the only time they had seen each other recently. And, in a devastating twist, she learned that Franklin and Eleanor's daughter Anna had been involved in orchestrating the secret meetings.

THE WHITE HOUSE QUICKLY arranged a swearing-in ceremony for the new President. It took place at 7:08 that evening in the Cabinet Room of the White House.

Chief Justice Stone was summoned to perform the task he had conducted with FDR just twelve weeks earlier. Stone had come so quickly that he was in his business suit, not having had time to get his judicial robe. White House aides scrambled to find a Bible. Congressional leaders and members of the Roosevelt Cabinet looked on with stricken faces as Truman, in his gray suit and polka-dot bow tie, faced Stone and officially became the country's thirty-third President.

The Justices were thunderstruck. Douglas was driving on Constitution Avenue in Washington when the news blared on his car radio. "I parked the car and walked for hours," he noted in his memoir, "trying to adjust myself to the great void that his death had created." Black had a similar reaction: "'President Roosevelt is dead.' When these words sounded in my ears, I repeated them—I could say no more."

Hearing the news flash from his household handyman, Jackson was just as dazed. "It took a good time for the fact to penetrate." A few weeks previously, Jackson and his wife Irene had joined FDR and Eleanor at the White House, along with a small group, to celebrate St. Patrick's Day and the Roosevelts' fortieth wedding anniversary. On their way home, worried about the President's appearance, Irene gloomily stated, "I do not think we will ever see the President again." Jackson barked, "That's damn nonsense!" Suddenly he realized how right she had been.

Justices publicly expressed their grief. Frankfurter called FDR's death "a cruel and monstrous loss." Douglas observed that "President Roosevelt gave his life for his nation the same as those who stormed Iwo Jima or fell at the Rhine." Black somberly noted that "it will be a long time before we have another who will meet situations as he met them"; FDR was "the man for the time at every recurring emergency."

Jackson told an assembly of grieving Justice Department employees that FDR had been "one of the most commanding figures of world history.... His personality, his serene self-confidence, and his gentle firmness were gifts of the gods." And Rutledge wrote a friend, "Not for one instant after his inauguration in 1933 did I waver in my faith either in his ultimate integrity or in his basic direction."

❖ ❖ ❖

THE FUNERAL TRAIN BEARING the presidential casket left Warm Springs on Friday morning and arrived at Washington's Union Station more than twenty-four hours later on a sunny Saturday. A crowd of twenty-five thousand swelled outside the station. A solemn procession of dignitaries slowly boarded the train to pay their respects to the First Lady, beginning with the new President, followed by the Cabinet, and then the Supreme Court Justices. When Truman entered the train, he deliberately flanked himself with former Vice President (and now Secretary of Commerce) Henry Wallace on one side and former Justice Jimmy Byrnes on the other—a sign of unity after the vice-presidential battle the preceding summer. If the vice-presidential contest had unfolded differently, reported one wire service, "the new President of the United States...might have been Henry A. Wallace, James F. Byrnes,...or perhaps William O. Douglas."

The cortege snaked through the Washington streets, where a hushed crowd of five hundred thousand lined the route, many in tears and anguish. Six horses drew the caisson carrying FDR's body, with a seventh horse in front. The procession stopped silently in front of the Capitol for several minutes and then resumed its trek to the White House. Members of the military accompanied the procession, including a company of African American soldiers and a group of women auxiliary forces from all three branches of the armed forces. One reporter noted that, in the "long line of cars" behind the caisson, Justice Frank Murphy sat with "eyes red-rimmed, face infinitely sad."

At 4 p.m. on Saturday, in the East Room of the White House, the Right Reverend Angus Dunn, the Episcopal Bishop of Washington, presided at a twenty-three-minute funeral service. Those in attendance were invited guests—ambassadors, Cabinet secretaries, Roosevelt's family and friends, members of the House and Senators, and all nine Supreme Court Justices.

At 10 p.m. that evening, the presidential train headed to Hyde Park. The Justices were on board. As the train rolled north toward the President's lifelong home, rows of onlookers solemnly greeted it, lining the tracks and standing by bonfires in the evening air. When the morning dawned, Attorney General Biddle and his wife, writer Katherine Garrison Chapin, joined Chief Justice Stone in the train's dining car for breakfast, gazing out at the Hudson River as the train steamed through New York State.

At 8:40 a.m. Sunday, following a journey beset by delays and layovers, the train pulled into Hyde Park. Later that morning, three hundred mourners gathered in the garden for the burial ceremony. Administration officials and members of Congress assembled on the east side of the grave, Supreme Court Justices on the west side. Other visitors, including local neighbors who had known the President and his family, hovered nearby. West Point cadets fired their rifles into the air for three volleys; FDR's dog Fala barked after each. After a twenty-one-gun salute fired by howitzers, the body of Franklin Delano Roosevelt, the thirty-second President of the United States, was lowered into the burial spot that he had long ago selected at Hyde Park—"where the sundial stands in the garden."

As soon as the presidential train headed back to Washington, the passengers jockeyed for position with the new President. "On the return trip," Jackson noted, "politics began to buzz. There was much rushing about by those who had political axes to grind.... The subdued tone of the train changed considerably on the return trip. The loyalties of politicians shift quickly." Jackson recounted that he "visited with Justice Roberts, Justice Reed, Chief Justice Stone, and Justice Frankfurter"—a list that conspicuously omits the four Justices that Frankfurter called the Axis (Black, Douglas, Murphy, and Rutledge). Jackson also included a jab at Douglas: "Brother Douglas was sent for by former Vice President Wallace and was exceedingly busy on conferences."

The political maneuvering continued until the train rolled into Washington's Union Station that Sunday evening. One man had clearly emerged as a close adviser and confidant of the new President: former Justice Jimmy Byrnes. He had resigned from the Roosevelt Administration only a few weeks previously, but suddenly he was inseparable from

Truman. Attorney General Biddle recalled in his memoir that Byrnes "clung to [Truman] as if... afraid that he might be captured by someone else." Within weeks, Truman would name Byrnes as his new Secretary of State.

The day after the return to Washington, on Monday, April 16, Harry Truman addressed a joint session of Congress for the first time as President. His wife Bess and daughter Margaret were in the gallery; the crowd included Representatives, Senators, and foreign diplomats, headed by the British Foreign Minister Anthony Eden and Soviet Ambassador Andrei Gromyko. As at FDR's speeches, the Justices sat in a row at the front of the packed House chamber, all except Frank Murphy, who was in New York receiving an award from a Jewish organization for his efforts at promoting brotherhood.

Truman made clear that he would continue Roosevelt's policies, foreign and domestic. He pledged to follow FDR's requirement of "unconditional surrender" by the Axis enemies. The cheering audience interrupted his speech with applause thirteen times.

Amid the adulation, some in the audience still appeared shell-shocked about the loss of FDR. One syndicated columnist reported that several Justices seemed "obviously nervous and upset. Felix Frankfurter clasped and unclasped his patrician fingers. Justices Hugo Black, William O. Douglas, and Wiley Rutledge shifted in their seats uneasily. The expressions on their faces were black.... The black-robed New Deal judges enjoyed close relationships with President Roosevelt, and they tried to carry out his wishes. Now they seem to feel themselves in eclipse, personally and judicially."

At least one Justice confided that, along with grief, he felt newly liberated. According to Frankfurter's private memo to his file, Reed told Frankfurter that the change would greatly affect him. "After all," Reed said with a grave face and a low voice, "Roosevelt was trying to further the things that I am interested in. And naturally I wanted to help him and not hinder him in matters that came before the Court, and I have found it very difficult not to decide things in the way in which I think he would be helped, and I, myself, as a result of his death, feel very much more free and expect to be much more free in the future."

Perhaps creating a record for posterity, Frankfurter stated in his memo that he told Reed, "I really do not know what you are talking about. It never occurred to me when I was working on a case to think about Roosevelt. Or, if I had thought about him, to care what he would think." Notably, even in his vehement denial, Frankfurter felt the need to argue in the alternative—to say that, "if he *had*" thought of FDR's reaction, he would not have let it affect him. It may have been a classic example of protesting too much.

TENSIONS BOILED AT THE Supreme Court in the spring of 1945. Even seemingly prosaic events—an awards dinner, a letter of appreciation—became fiercely contested battlegrounds.

The week before FDR's death, the Southern Conference for Human Welfare, a liberal organization promoting progressive change in the South, awarded Black its annual Thomas Jefferson Award at a festive dinner at the Statler Hotel in Washington. Eleanor Roosevelt spoke, and Majority Leader Alben Barkley read an adulatory letter from the President. Four Justices attended with Black—Douglas, Murphy, Rutledge, and Reed. But four others—Stone, Frankfurter, Jackson, and Roberts—refused to participate. Jackson privately excoriated the dinner. He thought it "grossly improper." In the "old days," if a "big business association" had feted a Justice for his pro-business views, "every liberal in the country would have screamed his head off over it." He acidly noted that three of the dinner "sponsors" were lawyers with cases before the Supreme Court. A friend wrote Frankfurter commending him for not attending and stating that "the perfume of public praise from people who ought to know better cannot eliminate the odor of the skunk."

Owen Roberts decided that he had had enough. He had grown increasingly alienated and disaffected, dissenting 30 percent of the time in the 1944 term, nearly twice as often as any other Justice. And he had become distrustful of some of his colleagues. On three occasions in 1944 and 1945, syndicated columnist Drew Pearson correctly predicted the outcome of pending Supreme Court cases. Roberts became convinced that Douglas, or perhaps Murphy, was leaking to Pearson, a breach that infuriated and embittered him.

On June 30, 1945, Roberts sent President Truman a letter of resignation, effective July 31. His letter noted that that he was now seventy and had served fifteen years; he would take advantage of retirement benefits provided by Congress in 1937 for Justices reaching that age and level of service.

Stone circulated a routine draft letter on behalf of the Justices, wishing Roberts well. But Black objected to two statements in Stone's draft—apparently innocuous comments that Roberts's "fidelity to principle" had been his "guide to decisions" and that the Justices regretted the end to their "association" with him. Black's proposed deletions incensed Jackson and Frankfurter. They refused to sign the letter if Black's changes were made, and Black refused to sign the letter without his changes. In the end, the Justices sent no farewell missive to Roberts.

One issue that roiled the Court internally in the spring of 1945 involved an obscure case that would generate an intensely personal confrontation between Jackson and Black, with Jackson accusing Black of a possible conflict of interest and Black feeling aggrieved at the challenge to his honor. The case, *Jewell Ridge Coal Corporation v. Local No. 6167, United Mine Workers of America*, presented the question whether a miner's travel time getting to a mine site counted as compensable work time under the Fair Labor Standards Act, a hotly disputed matter between the union and the mining companies. The Court voted 5–4 for the union; Black, the senior Justice in the majority, assigned the opinion to Murphy. As the decision writing unfolded, three points irked Jackson. First, in Jackson's view, as a Senator, Black had expressed a contrary position about the law to the one he favored now, which boosted the union. Second, when Murphy told Jackson that Black was hurrying him to issue the *Jewell Ridge* decision, Jackson thought that Black was inappropriately trying to aid the United Mine Workers in its ongoing negotiations with mining companies. And third, Jackson was bothered by the fact that the union's lawyer in the Supreme Court, Crampton Harris, had close ties to Black: he was Black's former law partner and personal lawyer.

The Court's opinion ruling for the union came down on May 7, a few weeks after FDR's death. Writing for the four dissenting Justices, Jackson extensively quoted Black's senatorial comments. That was the only public inkling of the divisions within the Court. The company's lawyers then filed a petition arguing that Black should not have participated in the case in light of his past relationship with Crampton Harris. Stone initially thought a brief statement by the Court that recusal decisions are up to each individual Justice would be appropriate. But Black took umbrage, and Stone yielded. At a Court conference on June 16, however, Jackson announced that he viewed a statement explaining that other Justices have no control over whether an individual Justice sits in a case was essential; he wished to avoid the appearance that he had approved Black's participation. Black was furious. He vowed that any statement would be "a declaration of war." Jackson responded that he would not capitulate to Black's "bullying."

When the Court denied the company's rehearing petition on June 18, Jackson issued a brief concurrence emphasizing that recusal decisions were left to each individual Justice and that the Court had no authority over such individual decisions. While Jackson's language was cryptic, its meaning was clear: he was distancing himself and other Justices from any involvement in the decision about whether Black's participation had been proper. Frankfurter joined the Jackson concurrence.

Nothing further became public at that point, and it was little noticed. But the controversy would explode the following year.

IN 1945, ROBERT JACKSON left the Supreme Court for a year. On April 26, two weeks after FDR's death, Truman sent an emissary, FDR confidant Judge Samuel Rosenman, to visit Jackson in his Supreme Court chambers and ask if he would lead the prosecution for the United States of war criminals in a postwar international proceeding. The pathbreaking position would vindicate the principle of legal accountability for the horrors of the Nazi regime.

Jackson agreed to head the American team in the historic trials that would take place at Nuremberg. He felt strongly about the undertaking and its importance. Jackson had been a leading voice urging FDR that Nazi leaders should be held responsible for war crimes in fair and orderly legal tribunals as an example to the world.

Jackson also later recalled that he "accepted this task because... there was a relief from the frustration at being in a back eddy with important things going on in the world." And he acknowledged that, "if internal matters at the court had been pleasant and agreeable, and if I had not already considered leaving the court, I probably would not have undertaken it. All things considered I didn't know but that it might prove to be a good exit from the court, and I wasn't at all sure that if I took it on I ever would return to the court."

Jackson plunged into preparations during the summer of 1945 and then decamped for Europe. He remained a Justice, although he was away the entire term beginning in October 1945. Stone, always skeptical of extrajudicial activities, was not pleased. He complained to a prominent lawyer, "Work, of course, is not any less because of Jackson's absence. Others must do his work in opinion writing, and cases in which the vote is four-to-four must be reargued or await his return." Even more caustically, Stone wrote a friend, "Jackson is over conducting his high-grade lynching party in Nu[rem]berg.... I don't mind what he does to the Nazis, but I hate to see the pretense that he is running a court or proceeding according to common law. That is a little too sanctimonious a fraud to meet my old-fashioned ideas."

GERMANY OFFICIALLY SURRENDERED ON May 7. Wild exuberance and joy erupted throughout the country. In Washington, crowds gathered everywhere—in Lafayette Park across from the White House; in front of the *Washington Post* building; around cars with radios blaring. At night, lights illuminated the Capitol dome for the first time since the blackout imposed on Pearl Harbor Day. The mood of "rejoicing" in the nation's capital, the *New York Times* noted, was accompanied by a "grim determination to fight on for quickest victory over Japan and for lasting peace."

Like all Americans, the Justices reveled in the victory. Speaking at a war bonds rally in Indianapolis, Douglas exulted, "We beat not only the German Army—we beat the Nazi idea." Black wrote his sons in the military, asking whether the triumph in Europe meant their military service now might end. And shortly before V-E Day, Stone jubilantly exulted to his son about the deaths of Mussolini and Hitler.

When Japan surrendered three months later, on August 14, the war was truly over. Black wrote to his wife of "the bedlam that broke loose last night immediately after Truman announced the Japanese surrender." The streets were filled with "racing, blowing cars," the joyful noises of celebration sounding in the night.

Truman joined the merriment. "Twenty minutes after he had announced the end of the war," reported the *Washington Post*, "President Truman walked out on the White House lawn with Mrs. Truman and waved to a crowd of ten thousand gathered along Pennsylvania Ave and Lafayette Park. The crowd gave the President and the First Lady a tremendous cheer. They waved flags, blew horns and rang cowbells in an ecstasy of joy."

Douglas again gave a speech punctuating the victory, this time to a Missouri bar association. "We beat [Japan]," he proclaimed. "...Let us be clear that, thanks to our victory, life for us can now be as good as we dare to make it."

WITH FDR'S DEATH, THE Justices had lost their patron and a man with whom they felt a close connection. Some tried to give Truman the benefit of the doubt or create a relationship with him as well. Reed had hosted Truman and his wife Bess at a dinner the night before FDR's fourth-term inauguration. Black, who had overlapped briefly with Truman in the Senate, was delighted by Truman's manner at a White

House dinner in August. He found Truman's "conduct as natural as it would have been in Independence, Missouri.... The country boy was at home. If he can keep this attitude, his success is certain." And although Frankfurter lacked a personal relationship with Truman, he continued his energetic efforts to affect Administration policies through intermediaries, such as his former student and close friend Dean Acheson, who had become Under Secretary of State. But it was nothing like the days of FDR.

On April 22, 1946, exactly one year and ten days after FDR's death, Chief Justice Harlan Fiske Stone sat in his usual seat at the center of the Supreme Court bench as he announced opinions. He began mumbling incoherently, and his fellow Justices rushed to help him and immediately adjourned the Court. Within hours, Stone died from a cerebral hemorrhage.

"Washington adores a funeral—especially if it ushers in a vacancy," Robert Jackson once wrote. Speculation about the new Chief Justice began immediately. Jackson himself was an early favorite. One commentator noted that he had "the inside track" and was "the logical choice." It was well known that FDR had told Jackson he would name him Chief after Stone's likely brief tenure. Truman had shown his regard for Jackson by appointing him to the Nuremberg position.

But soon after Stone's death, Drew Pearson wrote a column suggesting that, if Truman elevated Jackson to be Chief, two members of the Court would resign, a widely understood reference to Black and Douglas. Syndicated columnist Doris Fleeson likewise detailed what she called "the blood feud raging on the Supreme Court." Reprising the acrimony in the *Jewell Ridge* coal mining case, she reported that "Black and his friends" viewed Jackson's conduct as "reprehensible"—in their view, Jackson had launched an irresponsible personal attack—and that Black or Jackson would resign if the other became Chief.

More than four thousand miles away in Nuremberg, Jackson was furious. He already was under great pressure with the strains and challenges of the Nuremberg prosecutions. Jackson privately exploded at the columns and other rumors that reached him about a campaign by Black

and Douglas to deny him the Chief Justice position. His vehement reaction was driven partly by personal ambition, partly by personal pride,
and partly by stress from his isolation and the intensity in Germany. On
June 6, Truman announced his choice for the new Chief Justice: his
friend Treasury Secretary (and former congressman and federal judge)
Fred Vinson. Steering clear of both Black and Jackson, Truman was putting his own stamp on the Court.

The next day, Jackson sent Truman a private cable blasting Black
for his conduct in the mining case. When Truman declined Jackson's
request to make his cable public, Jackson sent a version of his diatribe
to the chairmen of the House and Senate Judiciary Committees and released it publicly. Jackson lambasted Black and detailed his concerns—
the involvement of Black's former law partner and lawyer; Black's
reversal from the position he had expressed in the Senate; and the
supposed pressure Black put on Murphy to release the decision hastily
(which had not previously been public). Declaring that such practices
threatened to bring the Court into "disrepute," Jackson vowed, "If it is
ever repeated while I am on the bench I will make my Jewell Ridge
opinion look like a letter of recommendation." Jackson also defended
his public attack on a fellow Justice. "If war is declared on me," he asserted, "I propose to wage it with the weapons of the open warrior, not
those of the stealthy assassin."

Jackson's cable received widespread publicity, with critical com-
mentary of both Jackson and Black. Black declined to respond publicly.
Truman wrote to his wife Bess, "I'm sure lucky I didn't appoint [Jackson]
Chief Justice. Wouldn't that have been a mistake!"

On June 20, 1946, the Senate confirmed Vinson by a voice vote.
The era of the Stone Court, begun on July 3, 1941, was officially over.
Stone's was the third-shortest tenure by a Chief Justice in American his-
tory and the briefest service by a Chief Justice since 1800.

❖ ❖ ❖

WHAT ACCOUNTS FOR THE rancor that developed on the Court? It arose
from three principal causes. First, substantive differences played an

important part. One wing of the Court—led by Frankfurter and Jackson, and often joined by Roberts and Reed—favored a limited role for the courts as the best response to the pre–New Deal Supreme Court abuses. Another wing of the Court—led by Black and Douglas, and often joined by Murphy and Rutledge—viewed the Court as an essential guarantor of constitutional rights and saw a broader role for the courts. For Black, the best jurisprudential response to the excesses of the pre–New Deal Court was a literal reading of the Constitution—a reading that, in his view, gave powerful and unassailable protections to every American. Stone, meanwhile, migrated between the two camps.

The Supreme Court can be a complex institution, sometimes varying according to cases and contexts, and these generalities did not universally hold. The civil libertarians Black and Douglas, for example, rejected Korematsu's claims, while Jackson and Roberts, along with Murphy, supported Korematsu. It was Jackson, moreover, who wrote the Court's iconic defense of civil liberties in wartime in *West Virginia State Board of Education v. Barnette*. But the generalization held in a number of cases, and it corresponded to the Justices' own views of their jurisprudential approaches.

The second major reason for the Court's divisions was the personalities of the Justices. Frankfurter, Black, Douglas, and Jackson were supremely ambitious and confident individuals, each certain that he should be the acknowledged leader on the Court. Frankfurter—the Austrian immigrant who became a leading authority on the Supreme Court and a trusted confidant of Brandeis and Holmes, and of the President. Black— the populist Senator who had wooed juries and voters. Douglas—the prodigy from rural Washington who rocketed to academic and public stardom and became a leading candidate for Vice President. Jackson— the savvy, self-styled country lawyer who dazzled in his time as Attorney General and Solicitor General. Each jockeyed for leadership, frequently disdaining one or another of his rivals.

Third, Harlan Fiske Stone was a weak Chief Justice. In those days, the Supreme Court generally held its case-deciding conferences on Saturdays. *Life* magazine profiled Stone and the other Justices in January

1945. The magazine reported that "the Saturday sessions" under Stone's predecessor Chief Justice Charles Evans Hughes "ended promptly at 4:30." But Stone, in contrast, was "a New England town-meeting democrat; he allows full discussion carrying on to Saturday night and the judges usually talk themselves into a session on Monday morning." Jackson later acknowledged that Stone "was not a very effective administrator." Douglas recalled conferences under Stone as "the great extreme of detail, long, lengthy discussions, almost interminable.... The thing went on and on and on." In addition to his unwieldy conferences, Stone lacked the skill of outstanding Chiefs to "mass the Court" (as Chief Justice William Howard Taft put it) for a particular outcome or opinion.

❖ ❖ ❖

BEYOND ITS INTERNAL SQUABBLES and its weak, if well-intentioned, Chief Justice, the War Court's legacy was profound. Forged amid the largest and most destructive war in human history, that legacy included some of the best and worst decisions since the founding of the republic.

On the negative side, the War Court is a cautionary tale about the problems of Justices being too close to the President who appointed them. In cases involving important war decisions by Franklin Roosevelt, the Justices were unwilling to confront him. In the Court's rush to judgment in *Ex parte Quirin*, they allowed accused Nazi saboteurs to be executed even though the Justices had not yet agreed on—or even figured out—the rationale for their decision. They knew that FDR had said he would defy a contrary judgment in the case; they so revered and admired him that they would not challenge him, even temporarily and even if the lack of a challenge meant failing to adhere to judicial principles.

Similarly, in *Hirabayashi* and *Korematsu*, the Justices refused to invalidate military conduct flowing from FDR's own executive order despite the discriminatory and unjust deprivations of liberty. To their great credit, Murphy, Jackson, and Roberts refused to go along with the majority—and with the President and his Administration—in *Korematsu*. But the pain and hardship inflicted by the other Roosevelt appointees was indelible and incalculable. Moreover, the Court's unanimous decision in *Endo* terminating indefinite detention, while welcome, did not begin to undo the damage wrought by *Hirabayashi* and *Korematsu*. And the Court's deliberate delay in releasing the *Endo* opinion to give the Roosevelt Administration time for stage-managed damage control further stained the Court's record on this shameful policy.

Particularly in our current era, when party affiliations correlate to Justices' positions and divisions more than at any time in our history, the War Court's failings send an important message. Justices must not be afraid to challenge the President who appointed them, even at the risk of alienating or infuriating that President or the President's supporters.

Of course, it was not only the Justices' deep affection for FDR that explains their posture on these war-related issues. Like almost all Americans, the Justices fervently supported the US contest against the Axis nations. The decisions in the Nazi saboteur case and Japanese American curfew and incarceration cases to some extent reflected the Justices' patriotic fervor. But, in that sense also, the Roosevelt Court is a cautionary tale—a story of excessive deference to the Executive Branch and its inflated claims of national security at times of severe national stress.

Even with these substantial failings, the War Court was an enormously consequential Court. It had a major impact in four areas of particular importance today: reproductive rights; voting rights; civil rights and civil liberties; and the constitutional authority of political branches to respond innovatively to evolving needs and crises. In all of these areas, the context of the war against fascist and authoritarian foes provided a vitally important backdrop. The Justices explicitly embraced American constitutional principles that stood in sharp contrast to their enemies.

The *Skinner v. Oklahoma* decision striking down forced sterilization is a landmark decision that set the Court on the path to reproductive freedom—a path that the current Court is abruptly jettisoning. In the present controversy, it is especially important to recall that a refusal to recognize constitutional protection in reproductive rights can logically permit forced sterilization as well as forced birth. In the wake of the Supreme Court's overruling of *Roe v. Wade*, the lessons of *Skinner* are more important than ever. The War Court recognized, in its equal-protection analysis, that an individual's freedom to determine whether to have a child is "a basic liberty" that a state legislature could not invade. The current Court has reached the opposite decision about reproductive choice (what it derided as the "right to procure an abortion")—a sharp, unwarranted, and tragic deviation from the War Court's insight.

The *Smith v. Allwright* decision invalidating the white primary was a momentous civil rights inflection point, launching a ten-year trajectory that culminated in *Brown v. Board of Education*. It is fitting, in light of the battle against fascism abroad and for civil rights at home, that Thurgood Marshall's sensational career as a Supreme Court advocate began and flourished in the war years, with his first major victory arriving in *Smith v. Allwright*. And here, too, the War Court's teaching is especially important at a time when the current Court drastically constricts judicially enforceable voting rights. In *Allwright*, the Court emphasized the Constitution's broad prohibition against racial discrimination in voting rights; in *Shelby County v. Holder* in 2013, the Supreme Court adopted an unprecedented, narrow, and stinting view of congressional authority on voting rights. The War Court's historic *Allwright* decision opened the doors of polling places for those who had been excluded; the current Court's *Shelby County* decision and subsequent voting rights opinions have shut them.

West Virginia State Board of Education v. Barnette, the decision rejecting a compulsory flag salute in public schools at the height of the war, is one of the most profound constitutional rights decisions ever issued by the Supreme Court. *Barnette* reflected a deep concern for the free-speech rights of unpopular and disfavored religious minorities. Here, too, at a time when religious protection under the Constitution seems increasingly tilted to favor majority religions and denominations, the War Court's protection for the despised religious-minority children in *Barnette* is a powerful and illuminating guidepost.

And finally, the War Court embraced a constitutional position of broad flexibility for government to innovate in response to new challenges—the doctrine that, perhaps more than any other, united the post-1937 Court. It is an approach as deeply rooted as Chief Justice John Marshall's exhortation in 1819 that "it is *a Constitution* we are expounding"—a Constitution that is "intended to endure for ages to come, and consequently to be adapted to the various crises of human affairs." As we face aggressive new Supreme Court doctrines choking the ability of government to respond to evolving circumstances, the War Court provides important lessons. The current Court has announced novel, far-reaching restrictions that put the Court aggressively back in the business of blocking government programs on issues ranging from public health in a pandemic to climate change; one example is the current Court's newly minted major questions doctrine, in which the Supreme Court will not permit the Executive Branch to address what the Court finds to be "major questions" unless Congress has legislated on that precise issue with great specificity. The War Court, in contrast, understood that, under the Constitution and its intentionally broad language, the government has wide and necessary latitude in addressing vexing social, economic, and administrative issues.

THE ROOSEVELT COURT FAILED badly in some of its wartime challenges. But, at a time when the fate of constitutional democracy hung in the balance, it issued pathbreaking decisions on issues from reproductive choice and voting rights to civil liberties and government structure. FDR's Justices built a legacy that, for all of its inconsistencies and serious imperfections, lit the path for the great achievements of three-quarters of a century after the war. It provided that the constitutional guarantees of liberty and equality would include the excluded, and it ensured that, as John Marshall emphasized, the general provisions of the Constitution would permit bold and flexible government innovations.

On all fronts, that vision is under fire. For all of the War Court Justices' shortcomings and feuds, as we face the current constitutional crossroads, we would do well to heed their insights on these fundamental issues. Now as then, the character of our constitutional democracy depends on it.

EPILOGUE

T HE WAR COURT JUSTICES LEFT VARYING LEGACIES.
Frank Murphy and Wiley Rutledge had their Supreme Court
service cut short by untimely deaths. Murphy died at fifty-nine in Detroit
in July 1949 of a coronary thrombosis after illness and hospitalizations.
His legacy remains that of a Justice who had a powerful social-justice
framework but whose shortcomings in judicial craft kept him from the
upper tier of Justices.

In August 1949, Wiley Rutledge suffered a stroke in Ogunquit, Maine,
slumping over the steering wheel while driving his wife home from a pot-
luck supper at a local church. He died two weeks later. Rutledge was only
fifty-five. When FDR appointed him in 1943, one of Rutledge's appealing
characteristics for FDR was his youth and expected longevity. But in the
end, he had the briefest tenure of any FDR Justice except Byrnes.

One of the least-known Justices, Rutledge emerged as a thought-
ful, careful, and insightful Justice, and his opinions continue to instruct.
One Rutledge dissent became a foundation of the Court's later opinion that Guantanamo detainees were entitled to judicial review of their

imprisonment—in an opinion by Rutledge's former clerk, Justice John Paul Stevens.

Four years after FDR's death, with the passing of Murphy and Rutledge and the appointment of their successors, Truman had filled four Supreme Court vacancies (the seats left by Roberts, Stone, Murphy, and Rutledge)—nearly half the Court.

ON MARCH 30, 1954, Robert Jackson, sixty-two years old, suffered a heart attack, leading to an extended hospital stay. Jackson left his hospital bed on May 17 to join his fellow Justices for the public announcement of the momentous unanimous decision in *Brown v. Board of Education*. Later that year, Jackson died of a second heart attack.

Through the power of his pen and his mind, Jackson ranks as one of the Court's most influential members. Current Justices ranging from John Roberts to Elena Kagan have praised him as an inspiration in their confirmation hearings. Drawing on his knowledge and experience as Attorney General and Solicitor General, Jackson wrote an iconic concurrence in 1952 about the scope and limits of presidential power. In that case, the Supreme Court ruled against Truman in a high-profile showdown over Truman's seizure of the nation's steel mills. For decades, Jackson's eloquent and incisive separate opinion has provided the governing legal framework for the Supreme Court's analysis of the President's authority in our constitutional system.

STANLEY REED RETIRED FROM the Court in 1957. Although he had written the opinion striking down the all-white primary, Reed clung to some of the racial attitudes of his Kentucky upbringing. In *Brown v. Board of Education*, Reed was the Court's last holdout. But the new Chief Justice, Earl Warren, masterfully steered the Court to unanimity and eventually brought even Reed on board. Reed died in 1980 at the age of ninety-five, living his last year in a Long Island nursing home.

Former FDR Justice James Byrnes also played a significant role in *Brown v. Board of Education*. Byrnes was elected Governor of South Carolina in 1950; he had left his position as Truman's Secretary of State in 1947. One of the five school-segregation cases in *Brown* came from South Carolina. Throughout the *Brown* litigation and its aftermath, Byrnes ardently defended the constitutionality and desirability of segregation. It seems very likely that, if he had remained on the Court, *Brown* would have lost its unanimity, a powerful and important message in that landmark decision. Byrnes, the "Assistant President" who so desperately wanted to be FDR's running mate, became a vigorous supporter of Richard Nixon's 1960 presidential campaign, Barry Goldwater's 1964 presidential campaign, and Nixon's 1968 campaign. He died in 1972.

IN 1965, FELIX FRANKFURTER lay on his deathbed. He had retired from the Supreme Court in 1962 after suffering a stroke—triggered, some thought, by Frankfurter's outrage at the Warren Court's *Baker v. Carr* decision, which led to a judicially enforceable one-person, one-vote constitutional command. On his deathbed, Frankfurter clutched the hand of Max Freedman, a historian editing a volume of Frankfurter's correspondence with FDR, and implored, "Tell the whole story. Let people see how much I loved Roosevelt, how much I loved my country, and let them see how great a man Roosevelt really was." He was a Roosevelt man, first and foremost, to the very end. He died two days later.

Frankfurter came to be viewed as a conservative on the Court, staunchly opposing what he saw as judicial intrusion on the political branches, regardless of the issue. Frankfurter's legacy, which includes notable leadership on civil rights issues, is complex. It contains significant blind spots, such as in his vehement attack on *Baker v. Carr* itself. But today, with a newly aggressive Supreme Court, some have expressed a renewed interest in Frankfurter's hands-off approach.

HUGO BLACK AND WILLIAM O. Douglas served until the 1970s. The two allies splintered toward the end.

Black, Roosevelt's first court pick, hewed to his plain-text interpretation of the Constitution. In some respects, Black was an originalist and a textualist long before Justices Antonin Scalia and Clarence Thomas. But in much of Black's career, originalism and textualism took him to conclusions very different from those of the later exponents of originalism—conclusions that often aligned with rights expansion rather than rights constriction. During the protests and disturbances of the 1960s, he sometimes dissented from the Warren Court's expansive decisions on constitutional rights and civil liberties, as in his disagreement with the Court's opinion upholding the First Amendment right of students protesting the Vietnam War to wear black armbands to school. Black retired in poor health in September 1971 and died eight days later.

Douglas, meanwhile, moved in the other direction, becoming evermore liberal and iconoclastic. Truman offered Douglas the Cabinet post of Secretary of the Interior and then the vice-presidential slot on his 1948 ticket, a role which Douglas had coveted in 1944. With Henry Wallace challenging on his left flank, Truman sought a well-respected liberal associated with FDR, and Douglas fit the bill. But Douglas turned down both offers, convinced he should be President. Douglas scornfully told friends regarding Truman's vice-presidential offer that he did not "want to play second fiddle to a second fiddle."

Douglas served until 1975. He was a quick thinker and a quick writer—too quick, in the eyes of his detractors. Though widely criticized for the superficiality of some of his opinions, Douglas became a leading defender of civil liberties and environmental protection. In his final year on the Court, Douglas suffered from illness and erratic behavior. The other Justices privately refused to decide cases if Douglas's vote would provide the fifth in a 5–4 case. Douglas survived until 1980, cared for by his fourth wife Cathy Douglas, who was four decades younger than him, a waitress when she met him who became a prominent lawyer in her own right. At thirty-six years on the Court, Douglas reigns as the longest-serving Justice in the nation's history.

❖ ❖ ❖

SHORTLY BEFORE AMERICA ENTERED World War II, FDR articulated the Four Freedoms that would famously inspire the nation in its global struggle: freedom of speech and expression; freedom of worship; freedom from want; and freedom from fear.

Although the War Court sometimes failed to maintain adequate independence from the much-loved President, and although at times it faltered badly in fulfilling its constitutional responsibilities, at its best, it provided a constitutional framework that furthered and enabled the Four Freedoms. At the height of nationalistic and patriotic fervor, the Court, at least in some cases, ensured constitutional protection for unpopular speakers, religions, and races. Crucially, it also assured constitutional flexibility for federal, state, and local governments to provide freedom from want and freedom from fear. And when the War Court abysmally failed to protect fundamental freedoms in *Korematsu*—a monumental injustice that cannot be ignored or whitewashed—the dissenting voices of Justices Murphy, Jackson, and Roberts powerfully bore witness and eventually won the historical argument.

The principles that the War Court, at its finest, articulated and enforced should continue to be, in Robert Jackson's words, a fixed star in our constitutional constellation.

Acknowledgments

It is said that every book is a journey. My companions on this trek have been extraordinary.

The friends of a lifetime generously shared time and encouragement, as well as invaluable comments on drafts. Jon Alter, John Barrett, David McKean, Pete Romatowski, Michael Waldman, and many others—thank you. I could not have made this trip without you.

Several people provided rich insights in interviews and conversations. I especially want to thank George Hutchinson, the eighteen-year-old Supreme Court aide who saw armed soldiers burst into the Court the day after the Pearl Harbor attack, and Jim Rowe, an esteemed Washington lawyer who is immensely knowledgeable about his father's heroic fight to prevent incarceration of Japanese Americans. A special word of gratitude to the late, great Justice John Paul Stevens, my former boss and my lifelong inspiration. He strongly encouraged me to write this book and shared his memories of clerking for Justice Wiley Rutledge soon after the war, in the 1947 Supreme Court term.

My professional home now is Georgetown Law School, an exceptional place to teach and write. Dean Bill Treanor and the entire faculty have been welcoming and supportive. Two of my colleagues, Victoria Nourse and Brad Snyder, have written powerful and definitive books on fundamental aspects of the War Court—the *Skinner v. Oklahoma* sterilization case and the life of Felix Frankfurter, respectively. I have benefited greatly from their work and their insights.

The Georgetown Law Library personnel, under the direction of Library Director Austin Williams, were outstanding. Suzanne Miller skillfully and tenaciously ferreted out hard-to-find information and documents. Thanh Nguyen also was enormously helpful and resourceful. I benefited from a dream team of student research assistants: in order of their work on the book, Kerry Walsh, Austin Beaudoin, Aaron Cheese, Lauren Manning, Shaun Rogers, Evan Crumb, and Abby West. They made crucial contributions, and I am deeply grateful.

Many research institutions house extensive collections on the Justices during the war years, including the Library of Congress; the National Archives; the Supreme Court; the Franklin D. Roosevelt Presidential Library and Museum in Hyde Park, New York; the Harry S. Truman Presidential Library and Museum in Independence, Missouri; the University of Michigan's Bentley Historical Library; the University of Kentucky's Special Collections Research Center; and Whitman College. Their dedicated employees were responsive and unstinting.

I am especially indebted to three remarkable professionals. My agent, Rafe Sagalyn, and my editor, Clive Priddle, enthusiastically supported this book from the first time I mentioned it. They both provided helpful ideas and welcome suggestions when I most needed them. Nancy Buckner, my colleague from my former professional home at Skadden, Arps, Slate, Meagher & Flom, played an indispensable role from the very beginning to the very end, always with her characteristic skill, calm, and joy.

Katie Dunn expertly identified and secured historical photos, and Franz Jantzen of the Supreme Court Curator's office generously shared his encyclopedic knowledge and insights. Several people played a key role in the final stages of this book, including Kiyo Saso, Melissa Raymond, Katie Carruthers-Busser, and Erin Granville of PublicAffairs.

On this journey, as on all others, my most important fellow travelers have been my family: Sarah and Michele and our grandson Henry, Annie and Allie, and Nick. Through it all, they cheerfully indulged—and even at times encouraged—my never-ending conversations on the War Court and its Justices.

And the greatest thanks, of course, goes to my wife, Mary Lou Hartman. She helped in every possible way, including providing wisdom, insights, and suggestions. She even arranged a "vacation" for us at the FDR Library in Hyde Park and joined in the research. This book, like everything else in my life, would be unimaginable without her.

Notes

PROLOGUE

5   **"marble palace"**: Peter Edson, "Supreme Court Hearing Case of Indigent Man Jailed for Bringing Poor Friend in California," *Burlington (VT) Daily News*, October 30, 1941, 6; "Stone's Fight for Liberalism Astounded Erstwhile Critics," *Washington Post*, June 13, 1941, 8.

5   **armed soldiers**: George Hutchinson, author interview, November 12, 2019.

7   **It heard the *Barnette* case**: The family's name was "Barnett"; it was misspelled "Barnette" in the Supreme Court and in other judicial decisions in the litigation. Jeffrey S. Sutton, 51 *Imperfect Solutions: States and the Making of American Constitutional Law* (Oxford University Press, 2018), 139. See *Barnette v. West Virginia Board of Education*, 47 F. Supp. 251 (S.D. W. Va. 1942); *West Virginia State Board of Education v. Barnette*, 319 U.S. 624 (1943). For consistency with the Supreme Court's opinion, the judicial spelling is used in this book.

7   **"fixed star in our constitutional constellation"**: *West Virginia State Board of Education v. Barnette*, 319 U.S. 624, 642 (1943).

8   **"Discrimination which would ordinarily be abhorrent"**: *Rottenberg v. United States*, 137 F.2d 850, 858 (1st Cir. 1943) (describing the Supreme Court's decision in *Hirabayashi v. United States*, 320 U.S. 81 (1943)), affirmed, *Yakus v. United States*, 321 U.S. 414 (1944).

8   **"war is an aggregation of hardships"**: *Korematsu v. United States*, 323
     U.S. 214, 219 (1944).

8   **"one-footed chicken thief"**: David L. Franklin, "Origin Story," *Slate*,
     June 29, 2015, https://slate.com/news-and-politics/2015/06/gay-marriage
     -supreme-court-ruling-how-skinner-v-oklahoma-laid-the-foundation-for
     -obergefell-v-hodges.html.

CHAPTER 1

11   **teasingly called each other "Governor"**: Noah Feldman, *Scorpions: The
     Battles and Triumphs of FDR's Great Justices* (Hachette, 2010), 201.

11   **FDR had told Jackson**: Alpheus Thomas Mason, *Harlan Fiske Stone: Pil-
     lar of the Law* (Viking, 1956), 567.

12   **recommended that FDR elevate Justice Harlan Fiske Stone**: John D.
     Fassett, *New Deal Justice: The Life of Stanley Reed of Kentucky* (Vantage,
     1994), 300–301; Mason, *Harlan Fiske Stone*, 566.

13   **"you mothers and fathers"**: Charles Hurd, "Roosevelt Says He Seeks to
     Supply 12,000 Planes, Other Arms, to Britain; Willkie Doubts His Anti-
     War Pledge," *New York Times*, October 31, 1940, 1.

13   **Gallup poll in April 1941**: Andrew Nagorski, *1941: The Year Germany
     Lost the War* (Simon and Schuster, 2019), 117.

13   **"On personal grounds...as Chief Justice"**: Mason, *Harlan Fiske Stone*,
     566–567. Frankfurter wrote a memo of the conversation from notes he
     made immediately following it. Mason, *Harlan Fiske Stone*, 857n12.

14   **FDR met with Stone and Jackson**: Mason, *Harlan Fiske Stone*, 567; "June
     10th, 1941," Franklin D. Roosevelt Day by Day (website), Pare Lorentz
     Center, FDR Presidential Library, accessed March 16, 2023, http://www
     .fdrlibrary.marist.edu/daybyday/daylog/june-10th-1941/.

14   **Public speculation predicted**: "Byrnes Great Help on Roosevelt Bills," *New
     York Times*, June 13, 1941, 3; William V. Nessly, "Chief Justice Hughes Re-
     tires July 1; Jackson Most Likely Successor," *Washington Post*, June 3, 1941, 1.

14   **floor manager at the 1940 Democratic convention**: Robert C. Albright,
     "A Great Dissenter Becomes Chief Justice in the Supreme Court's New
     Era of Liberalism," *Washington Post*, June 15, 1941, B9.

14   **"The lend-lease law came through"**: Joseph Alsop and Robert Kintner,
     "Byrnes and the Court," *Washington Post*, March 30, 1941, B5.

14   **"We talked about it in his library"**: Roger K. Newman, *Hugo Black: A
     Biography* (Fordham University Press, 1997), 312.

14   **participated even more extensively**: Brad Snyder, *Democratic Justice:
     Felix Frankfurter, the Supreme Court, and the Making of the Liberal Es-
     tablishment* (W. W. Norton, 2022), 373; Sidney Fine, *Frank Murphy: The
     Washington Years* (University of Michigan Press, 1984), 212.

15   **Byrnes ridiculed:** Edwin B. Haakinson, "Byrnes Passed Up Many High Honors Before Accepting Supreme Court Berth," *Washington Post*, June 13, 1941, 8. Lindbergh's Lend-Lease testimony is discussed in A. Scott Berg, *Lindbergh* (G. P. Putnam's Sons, 1998), 413–416.

15   **"All three appointments were received":** Hedley Donovan, "Stone Named Chief Justice, Bench Filled," *Washington Post*, June 13, 1941, 1.

15   **Stone and Jackson also were promptly confirmed:** "Jackson's Nomination Is Confirmed," *Washington Post*, July 8, 1941, 16. The *Washington Post* noted that, during the voice vote, "a single 'no' was shouted by Senator Tydings (Democrat), Maryland, who fought confirmation in committee and on the floor." Tydings had a grudge against Jackson over the handling of a Justice Department matter.

16   **"switch in time that saved nine":** John Q. Barrett has documented the obscure origin of the phrase, which quickly became pervasive. John Q. Barrett, "Attribution Time: Cal Tinney's 1937 Quip, 'A Switch in Time'll Save Nine,'" *Oklahoma Law Review* 73 (2021): 229–243.

16   **helped take the wind out of the sails:** Laura Kalman has challenged conventional wisdom about FDR's Court-packing plan, including the view that it was doomed to failure (either initially or after Roberts's switch) and that it reflected hubris by FDR. Laura Kalman, *FDR's Gambit: The Court Packing Fight and the Rise of Legal Liberalism* (Oxford University Press, 2022).

16   **It provided full retirement benefits:** William V. Nessly, "Chief Justice Hughes Retires July 1; Jackson Most Likely Successor," *Washington Post*, June 3, 1941, 1; Kalman, *FDR's Gambit*, 109–110, 264–265, 344n85; Judge Glock, "Unpacking the Supreme Court: Judicial Retirement, Judicial Independence, and the Road to the 1937 Court Battle," *Journal of American History* 106, no. 1 (2019): 47, 58–68.

16   **"All of his nominees":** "Our New Court," editorial, *Washington Post*, June 13, 1941, 16.

16   **Stone was sworn in:** Mason, *Harlan Fiske Stone*, 573–574; United Press, "Oath in Slacks," *Morning Post*, July 4, 1941, 5.

17   **country could "never survive":** FDR, radio address, July 4, 1941, transcript at "Radio Address of the President, F.D.R. Library, Hyde Park, July 4, 1941," Franklin D. Roosevelt Day by Day, Pare Lorentz Center, FDR Presidential Library, http://www.fdrlibrary.marist.edu/daybyday/resource /july-1941/.

17   **recitation of the pledge:** Associated Press, "Stone Leads Pledge," *Hartford Courant*, July 5, 1941, 2; "Greatest July 4 Program Yet Will Be Warning to Dictators; President to Speak, Stone Will Lead Oath of Allegiance," *Washington Post*, July 4, 1941, 1.

17   **Byrnes was sworn in:** Associated Press, "Justice Byrnes, Now," *Washington Post*, July 9, 1941, 7.

17   **Jackson's White House swearing-in:** International News Service, "The President's Day," *Washington Post,* July 12, 1941, 2.

18   **average age on the Court:** Associated Press, "Supreme Court Opens New Term," *Poughkeepsie (NY) Journal,* October 6, 1941, 12; Hedley Donovan, "Stone Named Chief Justice. Bench Filled," *Washington Post,* June 13, 1941, 1.

18   **judicial experience before joining the Court:** Alex R. George, Associated Press, "New Supreme Court Is Young, Beardless, Liberal," *Gettysburg Times,* October 1, 1941, 14.

18   **"whiskerless":** "New Court," *Sumter County (AL) Journal,* October 16, 1941, 1.

18   **"Young, Beardless, Liberal":** George, "New Supreme Court."

18   **private meeting:** International News Service, "President's Day," October 1, 1941, 3; "Timeline," Franklin D. Roosevelt Day by Day (website), Pare Lorentz Center, FDR Presidential Library, accessed January 25, 2023, http://www.fdrlibrary.marist.edu/daybyday/timeline/#1941-09-30.

18   **afternoon White House reception:** International News Service, "The President's Day: Supreme Court Tradition Upset," *Washington Post,* October 17, 1941, 2; "October 16th, 1941," Franklin D. Roosevelt Day by Day (website), Pare Lorentz Center, FDR Presidential Library, accessed January 25, 2023, http://www.fdrlibrary.marist.edu/daybyday/daylog/october-16th-1941/.

19   **Court's decision in *Edwards v. California*:** *Edwards v. California,* 314 U.S. 160 (1941).

19   **Twenty-seven other states:** Willis Thornton, "Yes, We Are One Country, One Nation," *Arizona Republic,* December 5, 1941, 26.

19   **"Poverty and immorality":** *Edwards,* 314 U.S. at 177.

19   **"The right of persons to move freely":** *Edwards,* 314 U.S. at 177 (Douglas, J., concurring).

20   **"a munificent bequest in a pauper's will":** *Edwards,* 314 U.S. at 186 (Jackson, J., concurring). Jackson's use of the phrase "a promise to the ear to be broken to the hope" echoes Shakespeare: Macbeth decries those who "keep the word of promise to our ear / And break it to our hope." William Shakespeare, *Macbeth,* act V, scene VIII.

20   **"non-democratic states...economic concentration camps":** Appellant's brief at 19, 21–23, *Edwards v. California,* 314 U.S. 160 (1941) (No. 588, 1940, and No. 17, 1941).

20   **"the suspicions, jealousies,...scheming and conniving":** Brief of John H. Tolan for the Select Committee of the House of Representatives to Investigate Interstate Migration of Destitute Citizens, at 43–45, *Edwards v. California,* 314 U.S. 160 (1941) (No. 17). Congressman Tolan participated

in the Supreme Court oral argument. "Banning of Indigents Argued in High Court," *Des Moines (IA) Register,* October 22, 1931, 11.

20 **"human rights are abridged"**: *New York Post* editorial, reprinted in "Be Proud You're American," *Daily Register* (Red Bank, NJ), December 4, 1941, 6.

20 **"un-American legislation"**: "Freedom to Move," editorial, *Washington Post,* November 26, 1941, 12.

20 **"Be Proud You're American"**: "Be Proud You're American," *Daily Register* (Red Bank, NJ), December 4, 1941, 6.

20 **"an unlimited national emergency"**: Franklin D. Roosevelt, "Fireside Chat 17: On an Unlimited National Emergency," speech, May 27, 1941, transcript and recording on Miller Center website, University of Virginia, https://millercenter.org/the-presidency/presidential-speeches/may-27 -1941-fireside-chat-17-unlimited-national-emergency.

21 **passed an extension**: Frederick R. Barkley, "House for 2½ Years Army Service by One Vote," *New York Times,* August 13, 1941.

21 **"unity of sentiment"**: Associated Press, "Justice Roberts Calls for Unity Behind Roosevelt," *Washington Post,* June 15, 1941, F7.

21 **"The Civil War settled slavery"**: Associated Press, "War Can Settle Much, Says Frankfurter," *Washington Post,* June 19, 1941, 3.

21 **"force must be met by force"**: "Reed Asks Nation for Defense Unity," *New York Times,* July 30, 1941, 8; Stanley Reed, "Bridgeport—Symbol of Working Democracy," 4–6, box 220, Stanley Forman Reed Papers, UK Libraries Special Collections Research Center, University of Kentucky.

21 **"We subscribe to every word"**: Associated Press, "Roberts Urges 'World Union to Force Peace,'" *Washington Post,* August 20, 1941, 2.

21 **"policy of aiding"**: Associated Press, "Murphy Calls on Catholics to Back Russia," *Washington Post,* August 20, 1941, 1; Frank Murphy, "The Greatest Danger," *Washington Post,* August 20, 1941, 7 (publication of Murphy's speech).

22 **"peaceably if we can, forcibly if we must"**: "Justice Black Warns Against Menace of Hitler and Axis Allies," *Birmingham News,* August 24, 1941, 10.

22 **"tickled to death"**: J. Woodford Howard Jr., *Mr. Justice Murphy: A Political Biography* (Princeton University Press, 1968), 253.

22 **"the sons of freedom"**: "Douglas Urges 'a Total Effort,'" *New York Times,* September 27, 1941, 8.

22 **"worth a tinker's damn"**: Associated Press, "Bar Told of Challenge in World Lawlessness," *Los Angeles Times,* October 3, 1941, 16.

22 **"served in the British Ambulance Corps"**: Elizabeth Henney, "Roosevelts Entertain Disabled War Veterans at Garden Party," *Washington Post,* May 23, 1941, 14. Jackson biographer John Barrett notes that the

Washington Post story about William Jackson may be inaccurate in light of a timeline of William Jackson's activities. Author conversation with John Q. Barrett, January 29, 2023.

23 **hosting three lively English children:** Snyder, *Democratic Justice*, 366–371; Matthew Josephson, "Profiles," *New Yorker*, December 14, 1940; Jon Meacham, *Franklin and Winston: An Intimate Portrait of an Epic Friendship* (Random House, 2003), 84; Joseph P. Lash, ed., *From the Diaries of Felix Frankfurter* (W. W. Norton, 1975), 193–194; Max Freedman, ed., *Roosevelt and Frankfurter: Their Correspondence, 1928–1945* (Little, Brown, 1967), 598.

23 **war relief efforts:** "Mrs. Stone Heads Yugoslav Group Formed Here," *Washington Post*, April 30, 1941, 14; "R.A.F. Fund to Get $16,000 from Arcade," *Washington Post*, April 6, 1941, 10; "Piccadilly Arcade," *Washington Post*, April 3, 1941, 10; "Bundles for Britain: Benefit Planned for British Relief at Erlebacher's," *Washington Post*, January 11, 1941, 26; Jessie Ash Arndt, "Organization Interested in Defense Needs, Local Problems," *Washington Post*, May 11, 1941, SA6.

23 **"What did we do with our time":** Lucia Giddens, "Seven American Women Respond to a Poem's Challenge," *Washington Post*, April 6, 1941, B6.

23 **Reporters raised the possibility:** Associated Press, "Daniels' Leave Causes Regret in Mexico City," *Tucson (AZ) Daily Citizen*, November 1, 1941, 2; W. H. Lawrence, "Murphy, President Discuss Far East," *New York Times*, July 19, 1941, 1; William V. Nessly, "Chief Justice Hughes Retires July 1; Jackson Most Likely Successor," *Washington Post*, June 3, 1941, 3.

23 **FDR and Murphy also directly discussed:** Fine, *Frank Murphy*, 207–212.

23 **serious conversations about Douglas leaving the Court:** Bruce Allen Murphy, *Wild Bill: The Legend and Life of William O. Douglas* (Random House, 2003), 191–196. One editorial in late 1941 noted that "Justice William O. Douglas is slated for a big defense job, inside Washington reports." "Justice Douglas Impatient," editorial, *Bradford (PA) Evening Star*, November 20, 1941, 1.

24 **Douglas met privately:** Murphy, *Wild Bill*, 195; "December 6th, 1941," Franklin D. Roosevelt Day by Day (website), Pare Lorentz Center, FDR Presidential Library, accessed January 25, 2023, http://www.fdrlibrary.marist.edu/daybyday/daylog/december-6th-1941/.

CHAPTER 2

25 **in his study on the second floor:** Nigel Hamilton, *The Mantle of Command: FDR at War, 1941–1942* (Houghton Mifflin, 2014), 53–55; Doris Kearns Goodwin, *No Ordinary Time: Franklin and Eleanor Roosevelt, The Home Front in World War II* (Simon and Schuster, 1994), 288–289.

25 **a relaxed Sunday lunch:** Roger K. Newman, *Hugo Black: A Biography* (Fordham University Press, 1997), 312–313; Harold Ickes, *The Secret Diary of Harold L. Ickes,* vol. 3, *The Lowering Clouds, 1939–1941* (Simon and Schuster, 1954), 661.

26 **"a deep sense of shock":** Robert H. Jackson, *That Man: An Insider's Portrait of Franklin D. Roosevelt,* ed. John Q. Barrett (Oxford University Press, 2003), 103.

26 **Frankfurter talked on the phone:** Brad Snyder, *Democratic Justice: Felix Frankfurter, the Supreme Court, and the Making of the Liberal Establishment* (W. W. Norton, 2022), 387–390.

26 **cheering on quarterback Sammy Baugh:** George Hutchinson, author interview, November 12, 2019.

26 **crowd outside the White House:** Scott Hart, "Crowds Gather at White House as News of Attack Spreads," *Washington Post,* December 8, 1941, 3.

27 **"If the President cannot get hold":** Max Freedman, ed., *Roosevelt and Frankfurter: Their Correspondence, 1928–1945* (Little, Brown, 1967), 626; Snyder, *Democratic Justice,* 389.

27 **"the whole American people are behind you":** Freedman, *Roosevelt and Frankfurter,* 625.

27 **"what's this about Japan":** Jon Meacham, *Franklin and Winston: An Intimate Portrait of an Epic Friendship* (Random House, 2003), 130. Churchill had served as First Lord of the Admiralty and FDR as Assistant Secretary of the Navy.

27 **Roosevelt met with his Cabinet:** Hamilton, *Mantle of Command,* 68–72; Goodwin, *No Ordinary Time,* 292–293.

28 **"I am amazed by the attack":** Hamilton, *Mantle of Command,* 72.

28 **anticipation built for the President's arrival:** "'We Will Gain the Inevitable Triumph,'" *Washington Post,* December 9, 1941, 12.

28 **unusual step of adjourning the Court:** *Journal of the Supreme Court of the United States,* October Term 1941, December 8, 1941, 86; Associated Press, "L.A. Times Wins Appeal to High Court," *Detroit Free Press,* December 9, 1941, 4.

28 **"Then through the door":** "Rep. Rankin Again Votes Against War," *Washington Post,* December 9, 1941, 2. Consistent with the press mores at the time, the article did not mention that FDR leaned on his son's arm because he could not walk.

29 **"Yesterday, December 7, 1941":** "The President's Message," *New York Times,* December 8, 1941, 1.

29 **Black wiped tears from his eyes:** "Rep. Rankin Again Votes."

29 **Within an hour:** "Rep. Rankin Again Votes."

30 **America First Committee announced:** "America First Acts to End Organization," *New York Times,* December 12, 1941, 22.

30   **Lindbergh stated that he no longer opposed the war:** "Isolation Groups Back Roosevelt," *New York Times*, December 9, 1941, 44.

30   **railroad case from Texas:** *Journal of the Supreme Court of the United States*, October Term 1941, December 8, 1941, 92 (argument in *Ex parte Texas*); *Ex parte Texas*, 315 U.S. 8 (1942).

30   **The Justices also announced eleven decisions:** *United States v. Kales*, 314 U.S. 186 (1941); *Pink v. A.A.A. Highway Express, Inc.*, 314 U.S. 201 (1941); *United States v. Kansas Flour Mills Corp.*, 314 U.S. 212 (1941); *Lisenba v. California*, 314 U.S. 219 (1941); *Parker v. Motor Boat Sales*, 314 U.S. 244 (1941); *Bridges v. California*, 314 U.S. 252 (1941); *Pierce v. United States*, 314 U.S. 306 (1941); *American Surety Company of New York v. Bethlehem National Bank*, 314 U.S. 314 (1941); *Textile Mills Securities Corp. v. Commissioner*, 314 U.S. 326 (1941); *United States v. Santa Fe Pacific Railroad Company*, 314 U.S. 339 (1941); *New York, Chicago & St. Louis Railroad Company v. Frank*, 314 U.S. 360 (1941).

30   **"It seems difficult to concentrate":** Newman, *Hugo Black*, 313.

30   **Harry Bridges and the *Los Angeles Times*:** *Bridges v. California*, 314 U.S. 252 (1941).

30   **"The legend that a 'packed' court":** "A Legend Dies," editorial, *St. Louis Star and Times*, December 16, 1941, 14.

31   **Frankfurter incessantly lobbied Reed:** John D. Fassett, *New Deal Justice: The Life of Stanley Reed of Kentucky* (Vantage, 1994), 314–317. Fassett describes the *Bridges* case, with Black's triumph and Frankfurter's bitter disappointment, as "a significant milestone for the FDR justices" (316).

31   **"a command of the broadest scope":** *Bridges v. California*, 314 U.S. at 263.

31   **"at a time when it is repudiated":** *Bridges v. California*, 314 U.S. at 290–291 (Frankfurter, J., dissenting).

31   **"We must be fastidiously careful":** *Bridges v. California*, 314 U.S. at 293 (Frankfurter, J., dissenting).

31   **"As I listened to the arguments":** James F. Byrnes, *All in One Lifetime* (Harper and Brothers, 1958), 147. Byrnes had the date of the *Bethlehem Ship Building* argument wrong: it took place on Tuesday, December 9, not Monday, December 8.

32   **"His appearance shocked me":** Byrnes, *All in One Lifetime*, 147–148. Byrnes stated that his meeting with FDR occurred on the morning after the *Bethlehem Ship Building* argument, which would have been on December 10. According to the presidential calendars, the only recorded meeting between FDR and Byrnes that week was on Thursday, December 11, at 11 a.m. "December 11th, 1941," Franklin D. Roosevelt Day by Day (website), Pare Lorentz Center, FDR Presidential Library, accessed January 25, 2023, http://www.fdrlibrary.marist.edu/daybyday/daylog/december-11th-1941/.

32   **Biddle reassured FDR:** Byrnes, *All in One Lifetime*, 148.

32 **"make such redistribution of functions":** First War Powers Act of 1941, Pub. L. No. 354, 55 Stat. 838 (1941).

33 **Byrnes played a major role:** Byrnes, *All in One Lifetime,* 148.

33 **"It was a very depressing time":** "The Reminiscences of Robert H. Jackson," Columbia Center for Oral History, p. 1000, located in Robert H. Jackson Papers, folder 2, box 191, Manuscript Division, Library of Congress, Washington, DC. Jackson recalled that the arguments in the two country club tax cases took place "the Monday after Pearl Harbor," but they actually occurred on the Friday after Pearl Harbor (December 12). The two cases were *White v. Winchester Country Club,* 315 U.S. 32 (1942), and *Merion Cricket Club v. United States,* 315 U.S. 42 (1942).

33 **"I take this occasion":** Robert Jackson to Franklin Roosevelt, December 29, 1941, folder 4, box 19, Robert H. Jackson Papers, Manuscript Division, Library of Congress, Washington, DC.

33 **"soberly confident voice":** Felix Frankfurter to Franklin Roosevelt, telegram, December 9, 1941, in Freedman, *Roosevelt and Frankfurter,* 626.

34 **"a good many talks":** Felix Frankfurter to Franklin Roosevelt, December 17, 1941, in Freedman, *Roosevelt and Frankfurter,* 628.

34 **"live in history":** Felix Frankfurter to Franklin Roosevelt, December 18, 1941, in Freedman, *Roosevelt and Frankfurter,* 632. FDR's condolence letter was addressed to a future President asking that the son of a soldier killed in the war be admitted to West Point.

34 **Christmas message from Dorothy Thompson:** Felix Frankfurter to Franklin Roosevelt, December 23, 1941, in Freedman, *Roosevelt and Frankfurter,* 633–635.

34 **"wish I was back in the islands":** International News Service, "Murphy Wishes He Were in Philippines Helping Their Fight," *Port Huron (MI) Times-Herald,* December 30, 1941, 1.

34 **"Show them that it matters not":** Associated Press, " 'Contest Every Foot,' Murphy Tells Manila," *Philadelphia Inquirer,* December 31, 1941, 1.

34 **neighborhood defense preparation meeting:** "Be on Guard Against Surprise Bombing Raids, Bolles Warns," *Washington Post,* December 16, 1941, 25; Jack Stinnett, "Washington Daybook," *High Point (NC) Enterprise,* December 27, 1941, 9.

34 **"We have no defense":** Harlan Fiske Stone to Marshall Stone and Lauson Stone, December 18, 1941, Harlan Fiske Stone Papers, folder 7, box 3, Manuscript Division, Library of Congress, Washington, DC.

35 **"If you don't want to bump into somebody":** Associated Press, "Tips for Blackout Victims," *Amarillo (TX) Daily News,* December 27, 1941, 10.

35 **"runs on black cloth":** Stinnett, "Washington Daybook."

35 **"For the first time since floodlighting was introduced":** Stinnett, "Washington Daybook."

35   **heavy curtains blocked windows:** Author interview with George Hutchinson, November 12, 2019.

36   **appointment of the Roberts Commission:** "Board Named to Investigate Pearl Harbor," *Baltimore Sun*, December 17, 1941, 1; United Press, "Justice Roberts Heads Pearl Harbor Probe," *Scranton (PA) Tribune*, December 17, 1941, 1; "December 16th, 1941," Franklin D. Roosevelt Day by Day (website), Pare Lorentz Center, FDR Presidential Library, accessed January 25, 2023, http://www.fdrlibrary.marist.edu/daybyday/daylog/december -16th-1941/; Snyder, *Democratic Justice*, 390. Stimson had recommended Roberts to FDR. Kenneth Kitts, *Presidential Commissions and National Security: The Politics of Damage Control* (Lynne Rienner Publisher, 2006), 35–36.

36   **new Commission on Pearl Harbor met for ninety minutes:** "Justice Roberts Heads Hawaiian Bombing Inquiry," *The Gazette* (Cedar Rapids, IA), December 17, 1941, 1; Lyle C. Wilson, "Hawaii Probe Board Named by F.D.R.," *Oshkosh (WI) Northwestern*, December 17, 1941, 1.

36   **"the President has named...commendable":** Hedley Donovan, "Justice Roberts Heads Pearl Harbor Inquiry Board," *Washington Post*, December 17, 1941, 1.

36   **subpoena power:** "Congress Approves Civilian Aid Funds," *New York Daily News*, December 20, 1941, 8.

36   **"The outstanding characteristic":** Jay Hayden, "Hawaii Investigation Board Free to Condemn Even F.D. In Findings," *Boston Globe*, December 18, 1941, 21.

37   **"the board of inquiry appointed":** "No More Pearl Harbors!," editorial, *St. Louis Post-Dispatch*, December 28, 1941, 24.

37   **"Selection of Roberts rocked the capital":** "Justice Roberts Heads Hawaiian Attack Inquiry," *New York Daily News*, December 17, 1941, 2.

37   **"Once a man ascends":** Frank R. Kent, "The Great Game of Politics," *Baltimore Sun*, December 19, 1941, 17. Kent was an influential columnist. He also was very close to FDR-loathing Alice Roosevelt Longworth— Theodore Roosevelt's daughter, Eleanor Roosevelt's first cousin, and a Washington fixture and acerbic gossip; Kent was rumored to be her lover. Theo Lippman Jr., "First One 'Inside the Beltway,'" *Baltimore Sun*, April 16, 1997, 2A.

37   **"You have probably seen":** Harlan Fiske Stone to Marshall Stone and Lauson Stone, December 18, 1941, Harlan Fiske Stone Papers, folder 7, box 3, Manuscript Division, Library of Congress, Washington, DC.

38   **Churchill was a guest:** Meacham, *Franklin and Winston*, 139–152; Goodwin, *No Ordinary Time*, 300–311.

38   **"nothing to conceal":** Robert E. Sherwood, *Roosevelt and Hopkins: An Intimate History* (Harper and Brothers, 1948), pp. 442–443. Doris Kearns

Goodwin notes that "accounts vary." According to Sherwood, Churchill denied it.

38   **"pink and white all over"**: Grace Tully, *F.D.R., My Boss* (Charles Scribner's Sons, 1949), 305.

38   **"pink cherub"**: Geoffrey C. Ward, ed., *Closest Companion: The Unknown Story of the Intimate Friendship Between Franklin Roosevelt and Margaret Suckley* (Simon and Schuster, 2009), 385.

38   **"For one night only"**: Meacham, *Franklin and Winston,* 147–148.

38   **joint session of Congress…glimpse of the Prime Minister:** Marquis W. Childs, "Congress Cheers Often as Churchill Speaks, but in Main Is Solemn," *St. Louis Post-Dispatch,* 2A; Richard L. Harkness, "Churchill's 'V for Victory' Salute Brings Wild Cheers in Capitol," *Philadelphia Inquirer,* December 27, 1941, 5.

39   **"The fact that my American forbears…will never forget?":** "Text of the Address of Prime Minister Churchill Before Congress on Our Joint War Effort," *New York Times,* December 27, 1941, 4; Robert C. Albright, "Alliance of U.S. and Britain Is Forecast After Victory Is Won," *Washington Post,* December 27, 1941, 1; Meacham, *Franklin and Winston,* 152–153. Meacham notes that Churchill's subsequent comments reflect self-awareness: Churchill said that, if he had been a member of Congress, "I should not have needed any invitation, but if I had, it is hardly likely it would have been unanimous. So perhaps things are better as they are." His statement also was a signal to his audience that he well understood the rough-and-tumble of a legislative body.

39   **"beat his hands together"**: Harkness, "Churchill's 'V for Victory' Salute."

39   **"fidgeted in his seat"**: "Few from State Hear Churchill," *Hartford Courant,* December 27, 1941, 3.

40   **raised his own hand:** United Press, "Churchill and Stone Signal V for Victory as Prime Minister Bids Congress Farewell," *New York Times,* December 27, 1941, 4; Robert De Vore, "Prime Minister Gives Sign of V While Congress Cheers Speech," *Washington Post,* December 27, 1941, 1; "Chief Justice Stone Exchanges Victory Sign with Premier," *St. Louis Post-Dispatch,* December 26, 1941, 1; Alpheus Thomas Mason, *Harlan Fiske Stone: Pillar of the Law* (Viking, 1956), 648.

CHAPTER 3

41   **services at Christ Church:** David Bercuson and Holger Herwig, *One Christmas in Washington* (Overlook, 2005), 204–205, 211–213.

41   **ceremony at Nuuanu Memorial Park:** "Day Dedicated to Memory of Fallen Heroes," *Honolulu Advertiser,* January 1, 1942, 1; "Tribute Paid to Memory of Isle Defenders," *Honolulu Star-Bulletin,* January 1, 1942, 8;

"Noted Visitors Join in Memorial Services," *Honolulu Advertiser*, January 2, 1942, 1; Associated Press, "Memorial Service in Hawaii For War Dead," *Helena (MT) Independent*, January 2, 1942, 2; "Honolulu Marks Memorial Day for Raid Victims," *Chicago Tribune*, January 2, 1942, 3; Associated Press, "Justice Roberts Lays Leis on Graves of War Dead to Chant of 'Aloha Oe,'" *St. Louis Post-Dispatch*, January 2, 1942, 1.

42 **Commissioners had arrived in Hawaii...morning of the attack:** Foster Hailey, "Civilians Asked to Aid Quiz on Pearl Harbor," *Washington Post*, January 6, 1942, 14; United Press, "Hearings Started on Pearl Harbor Attack," *Bakersfield Californian*, January 6, 1942; Associated Press, "Roberts Committee to Call Witnesses," *Valley Morning Star* (Harlingen, TX), January 6, 1942, 2; United Press, "Pearl Harbor Responsibility Is Determined," *Hanford (CA) Sentinel*, January 24, 1942, 1; International News Service, "Roberts Fixes Blame for Dec. 7," *Austin (TX) American-Statesman*, January 24, 1942, 1.

42 **Royal Hawaiian Hotel:** United Press, "Royal Hawaiian Leased by Navy," *Hawaii Tribune-Herald*, January 17, 1942, 1; Jay Jones, "At 90, Honolulu's Royal Hawaiian Resort Is Still Pink and Oh-So-Dreamy," *Los Angeles Times*, February 1, 2017.

42 **Owen Josephus Roberts...civil liberties issues:** Leon Friedman and Fred Israel, eds., *The Justices of the United States Supreme Court, 1789–1969: Their Lives and Major Opinions*, vol. 3 (Chelsea House, 1969), 2253–2263; Jay S. Bybee, "Owen J. Roberts," in *The Supreme Court Justices: Illustrated Biographies, 1789–1993*, ed. Clare Cushman (Congressional Quarterly, 1993), 366–370. As a general matter, many of the World War I–era Espionage Act prosecutions have come to be viewed as overly aggressive and inconsistent with principles of free speech. See Geoffrey Stone, *Perilous Times: Free Speech in Wartime* (W. W. Norton, 2004), 226–232.

43 **commanding courtroom presence:** Robert T. McCracken, "Owen J. Roberts—Master Advocate," *University of Pennsylvania Law Review* 104, no. 3 (1955): 322.

43 **White House meeting with Roberts and Pepper..."come to light":** Leslie E. Bennett, "One Lesson from History: Appointment of Special Counsel and the Investigation of the Teapot Dome Scandal," Brookings Institution, 1999, http://academic.brooklyn.cuny.edu/history/johnson/teapotdome.htm; M. R. Werner and John Starr, *Teapot Dome* (Viking, 1959), 153–154. Roberts and the prosecution team also received acquittals on some defendants. Bennett, "One Lesson from History."

44 **Supreme Court decisions regarding Teapot Dome:** *Mammoth Oil Co. v. United States*, 275 U.S. 13 (1927); *Sinclair v. United States*, 279 U.S. 749 (1929).

44 **"uncommonly good impression":** Bybee, "Owen J. Roberts," 367.

44   **ran into trouble in the Senate:** Richard L. Watson Jr., "The Defeat of
      Judge Parker: A Study in Pressure Groups and Politics," *Mississippi Valley
      Historical Review* 50, no. 2 (1963): 213–234; "To Advise and Consent to
      the Nomination of Judge John J. Parker as Associate Justice of Supreme
      Court," May 7, 1930, GovTrack, accessed January 27, 2023, www.govtrack
      .us/congress/votes/71-2/s321.

44   **One wing of the Court…Charles Evans Hughes:** Friedman and Israel,
      Justices of the United States, 3:1945–1953, 2023–2040, 2123–2143, 2183–
      2191; Clare Cushman, ed., *The Supreme Court Justices: Illustrated Biog-
      raphies, 1789–1993* (Congressional Quarterly, 1993), 286–290, 311–315,
      326–330, 331–335, 346–355, 361–365, 371–375.

45   **Roberts votes in opinions:** *Morehead v. New York ex rel. Tipaldo*, 298
      U.S. 587 (1936); *West Coast Hotel Co. v. Parrish*, 300 U.S. 379 (1937); *Na-
      tional Labor Relations Board v. Jones & Laughlin Steel Corp.*, 301 U.S. 1
      (1937).

45   **Roberts later contended:** Felix Frankfurter, "Mr. Justice Roberts," *Univer-
      sity of Pennsylvania Law Review* 104, no. 3 (1955): 313–316; Brad Snyder,
      *Democratic Justice: Felix Frankfurter, the Supreme Court, and the Making
      of the Liberal Establishment* (W. W. Norton, 2022), 274–275. After Rob-
      erts's death, Frankfurter publicly defended him against the claim that he
      had "switched" his vote to defuse the Court-packing controversy. Frank-
      furter, "Mr. Justice Roberts," 313–316.

45   **legal historians debate:** Barry Cushman, "The Hughes-Robert Visit," *Green
      Bag* 15, no. 2 (2012): 125–137; Daniel R. Ernst, "The Hughes-Roberts Visit
      Revisited," *Green Bag* 18, no. 1 (2014): 5–11; and Barry Cushman, "Inter-
      preting Secretary Perkins," *Green Bag* 18, no. 1 (2014): 13–25.

46   **"Black Tom" disputes:** John J. McCloy, "Owen J. Roberts' Extra Curiam
      Activities," *University of Pennsylvania Law Review* 104, no. 3 (1955): 350;
      Sam Roberts, "An Attack That Turned Out to Be German Terrorism Has a
      Modest Legacy 100 Years Later," *New York Times*, July 24, 2016.

46   **"the towering figure…to the very end":** McCloy, "Owen J. Roberts' Ex-
      tra Curiam Activities," 351.

47   **"the most forthright of men":** Max Freedman, ed., *Roosevelt and Frank-
      furter: Their Correspondence, 1928–1945* (Little, Brown, 1967), 644.

47   **Roberts met with FDR:** "January 18, 1942," Franklin D. Roosevelt Day
      by Day (website), Pare Lorentz Center, FDR Presidential Library, ac-
      cessed January 25, 2023, http://www.fdrlibrary.marist.edu/daybyday/daylog
      /january-18th-1942/.

47   **session with reporters:** Arthur Sears Harding, "Pearl Harbor Report Is
      Near, Says President," *Chicago Tribune*, January 24, 1942, 1.

47   **He and the president met:** Associated Press, "Pearl Harbor Report Given
      to Roosevelt," *Sheboygan (WI) Press*, January 24, 1942, 1; William S.

White, "Roberts Says Pearl Harbor Received Ample Warning," *New York Times*, January 29, 1946, 1.

47   **"running commentary"**: White, "Roberts Says," 1.

47   **"what reasons the officers out there"**: White, "Roberts Says," 1.

47   **the entire report:** *Attack upon Pearl Harbor by Japanese Armed Forces: Report of the Commission Appointed by the President of the United States to Investigate and Report the Facts Relating to the Attack Made by Japanese Armed Forces upon Pearl Harbor in the Territory of Hawaii on December 7, 1941,* 77th Cong., 2d sess., S. Doc. No. 159 (1942).

48   **"Mac, give this"**: White, "Roberts Says," 1.

48   **mobbed by reporters:** Photos of Roberts surrounded by reporters as he left the White House and as he later sat in his car appeared in the *Bennington (VT) Evening Banner*, January 28, 1942, 5; the *Okfuskee County (OK) News*, January 29, 1942, 4; and the *Anniston (AL) Star*, January 29, 1942, 14.

48   **spoke in generalities:** Associated Press, "Pearl Harbor Report Given to Roosevelt," 1; United Press, "Report of Attack on Pearl Harbor Filed with FDR," *Princeton (IN) Daily Clarion*, January 24, 1942, 1.

48   **"most thorough investigation"**: Associated Press, "Pearl Harbor Report Given to Roosevelt," 1.

48   **"fifty-one page report"**: Associated Press, "Pearl Harbor Report Given to Congress," 1. When Congress published the report, its printed version totaled twenty-one pages. *Attack upon Pearl Harbor.*

48   **"a complete surprise to the commanders"**: *Attack upon Pearl Harbor*, 21.

49   **"Subordinate commanders...their efficiency"**: *Attack upon Pearl Harbor*, 21.

49   **Commentators praised the report:** Drew Pearson and Robert Allen, "The Washington Merry Go-Round," *Courier* (Waterloo, IA), January 29, 1942, 4; "Observation and Comment," editorial, *Aiken (SC) Standard*, January 28, 1942, 4; "'Dereliction of Duty,'" *Daily Times* (Davenport, IA) (quoting the *Kewanee (IL) Star Courier*), January 28, 1942, 3.

49   **both parties hailed the report:** United Press, "Frank Nature of Hawaiian Probe Report Pleases," *Greenville (SC) News*, January 25, 1942, 7.

50   **Controversies about the accuracy:** Lance Cole, "Special National Investigative Commissions: Essential Powers and Procedures (Some Lessons from the Pearl Harbor, Warren Commission, and 9/11 Commission Investigations)," *McGeorge Law Review* 41, no. 1 (2009): 1, 8–15, 45–46; Kenneth Kitts, *Presidential Commissions and National Security: The Politics of Damage Control* (Lynne Rienner Publisher, 2006), 17–45.

50   **"rush to judgments" and "an ill-considered effort"**: Cole, "Special National Investigative Commissions," 45–46.

50 **"complacency," "smugness"**: "Smugness Blamed by Justice Roberts for Hawaii Tragedy," *Philadelphia Inquirer,* January 29, 1942, 1; "Roberts Condemns Our Complacency," *New York Times,* January 29, 1942, 4; Associated Press, "Smugness of Nation Puzzling to Roberts," *Hartford (CT) Courant,* January 29, 1942, 1; "Justice Roberts Blames American 'Smugness' for Pearl Harbor Disaster," *Capital Times* (Madison, WI), January 29, 1942, 2.

51 **"keep the wheels turning"**: Franklin D. Roosevelt, State of the Union address, January 6, 1942, transcript at the American Presidency Project, https://www.presidency.ucsb.edu/documents/state-the-union-address-1.

51 **Newspapers reported that the shortlist**: Marquis W. Childs, "Byrnes, Douglas Considered for War Output Job," *St. Louis Post-Dispatch,* January 6, 1942, 1; Ernest Lindley, "No More Makeshifts," *Washington Post,* January 2, 1942, 11; Jerry Klutz, "The Federal Diary," *Washington Post,* January 2, 1942, 17; Jack Bell, Associated Press, "Byrnes Rumored to Head Production," *Washington Post,* January 11, 1942, 3; Leonard Lyons, "The Lyons Den," *Miami News,* January 16, 1942, 9; Associated Press, "Byrnes May Be Asked to Handle Production Setup," *Carlsbad (NM) Current-Argus,* January 11, 1942, 1.

51 **"Now that we are in…personal swat"**: William O. Douglas to A. Howard Meneely, December 13, 1941, quoted in Bruce Allen Murphy, *Wild Bill: The Legend and Life of William O. Douglas* (Random House, 2003), 195–196.

51 **open letter**: Ralph Smith, "Drive Opens for Douglas as U.S. Chief Mobilizer," *Miami Daily News,* January 14, 1942, 17; John W. Kelly, "At the National Capitol," *Bend (OR) Bulletin,* January 21, 1942, 1.

51 **Donald Nelson**: Alfred Friendly, "Nelson Gets Full Power over War Production," *Washington Post,* January 17, 1942, 1; Alfred Friendly, "Nelson's Job Is to Turn Nation into World's Greatest Arsenal," *Washington Post,* January 18, 1942, B1.

51 **"It took Lincoln three years"**: Frankfurter to Roosevelt, January 17, 1942, in Freedman, *Roosevelt and Frankfurter,* 644.

52 **"even as a messenger boy"**: International News Service, "Justice Byrnes Will Remain on High Court," *Evening News* (Harrisburg, PA), January 21, 1942, 4.

52 **Byrnes sent a memo**: David Robertson, *Sly and Able: A Political Biography of James F. Byrnes* (W. W. Norton, 1994), 312–315.

52 **Second War Powers Act**: Second War Powers Act, Pub. L. No. 507, 56 Stat. 176 (1942).

53 **"intermediary between congress and the White House"**: Louis J. Schaefle, "National Whirligig," *News-Press* (Fort Myers, FL), March 1, 1942, 4.

53   **"They're fiddling while Byrnes roams":** Leonard Lyons, "The Lyons Den," *South Bend (IN) Tribune*, January 18, 1942, 23.

53   *Taylor v. Georgia* **opinion:** *Taylor v. Georgia*, 315 U.S. 28 (1942); Associated Press, "Supreme Court Kills Georgia 'Peonage' Law," *Washington Post*, January 13, 1942, 6. In *Taylor*, the Court relied extensively on its prior decision in *Bailey v. Alabama*, 219 U.S. 219 (1911), which likewise had found an Alabama criminal-debt-and-forced-service law unconstitutional; that opinion discussed race and found it irrelevant.

53   **Taylor's Supreme Court brief:** Appellant's Brief at 4, 11–13, 29, *Taylor v. Georgia*, 315 U.S. 25 (1942) (No. 70).

54   **"conferring with President Roosevelt":** "Byrnes Not Present When Decision Read," *Greenville (SC) News*, January 13, 1942, 5. White House logs reveal that Byrnes met with FDR from 11:40 a.m. to 12:05 p.m. on January 12, 1942, the day that *Taylor* was announced. "January 12, 1942," Franklin D. Roosevelt Day by Day (website), Pare Lorentz Center, FDR Presidential Library, accessed January 18, 2023, http://www .fdrlibrary.marist.edu/daybyday/daylog/january-12th-1942/. The Supreme Court convened to announce its decisions, including *Taylor*, at noon. *Journal of the Supreme Court of the United States*, October Term 1941, 122–123. Byrnes biographer David Robertson identifies January 12 as the day when FDR and Byrnes discussed the memo to Hopkins. Robertson, *Sly and Able*, 314.

54   **Bethlehem Steel Corporation:** *United States v. Bethlehem Steel Corp.*, 315 U.S. 289 (1942).

55   **pounded his fist on the bench:** United Press, "Regulation of War Profits Devolves on FDR, Congress," *Muskogee (OK) Daily Phoenix*, February 17, 1942, 4.

55   **Frankfurter's dissent:** *Bethlehem Steel Corp.*, 315 U.S. at 326, 336. Douglas also separately dissented.

55   **released a major report:** William Edwards, "Tommy the Cork Is Getting His Million," *Chicago Tribune*, February 8, 1942, 8.

55   **sparked legislation:** 88 Cong. Rec. 3398-99 (April 7, 1942); Sixth National Defense Appropriation Act, 1942, Pub. L. No. 528, 56 Stat. 245 (1942), 77th Cong., 2d Sess., section 403 (April 28, 1942). The new legislation directed the Army, Navy, and Federal Maritime Commission to renegotiate existing and future contracts whenever "excessive profits" would result; it also provided that all defense war contracts should have a clause permitting renegotiation at any time. James C. Withrow Jr., "The Control of War Profits in the United States and Canada," *University of Pennsylvania Law Review* 91, no. 3 (1942): 194, 209–211.

55   **"absolutely defenseless":** Senator Homer T. Bone (D, WA), *Congressional Record*, April 7, 1942, 3398–3399.

55   **"If the provisions embodied in this bill":** Senator Walter F. George (D, GA), *Congressional Record*, April 7, 1942, 3399.

55   **launch of the *Alabama*:** Associated Press, "Newest Naval Unit Launched," *Arizona Daily Star*, February 17, 1942, 12.

56   **When Senator Hugo Black:** Hugo Black Jr., "Hugo L. Black," in *The Supreme Court Justices: Illustrated Biographies, 1789–1993*, ed. Clare Cushman (Congressional Quarterly: 1993), 376–380; Henry J. Abraham, *Justices and Presidents: A Political History of Appointments to the Supreme Court*, 2nd ed. (Oxford University Press, 1985), 210–217; Newman, *Hugo Black*, 3–121.

57   **"Hugo, I'd like to write your name here":** Abraham, *Justices and Presidents*, 211.

57   **"Mr. President, are you sure":** Newman, *Hugo Black*, 236.

57   **"four-track mind":** Joseph Lelyveld, *His Final Battle: The Last Months of Franklin Roosevelt* (Knopf, 2016), 15.

57   **"Hugo went a little too far":** Newman, *Hugo Black*, 239. The *Washington Post* similarly reported that one defender of Black on the Senate floor charged that "opposition [to Black] actually was aimed at his liberal legislative record." Robert C. Albright, "Black Voted to Supreme Court Despite Klan Charge," *Washington Post*, August 18, 1937, 1.

57   **Conservative opponents:** Albright, "Black Voted to Supreme Court Despite Klan Charge," 1. The legal objection was that, because Black had been in the Senate when Congress increased retirement benefits for Justices, he was barred by Article I, Section 6, of the Constitution from serving in a position for which the "emoluments" had been increased. The Supreme Court later rejected an attempted objection to Black along these lines on the ground that the person raising the objection lacked standing. *Ex parte Levitt*, 302 U.S. 633 (1937). Professor William Baude has challenged the Supreme Court's reasoning. William Baude, "The Unconstitutionality of Justice Black," *Texas Law Review* 98, no. 2 (2019): 327.

57   **"ardent opponent of the New Deal":** "Copeland Enemy of the New Deal," *New York Times*, July 17, 1937, 13.

58   **he rose on the Senate floor:** "The New Associate Justice," *Washington Post*, October 3, 1937, B8; Albright, "Black Voted to Supreme Court."

58   **Sprigle's series provided definitive proof:** Ray Sprigle, "Justice Black Revealed as Ku Klux Klansman," *Pittsburgh (PA) Post-Gazette*, September 13, 1937, 1; United Press, "Story Linking Black to Klan Stirs Capital," *Pittsburgh (PA) Press*, September 14, 1937, 1; Ray Sprigle, "Black's Loyalty to Klan Shown in Fervid Pledge," *Pittsburgh (PA) Post-Gazette*, September 15, 1937, 1; Ray Sprigle, "Ku Klux Bigotry Shown by Wizard at Klan Ceremony," *Pittsburgh (PA) Post-Gazette*, September 16, 1937, 1; Ray Sprigle, "Imperial Wizard Proud of Klan's Political Inroads," *Pittsburgh (PA)*

Post-Gazette, September 17, 1937, 1; Ray Sprigle, "Klansman Black Minus His Mask Is Now Justice," *Pittsburgh (PA) Post-Gazette*, September 18, 1937, 1; Newman, *Hugo Black*, 246–251.

58   **"keep this man from wearing the black robe":** United Press, "Senator Urges Move to Oust Justice Black," *Pittsburgh (PA) Press*, September 13, 1937, 23.

59   **FDR kept a watchful distance:** Associated Press, "Black Takes Seat at Noon Today Before Court Throng," *Washington Post*, October 4, 1937, 1; Newman, *Hugo Black*, 251.

59   **Black and his wife arrived:** "Black Facing Reporters' Barrage of Questions," *Pittsburgh (PA) Post-Gazette*, September 30, 1937, 1; Ray Sprigle, "Black Home, Still Silent on His Klan Membership," *Pittsburgh (PA) Post-Gazette*, September 30, 1937, 1.

59   **Black's radio audience:** Associated Press, "Black's Audience Put at 50,000,000," *Pittsburgh (PA) Post-Gazette*, October 2, 1937, 2. Black biographer Roger Newman estimated the radio audience at forty million and noted that it was "the largest ever except for that which heard King Edward VIII abdicate the throne the year before." Newman, *Hugo Black*, 258.

59   **Black's speech:** Associated Press, "Text of Justice Black's Radio Talk Admitting He Joined Ku Klux Klan," *Pittsburgh (PA) Post-Gazette*, October 2, 1937, 2.

59   **Black's varying explanations:** Newman, *Hugo Black*, 96–98.

59   **"If the President had known":** United Press, "Usefulness of Black Limited," *Pittsburgh (PA) Press*, October 2, 1937, 3.

59   ***New York Times* decried:** "Mr. Black's Reply," *New York Times*, October 2, 1937, 20.

59   ***Pittsburgh Post-Gazette* editorialized:** "Justice Black's Radio Speech," *Pittsburgh (PA) Post-Gazette*, October 4, 1937, 8.

59   ***Washington Post* observed:** "The New Associate Justice," editorial, *Washington Post*, October 3, 1937, B8.

60   **Walter Chaplinsky:** *Chaplinsky v. New Hampshire*, 315 U.S. 568 (1942); Appellant's Brief and Appellee's Brief, *Chaplinsky v. New Hampshire*, 315 U.S. 568 (1942) (No. 255). Later cases interpreting *Chaplinsky* include *Terminiello v. City of Chicago*, 337 U.S. 1 (1949), *Texas v. Johnson*, 491 US. 397 (1989), and *R.A.V. v. City of St. Paul*, 505 U.S. 377 (1992).

60   **"offensive, derisive or annoying word":** *Chaplinsky v. New Hampshire*, 315 U.S. at 569.

60   **"what men of common intelligence...breach of the peace":** *Chaplinsky v. New Hampshire*, 315 U.S. at 572–574.

CHAPTER 4

63 **"The sky was gray"**: "Today's Great News," editorial, *Evening Times* (Sayre, PA), April 18, 1942, 4; Associated Press, "It's Just the Beginning, Beams a Smiling and Elated Washington," *Atlanta Constitution*, April 19, 1942, 2A. Seventy-seven years later, Washington cheered a Doolittle family member for another reason: Sean Doolittle, the star reliever on the Washington Nationals' World Series championship team in 2019, is a distant cousin of General Jimmy Doolittle. Janie McCauley, "Sean Doolittle Gets Lesson on Gen. James Doolittle," ESPN.com, August 22, 2013, http://www.espn.com/espn/wire/_/section/mlb/id/9592565.

64 **Jack Skinner**: Victoria F. Nourse, *In Reckless Hands: Skinner v. Oklahoma and the Near Triumph of American Eugenics* (W. W. Norton, 2008), 89–109.

64 **"felony involving" ... "revenue acts"**: Habitual Criminal Sterilization Act, 57 Okla. Stat. Ann. Tit. § 171 et seq. (1935), pp. 94 et seq. Oklahoma enacted its 1935 statute after two prior versions of sterilization statutes. Nourse, *In Reckless Hands*, 84–87.

64 **"Three generations"**: *Buck v. Bell*, 274 U.S. 200, 207 (1927).

64 **later research**: Adam Cohen, *Imbeciles: The Supreme Court, American Eugenics, and the Sterilization of Carrie Buck* (Penguin, 2017).

65 **twenty-seven states**: Nourse, *In Reckless Hands*, 20.

65 **parallels between the Nazis' program**: Nourse, *In Reckless Hands*, 16–37.

65 **Oklahoma prisoners rebelled**: Nourse, *In Reckless Hands*, 56–92.

66 **Oklahoma Supreme Court rejected**: *Skinner v. State ex rel. Williamson*, 115 P.3d 183 (Okla. 1941).

66 **Court decided to require**: The Supreme Court's order "request[ing]" the Oklahoma Attorney General (or his representative)—but not Skinner's lawyers—to appear at oral argument is in *Skinner v. Oklahoma, Journal of the Supreme Court of the United States*, October Term 1941, No. 782, April 13, 1942, 222.

66 **At argument**: Nourse, *In Reckless Hands*, 146; Associated Press, "Sterilization Law Is Before High Tribunal," *Baltimore Sun*, May 7, 1942, 2.

66 **"elements of violence ... no such evidence"**: Nourse, *In Reckless Hands*, 146.

66 **Frankfurter took the lead**: Nourse, *In Reckless Hands*, 144–145. In addition to pushing for the equal protection rationale, Frankfurter made an important stylistic edit to Douglas's draft, with an insertion that the equal protection clause "clearly condemns" the Oklahoma law. Nourse, *In Reckless Hands*, 152.

67 **"This case touches" ... "wither and disappear"**: *Skinner v. Oklahoma*, 316 U.S. 535, 536–539 (1942). Two Justices agreed with striking down the

law but wrote separately. Stone—the only Justice who had been on the Court when *Buck v. Bell* was decided—stated that he would rest on the ground that, unlike the law at issue in *Buck v. Bell*, the Oklahoma law did not permit a defense to sterilization based on the individual's characteristics. *Skinner*, 316 U.S. at 543 (Stone, C.J., concurring). Jackson, meanwhile, wrote that he saw no contradiction between Douglas's approach and Stone's approach, and he agreed with both. Jackson pointedly added that "there are limits to the extent to which a legislatively represented majority may conduct biological experiments at the expense of the dignity and personality and natural powers of a minority." *Skinner*, 316 U.S. at 546 (Jackson, J., concurring).

67   ***Carolene Products:*** *United States v. Carolene Products*, 304 U.S. 144, 152 n.4 (1938). Stone's famous footnote suggested that more-searching judicial review may be appropriate when there is legislation "directed at particular religious…or national…or racial minorities"; when there is "prejudice against discrete and insular minorities…which tends seriously to curtail the operation of those political processes ordinarily to be relied upon to protect minorities; and when there is a deprivation of a fundamental right." Stone's concurrence in *Skinner* cited his *Carolene Products* footnote 4. 316 U.S. at 544.

68   **more than a thousand individuals:** Nourse, *In Reckless Hands*, 127.

68   **landmark personal-liberty decisions:** *Griswold v. Connecticut*, 381 U.S. 479, 484 (1965) (birth control for married couples); *Loving v. Virginia*, 388 U.S. 1, 7 (1967) (interracial marriage); *Roe v. Wade*, 410 U.S. 113, 152 (1973) (reproductive rights); *Planned Parenthood v. Casey*, 505 U.S. 833, 834 (1992) (reproductive rights); *Obergefell v. Hodges*, 135 S. Ct. 2584, 2598 (2016) (marriage equality). As Victoria Nourse emphasizes, the core rationale of *Skinner* rested on equal protection grounds (*In Reckless Hands*, 15–16, 165); at the same time, *Skinner* emphasized the fundamental nature of the right at issue and applied strict scrutiny on that basis, and the Supreme Court repeatedly has highlighted *Skinner*'s emphasis on the personal-liberty right in objecting to forced sterilization.

68   **"one-footed chicken thief":** David L. Franklin, "Origin Story," *Slate*, June 29, 2015, https://slate.com/news-and-politics/2015/06/gay-marriage -supreme-court-ruling-how-skinner-v-oklahoma-laid-the-foundation-for -obergefell-v-hodges.html.

68   **"our cases represent":** *Thornburgh v. American College of Obstetricians and Gynecologists*, 476 U.S. 747, 778 n.6 (1986) (Stevens, J., concurring) (citations omitted).

68   **"improper" and "intellectually empty":** Robert H. Bork, "Neutral Principles and Some First Amendment Problems," *Indiana Law Journal* 47, no. 1 (1971): 1, 12.

68   *Dobbs v. Jackson Women's Health Organization*: 142 S. Ct. 2228, 2257, 2268, 2277–2278 (2022).

69   Thomas, while not mentioning *Skinner*: *Dobbs*, 142 S. Ct. at 2301–2302 (Thomas, J., concurring).

69   "if the majority is right": *Dobbs*, 142 S. Ct. at 2332 (Breyer, Sotomayor, and Kagan, JJ., dissenting).

69   two decisions vindicating: *Ward v. Texas*, 316 U.S. 547 (1942); *Hill v. Texas*, 316 U.S. 400 (1942).

70   Douglas had meetings: "April 10th, 1942," "April 16th, 1942," "May 15th, 1942," "May 28th, 1942," "June 7th, 1942," all on Franklin D. Roosevelt Day by Day (website), Pare Lorentz Center, FDR Presidential Library, http://www.fdrlibrary.marist.edu/daybyday/.

70   manpower mobilization board: Jerry Klutz, "The Federal Diary," *Washington Post*, April 10, 1942, 22; "McNutt Slated to Head Draft of Man Power," *Indianapolis News*, April 15, 1942, 8; Drew Pearson and Robert Allen, "The Daily Washington Merry-Go-Round," *Times and Democrat* (Orangeburg, SC), April 17, 1942, 4.

70   weekend in Charlottesville: Robert H. Jackson, *That Man: An Insider's Portrait of Franklin D. Roosevelt*, ed. John Q. Barrett (Oxford University Press, 2003), 64–65, 106–107, 235n15; "April 11th, 1942," Franklin D. Roosevelt Day by Day (website), Pare Lorentz Center, FDR Presidential Library, http://www.fdrlibrary.marist.edu/daybyday/daylog/april-11th-1942/. Jackson also had a private lunch with FDR at the White House in February. "February 7th, 1942," Franklin D. Roosevelt Day by Day (website), Pare Lorentz Center, FDR Presidential Library, http://www.fdrlibrary.marist.edu/daybyday/daylog/february-7th-1942/.

70   delegation to greet the King of Greece: "Greek King Is Visitor to Capital," *New York Daily News*, June 11, 1942, 52; United Press, "Greek King Will Visit 2 Shrines," *Evening News* (Harrisburg, PA), June 11, 1942, 3; "June 10th, 1942," Franklin D. Roosevelt Day by Day (website), Pare Lorentz Center, FDR Presidential Library, http://www.fdrlibrary.marist.edu/daybyday/daylog/june-10th-1942/.

70   Black addressed a record crowd: "Million New Yorkers Mark 'I Am American Day' in Park," *New York Daily News*, May 18, 1942, 4; Associated Press, "Justice Black Leads Rally," *Daily Oklahoman*, May 18, 1942, 9; United Press, "Largest Crowd in History at N.Y. Observance," *Hawaii Tribune-Herald*, May 18, 1942, 2.

70   Murphy headlined: Marjorie Avery, "Pied Pipers Again Ready to Start Summer Work," *Detroit Free Press*, May 26, 1942, 9; "War Rally Lists Great Opera Stars," *Detroit Free Press*, May 31, 1942, part 3, 10; "War-Bond Sale Boosted at Big Rally in City," *Detroit Free Press*, June 1, 1942,

1; Associated Press, "Murphy, Joe Louis Lead Bond Rally," *Lansing (MI) State Journal*, June 1, 1942, 3.

70   **Frankfurter continued to send FDR:** Max Freedman, ed., *Roosevelt and Frankfurter: Their Correspondence, 1928–1945* (Little, Brown, 1967), 639–661. Between January 1, 1942, and June 30, 1942, Frankfurter and FDR had at least three in-person meetings, including a one-on-one lunch. "March 19th, 1942," "April 3rd, 1942," and "May 26th, 1942," all on Franklin D. Roosevelt Day by Day (website), Pare Lorentz Center, FDR Presidential Library, http://www.fdrlibrary.marist.edu/daybyday/.

71   **make its opinions more dramatic:** FDR to Frankfurter, May 1, 1942; Frankfurter to FDR, May 26, 1942, both in Freedman, *Roosevelt and Frankfurter*, 658, 660.

71   **"As your Commander-in-Chief":** FDR to Frankfurter, January 16, 1942, in Freedman, *Roosevelt and Frankfurter*, 643.

71   *Betts v. Brady:* 316 U.S. 455 (1942).

73   *Jones v. City of Opelika:* 316 U.S. 584 (1942).

73   **"This is but another step":** *Jones v. City of Opelika*, 316 U.S. at 623–624 (Black, Douglas, and Murphy, dissenting).

74   **jump in 5–4 decisions:** John D. Fassett, *New Deal Justice: The Life of Stanley Reed of Kentucky* (Vantage, 1994), 318; C. Herman Pritchett, *The Roosevelt Court: A Study in Judicial Politics and Values, 1937–1947* (MacMillan, 1948), 25. In the preceding four terms, the Court had had less than a full Court for part of the term (Pritchett, *Roosevelt Court*, 25); during at least part of the 1941 term, the Court also had less than a full Court because of Justice Roberts's leave of absence.

74   **"If President Roosevelt expected":** Jay C. Hayden, "Justices Frankfurter and Black at Odds in 30 out of 45 High Court Cases," *Boston Globe*, June 2, 1942, 7. Hayden's column appeared before the final day of the term, June 8, when the divided *Opelika* decision was released. As Hayden explained, the Court was scheduled to finish on June 1, but "remaining contests forced the court to continue for another week the term which had been scheduled to end Monday." Shortly after the term ended, Stone told a group of judges, "Any high expectations that the Justices of the newly reorganized Court would have minds with but a single thought and hearts that beat as one were speedily dissipated. There have been quite a number of 5 to 4 decisions and a goodly number of dissents—more in fact than during any recent years." Quoted in Alpheus Thomas Mason, *Harlan Fiske Stone: Pillar of the Law* (Viking, 1956), 591.

75   **"independence of the judiciary":** "Supreme Court Ends Big Term," *Spokesman-Review* (Spokane, WA), June 1, 1942, 2.

75   **"the Axis":** Joseph P. Lash, ed., *From the Diaries of Felix Frankfurter* (W. W. Norton, 1975), 176. Other examples of Frankfurter using the term

are in Lash, *Diaries*, 197, 198, and 209. Frankfurter described it as "a common sobriquet" for Black, Douglas, and Murphy; he noted on one occasion that Stone had used it "laughingly" with him in a private conversation, and that Jackson had employed it as well (197, 209). Frankfurter also regularly used the term "Axis" with its public meaning of the countries that the United States was fighting—see, e.g., Lash, *Diaries*, 172, 173.

CHAPTER 5

78   **Royall had gone to see Black...at a loss:** Louis Fisher, *Military Tribunals and Presidential Power: American Revolution to the War on Terrorism* (University Press of Kansas, 2005), 106–107; "The Reminiscences of Kenneth Claiborne Royall, 1963," Individual Interviews Oral History Collection, Columbia Center for Oral History, Columbia University, 35–36.

78   **Royall went to Roberts's chambers:** Fisher, *Military Tribunals*, 106; "Reminiscences of Kenneth Claiborne Royall," 36; Michael Dobbs, *Saboteurs: The Nazi Raid on America* (Vintage, 2005), 235; Eugene Rachlis, *They Came to Kill: The Story of Eight Nazi Saboteurs in America* (Popular Library, 1962), 165–166. Accounts vary about the date that Royall saw the article regarding Sutherland's funeral and the date that Royall met with Roberts. In light of the available evidence (including the paucity of newspaper stories mentioning Roberts's attendance at the funeral), the most likely scenario is that Royall saw an article about Roberts attending the Sutherland funeral on Wednesday, July 22 (the day of the funeral), in the Washington, DC, *Evening Star* ("High Officials Attend Cathedral Services for Sutherland," *Evening Star*, July 22, 1942, B-1) and that he then quickly made his way to Roberts's chambers.

79   **After consulting with the White House:** Dobbs, *Saboteurs*, 236.

79   **they met with Roberts and Black:** Dobbs, *Saboteurs*, 236–237; Rachlis, *They Came to Kill*, 191–192; Fisher, *Military Tribunals*, 106–107; David J. Danelski, "The Saboteurs' Case," *Journal of Supreme Court History* 61, no. 1 (1996), 68; "The Blacks to Visit the Robertses in PA," *Washington Post*, July 22, 1942, 14.

80   **a sore point:** Sidney Fine, *Frank Murphy: The Washington Years* (University of Michigan Press, 1984), 217.

80   **Newsreels in movie theaters:** "War Conference in News Reels," *Oakland (CA) Tribune*, July 2, 1942, 15; "Paramount News Specials," *St. Mary and Franklin (LA) Banner-Tribune*, July 10, 1942, 5.

80   **made a point of declining:** Fine, *Frank Murphy*, 218.

80   **"swank tailor":** "Walter Winchell on Broadway," *Honolulu Advertiser*, July 17, 1942, 6.

80   **reviewing Supreme Court filings:** Fine, *Frank Murphy*, 218; Davenport
      Steward, "Justice Murphy Works at Night," *Reno Gazette-Journal*, July 2,
      1942, 10.

80   **"sets a splendid example"..."recess is over":** Associated Press, "Justice
      Frank Murphy Now at Fort Benning," *Montgomery (AL) Advertiser*, June
      16, 1942, 2; "Justice Murphy in Army," *Daily Times-News* (Burlington,
      NC), June 12, 1942; "Justice Murphy Ought to Have Resigned," editorial,
      Courier-Journal (Louisville, KY), June 12, 1942, 6; "Politics in Army," ed-
      itorial, *Times Recorder* (Zanesville, OH), July 14, 1942, 4; Drew Pearson
      and Robert Allen, "The Washington Merry-Go-Round," *Sheboygan (WI)
      Press*, June 16, 1942, 18.

81   **reached on a field telephone:** "Recalled from Army to Judicial Duty,"
      New York Times, July 28, 1942, 1 (photo caption).

81   **covert fact-finding mission..."comfort to the enemy":** Roger K. New-
      man, *Hugo Black: A Biography* (Fordham University Press, 1997), 313;
      Associated Press, "Justice Black Addresses War Mass Meeting," *Asheville
      (NC) Citizen-Times*, July 15, 1942, 8; Associated Press, "Consequences
      of Lost War Are Emphasized in Hugo Black Speech," *Birmingham (AL)
      News*, July 15, 1942, 18; "Black Asserts U.S. Owes Debt to China, Russia,
      and Britain," *Chicago Tribune*, July 15, 1942, 3.

81   **put his arm around the envoy:** *Baltimore Sun*, July 17, 1942, 3; *Atlanta
      Constitution*, July 17, 1942, 3.

81   **Stanley Reed spoke..."disunity":** John D. Fassett, *New Deal Justice: The
      Life of Stanley Reed of Kentucky* (Vantage, 1994), 329–330; "10,000 Cheer
      'Victory Rally' Speeches Here," *Capital Times* (Madison, WI); Associ-
      ated Press, "Liberties in Pawn, Justice Declares," *Rhinelander (WI) Daily
      News*, July 1, 1942, 9.

81   **"Whenever an American utters"..."on our side":** Associated Press,
      "Byrnes Hits Those Quoted by Axis Propagandists," *Tribune* (Scranton,
      PA), June 5, 1942, 2; "Spartanburg Hears Byrnes," *Charlotte (NC) Ob-
      server*, July 5, 1942, 13; Associated Press, "Justice Byrnes Speaks to Home
      Town People; 'God, Russia on Our Side,'" *Albuquerque (NM) Journal*,
      July 5, 1942, 5.

82   **"personification of evil":** United Press, "Allied Unity Held Essential in
      Axis' Defeat," *Pittsburgh (PA) Post-Gazette*, July 6, 1942, 2; "Have Faith in
      Our Allies," editorial, *Rock Island (IL) Argus*, July 9, 1942, 4.

82   **"no half victory":** International News Service, "Dallas Bar Hears Jack-
      son," *Fort Worth (TX) Star Telegram*, July 2, 1942, 16.

82   **two German submarines...instructions to commit sabotage:** Dobbs,
      Saboteurs, 15–86; Rachlis, *They Came to Kill*, 7–70; Danelski, "Saboteurs'
      Case," 61–65; Louis Fisher, *Nazi Saboteurs on Trial: A Military Tribunal
      and American Law* (University Press of Kansas, 2003), 1–36; W. A.

Swanberg, "The Spies Who Came In from the Sea," *American Heritage*, April 1970; Associated Press, "Nazi Saboteurs Land in U.S.," *South Bend (IN) Tribune*, June 28, 1942, 1.

84   **"military as well as political value"**: Dobbs, *Saboteurs*, 140.

84   **The press hailed**: Dobbs, *Saboteurs*, 194 (Winchell); "FBI Grabs 8 Berlin Saboteurs Landed from U-Boats with Powerful Explosives to Blow Up American Munitions Plants," *St. Louis Globe-Democrat*, June 28, 1942, 1.

84   **"Nothing was said"**: Francis Biddle, *In Brief Authority* (Doubleday, 1962), 328.

85   **"Let's make real money out of them"**: Biddle, *In Brief Authority*, 327.

85   **criminal charges in the civilian courts**: Danelski, "Saboteurs' Case," 65–68. As Biddle later described the problem, "If a man buys a pistol, intending murder, that is not an attempt at murder. The broad federal law covering conspiracies to commit crimes applied; but carried a penalty grossly disproportionate to their acts—three years, as I remember." Biddle, *In Brief Authority*, 328.

86   **FDR sent Biddle a memo**: Franklin D. Roosevelt to Attorney General, memorandum, June 30, 1942, quoted in Danelski, "Saboteurs' Case," 65; Biddle, *In Brief Authority*, 330.

86   **"bug of publicity"**: Stimson diary, July 1, 1942, quoted in Dobbs, *Saboteurs*, 201. In his memoir, Biddle recalled that Stimson initially opposed Biddle's proposal but later relented: "The Secretary of War did not like it, it was most irregular, it had never been done before—a civilian prosecuting for the Army." Biddle, *In Brief Authority*, 331.

86   **"We have to win"**: Biddle, *In Brief Authority*, 331.

86   **"I want one thing clearly understood"**: Biddle, *In Brief Authority*, 331.

86   **general proclamation**: Proclamation 2561, "Denying Certain Enemies Access to the Courts of the United States," 7 Fed. Reg. 5101 (July 7, 1942).

87   **FDR's order**: Appointment of a Military Commission, 7 Fed. Reg. 5103 (July 7, 1942).

87   **"Hanging would afford"**: Quoted in William D. Hassett, *Off the Record with FDR* (Enigma, 2016), 72.

88   **On the first day**: Dobbs, *Saboteurs*, 211–212.

88   **requested White House approval…best judgment**: Danelski, "Saboteurs' Case," 68; Dobbs, *Saboteurs*, 208.

88   **"a good cigar"**: Dobbs, *Saboteurs*, 211–212.

88   **The trial proceeded…defense rested**: Dobbs, *Saboteurs*, 210–229; Michal R. Belknap, "The Supreme Court Goes to War: The Meaning and Implications of the Nazi Saboteur Case," *Military Law Review* 89 (1980): 66; Biddle, *In Brief Authority*, 334–335.

89   **"convene a special term"…"against that of the President"**: Rachlis, *They Came to Kill*, 192; Lewis Wood, "Supreme Court Is Called in

Unprecedented Session," *New York Times*, July 28, 1942, 1; "Call Supreme
Court on Plea of Saboteurs," *New York Daily News*, July 28, 1942, 2.

89   **Many denounced... "do us injury":** *Los Angeles Times*, July 29, 1942, and
Washington Post, July 31, 1942, quoted in Belknap, "Supreme Court Goes
to War," 69–70; *Detroit Free Press*, quoted in Rachlis, *They Came to Kill*,
194; "Habeas Corpus," *Washington Post*, July 31, 1942, 12.

90   **left Royall a troubling phone message:** Alpheus Thomas Mason, *Harlan
Fiske Stone: Pillar of the Law* (Viking, 1956), 657n*. Mason quotes a letter
from Lauson Stone, who was on Royall's staff at the time: "Two days before
the Court hearing, Justice Roberts sent Colonel Royall a phone message
citing *Marbury v. Madison*—thus indicating that he doubted the Court's
direct jurisdiction. Accordingly, it was decided to prepare petitions to a district judge." The lawyers' scramble to establish jurisdiction is described in
Boris I. Bittker, "The World War II German Saboteurs' Case and Writs of
Certiorari Before Judgment by the Court of Appeals: A Tale of Nunc Pro
Tunc Jurisdiction," *Constitutional Commentary* 14 (1997): 431–451.

91   **"Colonel Royall did not entrust me":** Bittker, "German Saboteurs' Case,"
441n21.

91   **terse two-paragraph opinion:** *Ex parte Quirin*, 47 F. Supp. 431 (D.D.C.
1942).

91   **Murphy showed up in his military uniform:** Danelski, "Saboteurs'
Case," 69; Fine, *Frank Murphy*, 404; Albert Cox, "The Saboteur Story,"
Records of the Columbia Historical Society 57/59 (1957/1959): 17. Numerous accounts report that Murphy attended the Supreme Court conference
and hearing in his uniform. An Associated Press photo of Murphy taken at
some point on July 29 shows him sitting on the steps outside the Court in
civilian clothes; the photo may have been taken after Murphy changed out
of his uniform. See, e.g., Associated Press Wirefoto, *New York Daily News*,
July 30, 1942, 2.

91   **Frankfurter immediately objected:** Danelski, "Saboteurs' Case," 69;
Fine, *Frank Murphy*, 218.

92   **"keeper of his own conscience":** Wood, "Supreme Court Is Called."

92   **Frankfurter "shared Patterson's view":** Stimson diary, June 29, 1942,
quoted in Danelski, "Saboteurs' Case," 66.

92   **Stimson noted that "Frankfurter asked me":** Stimson diary, July 8, 1942,
quoted in Danelski, "Saboteurs' Case," 81n18. Frankfurter biographer
Brad Snyder summarizes, "As a justice likely to hear the Nazi saboteurs'
case, Frankfurter never should have offered advice about the composition
of the military commission, asked about the trial, or revealed his views
about Attorney General Biddle.... On two occasions with Stimson, Frankfurter had opined about the Nazi saboteurs' case. He also was a major on
inactive status in the army's Judge Advocate General's Corps reserve [a

position dating back to his World War I service in the War Department]. Frankfurter should have recognized the appearance of a conflict of interest and disqualified himself." Brad Snyder, *Democratic Justice: Felix Frankfurter, the Supreme Court, and the Making of the Liberal Establishment* (W. W. Norton, 2022), 396–397.

92 **extensive involvement with the President:** James F. Byrnes, *All in One Lifetime* (Harper and Brothers, 1958), 147–157.

93 **Stone advised his colleagues:** Danelski, "Saboteurs' Case," 69.

93 **Roberts shared:** Danelski, "Saboteurs' Case," 69.

93 **"That would be a dreadful thing":** Fine, *Frank Murphy*, 404–405; Danelski, "Saboteurs' Case," 69; Biddle, *In Brief Authority*, 331.

93 **audience in the courtroom:** International News Service, "Biddle Urges New Doctrine in Spy Trials," *Salt Lake Telegram* (Salt Lake City, UT), July 30, 1942, 1; Associated Press, "Stone and Murphy May Refuse to Hear Appeals from Saboteurs," *Daily Oklahoman* (Oklahoma City, OK), July 29, 1942, 1; Thomas O'Neill, "Accused Nazis' Plea Likened to '61 Case," *Evening Sun* (Baltimore, MD), July 29, 1942, 1; Biddle, *In Brief Authority*, 337.

93 **"event of the season":** Dobbs, *Saboteurs*, 238.

94 **"you can crack 'em":** O'Neill, "Accused Nazis' Plea."

94 **Royall's written argument…"an element of public clamor":** Petitioners' Brief at 20–64, *Ex parte Quirin*, 317 U.S. 1 (1942) (Nos. 1–7), July 1942.

95 **"In the year 1942":** Respondent's Brief at 10, 46, *Ex parte Quirin*.

95 **began by announcing…acquiesced and remained:** Philip B. Kurland and Gerhard Casper, eds., *Landmark Briefs and Arguments of the Supreme Court of the United States: Constitutional Law*, vol. 39 (University Publications of America, 1975), 496–497; *Ex parte Quirin*, 317 U.S. 1, 5 (1942). Lauson Stone later recalled that his father "cross-examined [him] as to [his] exact involvement" and initially "decided to disqualify himself" before deciding that he would sit on the case if the lawyers on both sides wanted him to do so after full disclosure. Lauson H. Stone, "My Father the Chief Justice," in *Supreme Court Historical Society Yearbook 1978* (Supreme Court Historical Society, 1977), 15. Lauson also told Stone's authorized biographer, Alpheus Thomas Mason, that he was the one on the defense team who first noticed the *Ex parte Milligan* case and brought it to Royall's attention; fearing that it might lead to the Chief Justice's recusal, Royall then instructed Stone not to work on constitutional issues. Alpheus Thomas Mason, "Inter Arma Silent Leges: Chief Justice Stone's Views," *Harvard Law Review* 69, no. 5 (1956): 806, 814.

95 **barrage of jurisdictional questions…"Milligan case granted":** Kurland and Casper, *Landmark Briefs*, 495–666; see also Rachlis, *They Came to Kill*, 200–209.

96   "technically correct": Danelski, "Saboteurs' Case," 70.

97   "The justices sweltered": O'Neill, "Accused Nazis' Plea."

97   Biddle, dressed in a white linen suit: Rachlis, *They Came to Kill*, 205.

98   filed the "piece of paper": Rachlis, *They Came to Kill*, 207.

98   Biddle began his argument: Kurland and Casper, *Landmark Briefs*, 495–666.

99   would not "assume in advance": Danelski, "Saboteurs' Case," 71.

99   But four justices...objected: G. Edward White, "Felix Frankfurter's 'Soliloquy' in *Ex parte Quirin*," *Green Bag* 5, no. 4 (2002): 423, 432.

99   At 11:59 a.m.: Myron C. Cramer, "Military Commissions: Trial of the Eight Saboteurs," *Washington Law Review* 17, no. 4 (1942): 247, 253, quoted in Fisher, *Military Tribunals*, 113.

99   "The Court's jurisdiction caught up": Robert E. Cushman, "*Ex parte Quirin et al*—The Nazi Saboteur Case," *Cornell Law Review* 28, no. 1 (1942): 54, 58, quoted in Mason, *Harlan Fiske Stone*, 657.

99   "an offense or offenses": *Ex parte Quirin*, 317 U.S. 1, 18–19 (1942).

100 found all eight defendants guilty...President's review: Danelski, "Saboteurs' Case," 71–72. As Danelski notes, on August 3, the day FDR received the verdict, sentence, and record, he signed a bill awarding a medal to J. Edgar Hoover for his heroism in capturing the saboteurs.

100 Army major ferried: Hassett, *Off the Record with FDR*, 86.

100 "What should be done": Hassett, *Off the Record with FDR*, 78, 85.

101 Saturday morning, August 8: Swanberg, "Spies Who Came In"; Rachlis, *They Came to Kill*, 224; Dobbs, *Saboteurs*, 262.

101 White House announced: Rachlis, *They Came to Kill*, 224–225.

101 Dasch and Burger: In 1948, upon the Justice Department's recommendation, President Harry Truman agreed to terminate the sentences for both Dasch and Burger and deport them to Germany. Rachlis, *They Came to Kill*, 233; Dobbs, *Saboteurs*, 273.

101 "inspired," Dorothy Rosenman recalled: Samuel Rosenman, *Working with Roosevelt* (Harper and Brothers, 1952), 351.

101 tales of murder and cannibalism: Rosenman, *Working with Roosevelt*, 351–355; Fisher, *Nazi Saboteurs on Trial*, 67–68. FDR's murderous barber tale is a clear echo, though apparently unspoken, of the popular nineteenth-century story of the fictional Sweeney Todd, which later would become a play and then a Stephen Sondheim musical in the 1970s. Aaron C. Thomas, *Sondheim and Wheeler's Sweeney Todd* (Routledge, 2018), 1–6.

CHAPTER 6

103   **"extremely cold Pullman car"**: Alpheus Thomas Mason, *Harlan Fiske Stone: Pillar of the Law* (Viking, 1956), 658, 658n*; Alpheus Thomas Mason, "Inter Arma Silent Leges: Chief Justice Stone's Views," *Harvard Law Review* 69, no. 5 (1956): 806, 820n58; Louis Fisher, *Nazi Saboteurs on Trial: A Military Tribunal and American Law* (University Press of Kansas, 2003), 392.

103   **"mortification of the flesh"**: Mason, *Harlan Fiske Stone*, 659; Mason, "Inter Arma Silent Leges"; David J. Danelski, "The Saboteurs' Case," *Journal of Supreme Court History* 61, no. 1 (1996), 72.

103   **"Both briefs have done their best"**: Harlan Fiske Stone to Bennett Boskey, August 5, 1942, folder 29, box 69, Harlan Fiske Stone Papers, Manuscript Division, Library of Congress, Washington, DC; Mason, "Inter Arma Silent Leges," 819; Mason, *Harlan Fiske Stone*, 658; Danelski, "Saboteurs' Case," 72.

103   **"I sincerely hope the military is better"**: Harlan Fiske Stone to Bennett Boskey, August 20, 1942, folder 29, box 69, Harlan Fiske Stone Papers, Manuscript Division, Library of Congress, Washington, DC; Danelski, "Saboteurs' Case," 72.

103   *New York Times* **had printed a draft**: Harlan Fiske Stone to Bennett Boskey, August 2, 1942, folder 29, box 69, Harlan Fiske Stone Papers, Manuscript Division, Library of Congress, Washington, DC; G. Edward White, "Felix Frankfurter's 'Soliloquy' in *Ex parte Quirin*," *Green Bag* 5, no. 4 (2002): 423, 428n6; Fisher, *Nazi Saboteurs on Trial*, 109; Danelski, "Saboteurs' Case," 71.

104   **military commissions as a "routine" matter**: Mason, *Harlan Fiske Stone*, 665–666.

104   **Harlan Fiske Stone did not always seem destined**: Louis Lusky, "Harlan Fiske Stone," in *The Supreme Court Justices: Illustrated Biographies, 1789–1993*, ed. Clare Cushman (Congressional Quarterly, 1993), 361–365; Warner Gardner, "Mr. Chief Justice Stone," *Harvard Law Review* 59, no. 8 (1946): 1203–1209; Mason, *Harlan Fiske Stone*, 42–64.

104   **kicked out after a melee**: Mason, *Harlan Fiske Stone*, 37–39.

104   **"bone-crushing era"**: "Stone's Fight for Liberalism Astounded Erstwhile Critics," *Washington Post*, June 13, 1941, 8.

105   **appointment of a serious young civil servant**: Beverly Gage, *G-Man: J. Edgar Hoover and the Making of the American Century* (Viking, 2022), 105–107. The Bureau of Investigation was renamed the Federal Bureau of Investigation in 1934.

105   **prosecution of Montana Senator Burton K. Wheeler**: Mason, *Harlan Fiske Stone*, 194–199; "First Supreme Court Nominee Appears Before the Judiciary Committee," United States Senate (website), accessed April 2,

2023, https://www.senate.gov/about/powers-procedures/nominations/first
-supreme-court-nominee-appears-judiciary-committee.htm. Wheeler was
acquitted in April 1925, two months after Stone's confirmation. The first
public Senate Judiciary Committee hearing for a Supreme Court nominee
was for Louis Brandeis in 1916, but Brandeis did not appear at the hearing.
Ronald G. Shafer, "The First Jewish Justice Was Also the First to Face Confirmation Hearings," *Washington Post*, April 4, 2022, https://www.washington
post.com/history/2022/04/04/louis-brandeis-jewish-confirmation-hearings/.

106   **Senator George Norris... "tool of the House of Morgan"**: Henry J.
      Abraham, *Justices and Presidents: A Political History of Appointments to
      the Supreme Court*, 2nd ed. (Oxford University Press, 1985), 194. See also
      William O. Douglas, "Chief Justice Stone," *Columbia Law Review* 46, no.
      5 (1946): 693, 694 ("Many thought when Stone came to the Court that his
      decisions would reflect the economic and social views of clients whom he
      had long represented. They were wrong."). As John Frank summarized,
      "Stone was a Wall Street lawyer, Republican Calvin Coolidge's Attorney
      General and Herbert Hoover's close friend. He was also perhaps the hard-
      est hitting opponent of the old Court's invalidation of the New Deal."
      John P. Frank, "Harlan Fiske Stone: An Estimate," *Stanford Law Review* 9,
      no. 3 (1957): 621, 621–622.

106   **Stone quickly... joined Justices Brandeis and Holmes:** Stone, Brandeis,
      and Holmes (and, later, Holmes's successor, Cardozo) were referred to
      by admirers as the "illustrious three" and "the great trio." Gardner, "Mr.
      Chief Justice Stone," 1203, 1205; Alpheus Thomas Mason, "Harlan Fiske
      Stone," in *The Justices of the United States Supreme Court, 1789–1969:
      Their Lives and Major Opinions*, ed. Leon Friedman and Fred L. Israel,
      vol. 3 (Chelsea House, 1969), 2225.

106   **"courts are not the only agency"**: *United States v. Butler*, 297 U.S. 1, 87
      (1936) (Stone, J., dissenting).

106   *Carolene Products* **footnote 4 in 1938**: 304 U.S. 144, 152 n.4 (1938).

106   **Stone's rugged football physique**: Lusky, "Harlan Fiske Stone," 363.

106   **medicine ball group:** Charles Evan Hughes Jr., who served as Hoover's So-
      licitor General until he resigned when his father returned to the Supreme
      Court as Chief Justice in 1930, was a medicine ball regular with Stone.
      He described their morning routine, including the stylized medicine-ball
      game and the postexercise White House breakfasts and discussions. Charles
      Evans Hughes Jr., "Mr. Chief Justice Stone," *Harvard Law Review* 59, no.
      8 (1946): 1193, 1195.

106   **self-deprecating humor:** "Stone's Fight for Liberalism Astounded Erst-
      while Critics," *Washington Post*, June 13, 1941, 8 ("elephants"); Mason,
      "Harlan Fiske Stone," 2221 ("leg by leg"); Lusky, "Harlan Fiske Stone,"
      361–362 ("pitchfork").

107 **Black resented Stone:** Noah Feldman, *Scorpions: The Battles and Triumphs of FDR's Great Supreme Court Justices* (Grand Central Publishing, 2010), 147–151, 294.

107 **Even Senator George Norris:** Mason, *Harlan Fiske Stone,* 572–573.

107 **Taft was concerned that Stone:** Frank, "Harlan Fiske Stone," 626n23; Mason, *Harlan Fiske Stone,* 275.

107 **After FDR hosted Frankfurter:** Alpheus Thomas Mason, "Extra-Judicial Work for Judges: The Views of Chief Justice Stone," *Harvard Law Review* 67, no. 2 (1953): 193, 196–197.

108 **medicine ball Stone had used:** Mason, "Extra-Judicial Work," 198.

108 **Eugene Meyer burst into a fistfight:** "Jesse Jones Shakes Eugene Meyer; Eyeglasses Broken in Encounter," *New York Times,* April 10, 1942, 1; International News Service, "Jesse Jones, Meyer in Fist Fight," *Pittsburgh (PA) Sun-Telegraph,* April 10, 1942, 6; Steven Fenberg, *Unprecedented Power: Jesse Jones, Capitalism, and the Common Good* (Texas A&M University Press, 2011), 41; William M. Tuttle Jr., "The Birth of an Industry: The Synthetic Rubber 'Mess' in World War II," *Technology and Culture* 22, no. 1 (1981): 35.

108 **President's proposed rubber assignment:** Mason, "Extra-Judicial Work," 202–205. On July 23 and 24, 1942, newspapers reported that FDR would appoint Stone to head the rubber survey. Stone told inquiring reporters, "I have not accepted and do not intend to." At a press conference on July 24, FDR acknowledged he had consulted Stone on a rubber survey but said he had not asked him to conduct it and "doubt[ed]" he would do so. In reality, FDR had asked Stone in his July 17 letter to take it on: "I have readily concluded that the most available and the most useful person I could call on for this task is none other than your good self. I am wondering if you would care to undertake this at your convenience?" "Chief Justice Will Probe Rubber Tangle," *Washington Post,* July 24, 1942, 1; Mason, "Extra-Judicial Work," 204; Press Conference 837, July 24, 1942, 22–23, Series 1: Press Conference Transcripts, Press Conferences of President Franklin D. Roosevelt, 1933–1945, Franklin D. Roosevelt Presidential Library and Museum, Hyde Park, NY.

110 **"if we had had a little more time":** Danelski, "Saboteurs' Case," 74.

110 **fortified "the conclusion":** Harlan Fiske Stone to Bennett Boskey, August 27, 1942, folder 29, box 69, Harlan Fiske Stone Papers, Manuscript Division, Library of Congress, Washington, DC.

110 **"seems almost brutal":** Fisher, *Nazi Saboteurs on Trial,* 110.

110 **"would not place the present Court in a very happy light":** Fisher, *Nazi Saboteurs on Trial,* 111.

111 **"I spelled it out":** Danelski, "Saboteurs' Case," 76.

111 **Stone sent his draft opinion:** Mason, *Harlan Fiske Stone,* 661–663.

111   **Reed advised him privately:** Danelski, "Saboteurs' Case," 76.

112   **met with Byrnes at the White House:** James F. Byrnes, *All in One Life-time* (Harper and Brothers, 1958), 154–155.

112   **"I get so damn lonely here":** David Robertson, *Sly and Able: A Political Biography of James F. Byrnes* (W. W. Norton, 1994), 307. Byrnes authored only sixteen opinions in his Supreme Court career, and not a single concurrence or dissent.

112   **"Let me tell you what I said to Jimmie":** Frankfurter to FDR, September 30, 1942, in *Roosevelt and Frankfurter: Their Correspondence, 1928–1945*, ed. Max Freedman (Little, Brown, 1967), 670–671.

112   **press reaction was generally favorable:** The *Washington Post* reported, "Justice Byrnes is one of the foremost authorities on government administration in the United States. He knows the economic problems of this country whether they concern labor, the farmer, the consumer, small retail store, or the manufacturer." "Byrnes Quits Supreme Court to Direct U.S. Economic Policy," *Washington Post*, October 4, 1942, 1.

112   **"Maybe we ought to pass":** David M. Kidney, "Let's Stabilize Supreme Court, Congress Says," *Pittsburgh (PA) Press*, October 9, 1942, 17 (quoting an unnamed Senator).

112   **"regards the Supreme Court as a part of his own Administration":** Merlo Pusey, "Wartime Washington," *Washington Post*, October 6, 1942, 9.

113   **"glad [they] had one member of the Court":** Alfred McCormack, "A Law Clerk's Recollections," *Columbia Law Review* 46, no. 5 (1946): 710, 718. One slightly different version has Stone telling Byrnes, "I am sorry to lose you from the Court, but I'm glad you can make up your mind whether you want to be a judge or something else." Mason, "Extra-Judicial Work," 206, 206n33.

113   **"This is no time for haggling":** Associated Press, "People Need to Know What to Do, Is Claim," *Deseret News* (Salt Lake City, UT), September 1, 1942, 2.

113   **"greatest encouragement":** Associated Press, "U.S. Leaders Laud Red Stand at Stalingrad," *Salt Lake Tribune* (Salt Lake City, UT), September 25, 1942, 3.

113   **"The Japanese attack":** United Press, "Justice Roberts Asserts People Need Waking Up," *Evening News* (Harrisburg, PA), 1.

113   **Roberts proudly gathering scrap metal:** Associated Press, *Knoxville (TN) Journal*, October 2, 1942, 10. Roberts proclaimed it was "'everybody's' war" as he posed with his scrap.

113   **"Bring in Scrap to Kill a Jap!":** *St. Louis Post-Dispatch*, September 25, 1942, 24.

113   **horse and buggy:** "Everybody's Weekly," *Philadelphia Inquirer*, September 20, 1942, 4; *Philadelphia Inquirer*, August 18, 1942, 16; *The Times*

(Munster, IN), August 19, 1942, 56. One newspaper cartoon showed Jackson behind a horse and buggy; the caption stated, "This is the life! That tire shortage is just a good excuse for horse-loving Robert H. Jackson to go buggy-riding behind his favorite mare." *Akron (OH) Beacon-Journal*, October 18, 1942, comics section, 16.

113   *Forbes* **named him:** "Men Behind the Scenes (From Forbes Magazine)," *Marion (OH) Star*, October 2, 1942, 6.

114   *Talk of the Town:* Harold V. Cohen, "The Drama Desk," *Pittsburgh (PA) Post-Gazette*, September 23, 1942, 9; "Dale Harrison's New York," *Scranton (PA) Times*, October 7, 1942, 5. Director George Stevens denied that the character was based on Frankfurter. "Dale Harrison's New York."

114   **"bad graces of the White House":** Ray Tucker, "National Whirligig," *Albuquerque (NM) Journal*, October 5, 1942, 4.

114   **"Busybody Justice Felix Frankfurter":** Drew Pearson, "Washington Merry-Go-Round," *Anniston (AL) Star*, September 3, 1942, 4.

114   **fifteen pounds lighter:** Associated Press, "Justice Murphy Warns Against Delay," *Clarion-Ledger* (Jackson, MS), September 21, 1942, 9.

114   **"harder than some of the rocks":** "Murphy Finishes Army Duty; Back in Washington," *Chicago Tribune*, September 17, 1942, 2.

114   **Rumored to be a candidate:** Ray Tucker, "The National Whirligig," *Salt Lake Telegram* (Salt Lake City, UT), September 23, 1942, 10.

114   **American weapons as the best in the world:** "Apathy on the Home Front Must End," *Detroit Free Press*, September 21, 1942, 13.

114   **"tanks made in Detroit":** International News Service, "Murphy Urges Labor Parley," *Morning News* (Wilmington, DE), September 29, 1942, 7.

114   **"cousin of Hirohito's":** "Apathy on the Home Front Must End," *Detroit Free Press*, September 21, 1942, 13. Hirohito was the Emperor of Japan during World War II. The article misspelled his name as "Hirohita."

114   **business and labor to work together:** United Press, "Strikes Endanger Nation," *Pittsburgh (PA) Press*, October 2, 1942, 16.

114   **should cooperate:** International News Service, "Murphy Urges Labor Parley."

114   **Murphy undertook a mission:** "Justice Frank Murphy Is Off to Speed Up Detroit Plants," *Chicago Tribune*, September 18, 1942, 18; "Justice Murphy to Report on Tour of War Industries," *The Robesonian* (Lumberton, NC), September 30, 1942, 6.

114   **"this nation is not mobilized":** Associated Press, "Says Nation Not Mobilized to Win," *Lincoln (NE) Journal Star*, October 2, 1942, 8.

114   **Justices arrived at the White House:** "October 13th, 1942," Franklin D. Roosevelt Day by Day (website), Pare Lorentz Center, FDR Presidential Library, http://www.fdrlibrary.marist.edu/daybyday. The meeting with the President lasted from 5:25 p.m. to 6:37 p.m.

115 **prominently mentioned for Byrnes's Court seat:** Associated Press, "Roosevelt to Name 8th Court Choice," *Washington Post*, October 4, 1942, 3; "Fahy Is Likely Choice to Fill Supreme Court," *Chicago Tribune*, October 27, 1942, 7.

115 **"Jovial Justices":** *Des Moines (IA) Register*, October 25, 1942, section 9, 1.

115 **consider the validity:** *Ex parte Quirin*, 317 U.S. 1, 25 (1942).

115 **Core constitutional rights:** *Ex parte Quirin*, 317 U.S. at 39–45.

115 **authority of Congress and the President:** *Ex parte Quirin*, 317 U.S. at 24–36. For examples of legal historians disputing Stone's interpretation, see Danelski, "Saboteurs' Case," 73, 79.

116 **one "specification" in the first charge:** *Ex parte Quirin*, 317 U.S. at 36–38. The charges are reprinted in Fisher, *Nazi Saboteurs on Trial*, 61–63. Stone's reliance on only one of the two specifications in the first charge meant that he actually was finding only one half of one charge sufficient.

116 **"I am troubled some":** Danelski, "Saboteurs' Case," 73, 82n55.

116 **"not an enemy belligerent" and not "associated with the armed forces of the enemy":** *Ex parte Quirin*, 317 U.S. at 45. For the facts in Milligan's case, see *Ex parte Milligan*, 71 U.S. 2, 6–7 (1866).

117 **that he was an American citizen:** *Ex parte Quirin*, 317 U.S. at 37–38; Amanda L. Tyler, *Habeas Corpus in Wartime: From the Tower of London to Guantanamo Bay* (Oxford University Press, 2017), 246–276. In the case involving the American initially held at Guantanamo, a four-Justice plurality relied on *Quirin* for the proposition that American citizens could be tried as enemy combatants; two Justices found it unnecessary to resolve the question; two Justices believed *Quirin* erroneous on this point; and one Justice approved treating an American citizen as an enemy combatant for reasons different from the plurality. See *Hamdi v. Rumsfeld*, 542 U.S. 507, 519 (2004) (plurality opinion of O'Connor, J.); *id.* at 549 (Souter, J., concurring in part, dissenting in part, and concurring in the judgment); *id.* at 570 (Scalia, J., dissenting); *id.* at 587 (Thomas, J., dissenting).

117 **Black, reflecting the concern he and Jackson:** Danelski, "Saboteurs' Case," 76. Black advised Stone, "In this case I want to go no further than to declare that these particular defendants are subject to the jurisdiction of a military tribunal because of the circumstances and purposes of their entry into this country as part of the enemy's war forces. Such a limitation…would leave the *Milligan* doctrine untouched, but to subject every person in the United States to trial by military tribunals for every violation of every rule of war which has been or may hereafter be adopted between nations among themselves, might go far to destroy the protections declared by the *Milligan* case."

117 **Douglas objected to a sentence:** Danelski, "Saboteurs' Case," 76.

118   **"This whole business of reviewing the President's Order"**: Jackson's draft concurrence is discussed in Jack Goldsmith, "Justice Jackson's Unpublished Opinion in *Ex parte Quirin*," *Green Bag* 9, no. 3 (2006): 223, and reprinted there as an appendix.

118   **"F.F.'s Soliloquy"**: Frankfurter's "Soliloquy" is discussed and reprinted in White, "Felix Frankfurter's 'Soliloquy.'" See also Michal Belknap, "Frankfurter and the Nazi Saboteurs," in *Supreme Court Historical Society Yearbook 1982* (Supreme Court Historical Society, 1982), 68–71.

118   **"one of the most unusual documents"**: Danelski, "Saboteurs," 76.

119   **"in as brief a form as possible"**: Danelski, "Saboteurs' Case," 78.

119   **"patient negotiations"**: Danelski, "Saboteurs' Case," 78.

119   **"majority...not agreed"**: *Ex parte Quirin*, 317 U.S. at 47–48 (1942).

119   **had the clerk's office**: United Press, "Supreme Court Rules on Nazi Sabotage Case," *Honolulu Star-Bulletin*, October 29, 1942, 4.

119   **"*Milligan* case is out of the way"**: Danelski, "Saboteurs' Case," 79.

120   **Cox-Stone correspondence**: Oscar Cox to Harlan Fiske Stone, October 31, 1942; Harlan Fiske Stone to Oscar Cox, November 15, 1942, both in box 61, Oscar S. Cox Papers, Franklin D. Roosevelt Presidential Library and Museum, Hyde Park, NY. Both Frankfurter and Jackson had sent letters to defense counsel Royall praising him for his representation of the saboteurs shortly after the Court issued its July 31 per curiam decision. Eugene Rachlis, *They Came to Kill: The Story of Eight Nazi Saboteurs in America* (Popular Library, 1962), 232; Michael Dobbs, *Saboteurs: The Nazi Raid on America* (Vintage, 2005), 251.

120   **editorials generally had praised**: "They That Take the Sword," editorial, *New York Times*, August 9, 1942, 8; "Justice Is Done," editorial, *Washington Post*, August 9, 1942, B6. Both editorials are cited in Louis Fisher, *Military Tribunals and Presidential Power: American Revolution to the War on Terrorism* (University Press of Kansas, 2005), 119.

120   **"make a farce out of justice"**: Norman Cousins, "The Saboteurs," *Saturday Review of Literature*, August 8, 1942, 8, cited in Fisher, *Military Tribunals*, 119.

120   **Court's full opinion**: United Press, "Narrow Court Decision Is Given in Spying Cases," *Dayton (OH) Herald*, October 30, 1942, 29.

120   **Frederick Bernays Wiener**: Danelski, "Saboteurs' Case," 79–80.

120   **"ceremonious detour"**: Edward S. Corwin, *Total War and the Constitution* (Alfred A. Knopf, 1947), 188, quoted in Mason, *Harlan Fiske Stone*, 665.

120   **"involvement in the trial"**: Mason, *Harlan Fiske Stone*, 663.

121   **"foundations of the Court's holding"**: Tyler, *Habeas Corpus*, 257. Tyler's observation concerns the Court's holding on the irrelevance of the citizen/noncitizen distinction.

121   "not a happy precedent": Danelski, "Saboteurs' Case," 80.

121   Douglas on *Quirin*: Fisher, *Military Tribunals*, 124; William O. Douglas, *The Court Years, 1939–1975: The Autobiography of William O. Douglas* (Random House, 1980), 138–139.

121   John Frank on *Quirin*: Danelski, "Saboteurs' Case," 80.

121   "not the Court's finest hour": *Hamdi v. Rumsfeld*, 542 U.S. 507, 569 (2004) (Scalia, J., dissenting, joined by Stevens, J.).

121   O'Connor invoked *Quirin*: *Hamdi*, 542 U.S. at 522–523.

121   Stevens cited it: *Rasul v. Bush*, 542 U.S. 466, 475 (2004).

122   draft of the opinion: Danelski, "Saboteurs' Case," 78–79.

122   majority decisions by 4–3 votes in 1942: *Mishawka Rubber & Woolen Manufacturing Co. v. S.S. Kresge Co.*, 316 U.S. 203 (1942); *United States v. Wayne Pump Co.*, 317 U.S. 200 (1942).

122   erroneously suggest the Court was evenly divided: Reed biographer John Fassett, for example, states that the Court was "equally divided" on the issue. John Fassett, *New Deal Justice: The Life of Stanley Reed of Kentucky* (Vantage, 1994), 333. Stone biographer Mason likewise mistakenly asserts that "the bench split down the middle on the meaning of the Articles." Mason, *Harlan Fiske Stone*, 663. The Court had been evenly divided on the issue until Byrnes left the Court, and after that point, it was a 4–3 division. Danelski, "Saboteurs' Case," 76–79.

122   glaring problems: A partial summary of the problems can be found in Fisher, *Military Tribunals*, 124–126.

122   "executive juggernaut": Mason, *Harlan Fiske Stone*, 666.

122   "carried water for the Administration": Fisher, *Nazi Saboteurs on Trial*, 19.

122   "If there is any lesson to be learned": Danelski, "Saboteurs' Case," 80.

123   "I hope you noticed": Harlan Fiske Stone to Sterling Carr, November 17, 1942, quoted in Mason, *Harlan Fiske Stone*, 664.

CHAPTER 7

125   "The courtroom was full": Associated Press, "Supreme Court Room Crowded as Willkie Defends Communist," *Cincinnati Enquirer*, November 10, 1942, 2.

126   "familiar lock of hair": Associated Press, "Supreme Court Room Crowded as Willkie Defends Communist," *Cincinnati Enquirer*, November 10, 1942, 2.

126   "simple, barefoot Wall Street lawyer": Turner Catledge, "Ickes Belittles Willkie Address as 'Demagoguery,'" *New York Times*, August 20, 1940, 1.

126 **Willkie on civil liberties:** Wendell L. Willkie, "Fair Trial," *New Republic*, March 18, 1940, 370–372; David Levering Lewis, *The Improbable Wendell Willkie: The Businessman Who Saved the Republican Party and His Country, and Conceived a New World Order* (Liveright, 2018), 272.

127 *Schneiderman* **decisions in lower courts:** District court: *United States v. Schneiderman*, 33 F. Supp. 510 (N.D. Cal. 1940); Court of Appeals: *United States v. Schneiderman*, 119 F.2d 500 (9th Cir. 1941).

127 **"A more incongruous meeting":** William Schneiderman, *Dissent on Trial: The Story of a Political Life* (MEP Publications, 1983), 79. Days before Willkie and Schneiderman met on December 8, the *New York Times* reported that Willkie would take on the representation. James C. Hagerty, "Willkie to Plead Case for U.S. Red," *New York Times*, November 29, 1941, 1.

127 **"shirt front" and "the brief had to be completely his":** Carol King, "The Willkie I Knew," *New Masses*, October 24, 1944, 10.

127 **"totalitarian":** Brief for Petitioner at 5, 26, *Schneiderman v. United States*, 320 U.S. 118 (1943) (No. 311).

128 **Welles, a close friend of FDR:** Jeffrey F. Liss, "The *Schneiderman* Case: An Inside View of the Roosevelt Court," *Michigan Law Review* 74, no. 3 (1976): 500, 507; J. Woodford Howard, *Mr. Justice Murphy: A Political Biography* (Princeton University Press, 1968), 310; Sidney Fine, *Frank Murphy: The Washington Years* (University of Michigan Press, 1984), 409; John D. Fassett, *New Deal Justice: The Life of Stanley Reed of Kentucky* (Vantage, 1994), 357.

128 **"It was an open secret":** Lewis Wood, "Red's Citizenship Declared Valid by Supreme Court in 5-to-3 Ruling," *New York Times*, June 22, 1943, 1.

128 **"embarrassing to proceed":** Mason, *Harlan Fiske Stone*, 686; Fine, *Frank Murphy*, 409.

128 **discussion in the Court's private conference on April 22:** Fine, *Frank Murphy*, 409; Liss, "*Schneiderman* Case," 500, 507.

129 **"near Stalingrad":** King, "Willkie I Knew," 10. Schneiderman later stated that Willkie "was stretching a point": Schneiderman believed he actually had been born "at least a thousand miles or more" from Stalingrad. Schneiderman, *Dissent on Trial*, 96.

130 **Willkie had met with Stalin:** "Willkie Is Toasted by Stalin as Guest at Kremlin Dinner," *New York Times*, September 28, 1942, 1; Lewis, *Improbable Wendell Willkie*, 223–265. FDR had given Willkie a private letter to Stalin with instructions that Willkie hand it to Stalin personally—but Willkie forgot to deliver the letter. Lewis, *Improbable Wendell Willkie*, 230, 248.

130 **"[whacked] the lectern with the flat of his fingers":** Associated Press, "Penalizing of Farmer Upheld," *Cincinnati Enquirer*, November 10, 1942, 26.

130   **Wilkie observed…Fahy, rising to answer:** Dewey L. Fleming, "Willkie Defends Communist's Case," *Baltimore Sun*, November 10, 1942, 1; Frederick R. Barkley, "Communist's Case Argued by Willkie," *New York Times*, November 10, 1942, 1; Associated Press, "Supreme Court Room Crowded as Willkie Defends Communist," *Cincinnati Enquirer*, November 10, 1942, 26; "Willkie, Defending Communist, Says Social Ideas Complicated," *Miami Herald*, November 10, 1942, 10-B; "California Communist Defended by Willkie," *Los Angeles Times*, November 10, 1942, 11; Associated Press, "Willkie Asks for Citizenship for Communist," *St. Albans (VT) Daily Messenger*, November 10, 1942, 3. Fahy later said that the Schneiderman matter was one of the few Supreme Court cases he had discussed with FDR directly and that the President had left him free to pursue the case as he saw fit. Liss, "*Schneiderman* Case," 506–507. Schneiderman, in turn, claimed that he learned "many years later of the behind-the-scenes role of President Roosevelt in the prosecution of the case," but he did not explain his statement or provide support for it. Schneiderman, *Dissent on Trial*, 83.

131   **At its conference:** Joseph P. Lash, ed., *From the Diaries of Felix Frankfurter* (W. W. Norton, 1975), 210–217; Fine, *Frank Murphy*, 410–411.

132   **"a new Court":** John Paul Stevens, *The Making of a Justice: Reflections on My First 94 Years* (Little, Brown, 2019), 135.

133   **Public speculation:** Associated Press, "Roosevelt to Name 8th Court Choice," *Washington Post*, October 4, 1942, 3; "Biddle Is Reported Cool to Court Post," *New York Times*, October 8, 1942, 16.

133   **an opportunity to promote:** Brad Snyder, *Democratic Justice: Felix Frankfurter, the Supreme Court, and the Making of the Liberal Establishment* (W.W. Norton, 2022), 406–409.

133   **"In time of national emergency":** Frankfurter to FDR, December 3, 1942, in *Roosevelt and Frankfurter: Their Correspondence, 1928–1945*, ed. Max Freedman (Little, Brown, 1967), 673.

133   **1942 midterm elections:** "Party Divisions of the House of Representatives, 1789 to Present," History, Art & Archives (website), United States House of Representatives, accessed January 21, 2023, https://history.house .gov/Institution/Party-Divisions/Party-Divisions/; "Party Division," United States Senate (website), accessed January 21, 2023, https://www.senate.gov /history/partydiv.htm.

133   **Democrats tried to spin:** Robert C. Albright, "Hill Leaders See Mandate for Tighter War Effort," *Washington Post*, November 6, 1942, 1; Henry N. Dorris, "Wallace Blames Light Vote Cast," *New York Times*, November 6, 1942, 17.

134   **"Felix overplayed his hand":** William O. Douglas, *Go East, Young Man: The Early Years* (Random House, 1974), 332 (ellipses omitted). Douglas's

recollection, decades after the poker game, contains at least one obvious error. He refers to the work of Missy LeHand on the Byrnes Supreme Court vacancy (in early 1943), but LeHand had suffered a debilitating stroke in June 1941 and was no longer working in the White House at that time—or working any place—during a prolonged and ultimately unsuccessful convalescence. Grace Tully, who had worked under LeHand, had assumed LeHand's responsibilities as FDR's personal secretary by the time of the Byrnes vacancy. Perhaps Douglas was thinking of Tully rather than LeHand.

134   **"Sometimes a fellow gets estopped by his own words and his own deeds"**: FDR to Frankfurter, December 4, 1942, in Freedman, *Roosevelt and Frankfurter,* 674.

134   **Rutledge's background:** Louis Pollak, "Wiley B. Rutledge," in *The Supreme Court Justices: Illustrated Biographies, 1789–1993,* ed. Clare Cushman (Congressional Quarterly, 1993), 411–415.

134   **"Wiley, you have geography!":** Henry J. Abraham, *Justices and Presidents: A Political History of Appointments to the Supreme Court,* 2nd ed. (Oxford University Press, 1985), 235.

134   **Rutledge's amiability:** Supreme Court historian Henry J. Abraham noted that Rutledge "genuinely loved people of all walks of life." Abraham, *Justices and Presidents,* 235. Rutledge once wrote to Harvard constitutional law professor Thomas Reed Powell, "I like people, have some sort of way of letting them know it, and in turn, they like me regardless of all the other deficiencies." John M. Ferren, *Salt of the Earth, Conscience of the Court: The Story of Justice Wiley Rutledge* (University of North Carolina Press, 2004), 219.

134   **"a quiet, dignified man":** William O. Douglas, *The Court Years, 1939–1975: The Autobiography of William O. Douglas* (Random House, 1980), 25.

135   **Irving Brant:** Ferren, *Salt of the Earth,* 218–219; Brad Snyder, *Democratic Justice: Felix Frankfurter, the Supreme Court, and the Making of the Liberal Establishment* (W. W. Norton, 2022), 303–307, 408.

135   **Stone also privately advised…devoted to its work:** Francis Biddle, *In Brief Authority* (Doubleday, 1962), 192–193.

135   **Rutledge wrote the President:** Ferren, *Salt of the Earth,* 221.

136   **Willkie, Fahy, and Rutledge at reargument:** Associated Press, "Willkie Speaks for Communist," *Wilkes-Barre (PA) Record,* March 13, 1943, 2; "Willkie in Fiery Plea," *Kansas City Times,* March 13, 1943, 7; "Willkie Presses Argument for Red," *New York Times,* March 13, 1943, 15. Decades later, Fahy told an interviewer that "Willkie's performance was far more 'lawyer-like' on reargument and, therefore, far more effective." Liss, "*Schneiderman* Case," 503n18. Willkie biographer David Levering

Lewis similarly noted that Willkie's reargument "was said to have been less flamboyant and technically tighter" than his first argument. *Improbable Wendell Willkie*, 274.

136 **Wilkie as top candidate:** "Governor Stassen to Discuss Post-war Planning and Fourth Term Talk Tonight," *Tampa (FL) Times*, March 13, 1943, 4. For Republican criticism of Willkie's Schneiderman representation, see Ellsworth Barnard, *Wendell Willkie: Fighter for Freedom* (Northern Michigan University Press, 1966), 400–405; and Lewis, *Improbable Wendell Willkie*, 271.

136 **Black elicited a concession:** Lash, *Diaries*, 209. The back-and-forth between Black and Frankfurter described by Frankfurter in his diary apparently was whispered and private; no contemporary news account reported the comments.

137 **"It is an awful thing":** Lash, *Diaries*, 209.

137 **"doctrine of imputed guilt":** Fine, *Frank Murphy*, 411.

137 **"clear, unequivocal, and convincing" evidence:** *Schneiderman v. United States*, 320 U.S. 118, 125 (1943).

137 **Frankfurter's reaction:** Lash, *Diaries*, 248–249.

138 **"plain as a pikestaff":** Fine, *Frank Murphy*, 415–416.

138 **Frankfurter tried various approaches to Murphy:** Fine, *Frank Murphy*, 416.

138 **Frankfurter-Murphy discussions:** Lash, *Diaries*, 249, 257–259.

139 **Irish "forbears":** Fine, *Frank Murphy*, 417.

139 **Frankfurter also sought to pry Reed:** Fine, *Frank Murphy*, 417; Liss, "*Schneiderman* Case," 516.

139 **"The case obviously has nothing to do":** *Schneiderman*, 320 U.S., at 171–172 (Stone, C.J., dissenting).

139 **"We agree with our brethren":** *Schneiderman*, 320 U.S. at 119.

140 **Douglas circulated a concurrence:** *Schneiderman*, 320 U.S. at 161–165.

140 **Douglas's…opinion offended Murphy:** Lash, *Diaries*, 257–258; Liss, "*Schneiderman* Case," 512.

140 **Rutledge's concurrence:** *Schneiderman*, 320 U.S. at 165–170.

140 **"This is a magnificent opinion":** Howard, *Mr. Justice Murphy*, 322.

140 **was "instituted":** *Schneiderman*, 320 U.S. at 207. In a pointed note to Murphy, Jackson stated, "As you know, I disqualified myself.…The inference from that is this case was my responsibility. That is true to a very limited extent only, as you know." Liss, "*Schneiderman* Case," 521.

141 **newspapers observed:** "Beliefs Are Personal," editorial, *Washington Post*, June 24, 1943, 12; *Philadelphia Record*, June 23, 1943, cited in Liss, "*Schneiderman* Case," 508; Arthur Sears Henning, "Court Upholds Naturalization of Communist," *Chicago Tribune*, June 22, 1943, 4; Wood, "Red's Citizenship Declared Valid."

141 **"I have always felt confident"**: "Willkie Baffled by Motive," *New York Times*, June 22, 1943, 6. Willkie entered the primaries for the Republican nomination for President in 1944 but withdrew in April 1944 after disappointing showings. He died on October 8, 1944, at the age of fifty-two.

141 **unanimous opinion by Felix Frankfurter**: *Baumgartner v. United States*, 322 U.S. 665 (1944). When prosecutions of Communists intensified in the late 1940s and 1950s, the federal government frequently targeted William Schneiderman and his ideological allies. Remarkably, Schneiderman was a party (with others) in two additional Supreme Court cases and was on the winning side in both. See *Stack v. Boyle*, 342 U.S. 1 (1951); and *Yates v. United States*, 354 U.S. 298 (1957).

CHAPTER 8

143 **Marshall's life and personality**: Susan Low Bloch, "Thurgood Marshall," in *The Supreme Court Justices: Illustrated Biographies, 1789–1993*, ed. Clare Cushman (Congressional Quarterly, 1993), 476–480; Mark V. Tushnet, *Making Civil Rights Law: Thurgood Marshall and the Supreme Court, 1936–1961* (Oxford University Press, 1994), 6–9; Larry S. Gibson, *Young Thurgood: The Making of a Supreme Court Justice* (Prometheus, 2012); Michael Carter, "Meet: NAACP's Top Sleuth—Tweedy Thurgood Marshall," *Baltimore Afro-American*, June 3, 1944, 2.

144 **1940 criminal case**: *Chambers v. Florida*, 309 U.S. 227 (1940).

144 **traveled thirty-five thousand to fifty thousand miles each year**: Carter, "NAACP's Top Sleuth."

144 **"amazing type of man"**: Carter, "NAACP's Top Sleuth."

144 **reluctant local attorneys**: Tushnet, *Making Civil Rights Law*, 65.

145 **Marshall took over**: Thomas J. Ward Jr., "Competent Counsel: Thurgood Marshall, the Black Press, and the Alexandria Soldiers' Rape Trials," *Louisiana History*, summer 2020, 229, 244–245.

145 **Marshall vigorously proclaimed**: Thurgood Marshall to Miss Harper, August 5, 1943, 1–2; "Court Martial Condemns Three Soldiers to Hang," August 6, 1943, both in NAACP Records, Manuscript Division, Library of Congress, Washington, DC, accessed via ProQuest.

145 **"until the men are released to fight Hitler"**: "Petition for Writ of Habeas Corpus in La. Rape Case," *New York Age*, January 30, 1943, 1.

145 **"the NAACP was called upon"**: Langston Hughes, *Fight for Freedom: The Story of the NAACP* (W. W. Norton, 1962), 92–94.

145 **"attitude of the Negro soldiers"**: Marshall to Truman K. Gibson Jr., Acting Civilian Aide to Secretary of War, August 3, 1943, NAACP Legal Defense and Educational Fund Records, Manuscript Division, Library of Congress, Washington, DC, accessed via ProQuest. Gibson was an

African American lawyer who succeeded William Henry Hastie as civilian adviser to Secretary of War Stimson after Hastie resigned.

145   **Marshall-Hastie NAACP report:** "Report Hits Lynch Evil, Indecency to Soldiers," *Pittsburgh (PA) Courier*, December 12, 1942, 15. William Henry Hastie, one of Marshall's Howard University School of Law professors, became an influential mentor to the young civil rights lawyer. Hastie's pathbreaking career included appointment by FDR in 1937 as the first African American federal judge. (He was appointed to the federal district court in the Virgin Islands.) Hastie resigned after two years on the bench to become Dean of Howard University School of Law. In 1940, he became a high-ranking adviser to Secretary of War Stimson, but in January 1943 he quit in protest over discrimination against African Americans in the military. In 1949, Truman appointed Hastie to the US Court of Appeals for the Third Circuit, the first African American federal appellate judge. Gilbert Ware, *William Hastie: Grace Under Pressure* (Oxford University Press, 1984). Frankfurter had been a mentor to Hastie at Harvard Law School. Brad Snyder, *Democratic Justice: Felix Frankfurter, the Supreme Court, and the Making of the Liberal Establishment* (W. W. Norton, 2022), 151.

146   **"Negro boys are fighting and dying":** Cliff Mackay, "Fight, Howl for Rights: Marshall," *Jackson (MS) Advocate*, November 7, 1942, 2.

146   **Marshall discovered an important technical issue:** Thurgood Marshall to A. P. Tureaud, December 31, 1942, NAACP Records, Manuscript Division, Library of Congress, Washington, DC, accessed via ProQuest; Tushnet, *Making Civil Rights Law*, 65.

146   **"It is another instance":** Thurgood Marshall to NAACP office, January 20, 1943, NAACP Records, Manuscript Division, Library of Congress, Washington, DC, accessed via ProQuest.

147   *Adams* **case:** *Adams v. United States*, 319 U.S. 312 (1943). After the Supreme Court decision, the Army brought charges against the three defendants in military court, where the technical issue did not present the same jurisdictional problem. Marshall continued to represent them and to advocate on their behalf. The soldiers were court-martialed, convicted, and again sentenced to death. In June 1944, FDR commuted their sentences to life imprisonment, and the sentences later were commuted to a shorter period. In 1947, the US government granted parole to at least one of the soldiers and ordered his release in an application process headed by Marshall. Tushnet, *Making Civil Rights Law*, 66; Fred S. Rogers to Thurgood Marshall, December 5, 1947; Thurgood Marshall to Fred S. Rogers, December 10, 1947; and Thurgood Marshall to Blanche Holmes, December 10 and 29, 1947, in NAACP Records, Manuscript Division, Library of Congress, Washington, DC, accessed via ProQuest. In 1947 Marshall wrote a letter of appreciation for the pardon to Attorney General Tom Clark—the

man he would replace on the Supreme Court twenty years later. Thurgood Marshall to Attorney General Tom C. Clark, December 29, 1947, NAACP Records, Manuscript Division, Library of Congress, Washington, DC, accessed via ProQuest.

CHAPTER 9

149   **Jehovah's Witnesses:** Shawn Francis Peters, *Judging Jehovah's Witnesses: Religious Persecution and the Dawn of the Rights Revolution* (University Press of Kansas, 2000), 28–35.

150   **"in view of the aid they give":** Peters, *Judging Jehovah's Witnesses*, 186.

150   **Jehovah's Witnesses refusing military conscription:** Jeffrey S. Sutton, *51 Imperfect Solutions: States and the Making of American Constitutional Law* (Oxford University Press, 2018), 137.

150   **numerous important cases involving the Witnesses:** Gregory L. Peterson et al., "Recollections of *West Virginia State Board of Education v. Barnette,*" *St. John's Law Review* 81, no. 4 (2007): 755, 758. In one of the decisions, *Cantwell v. Connecticut*, 310 U.S. 296 (1940), the Supreme Court held for the first time that the Constitution's protection of the free exercise of religion binds state governments as well as the federal government.

150   **Jackson's life:** William E. Leuchtenburg, foreword to *That Man: An Insider's Portrait of Franklin D. Roosevelt*, by Robert H. Jackson, ed. John Barrett (Oxford University Press, 2003), vii–xii; John Q. Barrett, introduction to Jackson, *That Man*, xiii–xviii; John Q. Barrett, "Justice Jackson in the Jehovah's Witness Cases," *FIU Law Review* 13, no. 4 (2019): 827; John Q. Barrett, "Albany in the Life Trajectory of Robert H. Jackson," *Albany Law Review* 68 (2005): 513–537; James M. Marsh, "Robert H. Jackson," in *The Supreme Court Justices: Illustrated Biographies, 1789–1993*, ed. Clare Cushman (Congressional Quarterly, 1993), 406–410.

152   **"Nothing that I did was significant":** Jackson, *That Man*, 8.

152   **"mastermind among the malefactors":** Quentin R. Skrabec, *Aluminum in America: A History* (McFarland, 2017), 126.

152   **belonged to Jackson:** Noah Feldman, *Scorpions: The Battles and Triumphs of FDR's Great Supreme Court Justices* (Grand Central Publishing, 2010), 101.

152   **"Solicitor General for life":** Barrett, introduction, xvi.

153   **Jackson's legendary speech to federal prosecutors:** Robert H. Jackson, "The Federal Prosecutor," speech, Second Annual Conference of United States Attorneys, Department of Justice Building, April 1, 1940, https://www.justice.gov/sites/default/files/ag/legacy/2011/09/16/04-01-1940.pdf.

153   **Jackson's best-seller:** Robert H. Jackson, *The Struggle for Judicial Supremacy: A Study of a Crisis in American Power Politics* (Vintage, 1941).

153   **bringing him on cozy cruises:** Jackson, *That Man*, ix, 8, 13, 34, 55, 69, 122, 130, 137–148, 253n12.

153   **President's poker games:** Jackson, *That Man*, 76, 137, 140–144, 146.

153   **"too much of a gentleman":** Leuchtenburg, foreword to Jackson, *That Man*, x.

154   **FDR…privately advised Jackson:** Jackson, *That Man*, 73–74, 239n39. The case was *Southern Steamship Co. v. NLRB*, 316 U.S. 31 (1942).

154   **flag salute controversy:** Sutton, *51 Imperfect Solutions*, 141; David R. Manwaring, *Render unto Caesar: The Flag-Salute Controversy* (University of Chicago Press, 1962), 208–211; *West Virginia Board of Education v. Barnette*, 319 U.S. 624, 625–630 (1943). The Barnette sisters recounted their memories in 2006. Peterson et al., "Recollections," 768–771.

155   **"criminally inclined juveniles":** *West Virginia Board of Education v. Barnette*, 319 U.S. at 630.

155   **spelling of Barnette family name:** As noted previously, the family's name—Barnett—was misspelled as "Barnette" in court decisions throughout the litigation, including in the Supreme Court. Sutton, *51 Imperfect Solutions*, 139. For consistency with the Supreme Court's opinion, the judicial spelling is used here.

155   *Gobitis: Gobitis v. Minersville School Dist.*, 310 U.S. 586 (1940). The Gobitis family's name also is misspelled in the Supreme Court and lower-court opinions; the actual spelling was "Gobitas." Sutton, *51 Imperfect Solutions*, 135. Here, too, the judicial spelling (Gobitis) is used for consistency with the Supreme Court's opinion.

155   **"school board for the country":** *Gobitis*, 310 U.S. at 598.

155   **"ultimate foundation of a free society":** *Gobitis*, 310 U.S. at 596.

156   **"hardly anything else has been on my mind":** Peters, *Judging Jehovah's Witnesses*, 55.

156   **"really not rational":** Harold L. Ickes, *The Secret Diary of Harold L. Ickes*, vol. 3, *The Lowering Clouds* (Simon and Schuster, 1954), 199; Peters, *Judging Jehovah's Witnesses*, 54.

156   **"Felix's Fall-of-France Opinion":** John Frank, "Review of the *Brandeis/Frankfurter Connection*, by Bruce Allen Murphy," *Journal of Legal Education*, September 1982, 442, quoted in Peters, *Judging Jehovah's Witnesses*, 65.

156   **"some of the worst anti-Witness violence":** Peters, *Judging Jehovah's Witnesses*, 9.

156   **vigilantes attacked Witnesses:** Peters, *Judging Jehovah's Witnesses*, 9–11; Justin Driver, *The Schoolhouse Gate: Public Education, the Supreme Court, and the Battle for the American Mind* (Pantheon, 2018), 63–64.

156   **"Ain't you heard?":** Peters, *Judging Jehovah's Witnesses*, 84.

156   **castor oil:** Peters, *Judging Jehovah's Witnesses*, 90–92.

157   **removed a testicle:** Peters, *Judging Jehovah's Witnesses*, 95.

157   **flare-up at the wedding:** Katharine Graham, *Personal History* (Alfred A. Knopf, 1997), 121–122.

157   **More than 170 newspapers:** Driver, *Schoolhouse Gate*, 7; Sutton, *51 Imperfect Solutions*, 139. Eugene Meyer's *Washington Post* was one of the few newspapers that supported the decision. It said that the Court had "skillfully drawn" a "delicate line." "Rights and Privileges," editorial, *Washington Post*, June 4, 1940, 6.

157   **"To compel school children to salute the flag":** "The Flag-Salute Issue," *New York Herald Tribune*, April 29, 1940, 14, quoted in Driver, *Schoolhouse Gate*, 64n*.

157   **Ickes recorded:** Ickes, *Secret Diary*, 3:199.

157   **cocktails at Hyde Park:** Joseph P. Lash, ed., *From the Diaries of Felix Frankfurter* (W. W. Norton, 1975), 70.

158   **"Something curious is happening":** Eleanor Roosevelt, My Day, June 23, 1940, in David Emblidge, ed., *My Day: The Best of Eleanor Roosevelt's Acclaimed Newspaper Columns, 1936–1962* (Da Capo, 2001), 46.

158   **Elliott Roosevelt . . . radio address:** Peters, *Judging Jehovah's Witnesses*, 74; Associated Press, "Mob Violence Scored by Elliott Roosevelt," *Los Angeles Times*, June 4, 1940, 8.

158   **"wrongly decided":** *Jones v. City of Opelika*, 316 U.S. 584, 624 (1942) (statement of Black, Douglas, and Murphy, JJ.).

158   **Murphy's draft dissent:** Peters, *Judging Jehovah's Witnesses*, 65–66.

158   **"he has read the papers":** Lash, *Diaries*, 209; Peters, *Judging Jehovah's Witnesses*, 238.

158   **mistakenly deferred to Frankfurter:** William O. Douglas, *The Court Years, 1939–1975: The Autobiography of William O. Douglas* (Random House, 1980), 44. Douglas and Black also later asserted that they had had doubts about the *Gobitis* opinion when Stone circulated his solitary dissent three days before it was announced, but that it was too late to change their positions. Peters, *Judging Jehovah's Witnesses*, 236–237; Robert L. Tsai, "Reconsidering *Gobitis*: An Exercise in Presidential Leadership," *Washington University Law Review* 86, no. 2 (2008): 363, 370–371.

159   **Jackson and Ickes at Cabinet meeting:** Ickes, *Secret Diary*, 3:211; Peterson et al., "Recollections," 795. Jackson also had singled out *Gobitis* publicly as a decision unlike those in which the Court had been "vigilant in stamping out attempts by local authorities to suppress the free dissemination of ideas." Jackson, *Judicial Supremacy*, 284, 284n48.

159   **Rutledge on *Gobitis*:** John M. Ferren, *Salt of the Earth, Conscience of the Court: The Story of Justice Wiley Rutledge* (University of North Carolina Press, 2004), 188. As a judge on the District of Columbia Court of Appeals, Rutledge also had vigorously dissented—in what his biographer

called "a broadside"—from a decision upholding Witness convictions for
failing to pay a license tax regarding their literature sales. Ferren, *Salt of
the Earth*, 190–191.

159   **Hayden Covington:** Ronald K. L. Collins, "Thoughts on Hayden C. Covington and the Paucity of Legal Scholarship," *FIU Law Review* 13, no. 4
(2019): 599.

160   **"a tall, Texas tornado":** "Witness's Angle," *Newsweek*, March 22, 1943, 68.

160   **"don't preach in a dead language":** "Witness's Angle."

160   **three-judge district court:** *Barnette v. West Virginia State Board of Education*, 47 F. Supp. 251, 253–255 (S.D. W.Va. 1942).

160   **"one of the greatest mistakes":** Peters, *Judging Jehovah's Witnesses*, 249;
David R. Manwaring, *Render unto Caesar: The Flag-Salute Controversy*
(University of Chicago Press, 1962), 208–224; John Q. Barrett, "Arguing
Barnette, et al. (1943)," *The Jackson List* (blog), March 11, 2013, http://
thejacksonlist.com/wp-content/uploads/2014/02/20130311-Jackson-List
-Arguing-Barnette.pdf.

160   **cited more than sixty separate biblical passages:** Appellees' Brief at viii–
ix, *West Virginia State Board of Education v. Barnette*, 319 U.S. 624 (1943)
(No. 591).

160   **"like that of the Nazi regime":** Appellees' Brief at 7 n.1, *Barnette*.

161   **"adequate national defense":** American Legion Amicus Curiae Brief at
18, *West Virginia State Board of Education v. Barnette*, 319 U.S. 624 (1943)
(No. 591).

161   **other cases argued on March 10 and 11:** The Supreme Court ruled for
the Witnesses in *Martin v. Struthers*, 319 U.S. 141 (1943), *Murdock v. Pennsylvania*, 319 U.S. 105 (1943), and *Jones v. City of Opelika*, 319 U.S. 103
(1943). The Witnesses' only defeat (on the technical issue) was in *Douglas v. Jeannette*, 319 U.S. 157 (1943). Jackson's views are presented in an
opinion combining his concurrence in the result in *Douglas* and a dissent in the other cases. *Douglas v. City of Jeannette*, 319 U.S. at 166 (Jackson, J., concurring in the result in *Douglas* and dissenting in *Murdock*
and *Struthers*). See also *Murdock*, 319 U.S. at 117 (Reed, J., dissenting)
and 134 (Frankfurter, J., dissenting); *Struthers*, 319 U.S. at 154 (Reed, J.,
dissenting). And, in one case, Frankfurter refused to label his opinion a
concurrence or a dissent (based on what he claimed was an ambiguity
in the Court's decision); the Court reporter labeled it a dissent in the official report of the case. *Struthers*, 319 U.S. at 152–154 (Frankfurter, J.,
dissenting).

161   **Stone's law clerk later confirmed:** Peterson et al., "Recollections," 755,
784–785.

161   **"rather too journalistic":** Peters, *Judging Jehovah's Witnesses*, 251.

162 **"We shall not defeat the Nazi evil"**: Francis Biddle, radio address, June 16, 1940, quoted in Tsai, "Reconsidering Gobitis," 406.

162 **Justice Department civil rights officials**: Victor W. Rotnem and F. G. Folsom Jr., "Recent Restrictions upon Religious Liberty," *American Political Science Review* 36, no. 6 (1942): 1053, 1062–1063.

162 **"ugly picture"**: Rotnem and Folsom, "Recent Restrictions upon Religious Liberty," 1063. Jackson's draft included references to Biddle's radio address and the Justice Department lawyers' article, but he eventually deleted them. Tsai, "Reconsidering Gobitis," 432.

162 **"We work in offices"**: *Douglas v. Jeannette*, 319 U.S. at 174 (Jackson, J., concurring in the result and dissenting).

163 **Roberts and Frankfurter…notes**: Barrett, "Justice Jackson," 827, 849–850.

163 **"If there is any fixed star"**: *West Virginia Board of Education v. Barnette*, 319 U.S. 624, 642 (1943).

163 **"As governmental pressure toward unity"**: *Barnette*, 319 U.S. at 641.

163 **"extension of the right arm"**: *Barnette*, 319 U.S. at 628 n.3 (internal quotation marks omitted).

163 **"Those who begin coercive"**: *Barnette*, 319 U.S. at 641.

164 **"very heart of the *Gobitis* opinion"**: *Barnette*, 319 U.S. at 640.

164 **"No issue of federal constitutional law"**: Sutton, *51 Imperfect Solutions*, 142.

164 **"reluctance to make the Federal Constitution"**: *Barnette*, 319 U.S. at 643 (Black and Douglas, JJ., concurring).

164 **Murphy stressed**: *Barnette*, 319 U.S. at 644 (Murphy, J., concurring).

164 **"[adhered] to the views expressed by the Court"**: *Barnette*, 319 U.S. at 642–643 (statement of Roberts and Reed, JJ.).

164 **"One who belongs to the most vilified"**: *Barnette*, 319 U.S. at 646 (Frankfurter, J., dissenting).

165 **"If the function of this Court"**: *Barnette*, 319 U.S. at 652 (Frankfurter, J., dissenting). Frankfurter also emphasized that, before *Gobitis*, the Court had rejected three constitutional challenges to flag salutes "for want of a substantial federal question" and summarily affirmed a lower-court opinion rejecting such a challenge. *Id.* at 664. As Frankfurter biographer Brad Snyder relates, former Chief Justice Charles Evans Hughes wrote to Frankfurter that he agreed with Frankfurter's dissent in *Barnette* and believed that Holmes, Brandeis, and Cardozo would have agreed as well. Brad Snyder, *Democratic Justice: Felix Frankfurter, the Supreme Court, and the Making of the Liberal Establishment* (W. W. Norton, 2022), 428.

165 **appalled by his reference to his religion**: Lash, *Diaries*, 253–254. Some commentators argue that Frankfurter's *Gobitis* opinion and *Barnette*

dissent have been unfairly criticized, even if his bottom-line conclusion was erroneous. See, e.g., Richard Morgan, "The *Flag Salute Cases* Reconsidered," *Journal of Supreme Court History* 34, no. 3 (2009): 275.

165   **"Blot removed"**: *Time*, June 21, 1943, 16, quoted in Driver, *Schoolhouse Gate*, 65n*.

166   **"clear contradiction of the Hitler method"**: W. H. Lawrence, "Civil Liberties Gain by the Flag Decision," *New York Times*, June 20, 1943, E10, quoted in Driver, *Schoolhouse Gate*, 69–70.

166   **"a gem"**: Sutton, *51 Imperfect Solutions*, 141.

166   **"majestic"**: Driver, *Schoolhouse Gate*, 65n*.

166   **"the single finest writer"**: Driver, *Schoolhouse Gate*, 65.

166   **"so as not to wake the baby"**: Barrett, "Justice Jackson," 827, 851–852.

167   **marriage equality**: *Obergefell v. Hodges*, 576 U.S. 644 (2015).

167   **free speech**: *Wooley v. Maynard*, 430 U.S. 705, 714 (1977).

CHAPTER 10

169   **Winston Churchill...speech**: Dewey L. Fleming, "Churchill Pledges Aid to the End in Japan," *The Sun* (UK), May 20, 1943, 1; "Brilliant Array of American and British Leaders Hears Churchill Speech," *Akron (OH) Beacon Journal*, May 20, 1943, 21; Joseph P. Lash, ed., *From the Diaries of Felix Frankfurter* (W. W. Norton, 1975), 243; *The Sun*, May 20, 1943. Justice Frank Murphy was out of town and did not attend.

169   **Behind the Justices**: "As Congress Listened to British Prime Minister," *San Francisco Examiner*, May 20, 1943, 18.

169   **Edward at the Capitol**: Arthur Sears Henning, "Pulverize Japs After Hitler: Churchill Vow," *Chicago Tribune*, May 20, 1943, 1.

169   **friendly visit to Hitler**: "When the Duke of Windsor met Adolf Hitler," BBC News, March 10, 2016, www.bbc.com/news/uk-england-35765793.

169   **"received an ovation"**: Henning, "Pulverize."

170   **first official airplane trip by an American President**: Tony Reichhart, "The First Presidential Flight," *Smithsonian*, January 18, 2013.

170   **screening of *Casablanca***: Doris Kearns Goodwin, *No Ordinary Time: Franklin and Eleanor Roosevelt, the Home Front in World War II* (Simon and Schuster, 1994), 399.

170   **FDR and Churchill at Casablanca**: Jon Meacham, *Franklin and Winston: An Intimate Portrait of an Epic Friendship* (Random House, 2003), 209–211; Nigel Hamilton, *Commander in Chief: FDR's Battle with Churchill, 1943* (Houghton Mifflin Harcourt, 2016), 127–129.

170   **Allies had triumphed in Tunisia**: Hamilton, *Commander in Chief*, ix, 207–208.

170 **Chandler of Kentucky:** Robert De Vore, "Anglo-Soviet Policy on Japs Criticized," *Washington Post*, May 18, 1943, 1; John Fisher, "U.S. Facing Lone War in Pacific, Senate Warned," *Chicago Tribune*, May 18, 1943, 1. Chandler also briefly criticized the Soviet Union, but it was his vehement denunciation of Great Britain that attracted attention. Chandler is best known today for his subsequent role as Commissioner of Major League Baseball from 1945 to 1951, a period that included Jackie Robinson's historic debut in 1947. Appraisals of Chandler's role in integrating Major League Baseball differ. Some accounts, including baseball's official narrative ("Happy Chandler," National Baseball Hall of Fame, accessed January 22, 2023, https:// baseballhall.org/hall-of-famers/chandler-happy), praise Chandler, but others are skeptical, arguing that Chandler's record was mixed at best and pointing to his later support for segregationist politicians. See, e.g., Ira Berkow, "Where Did Happy Stand on Jackie?" *New York Times*, June 29, 1991, 29.

171 **Churchill's speech:** "Text of Churchill's Address Before Congress," *Washington Post*, May 20, 1943, 12.

171 **"Pulverize Japs":** Henning, "Pulverize."

171 **"widespread impression":** C. P. Trussell, "Congress Pleased by Churchill Talk," *New York Times*, May 20, 1943, 3.

171 **"one of Mr. Churchill's greatest parliamentary efforts":** Harold Callender, "Churchill Takes Part in a Congress Debate," *New York Times*, May 23, 1943, E3.

172 **Justices cheered lustily:** Walter White, "People and Places: Churchill's Speech," *Chicago Defender*, May 29, 1943, 15.

172 **"Prime Minister had an auditor":** Inez Robb, International News Service, "Duke Gets Curtain Calls at Churchill Triumph," *Miami Herald*, May 20, 1943, 4. Two nights after Churchill's speech, Frankfurter and Stone attended an intimate British Embassy dinner honoring the Prime Minister; high-ranking officials from the State and War Departments and former Justice James Byrnes also attended. Lash, *Diaries*, 243.

172 **"Mr. Churchill talks a good Jap war":** Henning, "Pulverize." Chandler praised Churchill's speech but thought it fell short on concrete commitments. John Fisher, "Why Not Fight to Win Burma? Chandler Asks," *Chicago Tribune*, May 20, 1943, 1.

172 *Los Angeles Times*: "Death Sentence of a Mad Dog," editorial, *Los Angeles Times*, December 8, 1941, 2.

172 **Congressman John M. Coffee:** Geoffrey Stone, *Perilous Times: Free Speech in Wartime—from the Sedition Act of 1798 to the War on Terrorism* (W. W. Norton, 2004), 289; Commission on Wartime Relocation and Internment of Civilians, *Personal Justice Denied* (University of Washington Press, 1997), 48n*.

173   **"every effort will be made to protect"**: Peter Irons, *Justice at War: The Story of the Japanese American Internment Cases* (Oxford University Press, 1983), 23–24.

173   **Hoover on "practically all"**: Commission on Wartime Relocation, *Personal Justice Denied*, 55–56.

173   **limited immigration...prohibited land ownership**: Commission on Wartime Relocation, *Personal Justice Denied*, 4–5.

173   **"the most effective Fifth Column work"**: Commission on Wartime Relocation, *Personal Justice Denied*, 55. A few days after his public statement, Knox repeated his claim of "very active fifth column work" in Hawaii at a Cabinet meeting. Biddle recorded Knox's statement; it is not clear from Biddle's notes whether Knox made this comment to the entire Cabinet or only to Biddle. Commission on Wartime Relocation, *Personal Justice Denied*, 56.

174   **"fifth column treachery"**: Commission on Wartime Relocation, *Personal Justice Denied*, 56 (citing West Coast headlines proclaiming "Fifth Column Treachery Told," "Fifth Column Prepared Attack," and "Secretary of Navy Blames 5th Column for Raid"). As the Commission reported, FBI Director J. Edgar Hoover "did not believe that fifth column activities were prevalent in Hawaii." *Personal Justice Denied*, 56n*.

174   **Roberts Commission report**: Commission on Wartime Relocation, *Personal Justice Denied*, 57–58, 264.

174   **"conflicting opinions from the intelligence services"**: Commission on Wartime Relocation, *Personal Justice Denied*, 264.

174   **Los Angeles County Manager**: Irons, *Justice at War*, 40–41.

175   **Anti-Japanese groups...American Legion**: Commission on Wartime Relocation, *Personal Justice Denied*, 67–69.

175   **Congressman Leland Ford**: Commission on Wartime Relocation, *Personal Justice Denied*, 70.

175   **congressional delegations...sent FDR a letter**: Commission on Wartime Relocation, *Personal Justice Denied*, 81. The letter was sent by California Congressman Clarence Lea, the senior member of the delegations, on behalf of the Representatives from California, Oregon, and Washington.

175   **Earl Warren...Governor Culbert Olson**: Commission on Wartime Relocation, *Personal Justice Denied*, 70, 76; Jim Newton, *Justice for All: Earl Warren and the Nation He Made* (Riverhead, 2006), 127–138.

176   **Japanese share in California's agriculture**: Newton, *Justice for All*, 130.

176   **"We're charged with wanting"**: Frank J. Taylor, "The People Nobody Wants," *Saturday Evening Post*, May 9, 1942, quoted in Commission on Wartime Relocation, *Personal Justice Denied*, 69. In January and February 1942, the Western Growers Protective Association, the Grower-Shippers, and the California Farm Bureau Federation "all demanded stern measures

against the ethnic Japanese." Commission on Wartime Relocation, *Personal Justice Denied*, 69.

176   **James Rowe:** Irons, *Justice at War*, 32.

176   **Edward Ennis:** Irons, *Justice at War*, 14–15.

176   **John J. McCloy:** Irons, *Justice at War*, 15–16; Kai Bird, *The Chairman: John J. McCloy and the Making of the American Establishment* (Simon and Schuster, 1992), 170.

177   **McCloy's relationship … with Frankfurter:** Irons, *Justice at War*, 16; Brad Snyder, *Democratic Justice: Felix Frankfurter, the Supreme Court, and the Making of the Liberal Establishment* (W. W. Norton, 2022), 372–373, 379.

177   **Allen Gullion and his aide Karl Bendetsen**: Irons, *Justice at War*, 30–31.

177   **John L. DeWitt:** Irons, *Justice at War*, 24–26. DeWitt's initial vacillation is exemplified by his comment in early January that mass evacuation of the Japanese was "damned nonsense," followed by his embrace of that policy. Francis Biddle, *In Brief Authority* (Doubleday, 1962), 215.

177   **"a second General Short":** Commission on Wartime Relocation, *Personal Justice Denied*, 65; Irons, *Justice at War*, 27.

177   **"we cannot discriminate":** Irons, *Justice at War*, 46.

177   **Stimson spent a long evening:** Greg Robinson, *By Order of the President: FDR and the Internment of Japanese Americans* (Harvard University Press, 2001), 95; Commission on Wartime Relocation, *Personal Justice Denied*, 59.

178   **"since the publication of the Roberts report":** Irons, *Justice at War*, 41 (quoting a telephone conversation between DeWitt and Bendetsen on January 29, 1942). Peter Irons observes that a "discernible shift in public opinion from relative tolerance to active hostility toward Japanese Americans followed release of the Roberts Commission report." Irons, *Justice at War*, 40.

178   **"rigors of war demand":** Quoted in Irons, *Justice at War*, 7.

178   **meeting on February 1:** Irons, *Justice at War*, 44; Commission on Wartime Relocation, *Personal Justice Denied*, 74–75. J. Edgar Hoover's opposition to the War Department's expulsion and incarceration position is detailed in Beverly Gage, *G-Man: J. Edgar Hoover and the Making of the American Century* (Viking, 2022), 258–261.

178   **"just a scrap of paper":** Commission on Wartime Relocation, *Personal Justice Denied*, 380n142. The Commission notes that McCloy's comment occurred in a meeting with the Justice Department on February 4, but in light of the context, it seems clear that McCloy's quote is from the meeting on February 1. Forty years later, testifying before a government commission investigating the incarceration decision, McCloy denied making the "scrap of paper" statement contemporaneously attributed to him. Commission on Wartime Relocation, *Personal Justice Denied*, 380n142.

179 "One obvious thought": Irons, *Justice at War*, 20.

179 "as stupid as it is unjust": Franklin D. Roosevelt, "Statement Against Discharging Loyal Aliens from Jobs," January 2, 1942, American Presidency Project (website), University of California, Santa Barbara, https://www.presidency.ucsb.edu/documents/statement-against-discharging-loyal-aliens-from-jobs.

179 **Biddle advised Roosevelt:** Commission on Wartime Relocation, *Personal Justice Denied*, 78.

179 **Their memo stated:** Commission on Wartime Relocation, *Personal Justice Denied*, 73, 378n133; Irons, *Justice at War*, 53-55. Rauh later maintained that the trio's memo sought to head off incarceration and that Cohen was personally distraught by a photo of a Japanese child leaning out of a window and waving an American flag on a train heading to an internment camp. Commission on Wartime Relocation, *Personal Justice Denied*, 378n133.

180 "tremendous hole": Commission on Wartime Relocation, *Personal Justice Denied*, 79.

180 "a stiff proposition": Commission on Wartime Relocation, *Personal Justice Denied*, 79.

180 "I took up with him": Commission on Wartime Relocation, *Personal Justice Denied*, 79.

180 "We have carte blanche": Stetson Conn, Rose C. Engelman, and Byron Fairchild, "Japanese Evacuation from the West Coast," chapter 5 in *The United States Army in World War II: The Western Hemisphere, Guarding the United States and Its Outposts* (Washington, DC, 1964), 132, quoted in Irons, *Justice at War*, 58.

181 "the Pacific Coast is in imminent danger": Walter Lippmann, "The Fifth Column on the Coast," *Washington Post*, February 12, 1942, 9.

181 "I am for immediate removal": Henry McLemore, "Are We Too Courteous to Japanese in California?" *Louisville (KY) Courier-Journal*, January 30, 1942, 7; Commission on Wartime Relocation, *Personal Justice Denied*, 72.

181 "Do you get what [Lippmann] says?": Westbrook Pegler, "Fair Enough," *Scranton (PA) Tribune*, February 16, 1942, 4; Irons, *Justice at War*, 61.

181 last-ditch memo to FDR: Commission on Wartime Relocation, *Personal Justice Denied*, 83.

182 "I gave them twenty-four hours notice": Commission on Wartime Relocation, *Personal Justice Denied*, 84.

182 "In the war in which we are now engaged": Commission on Wartime Relocation, *Personal Justice Denied*, 82.

183 "a Jap is a Jap": Irons, *Justice at War*, 46. DeWitt made the same statement to reporters the following year after testifying at a congressional hearing. Commission on Wartime Relocation, *Personal Justice Denied*, 66.

183 **"The very fact that no sabotage has taken place"**: Commission on Wartime Relocation, *Personal Justice Denied*, 82. Walter Lippmann had made the same point in his column, undoubtedly based on discussions with DeWitt or others in the War Department. Walter Lippmann, "The Fifth Column on the Coast," *Washington Post*, February 12, 1942, 9. DeWitt's Orwellian reasoning is not merely a relic of the World War II era. When the author of this book served as Special Envoy for Guantanamo Closure in 2013 and 2014, he was advised by a Department of Defense official that a Guantanamo detainee's record of spotless conduct during confinement meant that the detainee was especially dangerous—even though that same official previously had said that other detainees' unruly conduct and defiance justified continued detention. "The most dangerous ones," he explained, "are the ones who haven't done anything yet."

183 **"fill in the application"**: Irons, *Justice at War*, 61.

183 **Biddle hosted a meeting**: Irons, *Justice at War*, 61–62.

183 **"The decision had been made by the President"**: Biddle, *In Brief Authority*, 219.

184 **"Ennis almost wept"**: Irons, *Justice at War*, 62.

184 **"a good piece of work"**: Commission on Wartime Relocation, *Personal Justice Denied*, 84–85.

184 **"not important enough"**: Irons, *Justice at War*, 62. Nearly four decades later, Ennis testified, "Now when I look back on it I don't know why I didn't resign." Commission on Wartime Relocation, *Personal Justice Denied*, 378n130. For insightful analysis of when government officials should resign because of personal conscience and principled opposition, see James C. Thomson, "How Could Vietnam Happen? An Autopsy," *The Atlantic*, April 1968; and David Luban, "Complicity and Lesser Evils: A Tale of Two Lawyers," *Georgetown Journal of Legal Ethics* 34, no. 3 (2021): 613.

184 **Rowe took the executive order**: Irons, *Justice at War*, 63.

185 **"it was a minor problem"**: Irons, *Justice at War*, 365.

185 **Biddle similarly observed**: Biddle, *In Brief Authority*, 219.

185 **Executive Order 9066**: Exec. Order 9066 (February 19, 1942), F.R. Doc. 42-1563.

185 **"The President is authorized"**: Commission on Wartime Relocation, *Personal Justice Denied*, 6. Biddle's February 20 memo to FDR confirming his legal authority is similar to the memo FDR previously had received from Ben Cohen, Joe Rauh, and Oscar Cox. Commission on Wartime Relocation, *Personal Justice Denied*, 6.

186 **DeWitt issued a blizzard**: Irons, *Justice at War*, 70–72; Commission on Wartime Relocation, *Personal Justice Denied*, 93–116, 135–137.

186 **number of those incarcerated**: Stone, *Perilous Times*, 287.

186   **"You can shoot a man":** Commission on Wartime Relocation, *Personal Justice Denied*, 95.

186   **Congress took up:** An Act... to Provide a Penalty for Violations of Restrictions or Orders with Respect to Persons Entering, Remaining in, Leaving, or Committing Any Act in Military Areas or Zones, Pub. L. No. 77-503, 56 Stat. 173 (1942).

186   **Senator Robert Taft:** Senator Taft, speaking on S. 2352, on March 19, 1942, 77th Cong., 2nd sess., *Congressional Record* 99, pt. 2:2726, quoted in Commission on Wartime Relocation, *Personal Justice Denied*, 99.

187   **One poll:** Commission on Wartime Relocation, *Personal Justice Denied*, 112 (citing Office of Facts and Figures, the Office for Emergency Management, April 21, 1942). The poll showed a "virtual consensus that the government had done the right thing in moving Japanese aliens away from the coast," with close to 60 percent of Americans "[favoring] moving American citizens of Japanese ancestry." Commission on Wartime Relocation, *Personal Justice Denied*, 112.

187   **Deutsch telegram to Frankfurter:** Deutsch to Frankfurter, telegram, March 28, 1942, quoted in Commission on Wartime Relocation, *Personal Justice Denied*, 113.

187   **"the President knows of the program and has approved it":** McCloy to Frankfurter, April 1, 1942, box 160, General Correspondence, 1941–1945, Records of the Office of the Assistant Secretary of War, National Archives and Records Administration, College Park, MD.

187   **Frankfurter praised his friend:** Frankfurter to McCloy, April 2, 1942, quoted in Commission on Wartime Relocation, *Personal Justice Denied*, 113.

CHAPTER 11

189   **"Why the hell am I running back?":** Peter Irons, *Justice at War: The Story of the Japanese American Internment Cases* (Oxford University Press, 1983), 90–91.

189   **"I received a lift":** Irons, *Justice at War*, 91.

190   **Gordon Hirabayashi grew up twenty miles:** Irons, *Justice at War*, 87–93.

190   **required the expulsion:** Civilian Exclusion Order No. 57, 7 Fed. Reg. 3725 (May 10, 1942). For a photocopy of the order as it appeared at the time, see the website of the Japanese American Veterans Association, http://www.javadc.org/java/docs/1942-05-10%3B%20WDC%20%20Civilian%20Exclusion%20Order%20No.57,pg4_dg%3Bay.pdf.

190   **Hirabayashi arrest and trial:** Irons, *Justice at War*, 154–159.

191   **Yasui biographical facts:** *Yasui v. United States*, 320 U.S. 115, 116–117 (1943); Irons, *Justice at War*, 81–87.

191 **"a relatively high opinion"**: Wayne Morse to ACLU Director Roger Baldwin, 1943, quoted in Irons, *Justice at War*, 82. Morse also noted that, "on many occasions," he had "detected a streak of blind stubbornness" in Min Yasui. Irons, *Justice at War*, 82.

192 **"There the general is wrong"**: Irons, *Justice at War*, 84. The curfew applied to noncitizens from Japan, Germany, and Italy, but only to American citizens "of Japanese ancestry."

192 **Yasui arrest and trial**: Irons, *Justice at War*, 135–142, 160–161. Irons explains that, shortly after Pearl Harbor, Yasui's father, a Japanese alien, was arrested as a possible sympathizer of Japan and assigned to the Justice Department's incarceration camp in Missoula, Montana. This process was different from the incarceration for the many "evacuated" Japanese Americans and Japanese noncitizens who were detained and imprisoned on no suspicion at all. The arrest and detention of Yasui's father were not a factor in the judicial decisions regarding Yasui's case. Irons, *Justice at War*, 83.

192 **Ninth Circuit**: Associated Press, "Argue Japanese Exclusion Edict," *Spokesman-Review* (Spokane, WA), February 20, 1943, 1; Irons, *Justice at War*, 175–180.

193 **Ninth Circuit...certified**: Brief for Appellant at 33–37, *Hirabayashi v. United States*, 320 U.S. 81 (1943) (No. 870). The Ninth Circuit's *Yasui* certification order is described in *American Civil Liberties Union News*, April 1943.

193 **"threat of penitentiary sentences"**: Denman dissent, reprinted as Appendix A to *Korematsu v. United States*, 140 F.2d 289, 300–304 (9th Cir. 1943) (Denman, J., concurring in the result and dissenting). Apparently scandalized by Denman's dissent, the Ninth Circuit ordered that it not be included in the official report of the court's decision. Denman released it to the press and included it as an appendix in a subsequent published opinion. Irons, *Justice at War*, 183–185. Denman's dissent included criticism of internment as being like the Nazis' internment of Jews, as well as bizarre observations and digressions about "Mongoloid" people. *Korematsu*, 140 F.2d at 300–304. In a later Supreme Court conference, Frankfurter mentioned that, while he disagreed with Denman's dissent, he opposed the Ninth Circuit's "scheme to gag a judge." Joseph P. Lash, ed., *From the Diaries of Felix Frankfurter* (W. W. Norton, 1975), 227.

193 **certification order...origin**: Irons, *Justice at War*, 182–183.

193 **Supreme Court agreed**: *Hirabayashi v. United States*, 63 S. Ct. 860 (1943); *Yasui v. United States*, 63 S. Ct. 860 (1943).

193 **"disgraceful situation"**: Appellant's Brief at 55, *Yasui v. United States*, 320 U.S. 115 (1943) (No. 871).

193 **didn't "want any Jap back on the Coast"**: Appellant's Reply Brief, Appendix, *Hirabayashi v. United States*, 320 U.S. 81 (1943) (No. 870), May

14, 1943; Appellant's Brief at 55, *Yasui*. Amicus briefs also quoted DeWitt's comment that "a Jap is a Jap." See, e.g., Brief of the American Civil Liberties Union, Amicus Curiae, at 8, *Hirabayashi v. United States* (No. 870) and *Yasui v. United States* (No. 871), October Term, 1942. As Peter Irons has detailed, the ACLU played a leading role in the strategy of Hirabayashi's Supreme Court case amid friction between the national organization and the local San Francisco branch. Consistent with a national ACLU policy position, the focus of the constitutional challenge in the Supreme Court was DeWitt's orders and the congressional statute rather than FDR's executive order; a significant contingent of the ACLU did not want to directly confront FDR. Nevertheless, in response to the government's reliance on the President's war power, Hirabayashi's reply brief did include a section arguing that the "war power of the president does not support the orders." Appellant's Reply Brief at 7–9, *Hirabayashi*, May 14, 1943; Irons, *Justice at War*, 186–192.

194   **Black and his wife:** Roger K. Newman, *Hugo Black: A Biography* (Fordham University Press, 1997), 314.

194   **Douglas also knew...the General:** Bruce Allen Murphy, *Wild Bill: The Legend and Life of William O. Douglas* (Random House, 2003), 206.

194   **Solicitor General's brief:** Brief for the United States, *Hirabayashi v. United States*, 320 U.S. 81 (1943) (No. 870), May 8, 1943.

194   **"might be regarded as loyal":** Brief for the United States at 61, *Hirabayashi*.

194   **Kenneth Ringle memos:** K. D. Ringle, "Ringle Report," January 26, 1942; Kenneth Ringle, "On the Japanese Question in the U.S.: A Compilation of Memoranda," June 19, 1942, http://www.mansell.com/eo9066/1942/42-01 /Ringle.html.

194   **Ringle..."black bag" break-in:** Ringle's son, journalist Ken Ringle, provided an overview of Ringle's activities, including his black bag job at the Japanese consulate, in "What Did You Do Before the War, Dad?," *Washington Post*, December 6, 1981, SM54. The black bag job incident did not come to light until later and is not mentioned in the Ringle report or other contemporaneous memos.

195   **"the entire 'Japanese Problem'...readily sifted out":** K. D. Ringle, "Ringle Report"; Ringle, "On the Japanese Question"; An Intelligence Officer, "The Japanese in America: The Problem and the Solution," *Harper's Magazine*, October 1942, 489–497.

195   **Ennis wrote:** The Ennis memo may be found at "Alien Enemy Control's Memo for Solicitor General," Famous Trials (website), Douglas O. Linder, accessed January 23, 2023, https://famous-trials.com/korem atsu/2569-alien-enemy-control-s-memo-for-solicitor-general. The quotes are from Edward J. Ennis, "Memorandum for the Solicitor General," April

30, 1943, 2–4. Ennis had read Ringle's memo on "The Japanese Question in the United States." Irons, *Justice at War*, 202.

196 **Fahy's grandson:** Charles J. Sheehan, "Solicitor General Charles Fahy and Honorable Defense of the Japanese-American Exclusion Cases," *American Journal of Legal History* 54, no. 4 (2014): 469. Peter Irons responded to Sheehan's article in "How Solicitor General Charles Fahy Misled the Supreme Court in the Japanese American Internment Cases," *American Journal of Legal History* 55, no. 2 (2015): 208–226, and Sheehan then replied to Irons's article in "Charles Fahy's 'Brilliant Public Service as Solicitor General,'" *American Journal of Legal History* 55, no. 3 (2015): 347–360. Sheehan emphasized that there was no proof that Fahy ever received or read the memo by Ennis addressed to him (349–350). It would be surprising if such a memo never reached its addressee. In 2011, Acting Solicitor General Neal Katyal highlighted the failure to disclose Ringle's analysis in a "confession of error" about the Solicitor General's handling of the Japanese American curfew and incarceration cases. Neal Katyal, "Confession of Error: The Solicitor General's Mistakes During the Japanese-American Internment Cases," Office of Public Affairs, US Department of Justice, May 20, 2011, https://www.justice.gov/archives/opa/blog/confession-error-solicitor-generals-mistakes-during-japanese-american-internment-cases.

197 **DeWitt... *Final Report*:** General DeWitt's initial *Final Report* is available on Jerry Kang's website, http://jerrykang.net/wp-content/blogs.dir/1/files/2010/10/Ex-D-reduced-size.pdf. It also is summarized in *Hirabayashi v. United States*, 627 F. Supp. 1445 (W.D. Wash. 1986), affirmed in part and reversed in part, *Hirabayashi v. United States*, 828 F.2d 591 (9th Cir. 1987).

198 **"duration of the present war":** DeWitt transmittal letter, April 15, 1943, quoted in *Hirabayashi*, 627 F. Supp. at 1449.

198 **"Because of the ties of race":** *Hirabayashi*, 627 F. Supp. at 1449.

198 **McCloy... made that clear:** Irons, *Justice at War*, 207–212.

198 **did not "desire to compromise":** DeWitt to War Department, May 5, 1943, quoted in *Hirabayashi*, 828 F.2d at 598.

198 **Bendetsen ordered the destruction:** Irons, *Justice at War*, 211.

198 **Aiko Herzig-Yoshinaga:** Lorraine Bannai, "Aiko Herzig-Yoshinaga: The Activist Who Discovered the Truth About WWII Internment," Politico, December 30, 2018, https://www.politico.com/magazine/story/2018/12/30/aiko-herzig-yoshinaga-obituary-discovered-japanese-american-internment-223314/.

199 **At oral arguments:** A summary of the oral arguments is in *United States Law Week*, May 18, 1943, 3345–3348. Most of the quotes from the oral argument presented here are from that account. See also International

News Service, "Justices Quiz Lawyers in Japanese Case," *St. Louis Star and Times*, May 11, 1943, 10.

199 **"Whispering Charlie":** On the nickname, see "Whispering Charlie," *New York Times*, September 20, 1979, A22.

200 **Justices met…to decide:** Irons, *Justice at War*, 227–234. Jackson initially had planned to support Hirabayashi on the ground that the policy should be left to the military, rather than enforced by the courts through criminal prosecutions, but Stone's narrow ground for opinion apparently convinced him not to do so. He also later prepared a draft concurrence but never circulated it. Dennis J. Hutchinson, "'The Achilles Heel' of the Constitution: Justice Jackson and the Japanese Exclusion Cases," *Supreme Court Review* 2002 (2002): 455, 459–476.

201 **"The Supreme Court tempers justice with Murphy":** Fine, "Frank Murphy," 398; Murphy and Price, *Courting Justice*, 21.

201 **William Francis Murphy:** Sidney Fine, "Frank Murphy," in *The Supreme Court Justices: Illustrated Biographies, 1789–1993*, ed. Clare Cushman (Congressional Quarterly, 1993), 396–400; Greg Zipes, *Justice and Faith: The Frank Murphy Story* (University of Michigan Press, 2021); John H. Pickering, "A Tribute to Justice Frank Murphy," *University of Detroit Mercy Law Review* 73, no. 4 (1996): 703.

201 **Ossian Sweet trial:** When a white mob attacked Dr. Ossian Sweet's home in a white neighborhood in Detroit, Sweet and others engaged in armed self-defense, in which a white man was killed. A first trial in 1925 presided over by Murphy for several defendants, including Dr. Sweet, led to a hung jury. After Murphy granted Darrow's motion for severance on the retrial (requiring separate trials for different defendants), Sweet's brother was acquitted; the prosecution then dropped all charges against all defendants. The leading account of the Sweet trials is Kevin Boyle, *Arc of Justice: A Saga of Race, Civil Rights, and Murder in the Jazz Age* (Henry Holt, 2004). See also Richard Bak, "(Frank) Murphy's Law," *Hour Detroit Magazine*, August 27, 2008; Douglas O. Linder, "The Sweet Trials: An Account," Famous Trials (website), accessed January 23, 2023, http://law2.umkc.edu/faculty/projects/ftrials/sweet/sweetaccount.HTM.

201 **"kindliest and most understanding man":** Clarence Darrow, *The Story of My Life* (Scribner, 1932), 306–307, quoted in Linder, "Sweet Trials."

202 **prosecutions of big-city bosses:** Pickering, "Tribute," 706–707.

202 **Douglas noted in his diary:** Zipes, *Justice and Faith*, 215; William O. Douglas, "The Court Diary of Justice William O. Douglas," ed. Philip E. Urofsky, in *Supreme Court Historical Society Yearbook 1995*, 89. Douglas noted that Jackson pressed to have Murphy leave the Justice Department and that Murphy was reluctant to take on the new assignment:

I hear that Frank did not want the job—in fact kicked like a steer. But the President was under great compulsion to appoint him not alone because he was a Catholic but also because he had to get rid of him as A.G. I know that the President had promised to make Bob Jackson A.G. on July 1, 1939. Bob was chafing under the delay & threatening to leave. He & Frank were at swords points. [Jackson was Solicitor General at the time.] So in spite of Frank's protestations he was kicked upstairs. After Frank was appointed, he indicated that he would stay on as A.G. until he had certain pending matters cleared up. Bob was furious & saw the President and got that plan changed. (Douglas, "Court Diary," 89)

202 **"Irishman of strawberry-colored eyebrows" and the "answer to ladies' prayers":** Quoted in Zipes, *Justice and Faith,* 185.

203 **FDR's offer to play matchmaker:** The FDR-Murphy correspondence regarding the Tennessee widow is in Supreme Court, 1938–44, box 166, President's Secretary's File, Franklin D. Roosevelt Presidential Library and Museum, Hyde Park, NY. The widow, Mrs. Rebecca L. R. Arky of Nashville, Tennessee, had written Democratic National Committee chairman James Farley that Murphy seemed to be "a high-class man" whom she would like to meet and marry, and Farley had forwarded the letter to FDR.

203 **"yet to meet a girl":** Zipes, *Justice and Faith,* 221.

203 **"Murphy's eyebrows":** James L. Wright, "Washington Sidelights," *Buffalo (NY) Evening News,* June 5, 1941, 24.

203 **Murphy was very close to Edward Kemp:** Joyce Murdoch and Deb Price, *Courting Justice: Gay Men and Lesbians v. the Supreme Court* (Basic Books, 2001), 18–21; Sidney Fine, *Frank Murphy: The Washington Years* (University of Michigan Press, 1984), 8–9, 201–202, 478–480; Zipes, *Justice and Faith,* 206–211, 301.

203 **"with modern-day gay eyes":** Murdoch and Price, *Courting Justice,* 18.

203 **Murphy shared…draft opinions:** Fine, *Frank Murphy,* 164, 170–171, 178; Murdoch and Price, *Courting Justice,* 20.

204 **"admitted that he was not a great legal scholar":** Pickering, "Tribute," 703, 705.

204 **"poisonous whispering campaign":** Douglas, "Court Diary," 89.

204 **"prevented [the] assimilation":** *Hirabayashi v. United States,* 320 U.S. 81, 96 (1943).

204 **"odious" classification:** *Hirabayashi,* 320 U.S. at 100.

204 **"cannot close our eyes to the fact":** *Hirabayashi,* 320 U.S. at 101.

204 **"espionage by persons in sympathy":** *Hirabayashi,* 320 U.S. at 96, 96n2.

204 **Douglas concurrence:** *Hirabayashi,* 320 U.S. at 105–109; Irons, *Justice at War,* 237–239.

205   "Douglas encountered DeWitt": Irons, *Justice at War*, 238.
205   Frankfurter's reaction to Douglas's opinion: Irons, *Justice at War*, 239–241.
205   "very close and devoted to Roosevelt": Irons, *Justice at War*, 239.
205   "saw himself": Irons, *Justice at War*, 239.
205   Frankfurter…met at length with McCloy: Lash, *Diaries*, 246–248.
205   "a thousand *habeas corpus* suits": Irons, *Justice at War*, 240. Frankfurter stated that he was quoting Black.
205   "if he were the Commanding General": Irons, *Justice at War*, 240.
205   "in time of war, somebody has to exercise authority": Lash, *Diaries*, 251.
205   "Overcome your natural hesitation": Irons, *Justice at War*, 240.
206   "most shocking thing" and "soap-box speech": Lash, *Diaries*, 251.
206   back-and-forth between Douglas and Stone: Irons, *Justice at War*, 237–242.
206   Rutledge added a brief concurrence: *Hirabayashi*, 320 U.S. at 114 (Rutledge, J., concurring).
206   "Catholic and other church schools": Irons, *Justice at War*, 243.
206   "Are you writing Indian cases": Irons, *Justice at War*, 243.
206   "Felix, I would protect": Irons, *Justice at War*, 243.
206   "Please, Frank": Irons, *Justice at War*, 244.
206   Murphy…circulated a vigorous dissent: Irons, *Justice at War*, 244–246.
206   "I shan't try to dissuade you": Irons, *Justice at War*, 246.
207   "strong sympathy with Mr. Justice Murphy's views": Irons, *Justice at War*, 247.
207   "unhappiness that he had not persisted": Irons, *Justice at War*, 247.
207   Murphy maintained: *Hirabayashi*, 320 U.S. at 110–114 (Murphy, J., concurring).
207   "wisdom of having been able to reach a concurrence": Irons, *Justice at War*, 247.
207   "worthy of the Torah": Irons, *Justice at War*, 250.
207   *Yasui* decision: *Yasui v. United States*, 320 U.S. 155 (1943).

CHAPTER 12

210   "idea men": Frank L. Weller, Associated Press, "White House Official Family Runs Home, War Fronts," *Miami Herald Magazine*, August 29, 1943, 1.
210   "Happy Hot Dogs": As early as 1935, the term "Happy Hot Dogs" was used to refer to "Prof. Felix Frankfurter's proteges"—"the group of bright young men from the Harvard Law School who occupy key posts in various

New Deal agencies." Henry M. Hyde, "The Washington Goldfish Bowl," *Evening Sun* (Baltimore, MD), October 22, 1935, 18.

210 **Frankfurter's policy portfolio:** Brad Snyder, *Democratic Justice: Felix Frankfurter, the Supreme Court, and the Making of the Liberal Establishment* (W. W. Norton, 2022), 226–228, 295, 341–342. The only Jew of comparable prominence to Frankfurter in the US government at the time was Treasury Secretary Henry Morgenthau Jr., with whom Frankfurter had a frosty and distrustful relationship. *Democratic Justice*, 284, 294.

210 **release of his uncle Salomon Frankfurter:** Snyder, *Democratic Justice*, 295–297. A number of sources spell the first name of Frankfurter's uncle as "Solomon," but Snyder uses "Salomon" based on original sources. See, e.g., *Democratic Justice*, 736, 825.

210 **"the threat of Nazi Germany was political and personal":** Snyder, *Democratic Justice*, 341.

211 **Karski was born:** The definitive biography of Karski is E. Thomas Wood and Stanislaw M. Jankowski, *Karski: How One Man Tried to Stop the Holocaust*, rev. ed. (Texas Tech University Press, 2014). Karski's life and activities before his trip to the United States are set forth in the first eight chapters, pp. 3–161. Karski's best-selling 1944 memoir reviews these events, but, as Wood and Jankowski explain, it contains errors and omissions because of the pressures of wartime confidentiality, mistaken recollections, and the stresses of prompt publication. Jan Karski, *Story of a Secret State: My Report to the World* (1944; Georgetown University Press, 2013).

212 **Jewish leaders…sought a public declaration:** Wood and Jankowski, *Karski*, 105–106.

213 **meeting with a wide range of British leaders:** Wood and Jankowski, *Karski*, 150–154. In response to Karski's harrowing descriptions, one high-ranking British official launched into a discussion of World War I rumors about German soldiers crushing the skulls of Belgian babies. He observed that these propaganda stories were false but useful for public morale—hardly the reaction to the ongoing horror that Karski sought. The Warsaw Ghetto uprising took place while Karski was in London, from April 19, 1943, to May 16, 1943.

214 **Frankfurter's life:** Brad Snyder's *Democratic Justice* is the definitive Frankfurter biography. Informative summaries of Frankfurter's life are presented in Joseph Lash's introductory essay in *From the Diaries of Felix Frankfurter* (W. W. Norton, 1975), 3–90; Philip B. Kurland's "Felix Frankfurter" in *The Supreme Court Justices: Illustrated Biographies, 1789–1993*, ed. Clare Cushman (Congressional Quarterly, 1993), 386–391; Albert Sacks's essay in *The Justices of the United States Supreme Court, 1789–1969: Their Lives and*

Major Opinions, ed. Leon Friedman and Fred L. Israel (Chelsea House, 1969), 3:2401–2443; Liva Baker, *Felix Frankfurter* (Coward-McCann, 1969), 15–21; and David B. Green, "A Controversial Judge Leery of Court Power Grabs Is Born," Haaretz, November 15, 2015, https://www.haaretz.com /jewish/a-controversial-judge-leery-of-court-power-grabs-is-born-1.5420964.

214   **"House of Truth":** Brad Snyder, *The House of Truth: A Washington Political Salon and the Foundations of American Liberalism* (Oxford University Press, 2017).

214   **"almost everybody who was interesting":** Brad Snyder, "The Washington Salon That Saved Liberalism," Politico, February 5, 2017, https://www.po litico.com/magazine/story/2017/02/washington-salon-liberalism-214731/.

215   **"Academic life is but half life":** Kurland, "Felix Frankfurter," in Cushman, *Supreme Court Justices*, 387.

215   **argue before the conservative Supreme Court:** Frankfurter argued in *Bunting v. Oregon*, 243 U.S. 426 (1917) (Oregon's maximum-hours law held to be constitutional), and *Adkins v. Children's Hospital*, 261 U.S. 525 (1923) (District of Columbia's minimum wage law held to be unconstitutional). Another wage-and-hours case argued by Frankfurter resulted in a no-decision affirmance by a divided Court, which left the law in place. *Stettler v. O'Hara*, 243 U.S. 629 (1917). Frankfurter also had argued Supreme Court cases on behalf of the United States in his stint at the War Department under Secretary Stimson. See, e.g., *Porto Rico v. Ramos*, 232 U.S. 627 (1914).

215   **Frankfurter went to Paris:** Snyder, *House of Truth*, 238–240.

215   **Brandeis even covertly subsidized:** Bruce Allen Murphy, *The Brandeis/ Frankfurter Connection: The Secret Political Activities of Two Supreme Court Justices* (Oxford University Press, 1982), 10.

216   **"Because I cannot compress life into a formula":** Lash, *Diaries*, 19.

216   **Frankfurter's mother…opposed the marriage:** Bruce Allen Murphy and Arthur Owens, "Felix Frankfurter (1882–1965)," in *Great American Judges*, ed. John R. Vile (ABC-Clio, 2003), 2:265.

216   **Marion confided to a friend:** Lash, *Diaries*, 39.

216   **"there are only two things wrong":** "Mrs. Frankfurter Is Dead; High Court Justice's Widow, 84," *New York Times*, June 11, 1975, 46. In a slightly different version, Marion said that Frankfurter had two faults: "One, he *always* gets off the subject, two, he *always* gets back on it again." Lash, *Diaries*, 30; emphasis in original.

216   **"interesting little man":** David Michaelis, *Eleanor* (Simon and Schuster, 2020), 137.

217   **"more ideas per minute":** Lash, *Diaries*, 46.

217   **"wherever I turn and to whomever I talk":** Lash, *Diaries*, 63.

217   **Frankfurter wrote to FDR:** Lash, *Diaries*, 65.

218 **knew about his boosters' efforts:** Henry J. Abraham, *Justices and Presidents: A Political History of Appointments to the Supreme Court*, 2nd ed. (Oxford University Press, 1985), 218–219.

218 **"All of us regard this":** Lash, *Diaries*, 64.

218 **"the most dangerous man":** Snyder, *Democratic Justice*, 125. Even while Frankfurter was on the Supreme Court, some in the intelligence community viewed him with suspicion. On January 25, 1943, a law clerk to Justice Black confided to Frankfurter that, in the course of a background investigation of a Harvard Law graduate, a Naval Intelligence officer advised the law clerk that "it might be very undesirable from [the job applicant's] view that his connection with [Frankfurter] be known." Lash, *Diaries*, 169.

218 **"conceive of a worse appointment":** Editorial, *Gazette and Daily* (York, PA), January 11, 1939, 6.

218 **first Supreme Court nominee to give public testimony on unrestricted topics:** Paul M. Collins Jr. and Lori A. Ringhand, "The Institutionalization of Supreme Court Confirmation Hearings," *Law and Social Inquiry* 41, no. 1 (2016): 126, 132.

218 **"I have never been" a Communist:** Snyder, *Democratic Justice*, 126; Chesly Manly, "Quiz Committee Votes Approval of Frankfurter," *Chicago Tribune*, January 13, 1939, 2.

219 **top tier of the New Deal:** Lash, *Diaries*, 66.

219 **In Frankfurter's view:** In October 1942, David Lilienthal, a Frankfurter protégé in the Roosevelt Administration, observed, "I sense that Felix is not too happy about his own standing with his own younger contemporaries, including those on the bench with him." Lash, *Diaries*, 70. For examples of Frankfurter's unhappiness with his colleagues, see, e.g., Lash, *Diaries*, 174–176, 181–182, 205, 229–230, 254.

219 **"pure bunk":** Lash, *Diaries*, 76.

219 **"the little bastard":** Fine, *Frank Murphy*, 254.

219 **"Der Fuehrer":** Fine, *Frank Murphy*, 254.

220 **"fifty minutes, no more or less":** Melvin I. Urofsky, "William O. Douglas and Felix Frankfurter: Ideology and Personality on the Supreme Court," *History Teacher* 24, no. 1 (November 1990): 7, 9.

220 **Paul Freund...compared:** Freund described Frankfurter to the author of this book in the early 1980s, when the author was a law student. Mary DeWolfe Howe, the wife of Frankfurter protégé and Harvard Law School professor Mark DeWolfe Howe, described Frankfurter's presence in similar terms: "It was like a champagne cork going off. Off he went and the conversation was marvelous." Lash, *Diaries*, 50–51.

220 **The five-foot-four-inch Justice:** Lash, *Diaries*, 3. The Supreme Court had a rule that no page could be taller than Frankfurter, the shortest Justice.

Todd C. Peppers, "The Chief Justice and the Page: Earl Warren, Charles Bush, and the Promise of *Brown v. Board of Education*," *Journal of Supreme Court History* 47, no. 1 (2022): 27, 30; author interview with George Hutchinson, November 12, 2019.

221 **Karski's experiences were "bloodcurdling" and "make your hair stand on end":** Wood and Jankowski, *Karski*, 167–168.

221 **Frankfurter wanted to hear:** This account of the Karski-Frankfurter discussion principally relies on Wood and Jankowski, *Karski*, 167–169. Details of the Karski-Frankfurter meeting differ in various sources. For example, some versions cite the Frankfurter meeting as one of Karski's last meetings in Washington, after Karski's session with Roosevelt, and attribute that sequence to Karski himself. See, e.g., David Engel, *Holocaust and Genocide Studies* 5, no. 4 (1990): 363, 378 n.55. Wood and Jankowski's book merits deference in light of its extensive documentation, the authors' numerous interviews with Karski, and their detailed efforts at corroboration. The details in Karski's own descriptions of his Frankfurter meeting also sometimes vary. In his interview with Claude Lanzmann for the documentary movie *Shoah*, for example, Karski said that the meeting with Frankfurter at the Polish Embassy took place in the morning ("Jan Karski Videos: On Meeting Justice Frankfurter," Brooklyn College Library, accessed January 23, 2023, https://libguides.brooklyn.cuny.edu/jankarskivideos/frankfurter); Karski's description to Wood and Jankowski, however, placed the meeting in the evening, after the dinner with Cox and Cohen. Research by Wood and Jankowski confirms the latter account.

222 **There is no record:** As Jill Lepore has detailed, a theft of Frankfurter papers from the Library of Congress leaves gaps in the historical record. Jill Lepore, "The Great Paper Caper," *The New Yorker*, December 1, 2014.

222 **harmful influence of Communist agents:** Engel, "'Western Allies and the Holocaust,'" 363, 369.

222 **"terrible, horrible things":** Wood and Jankowski, *Karski*, 170.

222 **Karski…met with FDR:** Wood and Jankowski, *Karski*, 175–180. The time of the meeting is listed in FDR's calendar as 10:50 a.m. to 11:50 a.m. on July 28, 1943, for "The Polish Ambassador, Mr. Karsky." "July 28th, 1943," Franklin D. Roosevelt Day by Day (website), Pare Lorentz Center, FDR Presidential Library, accessed January 23, 2023, http://www.fdrlibrary.marist.edu/daybyday/daylog/july-28th-1943/. In Karski's contemporaneous account, the meeting was scheduled for 10:30 a.m. and lasted for an hour and fifteen minutes. Wood and Jankowski, *Karski*, 175, 179.

222 **Karski then brought up atrocities facing the Jews:** Wood and Jankowski, *Karski*, 178. Karski noted the possibility of survival for Polish Jews "actively working in the Jewish underground in cooperation with us," presumably in hiding.

223   **"You will tell your leaders that we shall win this war!":** Harry James Cargas, *Voices from the Holocaust* (University Press of Kentucky, 1993), 63.

223   **"About the dead Jews, Roosevelt said nothing":** Cargas, *Voices from the Holocaust*, 63.

223   **"The president seems so thrilled":** Wood and Jankowski, *Karski*, 180.

223   **"indifference at best":** Wood and Jankowski, *Karski*, 180. Wood and Jankowski observe that "other factors...also motivated FDR to set up Pehle's agency—chiefly, pressure from treasury secretary Henry Morgenthau." The creation of the War Refugee Board was a complex tale, involving extensive efforts by Morgenthau, Pehle, and others in late 1943 and early 1944, and arising from many sources. Andrew Meier, *Morgenthau: Power, Privilege, and the Rise of an American Dynasty* (Random House, 2022), 341–358.

223   **quickly became a best-seller:** Madeleine Albright, foreword to *Story of a Secret State: My Report to the World*, by Jan Karski (Georgetown University Press, 2013), xvii; Wood and Jankowski, *Karski*, 202–204, 210–211.

224   **"everywhere there was hunger":** Jan Karski, *Story of a Secret State: My Report to the World* (Georgetown University Press, 2013.), 311.

224   **"the chaos, the squalor":** Karski, *Story of a Secret State*, 326–329.

224   **lauded...by Yad Vashem:** "Jan Karski," Yad Vashem, accessed January 23, 2023, https://www.yadvashem.org/righteous/stories/karski.html.

224   **death of Karski's wife:** Jennifer Dunning, "Pola Nirenska, a Choreographer and Teacher, Is a Suicide at 81," *New York Times*, July 31, 1992, D17; Wood and Jankowski, *Karski*, 234–235, 251. The death of Karski's wife was not his only postwar tragedy. In 1964, Karski's beloved older brother, Marian Kozielewski, a Warsaw police official who joined the Resistance and survived Auschwitz after his capture, also died by suicide in Washington, DC. Wood and Jankowski, *Karski*, 219.

225   **3 million of Poland's 3.3 million Jews:** "Murder of the Jews of Poland," Yad Vashem, accessed January 23, 2023, https://www.yadvashem.org/holocaust/about/fate-of-jews/poland.html.

CHAPTER 13

227   **"an important Weapon...all of us":** Franklin D. Roosevelt, "Statement on Signing the Emergency Price Control Act," January 30, 1942, American Presidency Project (website), University of California, Santa Barbara, https://www.presidency.ucsb.edu/documents/statement-signing-the-emergency-price-control-act.

228   **OPA released a torrent:** "Note: Price and Sovereignty," *Harvard Law Review* 135 (2021): 755, 773; Meg Jacobs, "'How About Some Meat?': The Office of Price Administration, Consumption Politics, and State Building

from the Bottom Up, 1941–1946," *Journal of American History* 84, no. 3 (1997): 910, 923–924.

228   **stockings:** Allan M. Winkler, *Home Front U.S.A.: America During World War II* (Harlan Davidson, 2012), 44.

228   **ban on the sale of sliced bread:** Richard R. Lingerman, *Don't You Know There's a War On? The American Home Front, 1941–1945* (G. P. Putnam's Sons, 1970), 354.

228   **thieves stole butter:** Lingerman, *Don't You Know,* 246.

228   **government exhorted:** Richard Polenberg, *War and Society: The United States, 1941–1945* (J. B. Lippincott, 1972), 133.

228   **posted a sign:** David Brinkley, *Washington Goes to War: The Extraordinary Story of the Transformation of a City and a Nation* (Knopf, 1988), 132.

228   **Justices were plunged:** "From the Capital," *Newsweek,* March 1, 1943; Harlan Fiske Stone to Mrs. John Vance Hewitt, December 30, 1942, box 16, folder 13, Harlan Fiske Stone Papers, Manuscript Division, Library of Congress, Washington, DC.

229   **Lucile Lomen:** Lucile Lomen, "Privileges and Immunities Under the Fourteenth Amendment," *Washington Law Review* 18, no. 3 (1943): 120–135; Robert S. Lasnik, "Go East, Young Woman: Breaking the Supreme Court Clerk Gender Barrier," *Western Legal History* 31, no. 1 (2020): 71–79; Mary Whisner, "Douglas Hires a Woman to Clerk," in *2020 Green Bag Almanac and Reader,* 297–310; Chandra, "Lucile Lomen," 198–216.

229   **seven million women in the workforce:** Jennie Berry Chandra, "Lucile Lomen: The First Female United States Supreme Court Law Clerk," in *In Chambers: Stories of Supreme Court Law Clerks and Their Justices,* ed. Todd Peppers and Artemus Ward (University of Virginia Press, 2012), 202.

229   **"When you say that you have 'no available graduates' ":** William O. Douglas to Judson P. Falknor, March 24, 1943, in *Selections from the Private Papers of Justice William O. Douglas,* ed. Melvin Urofsky (Adler and Adler, 1987), 46. Douglas ultimately agreed to hire Lomen as his law clerk on January 29, 1944, for the Supreme Court term beginning in October 1944. Chandra, "Lucile Lomen," 207.

229   **"the American woman does not give the man":** Helen Lombard, "Emil Ludwig Speaks Out Concerning American Women," Wartime Washington, *Boston Globe,* August 24, 1943, 8.

229   **The other Supreme Court clerks:** Lucile Lomen, interview by Marilyn Sparks, transcript, May 20, 1991, Whitman College Oral History Collection, 1960s–1999, Whitman College and Northwest Archives, 17–18. Lomen recalled that, while the other clerks "accepted me pretty well," "they all had something after law school but me. So, from that standpoint, I

never knew if my problem was because I was a woman or because I was too young, or what." She also thought it might be because she "was from the Northwest."

230 **Douglas found Lomen's work:** William O. Douglas to Lewis F. Huck, May 5, 1948, quoted in Chandra, "Lucile Lomen," 213.

230 **Frankfurter refused to hire…Ruth Bader Ginsburg:** Brad Snyder, *Democratic Justice: Felix Frankfurter, the Supreme Court, and the Making of the Liberal Establishment* (W. W. Norton, 2022), 662–664. In the summer of 1942, columnist Drew Pearson, a frequent Frankfurter critic, reported that Frankfurter told a friend who suggested hiring a woman clerk after Frankfurter's clerk joined the Army, "I won't have a woman law clerk. Can't stand them." Drew Pearson, "Washington Merry-Go-Round," *Raleigh News and Observer,* July 24, 1942, 4.

230 **OPA-imposed price controls:** The background of the squeeze on meat dealers is described in James R. Conde and Michael S. Greve, "*Yakus* and the Administrative State," *Harvard Journal of Law and Public Policy* 42, no. 3 (2019): 808, 826, 839.

230 **Yakus bio:** "Albert Yakus, 86, Was Head of Beef Company" obituary, *Boston Globe,* September 21, 1986, 55.

230 **Yakus indictment…OPA regime:** "12 Are Indicted for 'Black Market' Activities," *Boston Globe,* February 13, 1943, 2; "Meat Wholesalers Plead Not Guilty to Price Violations," *Boston Globe,* February 16, 1943, 9; Associated Press, "Violation of OPA Ceiling," *Barre (VT) Daily Times,* February 17, 1943, 2.

231 **Charles Wyzanski:** Peter H. Irons, *The New Deal Lawyers* (Princeton University Press, 1982), 23–24. Irons notes that Wyzanski reportedly voted for Hoover in 1932. But, as Irons also relates, Wyzanski was a devoted acolyte of Frankfurter and became one of the New Deal's legal luminaries.

231 **Emergency Price Control Act:** The statute is quoted and described in *Yakus v. United States,* 321 U.S. 414, 419–420 (1944).

231 **Wyzanski swatted away:** *United States v. Slobodkin,* 48 F. Supp. 913 (D. Mass. 1943).

231 **Rottenberg's trial and sentencing:** "Meat Dealer Tells Court of Black Market Prices," *Boston Globe,* March 3, 1943, 1; "Grocer Says He Was Forced to Pay Extra Cash for Meat," *Boston Globe,* March 4, 1943, 7; "Prosecution Rests in Case Against Meat Wholesaler," *Boston Globe,* March 5, 1943, 13; Associated Press, "Federal Jury Convicts Boston Meat Wholesalers," *Bangor (ME) Daily News,* March 6, 1943, 9; "'Black Market' Defendant Given Six Months' Term," *Boston Globe,* March 10, 1943, 1.

232 **Yakus's trial and sentencing:** "Motion to Quash in Black Market Case Under Advisement," *Boston Globe,* March 23, 1943, 16; "Butcher Tells of

Paying Extra in 'Black Market,'" *Boston Globe*, April 6, 1943, 14; "Brighton Packing Co. Held Guilty of Violating OPA Beef Ceilings," *Boston Globe*, April 8, 1943, 5; "Jail Sentences for Two in Black Market Case," *Boston Globe*, April 30, 1943, 1.

232 **Wyzanski met with...Frankfurter:** Joseph P. Lash, ed., *From the Diaries of Felix Frankfurter* (W. W. Norton, 1975), 236–237. It seems certain that Wyzanski was referring to Rottenberg. A *Boston Globe* article on August 24, 1943, listed the sentences for eleven of the seventeen black-market defendants in the meat-dealing prosecutions (including Rottenberg and Yakus). The only six-month sentences were imposed on Rottenberg, Yakus, and Joseph Keller (the treasurer at Yakus's company). Both Yakus and Keller had been sentenced by Judge Arthur D. Healey; Rottenberg was the only one of the three who had been sentenced by Wyzanski. "OPA Upheld by U.S. Court on Price Control," *Boston Globe*, August 24, 1943, 1.

233 **US Court of Appeals:** *Rottenberg v. United States*, 137 F.2d 850, 855–856, 858 (1st Cir. 1943).

233 **Court heard arguments:** Associated Press, "OPA Rulings Taken to Supreme Court," *Baltimore Sun*, January 8, 1944, 1. The oral argument is also described in "Arguments Before the Court: Power to Review Price Regulation," *United States Law Week*, January 11, 1944, 3225.

234 **State of the Union address:** Franklin D. Roosevelt, State of the Union address, January 11, 1944, transcript at Franklin Delano Roosevelt Presidential Library and Museum, http://www.fdrlibrary.marist.edu/archives /stateoftheunion.html; "President Asks Civilian Draft to Bar Strikes, Realistic Taxes, Subsidies, New Bill of Rights," *New York Times*, January 12, 1944, 1.

235 **Six Justices voted:** The decision and the quoted passages are at *Yakus v. United States*, 321 U.S. 414, 419–420, 432–435, 443 (1944).

235 **Rutledge...disagreed:** *Yakus*, 321 U.S. at 460–489 (Rutledge, J., dissenting).

235 **dissent—by Roberts:** *Yakus*, 321 U.S. at 448–460 (Roberts, J., dissenting).

236 **Kate Willingham:** *Bowles v. Willingham*, 321 U.S. 503 (1944). On March 27, 1944, the day that it announced the *Yakus* and *Willingham* decisions, the Supreme Court also announced a third economic regulation decision, *Vinson v. Washington Gas Co.*, 321 U.S. 489 (1944). That case concerned the scope of local governments' authority to grant utility rate increases. The District of Columbia Public Utilities Commission had approved a rate increase over the objection of the OPA and the Director of Economic Stabilization. Based on a reading of the Emergency Price Control Act's technical provision regarding utilities, the Supreme Court, in a 6–3 decision by Roberts, refused to set aside the approved rate increase. The case thus was a defeat for the Roosevelt Administration, but it was based

entirely on parsing the meaning of specialized statutory language. Doug-las, joined by Black and Murphy, dissented.

237 **"Price-fixing and rent control regulations"**: Associated Press, "Price Fixing, Rent Controls Upheld by High Court," *Boston Globe*, March 28, 1944, 4. Some criticized the *Yakus* decision. Wayne Morse, the University of Oregon School of Law dean running as a Republican for his first Senate term, blasted the *Yakus* decision as "another nail which present trends of government have driven into the coffin of individual and constitutional rights." Associated Press, "Morse Criticizes Court Decision," *Eugene (OR) Register-Guard*, April 25, 1944, 4. One editorial lamented that, despite the references to wartime exigencies, *Yakus* seemed to establish a "pattern for the peacetime mushroom growth of that bureaucracy which so thrives in the Washington political atmosphere." "Bureaucracy Bolstered," editorial, *Hartford (CT) Courant*, March 29, 1944, 10.

237 **Nixon...as an OPA lawyer**: Milton Viorst, "Nixon of the O.P.A.," *New York Times Magazine*, October 3, 1971, 70–76. As Viorst recounts, Nixon worked on tire rationing at the OPA and was very unhappy in his post. During much of his political career, he tried to conceal his OPA stint by saying that he had worked for the Office of Emergency Management.

237 **upholding Nixon's wage and price controls**: *Amalgamated Meat Cut-ters v. Connally*, 337 F. Supp. 737, 762 (D.D.C. 1971) (three-judge court); *United States v. Lieb*, 462 F.2d 1161 (Temporary Emergency Court of Ap-peals, 1972); *Salsburg's Meats, Inc. v. Shultz*, 363 F. Supp. 269 (ED Pa, 1973). The legal challenges to the Nixon wage and price controls are discussed in "Note: Price and Sovereignty," 755, 773. The context of the Nixon wage and price control orders—and the congressional surprise at his decision to issue them—are discussed in Gene Healy, "Remembering Nixon's Wage and Price Controls," Cato Institute, August 16, 2011, https://www.cato.org/commentary/remembering-nixons-wage-price-controls.

237 ***Yakus* reflected broad deference**: *Mistretta v. United States*, 488 U.S. 361, 373, 378–379 (1989); *Touby v. United States*, 500 U.S. 161, 165–169 (1991); *Gundy v. United States*, 139 S. Ct. 2116, 2123, 2129 (2019).

237 **"nondelegation" principle**: *Gundy v. United States*, 139 S. Ct. 2116, 2131 (2019) (Gorsuch, J., dissenting, joined by Roberts, C.J. and Thomas, J.). In a separate opinion in *Gundy*, Justice Samuel Alito wrote that "if a majority of this Court were willing to reconsider the approach we have taken for the past 84 years, I would support that effort." *Id.* at 2131 (Alito, J., concurring in the judgment).

237 **conservative scholars attack *Yakus***: See, e.g., Conde and Greve, "*Yakus* and the Administrative State," 807–813, 860–870.

237 **Justices...rely on *Yakus*...principle**: *Gundy v. United States*, 139 S. Ct. 2116 (2019) (Kagan, J., joined by Ginsburg, Breyer, and Sotomayor, JJ.).

With regard to the other aspect of *Yakus*—the preclusion of judicial review unless a claim has been raised in a specialized administrative channel— some Justices have stressed the wartime context of *Yakus*. See *PDR Network, LLC v. Carlton Harris Chiropractic, Inc.*, 139 S. Ct. 2051, 2065 (2019) (Kavanaugh, J., concurring in the judgment); *Adamo Wrecking Co. v. United States*, 434 U.S. 275, 290 (1978) (Powell, J., concurring).

CHAPTER 14

239   **Texas's white primary:** Darlene Clark Hine, *Black Victory: The Rise and Fall of the White Primary in Texas* (University of Missouri Press, 2003), 249. Political scientist Kevin McMahon has called the white primary the "device that was then thought to be *the* most effective legal measure for keeping African Americans out of the South's one-party political process." Kevin J. McMahon, *Reconsidering Roosevelt on Race: How the Presidency Paved the Road to* Brown (University of Chicago Press, 2004), 2.

240   *Grovey v. Townsend:* 295 U.S. 45 (1935). In two cases leading up to *Grovey*, the Court had found that, under Texas state law, the state was administering the primary and thus it was unconstitutional. But, in both, the Court left open the possibility that Texas could change its law to avoid the constitutional problem by making clear that the political party, not the state, ran the primary, and that is what Texas had tried to do before the *Grovey* decision. *Nixon v. Herndon*, 273 U.S. 536 (1927); *Nixon v. Condon*, 286 U.S. 73 (1932).

240   **Louisiana...election fraud during a primary:** *United States v. Classic*, 213 U.S. 299 (1941).

240   **case titled *Smith v. Allwright*:** Petition for Writ of Certiorari at 1–6, *Smith v. Allwright*, 321 U.S. 649 (1944) (No. 51), filed April 21, 1943; *Smith v. Allwright*, United States District of Court Findings of Facts and Conclusions of Law, May 11, 1942 (reprinted in Transcript of Record at 80–85, *Smith v. Allwright*, 321 U.S. 649 (1944) (No. 51); *Smith v. Allwright*, 131 F.2d 593 (5th Cir. 1942); *Smith v. Allwright*, 319 U.S. 738 (1943) (granting cert).

241   **"Grovey versus Townsend is out":** Transcript of Record at 112, *Smith v. Allwright*, 321 U.S. 649 (1944) (No. 51).

241   **"sound theory in the *Classic* case":** Petition for Writ of Certiorari at 23, *Allwright*.

241   **William Henry Hastie:** Brad Snyder, *Democratic Justice: Felix Frankfurter, the Supreme Court, and the Making of the Liberal Establishment* (W. W. Norton, 2022), 151, 372, 431.

242   **"Double V" campaign:** Rawn James Jr., *The Double V: How Wars, Protest, and Harry Truman Desegregated America's Military* (Bloomsbury, 2013), 141–143; Matthew F. Delmont, *Half American: The Epic Story of*

African Americans Fighting World War II at Home and Abroad (Penguin, 2022), 101–106; Henry L. Gates Jr., "What Was Black America's Double War?," *The Root*, May 24, 2013, https://www.theroot.com/what-was-black-americas-double-war-1790896568; William F. Yurasko, "The *Pittsburgh Courier* During World War II: An Advocate for Freedom," Yurasko.net, https://www.yurasko.net/wfy/vv-campaign/pittsburgh-courier-double-v-campaign.

242   **African American men and women served…during World War II**: *Selective Service and Victory: The 4th Report of the Director of Selective Service, 1944–45, with a Supplement for 1946–47* (US Government Printing Office, 1948), 187, 190; Micheal Clodfelter, *Warfare and Armed Conflicts: A Statistical Encyclopedia of Casualty and Other Figures, 1492–2015*, 4th ed. (McFarland, 2017), 529; Mattie Treadwell, "The Employment of Personnel: Minority Groups," in *Special Studies: The Women's Army Corps* (US Government Printing Office, 1954), 589–601.

242   **racial resentments…and violence**: Delmont, *Half American*, 151–167; Harvard Sitkoff, *Toward Freedom Land: The Long Struggle for Racial Equality in America* (University Press of Kentucky, 2010), 43–64; Daniel Kryder, *Divided Arsenal: Race and the American State During World War II* (Cambridge University Press, 2000), 146–153, 228–233; Joseph Lelyveld, "Riots Viewed Against History of Clashes Almost as Old as U.S.," *New York Times*, September 11, 1964, 23; "Race Riot of 1943," *Encyclopedia of Detroit*, Detroit Historical Society, https://detroithistorical.org/learn/encyclopedia-of-detroit/race-riot-1943. "Hate protests"—walkouts by white workers protesting the hiring and promotion of Black workers—occurred in at least twenty cities in the summer of 1943. Roderick N. Ryon, "When Baltimore's War Effort Tripped over Race," *Baltimore Sun*, April 11, 1993, 11A.

242   **Langston Hughes published his poem**: Langston Hughes, "Beaumont to Detroit: 1943," in *The Collected Poems of Langston Hughes*, ed. Arnold Rampersad and David Roessel (Vintage Classics, 1994), 281. The passage in the text is an excerpt from the poem.

243   **"regret"**: "President Condemns Rioting," *Pittsburgh Courier*, July 24, 1943, 1.

243   **Pauli Murray poem**: Pauli Murray, "Mr. Roosevelt Regrets (Detroit Riot, 1943)," in *Dark Testament and Other Poems* (Liveright, 2018), 27.

243   **"weak-kneed policy"**: Walter White and Thurgood Marshall, *What Caused the Detroit Riot? An Analysis* (1943; reprint, Leopold Classic Library, 2016), 30.

244   **Frankfurter and Murphy…NAACP**: "Justice Describes Former N.A.A.C.P. Tie," *New York Times*, September 30, 1958, 19 (Frankfurter); J. Woodford Howard Jr., *Mr. Justice Murphy: A Political Biography* (Princeton University Press, 1968), 203 (Murphy).

244   **Frankfurter and Black attended an NAACP meeting:** Donald K. Hill, "Social Separation in America: Thurgood Marshall and the Texas Connections," *Thurgood Marshall Law Review* 28 (2003): 177, 192.

244   **Rutledge…attended…in blackface:** "Nearly 1000 Attend 72d Annual Bar Dinner Devoted to Chiding District's Legal Colony," *Washington Post*, December 12, 1943, M16, in Clippings 1943 Aug.–Dec., Wiley Rutledge Papers, Manuscript Division, Library of Congress, Washington, DC. The caption on the *Washington Post* photo of the lawyers in blackface begins "Blackface Bar…risters." In the photo, the lawyers in blackface, arrayed around a piano, are joined by Solicitor General Charles Fahy, Assistant Attorney General James McGranery, and DC Bar Association President Milton King.

244   **Frankfurter hired William Coleman:** Snyder, *Democratic Justice*, 511–513.

244   **"last plantation":** Nina Totenberg, "The Supreme Court: The Last Plantation," *New Times*, July 26, 1974, 26.

245   **Marshall's meeting with Biddle and Wechsler:** Richard Kluger, *Simple Justice: The History of* Brown v. Board of Education *and Black America's Struggle for Equality* (Alfred Knopf, 1994), 234–235.

245   **"neutral principles":** Herbert Wechsler, "Toward Neutral Principles of Constitutional Law," *Harvard Law Review* 73, no. 1 (1959): 1–35.

245   **FDR raised the issue with Biddle:** McMahon, *Reconsidering Roosevelt*, 153; Francis Biddle, *In Brief Authority* (Doubleday, 1962), 187.

245   **"Although the legal questions":** McMahon, *Reconsidering Roosevelt*, 153.

246   **Folsom article:** Fred G. Folsom Jr., "Federal Elections and the 'White Primary,'" *Columbia Law Review* 43, no. 7 (1943): 1026, 1035.

246   **oral argument in November:** "Supreme Court Hears White Primary Case: Lawyers Depend on High Court Ruling in La. Case to Win," *Afro-American*, November 20, 1943; Associated Press, "Texas Negro Vote Urged Before Court," *Fort Worth (TX) Star Telegram*, November 11, 1943, 9.

246   **"the motion of the State of Texas for leave":** *Journal of the Supreme Court of the United States*, October 1943 Term, December 6, 1943, 74.

247   **Texas Attorney General filed an amicus brief:** Brief of Gerald C. Mann, Attorney General of Texas as Amicus Curiae, at 1, *Smith v. Allwright*, 321 U.S. 649 (1944) (No. 51), December 27, 1943.

247   **At the reargument:** Associated Press, "Barcus Asserts Texans' Rights to 'White' Primary," *Austin (TX) American-Statesman*, January 13, 1944, 11; Associated Press, "Supreme Court Hears Primary Voting Case," *Wichita Falls (TX) Tribune*, January 12, 1944, 2.

248   **"He thought it was a very great mistake":** Frankfurter, "Memorandum on Smith v. Allwright," April 10, 1944, 1–2, file 17, box 6, Felix Frank-

furter Papers, Modern Manuscripts Collection, Harvard Law School Library.

248   **Jackson wrote Stone:** Alpheus Thomas Mason, *Harlan Fiske Stone: Pillar of the Law* (Viking, 1956), 615.

249   **"one under a heavy burden":** Frankfurter, "Memorandum on Smith v. Allwright," 2. According to Frankfurter, Stone also "said how generous I was. I said that was nonsense, that there was nothing of generosity about it, that we were all on the same team and the problem was how best the team can do its work." With regard to the reassignment, Frankfurter noted in his memo, "I did not tell [Stone] what seemed to me to be the obvious thing, that the Chief Justice should write an opinion like this, particularly when he was helping to overrule an opinion in which he had joined only a few years ago." According to Frankfurter's memo, Jackson also had suggested Stone to him in their initial conversation. Stone, of course, suffered from two of the three problems Jackson mentioned to Frankfurter: Stone was from New England, and he was a Republican. If Jackson did suggest Stone as a possible author (and Frankfurter's recollection may have been clouded by pique), Jackson's suggestion would have been based on one of two judgments (or both): (1) Jackson thought that Stone's position as Chief Justice—and as a former Associate Justice who had joined the *Grovey* opinion—outweighed the disadvantages of regional origin and political party, or (2) Jackson thought that Frankfurter's Judaism actually was the most troubling problem. Notably, Jackson's memo to Stone about the need for reassignment mentions only the desirability of having the opinion "by a Southerner who has been a Democrat and is not one of those minorities which stir prejudices kindred to those against the Negro"; it says nothing about Stone possibly writing the opinion. Mason, *Harlan Fiske Stone*, 615.

250   **Stanley Forman Reed:** John D. Fassett, "Stanley F. Reed," in *The Supreme Court Justices: Illustrated Biographies, 1789–1993*, ed. Clare Cushman (Congressional Quarterly, 1993), 381–385; John D. Fassett, *New Deal Justice: The Life of Stanley Reed of Kentucky* (Vantage, 1994).

251   **Frankfurter...strongly urged FDR:** Peter H. Irons, *The New Deal Lawyers* (Princeton University Press, 1982), 12.

251   **"Black Monday":** *Schechter Poultry Corp. v. United States*, 295 U.S. 495 (1935) (National Industrial Recovery Act); *Louisville Joint Stock Land Bank v. Radford*, 295 U.S. 555 (1935) (Frazier-Lemke Bankruptcy Act); *Humphrey's Executor v. United States*, 295 U.S. 602 (1935) (FTC Commissioner).

251   **Reed...collapsed:** "Reed in Collapse; AAA Cases Halted," *New York Times*, December 11, 1935, 1. The next day, the Department of Justice "announced that the government's case before the Supreme Court in defense of the Bankhead Act would be completed through printed briefs instead

of oral argument. The reason given was the collapse yesterday of Solicitor General Stanley Reed while arguing the case." Felix Belair Jr., "Bankhead Defense Ignores a Warning by Wallace Aide," *New York Times*, December 12, 1935, 1.

251   **Reed offered FDR his resignation:** Fassett, *New Deal Justice*, 146.

252   **"realistic rather than radical":** "Stanley Reed Goes to Supreme Court," *New York Times*, January 16, 1938, 1.

252   **"tone and reception were perfect":** Reed to FDR, August 27, 1935, box 4877, President's Personal File, Franklin D. Roosevelt Presidential Library and Museum, Hyde Park, NY (hereafter PPF).

252   **Reed served as a Kentucky delegate:** "Kentucky Delegation to the 1936 Democratic National Convention," PoliticalGraveyard.com, accessed January 25, 2023, https://politicalgraveyard.com/parties/D/1936/KY.html.

252   **Reed gave dozens of speeches...in the fall of 1936:** Fassett, *New Deal Justice*, 133–136. Reed also was involved in discussions about FDR's Court-packing plan in late 1936 and early 1937, although, according to Fassett, Reed's involvement likely was peripheral. Fassett, *New Deal Justice*, 139, 146–150.

253   **"If I can be of any service":** Reed to FDR, June 6, 1942, box 4877, PPF.

253   **After FDR's reelection:** Reed to FDR, November 8, 1944, box 4877, PPF.

253   **Reed plied FDR with...Christmas presents:** Reed to FDR, "Xmas 1940"; FDR to Reed, January 18, 1942; FDR to Reed, February 2, 1943; Reed to FDR, December 1943, all in box 4877, PPF.

253   **"most intriguing" bottles:** FDR to Reed, January 4, 1940, box 4877, PPF.

253   **"Kentucky sunshine":** FDR to Reed, January 17, 1944, box 4877, PPF.

253   **"my understanding of your objectives":** Reed to FDR, October 26, 1938, box 4877, PPF.

253   **the President and the Justice dined:** FDR's calendar on November 1, 1938, six days after the date of Reed's note to him about FDR's "objectives," reports a lunch at the White House between FDR and Reed from 1 p.m. to 2 p.m. "November 1st, 1938," Franklin D. Roosevelt Day by Day (website), Pare Lorentz Center, FDR Presidential Library, accessed January 25, 2023, http://www.fdrlibrary.marist.edu/daybyday/daylog/november -1st-1938/. FDR wrote on Reed's note requesting a meeting to learn his objectives, "Have him into lunch some day next week." FDR, note on Reed, October 26, 1938, box 4877, PPF.

253   **Reed's opinion:** *Smith v. Allwright*, 321 U.S. 649, 660–666 (1944).

254   **"fundamental importance":** Michael J. Klarman, *From Jim Crow to Civil Rights: The Supreme Court and the Struggle for Racial Equality* (Oxford University Press, 2004), 200.

254   **Frankfurter..."concurred in the result":** *Allwright*, 321 U.S. at 666; Snyder, *Democratic Justice*, 438–440. Frankfurter's refusal to join the majority

opinion also may have been at least in part because he was miffed about the reassignment of the opinion, or because of the Court's recent overturning of his *Gobitis* decision by *Barnette*—an example that Reed mentioned in a footnote about the Court overturning constitutional precedents. *Allwright*, 321 U.S. at 665 n.10.

254 **[Frankfurter] had drafted a concurrence:** Mark V. Tushnet, *Making Civil Rights Law: Thurgood Marshall and the Supreme Court, 1936–1961* (Oxford University Press, 1994), 105–106; Snyder, *Democratic Justice*, 432–437.

254 **Roberts vehemently dissented:** *Allwright*, 321 U.S. at 666–670.

255 **"bold stroke for democracy":** "Open Primaries," editorial, *Washington Post*, April 4, 1944, 8. In a congratulatory note to Reed on April 5, Stone wrote, "I am glad to see that such papers as the *Washington Post* recognize it is sometimes our duty to do away with a bad precedent and that this was one of those times." Mason, *Harlan Fiske Stone*, 517.

255 **"real reason for the overturn":** Arthur Krock, "In the Nation," *New York Times*, April 4, 1944, 20.

255 **"May I ask the white politician":** W. L. Hillard, letter to the editor, *Pittsburgh Courier*, April 22, 1944, 11.

255 **southern states reacted:** Associated Press, "Southern Leaders Prepare to Resist," *New York Times*, April 4, 1944, 15; Ward E. Y. Elliott, *The Rise of Guardian Democracy: The Supreme Court's Role in Voting Rights Disputes, 1845–1969* (Harvard University Press, 1974), 80–81; McMahon, *Reconsidering Roosevelt*, 155.

256 **Efforts at resistance:** Elliott, *Rise of Guardian Democracy*, 81; Tushnet, *Making Civil Rights Law*, 107–108.

256 **At the NAACP…Murphy:** Richard Kluger, *Simple Justice: The History of* Brown v. Board of Education *and Black America's Struggle for Equality* (Notable Trials Library, 1994), 237.

256 **Marshall called it "one of the most important":** Marshall to Maceo Smith, December 31, 1943; Marshall to Sam Winter, May 10, 1944. Both letters are in Michael G. Long, ed., *Marshalling Justice: The Early Civil Rights Letters of Thurgood Marshall* (Harper Collins, 2011), 125, 134.

256 **Marshall's letter to Biddle:** Marshall to Biddle, April 3, 1944, in Long, *Marshalling Justice*, 128–129.

256 *Lyons: Lyons v. Oklahoma*, 322 U.S. 596 (1944).

257 **"watershed in the struggle for black rights":** Hine, *Black Victory*, 249.

257 **Lonnie Smith proudly cast his ballot:** Zelden, *Battle for the Black Ballot*, 109. Zelden notes that, "citywide, 2,618 Houston blacks joined Smith in exercising their franchise."

CHAPTER 15

260   **"vast potentialities"**: Roger K. Newman, *Hugo Black: A Biography* (Fordham University Press, 1997), 306.

260   **"a pitcher of warm spit"**: Anne Dingus, "John Nance Garner," *Texas Monthly*, November 1996. Dingus notes that Garner claimed that his "exact phrase" was "a pitcher of warm piss" but "those pantywaist writers wouldn't print it the way I said it."

260   **"favorite"**: Robert C. Albright, "Democrats Plan Stand on Record of New Deal," *Washington Post*, July 4, 1940, 1.

260   **"New Dealers' first choice"**: Ernest K. Lindley, "Roosevelt and Who? The Vice Presidential Field," *Washington Post*, July 10, 1940, 7.

260   **FDR told aides:** Bruce Allen Murphy, *Wild Bill: The Legend and Life of William O. Douglas* (Random House, 2003), 189; James F. Simon, *Independent Journey: The Life of William O. Douglas* (Harper & Row, 1980), 260–261.

260   **"I am delighted"**: William O. Douglas to A. Howard Meneely, August 21, 1940, William O. Douglas Papers, Library of Congress, box 10, in Murphy, *Wild Bill*, 189.

260   **Douglas also wrote Frankfurter:** William O. Douglas to Felix Frankfurter, July 2, 1940, in *The Douglas Letters: Selections from the Private Papers of Justice William O. Douglas*, ed. Melvin Urofsky (Adler and Adler, 1987), 215. Douglas wrote Frankfurter: "There is considerable talk in Washington about putting me on the ticket. I discount it very much. I do not really think it will come to anything. But it is sufficiently active to be disturbing. It is disturbing because I want none of it. I want to stay where I am. This line to you is to ask you, should the matter come your way, to scotch it."

260   **Arthur Krock:** Arthur Krock, "A Political Prowler, Which Should Be 'Liquidated,'" *New York Times*, October 26, 1939, 21.

261   **sharing his political observations:** Simon, *Independent Journey*, 260.

261   **Orville…future Justice:** James C. Duram and Judith Johnson, "William O. Douglas," in *The Supreme Court Justices: Illustrated Biographies, 1789–1993*, ed. Clare Cushman (Congressional Quarterly, 1993), 391–395; Simon, *Independent Journey*; Murphy, *Wild Bill*; Melvin Urofsky, "Introduction: William O. Douglas, 1898–1980," in Urofsky, *Douglas Letters*, ix–xxii.

261   **Orville nearly died:** Douglas maintained that he had suffered "infantile paralysis" and polio. William O. Douglas, *Go East, Young Man: The Early Years* (Random House, 1974), 31–32. Many accounts of his life repeat this characterization; biographer Bruce Allen Murphy, a critic of many Douglas claims, avoids identifying the malady and notes that, in contemporaneous accounts, "the precise nature of Orville's illness was not described." Murphy, *Wild Bill*, 10.

261 **Douglas flourished:** Duram and Johnson, "William O. Douglas," 391–392.

261 **Douglas taught English:** Murphy, *Wild Bill*, 37–39; Simon, *Independent Journey*, 60–62.

261 **left for Columbia law school:** Urofsky, "Introduction," xi–xii; Murphy, *Wild Bill*, 40–41.

261 **Douglas excelled in law school:** Murphy, *Wild Bill*, 43–80; Simon, *Independent Journey*, 66–75.

262 **jumped at the opportunity:** Duram and Johnson, "William O. Douglas," 392; Murphy, *Wild Bill*, 81–105.

262 **Douglas at SEC:** Duram and Johnson, "William O. Douglas," 392; Murphy, *Wild Bill*, 106–163.

262 **Brandeis announced his retirement:** Murphy, *Wild Bill*, 166; "Justice Brandeis Retires from the Supreme Court; Post May Go to the West," *New York Times*, February 14, 1939, 1. The *New York Times* reported that "Senator Schwellenbach of Washington was placed high on the list of possible appointees" and included Schwellenbach in its subheadline: "SCHWELLENBACH IS IN LINE—Conjecture on Post Puts Him High on List."

262 **he met Roosevelt:** William O. Douglas, *Go East, Young Man* (Random House, 1974), 462–463; Simon, *Independent Journey*, 194; Murphy, *Wild Bill*, 172–173.

263 **aggressive effort to secure:** Murphy, *Wild Bill*, 165–172; Urofsky, "Introduction," xvi–xvii; David J. Danelski, "The Appointment of William O. Douglas to The Supreme Court," *Journal of Supreme Court History* 40, No. 1 (March 2015).

263 **"best dry martinis":** William O. Douglas, *The Court Years, 1939–1975: The Autobiography of William O. Douglas* (Random House, 1975), 275.

264 **"hundreds of tables in the hallways":** Douglas, *Court Years*, 278.

264 **"there was nothing in the Constitution":** Douglas, *Court Years*, 281.

264 **"FDR would mull over his problems":** Douglas, *Court Years*, 273.

264 **sent FDR his view:** Douglas to FDR, June 16, 1941, in Supreme Court 1938–44, box 166, President's Secretary's File, Franklin D. Roosevelt Presidential Library, Hyde Park, NY. Johnson's campaign was a Senate special election primary between the young Congressman, who had already become an eager FDR acolyte, and Governor W. Lee "Pappy" O'Daniel, who was far less of a Roosevelt enthusiast. Douglas predicted victory for Johnson and flattered FDR: "Every time he mentioned your name the crowd cheered. Every time he mentioned Lindbergh the crowd booed. It was an enthusiastic Roosevelt crowd.... O'Daniel is trying to jump onto your coat tails. But the boys in Texas say that it is fooling few people." Douglas's political punditry missed the mark. Johnson narrowly lost and stayed in the House of Representatives. As Robert Caro recounts, the circumstances

regarding O'Daniel's 1941 victory were suspicious; one Johnson ally complained that O'Daniel "stole more votes than we did, that's all." Robert
Caro, *The Years of Lyndon Johnson*, vol. 1, *The Path to Power* (Vintage,
1983), 740. Johnson eventually made it to the Senate in the 1948 election
to succeed O'Daniel in a notoriously disputed election.

265   **Teddy Hayes's conversations with Flynn, Hannegan, and Douglas:**
      Teddy Hayes, *With the Gloves Off: My Life in the Boxing and Political
      Arenas* (Lancha, 1977), 140–142; Murphy, *Wild Bill*, 212–214. Murphy
      places the date of Flynn's report to Hayes as July 4, presumably because
      Hayes said that FDR's dinner with the political committee would be one
      week from that night and the dinner occurred on July 11. But FDR was
      in Hyde Park on July 4 and did not return to Washington until July 6.
      FDR's calendar, moreover, reveals that he met with Flynn on July 6 at
      12:15 p.m. In Hayes's telling, Flynn came from a dinner with FDR late
      at night to tell him of FDR's preference for Douglas. But FDR's calendar
      for July 6 lists dinner with the Boettigers (the President's daughter and
      son-in-law). It does not mention Flynn, although it is possible that he was
      there and that he told Hayes after returning from the dinner. It also is
      possible that Hayes, writing his memoir three decades later, was confused
      about the timing, and that Flynn spoke to him after his 12:15 p.m. meeting
      with FDR.

266   **Rosenman and Ickes's discussions with FDR and Wallace:** John W.
      Partin, "Roosevelt, Byrnes, and the 1944 Vice-Presidential Nomination,"
      Historian, November 1979, 90–91; Samuel Rosenman, *Working with Roo-
      sevelt* (Harper and Bros., 1952), 438–442; Brenda L. Heaster, "Who's on
      Second: The 1944 Democratic Vice Presidential Nomination," *Missouri
      Historical Review* 80, no. 2 (1986): 156–175.

267   **Wallace met with FDR:** Partin, "Roosevelt, Byrnes," 91; Henry A. Wal-
      lace, *The Price of Vision: The Diary of Henry A. Wallace, 1942–1946*, ed.
      Morton Blum (Houghton Mifflin, 1973), 361–362, 371.

267   **"The Hannegan game":** Wallace, *Price of Vision*, 365.

268   **FDR...distributed a letter:** "FDR Letter Says He Will Be Good Soldier,"
      Eugene (OR) Guard, July 11, 1944, 1.

268   **United Press:** United Press, "FDR Says He Would Accept Renomination,"
      Eugene (OR) Guard, July 11, 1944, 1. A transcript of FDR's July 11 press
      conference can be found in folder 960–963, July 7, 1944–August 15, 1944,
      Series 1: Press Conference Transcripts, Press Conferences of President
      Franklin D. Roosevelt, 1933–1945, Franklin D. Roosevelt Presidential
      Library and Museum, Hyde Park, NY, http://www.fdrlibrary.marist.edu
      /_resources/images/pc/pc0162.pdf. Immediately after FDR's announce-
      ment that he would run for a fourth term, a reporter asked the President

if his discussion with Wallace the previous day had any "bearing—" FDR interrupted and announced, "No. Talked about China. Now get out!" The press conference transcript notes "much laughter."

268 **FDR and Harry Hopkins...Byrnes:** James F. Byrnes, *All in One Lifetime* (Harper and Brothers, 1958), 219–223.

269 **July 11:** The description of the July 11 meeting is primarily drawn from Edwin Pauley with Richard English, "Why Truman Is President," box 25, White House Central Files, Confidential Files, Harry S. Truman Library and Museum, Independence, MO; Murphy, *Wild Bill*, 214–216; George Allen, *Presidents Who Have Known Me* (Simon & Schuster, 1950), 126–129; and Robert Ferrell, *Choosing Truman: The Democratic Convention of 1944* (University of Missouri Press, 1994), 11–14. The accounts differ in some details.

269 **Teddy Hayes...called Douglas:** Hayes, *With the Gloves Off*, 142; Murphy, *Wild Bill*, 214.

270 **"Roosevelt kept stressing Douglas":** Pauley with English, "Why Truman Is President," 14.

270 **"Douglas had no visible followers":** Allen, *Presidents*, 127–128.

270 **"When Roosevelt finished talking":** Ferrell, *Choosing Truman*, 13.

271 **party leaders decided...break the news:** Partin, "Roosevelt, Byrnes," 92–93; Byrnes, *All in One Lifetime*, 221–222; Ferrell, *Choosing Truman*, 28–29.

272 **FDR's meetings with de Gaulle and Lucy Mercer Rutherfurd:** Doris Kearns Goodwin, *No Ordinary Time: Franklin and Eleanor Roosevelt: The Home Front in World War II* (Simon & Schuster, 1994), 516–521; Joseph Persico, *Franklin and Lucy: Mrs. Rutherfurd and the Other Remarkable Women in Roosevelt's Life* (Random House, 2008), 301–304; "July 7th, 1944," "July 8th, 1944," "July 9th, 1944," all on Franklin D. Roosevelt Day by Day (website), Pare Lorentz Center, FDR Presidential Library, http://www.fdrlibrary.marist.edu/daybyday/. White House calendars reveal that FDR spent time with Lucy in the evenings at the White House on July 7 ("Mrs. Rutherford [*sic*]" at the White House from 8:45 p.m. to 11:10 p.m.) and July 8 (FDR "motoring" to Q Street at 6:20 p.m. "to call for Mrs. Rutherford [*sic*]"); followed by FDR's dinner with her and the Boettigers and movies at the White House; followed by FDR "accompanied by Mrs. Rutherford [*sic*]" in the study for approximately an hour until 11:00 p.m. FDR also spent the day with her at Shangri-La on July 9 ("motoring to 'Shangri-La' with Mrs. Rutherford [*sic*]" at 11:17 a.m.; "Returned from Shangri-La" at 10:30 p.m.). Doris Kearns Goodwin describes the possible sexual dimension of the relationship: "Were Lucy and Roosevelt lovers at this point? It is impossible to know, though, given the state of Roosevelt's

health, doubt remains. Still, even if they did not share the same bed, it is reasonable to imagine that there was a pleasing sexuality in their relationship." *No Ordinary Time*, 520.

273 **The Douglas team:** Murphy, *Wild Bill*, 217–219. Murphy relies in part on interviews with Janeway. In connection with the timing details of an unrelated topic, Janeway's son later wrote, "Alas, my father had suffered a stroke before the set of interviews Murphy conducted with him in 1990, and his command of details about the past became unreliable." Michael Janeway, *The Fall of the House of Roosevelt* (Columbia University Press, 2004), 65n*. For other points, however, Michael Janeway cited and relied on Murphy's interviews with his father. (239n42, 241n67).

273 **Corcoran similarly resented:** David McKean, *Tommy the Cork: Washington's Ultimate Insider from Roosevelt to Reagan* (Steerforth, 2004), 152–154; Brad Snyder, *Democratic Justice: Felix Frankfurter, the Supreme Court, and the Making of the Liberal Establishment* (W. W. Norton, 2022), 380.

273 **"knew the situation with Roosevelt's health":** Murphy, *Wild Bill*, 218. Janeway told James Simon that "Douglas thought he had the vice-presidential nomination in 1944 and he wanted it." Simon, *Independent Journey*, 265.

273 **"worse than Don Quixote wanted Dulcinea":** Murphy, *Wild Bill*, 218.

273 **FDR...met with Byrnes:** Byrnes, *All in One Lifetime*, 222–223; Partin, "Roosevelt, Byrnes," 94; David Robertson, *Sly and Able: A Political Biography of James F. Byrne* (W. W. Norton, 1994), 350.

274 **The President then had lunch:** Wallace, *Price of Vision*, 366–367. Hannegan's meeting with Wallace the previous day and Wallace's peremptory refusal to deal with him are described in Ferrell, *Choosing Truman*, 24. A reporter observed that Hannegan "emerged red-faced" from his conversation with the Vice President. Ferrell, *Choosing Truman*, 24.

275 **FDR had other political meetings that day:** "July 13th, 1944," Franklin D. Roosevelt Day by Day (website), Pare Lorentz Center, FDR Presidential Library, accessed January 25, 2023, http://www.fdrlibrary.marist .edu/daybyday/daylog/july-13th-1944/; Partin, "Roosevelt, Byrnes," 93–94; Matthew Josephson, *Sidney Hillman: Statesman of American Labor* (Doubleday, 1952), 617–618. Josephson mistakenly dates the FDR-Hillman meeting as July 14. FDR's calendar reveals the meeting to be on July 13, and FDR left Washington that night.

275 **Crowley...hosted a meeting:** Byrnes, *All in One Lifetime*, 223; Partin, "Roosevelt, Byrnes," 95.

275 **"We have to be damned careful about language":** Byrnes, *All in One Lifetime*, 224–225. According to Byrnes, FDR said that the party leaders "all agreed that Truman would cost fewer votes than anybody and probably Douglas second." Byrnes, who had learned shorthand as a youth, recorded

his July 14 conversation with FDR verbatim, and he also recounted other FDR quotes from the conversation in his memoir.

276 **Byrnes asked Truman:** Ferrell, *Choosing Truman*, 33; David McCullough, *Truman* (Simon & Schuster, 1992), 304.

276 **Cuneo in Chicago and Corcoran's efforts:** Murphy, *Wild Bill*, 219–221.

277 **Press accounts leading up:** Ralph Smith, "Won't Be Wallace, Heard More Often in Chicago," *Dayton (OH) Daily News*, July 17, 1944, 1.

277 **Douglas...wrote...Stone:** Murphy, *Wild Bill*, 221; William O. Douglas to Harlan Fiske Stone, July 12, 1944, Harlan Fiske Stone Papers, Library of Congress, box 74.

277 **he wrote...Senator Maloney:** Murphy, *Wild Bill*, 221; William O. Douglas to Frank Maloney, July 14, 1944, William O. Douglas Papers, Library of Congress, box 358.

277 **Maloney called Eliot Janeway:** Murphy, *Wild Bill*, 221–222. In addition to creating a record of his lack of interest, Douglas likely was aware that Truman had publicly disclaimed pursuit of the vice presidency; far from dampening public interest in Truman, it seemed to elevate him.

278 **in his specially designed train:** Murphy, *Wild Bill*, 222–223.

278 **"Dear Bob":** Ferrell, *Choosing Truman*, 81.

278 **Grace Tully later insisted:** Grace Tully, *Franklin Delano Roosevelt, My Boss* (Charles Scribner's Sons, 1949), pp. 276–277. Hannegan denied switching the order of the names. McCullough, *Truman*, 306.

279 **one Douglas biographer:** Murphy, *Wild Bill*, 605–608.

279 **"Grace Tully was not known":** McCullough, *Truman*, 307.

279 **Dorothy Brady corroborated:** Murphy, *Wild Bill*, 222, 606; Ferrell, *Choosing Truman*, 120n41.

279 **President told Hannegan:** Partin, "Roosevelt, Byrnes," 96. The details of the conversation aboard FDR's train are not clear; David McCullough concluded that Hannegan "was playing an extremely deceitful game" in the discussion and its aftermath. *Truman*, 307.

279 **"Clear it with Sidney":** McCullough, *Truman*, 306.

279 **Byrnes set up shop in Chicago:** Byrnes, *All in One Lifetime*, 226–227; Robertson, *Sly and Able*, 352–360; Partin, "Roosevelt, Byrnes," 96–97.

280 **Press accounts:** William K. Hutchinson, International News Service, "F.R. Names Four Alternatives to Wallace, Scribe Says," *Cedar Rapids (IA) Gazette*, July 16, 1944, 1; D. Harold Oliver, Associated Press, "Democratic Party Leaders Predict 'Wide Open' Battle for Second Place," *Billings (MT) Gazette*, July 16, 1944, 1.

280 **labor would oppose Byrnes:** Partin, "Roosevelt, Byrnes," 97.

280 **Flynn...effort to block him:** David M. Jordan, *FDR, Dewey, and the Election of 1944* (Indiana University Press, 2011), 157; Edward J. Flynn, *You're the Boss: The Practice of American Politics* (Viking, 1947), 182.

Byrnes thought that Flynn nursed a grudge against him because Byrnes had undermined Flynn's confirmation to be Ambassador to the Vatican; FDR was forced to withdraw Flynn's nomination because of a lack of support in the Senate. Byrnes, *All in One Lifetime*, 217–218.

281 **"kiss the Negro vote goodbye"**: Robertson, *Sly and Able*, 355.

281 **"Mr. Justice, you cannot be my candidate"**: Robertson, *Sly and Able*, 355.

281 **"political liability"**: Partin, "Roosevelt, Byrnes," 98.

281 **Crowley told Byrnes**: Robertson, *Sly and Able*, 358–359; Partin, "Roosevelt, Byrnes," 98; McCullough, *Truman*, 312. According to Byrnes, Truman, having heard from Hannegan that FDR now favored him, visited him Monday night and asked to be released from his pledge of support; Byrnes obliged. Byrnes, *All in One Lifetime*, 229. Byrnes's account of this conversation seems at odds with Truman's recollection that the following morning he told Hillman that he continued to support Byrnes for the nomination. Ferrell, *Choosing Truman*, 53–54.

281 **Byrnes called FDR early the next day**: Partin, "Roosevelt, Byrnes," 98–99; Ferrell, *Choosing Truman*, 48–49; Robertson, *Sly and Able*, 359.

281 **Byrnes met with Hannegan**: Partin, "Roosevelt, Byrnes," 98–99.

282 **He wrote a letter…to…Maybank**: Partin, "Roosevelt, Byrnes," 99.

282 **"I got off the Supreme Court"**: Byrnes, *All in One Lifetime*, 231.

282 ***New York Times* ran an explosive account**: Arthur Krock, "The Inflammatory Use of a Party Chairman," *New York Times*, July 25, 1944, 18. Krock's story reported FDR's quote as "Clear everything with Sidney," but it rapidly became popularized as "Clear it with Sidney." In his 1971 memoir, *New York Times* reporter Turner Catledge recalled that he heard the quote from Chicago Mayor Ed Kelly and passed it on to Krock for reporting under his byline because Catledge's "friendship with Byrnes and Kelly was well known." Turner Catledge, *My Life and the Times* (Harper and Row, 1971), 147–148. Byrnes biographer David Robertson concluded that Byrnes "managed to plant" the "Clear it with Sidney" story with the *New York Times* as an act of "revenge" against FDR. Robertson, *Sly and Able*, 361, 596.

282 **Byrnes "disappointed" and "hurt"**: Byrnes, *All in One Lifetime*, 230. Byrnes continued, likely with an eye to posterity, "I was angry with myself for permitting the President to get me in it. But I cherished no animosity toward him. I realized that he was looking after his own interests."

282 **"men were so many tools"**: Byrnes to former Senator Burton Wheeler, April 6, 1966, quoted in Robertson, *Sly and Able*, 360–361.

282 **a letter…expressing his views on the vice-presidential nomination**: Turner Catledge, "Wallace Left to Delegates by Roosevelt," *New York Times*, July 18, 1944, 1.

283 "reported to be [the President's] second choice": Turner Catledge, "President's Word on Wallace Choice Not Believed Order," *New York Times*, July 17, 1944, 1.

283 Hannegan met with Hillman and Murray over dinner: Partin, "Roosevelt, Byrnes," 98; Ferrell, *Choosing Truman*, 56.

283 Cuneo...in Chicago: Murphy, *Wild Bill*, 224.

283 Hillman was having breakfast with Harry Truman: Josephson, *Sidney Hillman*, 621; Jonathan Daniels, *The Man of Independence* (Kennikat, 1950), 245; McCullough, *Truman*, 311; Ferrell, *Choosing Truman*, 53–54; Harry Truman, *The Autobiography of Harry S. Truman*, ed. Robert H. Ferrell (1980; University of Missouri Press, 2002), 88. In Truman's recollection, Hillman mentioned both Douglas and Truman as backup choices to Wallace. Unlike some accounts, Truman does not state that Hillman ranked Truman as the first choice and Douglas as the second choice.

284 "Bob, you *are* a son-of-a-bitch": Murphy, *Wild Bill*, 225.

284 Cuneo reached out to...Murray: Murphy, *Wild Bill*, 225.

284 Hannegan and Kelly gathered several Senators: Murphy, *Wild Bill*, 225; Wallace, *Price of Vision*, 368.

285 "Hannegan worked one end of the table": Wallace, *Price of Vision*, 368.

285 the President joined the call: McCullough, *Truman*, 314.

285 "Hello, fellows": Murphy, *Wild Bill*, 226.

285 FDR delivered his acceptance speech: Jordan, *FDR, Dewey*, 169–172.

286 "too late for any Douglas forces to organize": Murphy, *Wild Bill*, 226.

286 Reporters barraged Hannegan: Murphy, *Wild Bill*, 226–227; Ferrell, *Choosing Truman*, 82; James A. Hagerty, "President Favors Truman, Douglas," *New York Times*, July 21, 1944, 1.

286 "Our throats were slit": Murphy, *Wild Bill*, 227.

286 "Fuck 'em": Murphy, *Wild Bill*, 227. Ickes also sometimes signaled a willingness to support Wallace despite their strained relationship. T. H. Watkins, *Righteous Pilgrim: The Life and Times of Harold L. Ickes, 1874–1952* (Henry Holt, 1990), 812.

287 Joe Kennedy: Murphy, *Wild Bill*, 227–228.

287 "within a nickel's phone call": Murphy, *Wild Bill*, 229.

287 Wallace's seconding speech: Turner Catledge, "Roosevelt Nominated for Fourth Term," *New York Times*, July 21, 1944, 1.

288 "I had been greatly impressed": Pauley with English, "Why Truman Is President," 12.

288 Kelly quickly proclaimed: Ferrell, *Choosing Truman*, 80.

288 Hannegan worked the floor: Murphy, *Wild Bill*, 229.

288 Ickes sent FDR a...telegram: Ferrell, *Choosing Truman*, 123n48.

289 "exemplar of the principles of justice": Hub M. George, "Nomination Dictated, Union Chief Charges," *Detroit Free Press*, July 22, 1944, 3.

289   "It's going to be an impasse": Ferrell, *Choosing Truman*, 87.

289   second ballot: Ferrell, *Choosing Truman*, 88; Murphy, *Wild Bill*, 229.

289   Douglas...was in the mountains: William O. Douglas, *The Court Years,
      1939–1975: The Autobiography of William O. Douglas* (Random House,
      1980), 283. A syndicated column by Leonard Lyons published on the day
      of the vice-presidential nomination stated that "Justice William O. Douglas
      still is on a pack trip in Oregon, out of reach of any telegram or telephone
      calls." Leonard Lyons, "Truman Probe," *Harrisburg Telegraph*, July 21,
      1944, p. 10.

290   Douglas actually was at the home of the Whitman College president:
      Murphy, *Wild Bill*, 230–231. Murphy relied for his conclusion on his inter-
      view with Janeway and on an interview with the former Whitman College
      President that had been conducted by a documentary filmmaker. Efforts
      to obtain the interviews have been unsuccessful.

290   "never threw his hat in the political ring": Simon, *Independent Jour-
      ney*, 266. James L. Moses has challenged the conventional wisdom and
      concluded that Douglas "made all reasonable efforts to stop his friends
      from promoting him for the vice-presidency." James L. Moses, "William
      O. Douglas's 'Political Ambitions' and the 1944 Vice-Presidential Nom-
      ination: A Reinterpretation," *The Historian*, volume 62, issue 2 (Winter
      2000): 325, 341. As Simon points out, however, Douglas never made a
      public statement disavowing efforts on his behalf. (In Douglas's letter to
      Maloney on July 14, he sought to justify the lack of a public statement by
      saying that "public denial of political aspirations has too often in our his-
      tory been actual public assertion of the very ambitions which are denied.")
      And there is no indication that Douglas ever sought to stop his close asso-
      ciate Corcoran, even though Corcoran's efforts on Douglas's behalf were
      publicly reported. Henry Wallace noted in his diary that, according to
      Frank Murphy, Corcoran and Janeway were frequent visitors to Douglas's
      chambers in the period leading up to the convention. Simon, *Independent
      Journey*, 266.

290   Douglas...wrote the President: Ferrell, *Choosing Truman*, 84.

290   "most outwardly chaotic in American political history": Heaster, "Who's
      on Second," 156.

290   In his memoir, Samuel Rosenman: Rosenman, *Working with Roosevelt*,
      438–454.

290   James Roosevelt: James Roosevelt and Sidney Shalett, *Affectionately,
      F.D.R.: A Son's Story of a Lonely Man* (Harcourt Brace, 1959), 351. James
      Roosevelt also noted that, even while seeming to prefer Douglas, FDR
      "professed not to 'give a damn' whether the delegates came up with Justice
      Douglas, Jimmy Byrnes, or Senator Harry Truman. His mind was on the
      war; the fourth-term race was simply a job that had to be accomplished,

and his attitude toward the coming political campaign was one of 'let's get on with it.'"

291   **FDR...persistently included Douglas's name:** Some commentators have speculated that FDR kept Douglas's name in the letter with Truman's so that it would not appear that he was dictating an outcome by listing only one name. See, e.g., Partin, "Roosevelt, Byrnes," 92. As the week progressed, FDR seems to have focused on Truman; as discussed, however, there also are abundant indications that he had a high personal regard for Douglas and thought that he would bring strength to the ticket.

291   **Party nominated Associate Justice Charles Evan Hughes:** James F. Simon, *FDR and Chief Justice Hughes: The President, the Supreme Court, and the Epic Battle over the New Deal* (Simon & Schuster, 2012), 95–99; Lewis L. Gould, *The First Modern Clash over Federal Power: Wilson versus Hoover in the Presidential Election of 1916* (University Press of Kansas, 2016), 73–75, Appendix A.

291   **John Jay:** Cliff Sloan and David McKean, *The Great Decision: Jefferson, Adams, Marshall, and the Battle for the Supreme Court* (PublicAffairs, 2009), xv.

292   **Stephen Field:** John P. Frank, *Marble Palace: The Supreme Court in American Life* (Knopf, 1958), 274–275; William J. Cibes, Jr., "Extra-Judicial Activities of Justices of the United States Supreme Court, 1790–1960" (PhD diss., Princeton University, 1975), 846–849; Paul Kens, *Justice Stephen Field: Shaping Liberty from the Gold Rush to the Gilded Age* (University Press of Kansas, 1997), 174–176, 227–231; "The Bourbons Stampeded," *New York Times*, June 25, 1880, 1. A few other Justices in the nineteenth century also sought the presidency. Kens (175); Frank (274–275).

292   **Morrison Waite:** Frank, *Marble Palace*, 275–276; Cibes, "Extra-Judicial Activities," 841–842.

CHAPTER 16

293   **Korematsu bio and arrest:** Peter Irons, *Justice at War: The Story of the Japanese American Internment Cases* (Oxford University Press, 1983), 93–99; Lorraine K. Bannai, *Enduring Conviction: Fred Korematsu and His Quest for Justice* (University of Washington Press, 2015), 7–37; Transcript of Record at 20–25, *Fred Toyosaburo Korematsu v. United States*, 321 U.S. 760 (1944) (No. 22). Some details of Korematsu's life differ in various accounts.

294   **General DeWitt issued Exclusion Order Number 34...and accompanying procedures:** Civilian Exclusion Order No. 34, 7 Fed. Reg. 3967 (May 28, 1942) https://hsp.org/education/primary-sources/civilian-exclusion-order-no -34; Brief for the American Civil Liberties Union, Amicus Curiae, at 2, *Fred Toyosaburo Korematsu v. United States*, 321 U.S. 760 (1944) (No. 22), 5–6.

295   **Korematsu acknowledged his real identity:** Irons, *Justice at War*, 94–96;
       Bannai, *Enduring Conviction*, 42.

295   **official charging document:** Transcript of Record at 1, *Fred Toyosaburo
       Korematsu v. United States*, 321 U.S. 760 (1944) (No. 22).

295   **Korematsu's trial and testimony:** Irons, *Justice at War*, 151–154; Tran-
       script of Record at 15–16, *Fred Toyosaburo Korematsu v. United States*, 321
       U.S. 760 (1944) (No. 22). The ACLU lawyer who recruited Korematsu
       was Ernest Besig. Even though Besig did not serve as Korematsu's lead
       lawyer, he remained supportive throughout Korematsu's legal travails; de-
       cades later, Korematsu expressed his continuing gratitude to Besig. John
       Q. Barrett, "A Commander's Power, A Civilian's Reason: Justice Jackson's
       Korematsu Dissent," *Law and Contemporary Problems* 68, no. 2 (2005): 57,
       79; Irons, *Justice at War*, 97, 117.

296   **Ninth Circuit opinion:** *Korematsu v. United States*, 140 F.2d 289 (9th Cir.
       1943). Judge Denman's separate opinion is at p. 291. The Ninth Circuit
       initially ruled that Korematsu's appeal was premature in light of the sen-
       tencing judge's order, but the Supreme Court reversed on this preliminary
       procedural point and sent the case back to the Ninth Circuit for consider-
       ation of the merits. *Korematsu v. United States*, 319 U.S. 432 (1943).

296   **agreed to hear the case:** *Korematsu v. United States*, 321 U.S. 760 (1944).

297   **Mitsuye Endo:** Irons, *Justice at War*, 99–103, 266–268; Lori Aratani, "She
       Fought the Internment of Japanese Americans During World War II and
       Won," *Washington Post*, December 18, 2019.

297   **district court rejected her claim:** Transcript of Record at 20, *Endo v. Ei-
       senhower* [later renamed *Ex parte Endo*], 323 U.S. 283 (1944) (No. 70).

297   **Ninth Circuit certification questions:** "War Relocation Authority,"
       United States Law Week, July 4, 1944, 3021; Brief of the United States at
       2–5, *Ex parte Endo*, 323 U.S. 283 (1944) (No. 70); Irons, *Justice at War*,
       266–267.

297   **Supreme Court accepted the…certification:** *Journal of the Supreme
       Court of the United States*, October Term 1943 (No. 932), May 8, 1944,
       206.

297   **"leave clearance":** Brief of the United States, *Ex parte Endo*, October
       Term 1944, No. 70, pp. 7–8, 15–22; Brief of the United States, *Korematsu
       v. United States*, 321 U.S. 760 (1944) (No. 22). According to the federal
       government, "as of July 29, 1944," 28,911 detainees had been granted "in-
       definite leave" under the two-step process. Brief of the United States at 36,
       Ex parte Endo.

297   **Korematsu's leave:** Irons, *Justice at War*, 312; Bannai, *Enduring Convic-
       tion*, 70–71, 83, 90–91. Before receiving indefinite leave, Korematsu had
       received short-term leave that allowed him to leave for work on a tempo-
       rary basis. Bannai, *Enduring Conviction*, 70.

298 **Endo...balked at the second step:** Brief of the United States at 7–8, 21–22, 37–38, *Ex parte Endo*; Amanda L. Tyler, *Habeas Corpus in Wartime: From the Tower of London to Guantanamo Bay* (Oxford University Press, 2017), 234–235; Irons, *Justice at War*, 257, 312; Aratani, "She Fought"; Associated Press, "Highest Court to Decide on Jap Problems," *Press Democrat* (Santa Rosa, CA), October 13, 1944, 1.

298 **"we of Japanese ancestry were not guilty of any crime":** Tyler, *Habeas Corpus*, 235.

298 **reported by General DeWitt:** Western Defense Command and Fourth Army, *Final Report: Japanese Evacuation from the West Coast, 1942* (Government Printing Office, 1943), 8, https://collections.nlm.nih.gov/ext/dw /01130040R/PDF/01130040R.pdf; James F. King, "DeWitt Cites Evidence of Wide Espionage in 1941–'42 Period," *Washington Post*, January 20, 1944, 2.

299 **reactions to DeWitt Report by the Justice Department, FBI, and FCC:** Peter Irons, *Justice Delayed: The Record of the Japanese American Internment Cases* (Wesleyan University Press, 1989), 158–160; Irons, *Justice at War*, 278–302.

299 **"no information in the possession of this Bureau":** Irons, *Justice at War*, 280–281.

299 **FCC's "investigations":** Irons, *Justice at War*, 282–284.

300 **"practice of keeping loyal American citizens":** Irons, *Justice at War*, 271.

300 **Ickes...sent Roosevelt a series of letters:** Irons, *Justice at War*, 271.

300 **At a Cabinet meeting on May 26, 1944:** Irons, *Justice at War*, 272. Stimson's statements are recorded in Biddle's notes of the Cabinet meeting and Stimson's diary entry.

300 **"likelihood of an adverse [court] decision":** Stimson diary entry, May 26, 1944, quoted in Irons, *Justice at War*, 272.

300 **"no longer any military necessity":** Irons, *Justice at War*, 272.

301 **"The more I think of the problem":** Irons, *Justice at War*, 273.

301 **"a substantial number":** Irons, *Justice at War*, 273.

301 **summoned John McCloy to the White House:** Irons, *Justice at War*, 273.

301 **"surrounded...by his political advisors":** FDR's White House calendar for June 13, 1944, shows a presidential meeting with McCloy at 3:45 p.m., with nobody else listed. Numerous political insiders—including DNC Chairman Robert Hannegan, DNC Publicity Director Paul Porter, former DNC Chairman Ed Flynn, and former FDR aide Tommy Corcoran—met with FDR in the White House earlier in the day. McCloy likely was referring to some or all of them; they may have stayed and joined the McCloy meeting. "June 13th, 1944," Franklin D. Roosevelt Day by Day (website), Pare Lorentz Center, FDR Presidential Library, accessed January 25, 2023, http://www.fdrlibrary.marist.edu/daybyday/daylog/june-13th-1944/.

301 "Roosevelt's desire for partisan advantage": Irons, *Justice at War*, 277.

301 **Burling prepared a footnote:** Irons, *Justice Delayed*, 161.

302 **archetypal "stop the presses" moment:** Irons, *Justice at War*, 288. Adrian Fisher was a former Supreme Court law clerk to Justices Brandeis and Frankfurter.

302 **Burling and Ennis urged Wechsler:** Irons, *Justice at War*, 287–288; Irons, *Justice Delayed*, 162–163.

303 **Wechsler's footnote:** Irons, *Justice at War*, 290–292; Brief of the United States at 11 n.2, *Korematsu*.

303 **"almost nonsensical":** Kai Bird, *The Chairman: John J. McCloy and the Making of the American Establishment* (Simon and Schuster, 1992), 173.

303 **"public relations problem":** Irons, *Justice at War*, 289.

304 **"veritable reign of terror":** Brief for Appellant at 30, *Korematsu v. United States*, 321 U.S. 760 (1944) (No. 22).

304 **"They are parts of one single program":** Brief for Appellant at 31, *Korematsu*.

304 **DeWitt's public statements:** Brief for Appellant at 52, *Korematsu* (citing Petition for Writ of Certiorari at 33, *Korematsu v. United States*, 321 U.S. 760 (1944)).

304 **DeWitt's "brutal evacuation program":** Brief for Appellant at 52, *Korematsu*.

305 **beneficent protection:** Brief of the United States at 52–55, *Korematsu*.

305 **Ennis's discussions with Baldwin and Horsky:** Irons, *Justice at War*, 260–261, 267–268, 315.

305 **"The true issue posed by this case":** Brief for the American Civil Liberties Union, Amicus Curiae, at 2, *Korematsu v. United States*, 321 U.S. 760 (1944) (No. 22). In addition to Horsky's brief for the national ACLU, the ACLU branch in Northern California filed its own amicus brief, partly because of the branch's anger at the national organization's initial timidity about challenging the Roosevelt Administration.

305 **"Americans of Japanese ancestry are well assimilated and loyal":** Brief of Japanese American Citizens League, Amicus Curiae, at 151, *Korematsu v. United States*, 321 U.S. 760 (1944) (No. 22).

306 **states' brief:** Brief of the States of California, Oregon, and Washington as Amici Curiae on Behalf of Appellee at 2–3, 16, 26, *Korematsu v. United States*, 321 U.S. 760 (1944) (No. 22).

306 **briefs in *Endo*:** Appellant's Brief, *Ex parte Endo*, 323 U.S. 283 (1944) (No. 70).

306 **"exclude" and "take such other steps":** Exec. Order 9066, 3 C.F.R. 1092–1093 (1942).

307 **"The government has no power":** Brief of American Civil Liberties Union, Amicus Curiae, at 3, 7, *Ex parte Endo*, 323 U.S. 283 (1944) (No. 70).

307   **two-step process:** Brief of the United States at 16–21, *Ex parte Endo.*
307   **The Justice Department argued:** Brief of the United States at 38, *Ex parte Endo* ("Summary of Argument"). Another procedural issue in the case was whether the San Francisco court where Endo's habeas petition had been filed lost jurisdiction when she was transferred to an incarceration camp in Utah. Although the district court had relied on that ground, the United States declined to rely on it, saying only that the "authorities" were "inconclusive." *Id.* 39.
307   **September 1943 report by James Byrnes:** Brief of the United States at 79–81, 79n67, *Ex parte Endo* (quoting James F. Byrnes, Director of War Mobilization, *Segregation of Loyal and Disloyal Japanese in Relocation Centers,* 78th Cong., 1st Sess., September 14, 1943, S. Doc. 96).
308   **"program which has been begun":** Brief of the United States at 82, *Ex parte Endo.*
308   **war news dominated national attention:** W. H. Lawrence, "Big 3 Peace Unity Toasted by Stalin," *New York Times,* October 11, 1944, 1; Robert Trumbull, "Carrier Planes Hit Japanese Homeland Isles," *New York Times,* October 11, 1944, 1; "War News Summarized," *New York Times,* October 11, 1944, 1; "War News Summarized," *New York Times,* October 12, 1944, 1; "War News Summarized," *New York Times,* October 13, 1944, 1.
308   **"[clawing] the guts out of the filthy Nazis":** W. H. Lawrence, "Big 3 Peace Unity Toasted by Stalin," *New York Times,* October 11, 1944, 1.
308   **Collins rose...to argue:** Associated Press, "Japanese Evacuation Is Hit as Nazified," *Sacramento Bee,* October 12, 1944, 20; Irons, *Justice at War,* 313–314.
308   **Horsky then argued:** United Press, "AJA Evacuation Comparable to Hitler Action, Court Told," *Honolulu Advertiser,* October 12, 1944, 8; Warren B. Francis, "Jap Exclusion Argued Before Supreme Court," *Los Angeles Times,* October 12, 1944, 2; Irons, *Justice at War,* 314–315.
309   **Purcell emphasized:** Warren B. Francis, "Supreme Court to Rule on Nisei Return to Coast," *Los Angeles Times,* October 13, 1944, 7; Associated Press, "Highest Court to Decide on Jap Problems," *Press Democrat* (Santa Rosa, CA), October 13, 1944, 1; Irons, *Justice at War,* 317–318.
309   **Justices "fired pointed questions frequently":** Associated Press, "Supreme Court Hears Jap Case," *Daily Oklahoman* (Oklahoma City, OK), October 13, 1944, 17.
309   **"By what standard":** Warren B. Francis, "Jap Exclusion Argued Before Supreme Court," *Los Angeles Times,* October 12, 1944, 2. The *Los Angeles Times* article noted that Douglas and Murphy also "wondered whether the court should review statutes enacted for national defense."
309   **"loyal in one place, and not loyal in another":** Associated Press, "Highest Court."

309   **Fahy acknowledged:** Charles Sheehan, "Solicitor General Charles Fahy
       and Honorable Defense of the Japanese-American Exclusion Cases,"
       American Journal of Legal History 54, no. 4 (October 2014): 469–520, 517;
       "Whispering Charlie," *New York Times*, September 20, 1979, A22. Irons
       noted that, in the *Endo* argument, Fahy's "defense of detention was half-
       hearted at best." Irons, *Justice at War*, 318. As with the *Hirabayashi* case,
       Sheehan vigorously defends Fahy's handling of the *Korematsu* and *Endo*
       cases. Sheehan, "Solicitor General Charles Fahy"; Charles J. Sheehan,
       "Charles Fahy's 'Brilliant Public Service as Solicitor General': A Reply to
       Peter Irons," *American Journal of Legal History* 55, no. 3 (September 2015):
       347–360.

309   **Fahy's arguments about the DeWitt Report:** Peter Irons, "Fancy Danc-
       ing in the Marble Palace," *Constitutional Commentary* 3 (1986): 35, 48–
       49 (Fahy argument transcript). At that time, the Supreme Court did not
       transcribe oral arguments. Fahy arranged for transcripts of his own argu-
       ments in *Korematsu* and *Endo*, but not those of other lawyers; Fahy's *Ko-
       rematsu* argument is printed in Irons, "Fancy Dancing," 46–60. Horsky's
       comment about the "extraordinary footnote" was recorded by an Army ob-
       server. Irons, *Justice at War*, 315.

311   **"by the whole executive…Congress":** Irons, "Fancy Dancing," 47, 54.

311   **humaneness of the government's actions:** Irons, "Fancy Dancing," 60.

311   **questions from the Justices:** Francis, "Supreme Court to Rule."

CHAPTER 17

313   **"we do our own work":** William H. Rehnquist, *The Supreme Court* (Vin-
       tage, 2001), 231.

313   **topic in the conference room:** Peter Irons, *Justice at War: The Story of
       the Japanese American Internment Cases* (Oxford University Press, 1983),
       319–325. Murphy's clerk reported that Black was not happy about being
       assigned *Korematsu*, especially without also being assigned *Endo*, because
       "he says he hates to write against civil liberties." Roger K. Newman, *Hugo
       Black: A Biography* (Fordham University Press, 1997), 316.

315   **toll on his wife Josephine:** Newman, *Hugo Black*, 308.

315   ***Chambers v. Florida:*** 309 U.S. 227, 241 (1940).

316   **circulated his draft majority opinion:** Irons, *Justice at War*, 325–341; *Ko-
       rematsu v. United States*, 323 U.S. 214 (1944).

316   **Black's opinion rested:** *Korematsu*, 323 U.S. at 214–224.

316   **"In the light of the principles":** *Korematsu*, 323 U.S. at 217–218.

316   **"We are not unmindful of the hardships":** *Korematsu*, 323 U.S. at 219.

317   **Douglas circulated:** Irons, *Justice at War*, 333–334, 338.

317   **For Roberts:** *Korematsu*, 323 U.S. at 225–233.

318 **Murphy...now attacked:** *Korematsu*, 323 U.S. at 233–242.

318 **Jackson...lacerating:** *Korematsu*, 323 U.S. at 242–248.

319 **Black...added a passage:** *Korematsu*, 323 U.S. at 223–224.

320 **Frankfurter...emphasized:** *Korematsu*, 323 U.S. at 224–225.

320 **Douglas's majority opinion:** *Ex parte Endo*, 323 U.S. 283 (1944).

320 **"Mitsuye Endo is entitled to an unconditional release":** *Endo*, 323 U.S. at 304. Patrick Gudridge has argued that, in addition to its statutory interpretation, *Endo* has a constitutional foundation. Gudridge, "Remember *Endo*?," *Harvard Law Review* 116, no. 7 (2003): 1933.

320 **"The fact that the Act and the orders are silent":** *Endo*, 323 U.S. at 301.

321 **Murphy added a concurrence:** *Endo*, 323 U.S. at 307–308.

321 **Roberts, meanwhile, refused:** *Endo*, 323 U.S. at 308–310.

322 **Douglas wrote Stone:** Irons, *Justice at War*, 344; Amanda L. Tyler, *Habeas Corpus in Wartime: From the Tower of London to Guantanamo Bay* (Oxford University Press, 2017), 404n129; William O. Douglas to Harlan Stone, memo, November 28, 1944, Folder No. 70, O.T. 1944, *Endo v. Eisenhower*, Certiorari, Conference & Misc. Memos, Box 116, Papers of William O. Douglas, Library of Congress.

322 **Cabinet meeting on Friday:** Greg Robinson, *By Order of the President: FDR and the Internment of Japanese Americans* (Harvard University Press, 2001), 227–229.

323 **Governor Earl Warren publicly stated:** Robinson, *By Order of the President*, 228.

323 **one of FDR's regular meetings with the press:** Robinson, *By Order of the President*, 1–3.

323 **issued by General H. C. Pratt:** Public Proclamation No. 21, 10 Fed. Reg. 53 (January 2, 1945), www.du.edu/behindbarbedwire/pp_21.html. General Pratt sought to calm the western states about the imminent return of the detainees: "The people of the states situated within the Western Defense Command are assured that the records of all persons of Japanese ancestry have been carefully examined.... They should be accorded the same treatment and allowed to enjoy the same privileges accorded other law aiding American citizens or residents."

323 **"an unusual Sunday press conference":** "Army Approves Return of Japs," *Oakland (CA) Tribune*, December 18, 1944, 1.

324 **"The government was tipped off":** Robinson, *By Order of the President*, 230.

324 **Roger Daniels...confidential source:** Irons, *Justice at War*, 345. Greg Robinson similarly attributes the tip to Frankfurter. *By Order of the President*, 230. As Patrick Gudridge has detailed, some observers think that Stone also may have been a source of the leak. Gudridge, "Remember *Endo*?," 1935n11.

324   **"If Japs in large numbers"**: "We Shan't Pretend to Like It," editorial, *Los Angeles Times*, December 19, 1944, section II, 4.

324   **"We are inclined to take our stand"**: "Legalization of Racism," editorial, *Washington Post*, December 22, 1944, 8. The *Pittsburgh Post-Gazette* expressed puzzlement about the "paradoxical decisions handed down at the same session." "Japanese Relocation," editorial, *Pittsburgh (PA) Post-Gazette*, December 20, 1944, 6.

324   **Dembitz...article**: Nanette Dembitz, "Racial Discrimination and the Military Judgment: The Supreme Court's *Korematsu* and *Endo* Decisions," *Columbia Law Review* 45, no. 2 (1945): 175n*, 239.

325   **Rostow...broadside**: Eugene V. Rostow, "The Japanese American Cases—A Disaster," *Yale Law Journal* 54, no. 3 (1945): 489, 490, 533.

325   **"I would do precisely the same thing today"**: "Justice Black, Champion of Civil Liberties for 34 Years on Court, Dies at 85," *New York Times*, September 26, 1971, 76; Newman, *Hugo Black*, 318.

325   **Reed likewise defended**: Irons, *Justice at War*, 356.

325   **"My vote to affirm was one of my mistakes"**: William O. Douglas, *The Court Years, 1939–1975: The Autobiography of William O. Douglas* (Random House, 1980), 39, 280.

326   **"I have since deeply regretted the removal order...their parents"**: Earl Warren, *The Memoirs of Earl Warren* (Doubleday, 1977), 149; Newman, *Hugo Black*, 319n*.

326   **"greatest deprivation of civil liberties"**: Edward Ennis, testimony to the Commission on Wartime Relocation and Internment of Civilians, quoted in Irons, *Justice at War*, 349.

326   **McCloy derided**: John J. McCloy, testimony to the Commission on Wartime Relocation and Internment of Civilians, quoted in Irons, *Justice at War*, 352–353.

327   **"anniversary of a sad day"**: Proclamation 4417, 41 Fed. Reg. 7741 (February 20, 1976), https://www.fordlibrarymuseum.gov/library/speeches/760 111p.htm.

327   **"was not justified by military necessity"**: Commission on Wartime Relocation and Internment of Civilians, *Personal Justice Denied* (University of Washington Press, 1997), 18.

327   **Civil Liberties Act**: Pub. L. No. 100-383, 102 Stat. 988 (1988).

327   **"We gather here today"**: Ronald Reagan, "Remarks on Signing the Bill Providing Restitution for the Wartime Internment of Japanese-American Civilians," speech, Washington, DC, August 10, 1988, transcript at https://www.reaganlibrary.gov/archives/speech/remarks-signing-bill-providing -restitution-wartime-internment-japanese-american.

327   **writ of coram nobis**: *Korematsu v. United States*, 584 F. Supp. 1406 (N.D. Cal. 1984); *Hirabayashi v. United States*, 828 F.2d 591 (9th Cir. 1987). The

Ninth Circuit's *Hirabayashi* opinion explains the sequence of the *Yasui* litigation. 828 F.2d at 594 n.4. In 2011, citing the judicial decisions overturning the convictions in the *Korematsu* and *Hirabayashi* cases, Acting Solicitor General Neal Katyal announced a "confession of error" about the government's failure to disclose relevant information to the Supreme Court. Neal Katyal, "Confession of Error: The Solicitor General's Mistakes During the Japanese-American Internment Cases," Office of Public Affairs, US Department of Justice, May 20, 2011, https://www.justice .gov/archives/opa/blog/confession-error-solicitor-generals-mistakes-during -japanese-american-internment-cases; Neal Kutmar Katyal, "The Solicitor General and Confession of Error," *Fordham Law Review* 81, no. 6 (May 2013): 3027–3038.

328 **Trump had called for:** *Trump v. Hawaii*, 138 S. Ct. 2392, 2435–2438 (2018) (Sotomayor, J., dissenting).

328 **Chief Justice Roberts's opinion:** *Trump v. Hawaii*, 138 S. Ct. at 2417–2423.

328 **"plausible":** *Trump v. Hawaii*, 138 S. Ct. at 2420. The Court articulated its standard as "whether the entry policy is plausibly related to the Government's stated objective to protect the country and improve vetting processes." *Id.*

328 **Sotomayor's dissent:** *Trump v. Hawaii*, 138 S. Ct. at 2447–2448. Justice Ginsburg joined Justice Sotomayor's dissent. Justice Breyer, joined by Justice Kagan, dissented separately.

329 **majority explicitly disavowed:** *Trump v. Hawaii*, 138 S. Ct. at 2423.

329 **"By blindly accepting":** *Trump v. Hawaii*, 138 S. Ct. at 2448.

CHAPTER 18

331 **President Franklin Roosevelt:** J. A. Fox, "Roosevelt Pledges Lasting Peace in Brief Inaugural Address at Simple White House Ceremony," *Evening Star*, January 20, 1945, 1; Associated Press, "FDR Pledges Nation to Total Victory in War, Durable Peace," *Shreveport (LA) Journal*, January 20, 1945, 1.

332 **Congress had...appropriated:** Bob Considine, International News Service, "Roosevelt Begins His Fourth Term in Somber Style," *Montgomery (AL) Advertiser*, January 25, 1945, 1.

332 **number of invited guests:** Fred Pasley, "First Twelve Years the Hardest, Quips F.D.R. on Inaugural Eve," *New York Daily News*, January 20, 1945, 1.

332 **wounded veterans:** Douglas B. Cornell, Associated Press, "Inauguration Takes Place in Capital," *Charlotte (NC) News*, January 20, 1945, 1.

332 **sober ceremony:** Edwin A. Lahey, "Roosevelt Takes Oath of Office, Dedicates Fourth Term to Peace," *Miami Herald*, January 21, 1945, 1.

332 **first twelve years were always the hardest:** Pasley, "First Twelve Years."

332 **Sitting on the…portico:** William K. Hutchinson, International News Service, "Roosevelt Promises Victory, Peace as He Takes Oath for Fourth Term," *Lexington (KY) Leader,* January 20, 1945, 1.

332 **Douglas looked "puckish":** Louis M. Lyons, "We Shall Not Fail Supreme Test—F.D.," *Boston Globe,* January 21, 1945, 1.

332 **Frankfurter…"shushed":** John C. O'Brien, "Inaugural Ceremonies Last Only 14 Minutes," *Philadelphia Inquirer,* January 21, 1945, 1.

332 **Dutch Bible:** Cornell, "Inauguration Takes Place."

332 **second briefest inaugural address:** Hutchinson, "Roosevelt Promises Victory"; Gary Ginsberg, *First Friends* (Twelve, 2021), 194.

333 **FDR was in fine shape:** Associated Press, "F.D.R. in 'Fine Shape' to Start Fourth Term," *Courier-Journal,* January 21, 1945, 1.

333 **the President began:** Franklin D. Roosevelt, fourth inaugural address, January 20, 1945, Washington, D.C., transcript from Miller Center, University of Virginia, https://millercenter.org/the-presidency/presidential-speeches/january-20-1945-fourth-inaugural-address.

333 **"Petty Feuding":** Jay Hayden, "Petty Feuding Splits Personnel of Supreme Court," *Atlanta Constitution,* February 13, 1944, 5-D. Other public commentary similarly highlighted the divisions on the Court: "Supreme Court Feud," editorial, *Decatur (IL) Daily Review,* March 18, 1944, 6; Charles G. Ross, "U.S. Supreme Court Disagreement Reaches New High in 1943–44 Term," *St. Louis Post-Dispatch,* September 10, 1944, 1.

333 **"increasing tendency":** Felix Frankfurter to Wiley Rutledge, May 10, 1945, Felix Frankfurter Papers, Reel 60, Manuscript Division, Library of Congress, Washington, DC.

333 **separate opinions and dissents at a higher rate:** John Chamberlain, "The Nine Young Men," *Life,* January 22, 1945, 77; C. Herman Pritchett, *The Roosevelt Court: A Study in Judicial Politics and Values, 1937–1947* (Macmillan, 1948), 25. The high level of nonunanimity has frequently reappeared since that time. Cass R. Sunstein, "Unanimity and Disagreement on the Supreme Court," *Cornell Law Review* 100, no. 4 (2015): 769.

334 **"slip a word to Felix or Bill":** Francis Biddle, memo re: cabinet meeting, March 16, 1945, Francis Biddle Papers, "Cabinet Meetings, Jan. 1944–May 1945," Franklin D. Roosevelt Presidential Library and Museum, Hyde Park, NY.

335 **FDR's death:** Doris Kearns Goodwin, *No Ordinary Time: Franklin and Eleanor Roosevelt, the Home Front in World War II* (Simon and Schuster, 1994), 602–603; Robert Klara, *FDR's Funeral Train: A Betrayed Widow, a Soviet Spy, and a Presidency in the Balance* (St. Martin's, 2010), 6–7, 17–18.

335 **fly Eleanor…to Warm Springs:** Goodwin, *No Ordinary Time,* 611–612.

335 **swearing-in ceremony:** Klara, *FDR's Funeral Train*, 39; Associated Press wirephoto, "I Will Faithfully Execute the Office of President," *Detroit Free Press*, April 13, 1945, 1; Francis Biddle, *In Brief Authority* (Doubleday, 1962), 360; James Forrestal, *The Forrestal Diaries*, ed. Walter Mills (Viking, 1951), 42.

336 **"I parked the car and walked for hours":** William O. Douglas, *The Court Years, 1939–1975: The Autobiography of William O. Douglas* (Random House, 1980), 285.

336 **"President Roosevelt is dead":** Newman, *Hugo Black*, 337.

336 **"It took a good time for the fact to penetrate":** Robert H. Jackson, *That Man: An Insider's Portrait of Franklin D. Roosevelt*, ed. John Q. Barrett (Oxford University Press, 2003), 165.

336 **"I do not think we will ever see the President again":** Jackson, *That Man*, 154.

336 **"a cruel and monstrous loss":** Felix Frankfurter, "Franklin Delano Roosevelt," *Harvard Alumni Bulletin*, April 28, 1945, quoted in *Roosevelt and Frankfurter: Their Correspondence, 1928–1945*, ed. Max Freedman (Little, Brown, 1967), 750.

336 **"President Roosevelt gave his life":** United Press, "Leaders See Death as World Tragedy," *Morning Post* (Camden, NJ), April 13, 1945, 1, 12.

336 **"a long time before we have another":** "Noted Pay Tribute to President," *Detroit Free Press*, April 13, 1945, 10.

336 **"one of the most commanding figures":** Jackson, *That Man*, 167–168.

336 **"Not for one instant":** Wiley Rutledge to Louise Larrabee, April 21, 1945, box 30, folder 6, Wiley Rutledge Jr. Papers, Library of Congress, Washington, DC.

337 **procession of dignitaries:** Klara, *FDR's Funeral Train*, 75–77.

337 **"new President of the United States…might have been":** United Press, "Might Have Been Wallace, Byrnes, Barkley, Douglas," *Piqua Daily Call* (Miami Valley, OH), April 14, 1945, 1.

337 **cortege snaked:** Alexander Kendrick, "500,000 Mourn in Historic Rites at Washington," *Philadelphia Inquirer*, 1, 2.

337 **"eyes red-rimmed":** John W. McCullough, "Washington Throngs Weep in Final Tribute," *Philadelphia Inquirer*, April 15, 1945, 1, 2.

338 **Biddle and Stone having breakfast:** Klara, *FDR's Funeral Train*,138; Biddle, *In Brief Authority*, 363.

338 **Justices on the west side:** Klara, *FDR's Funeral Train*, 153. According to one press account, Black stood "beside Secretary Ickes," across the grave from other Justices. Louis M. Lyons, "Great Men, Villagers Mingle While Guns Boom Final Salute," *Boston Globe*, 1, 7.

338 **West Point cadets:** Goodwin, *No Ordinary Time*, 615; Klara, *FDR's Funeral Train*, 152–156.

338   **"where the sundial stands":** Klara, *FDR's Funeral Train*, 152.

338   **"On the return trip":** Jackson, *That Man*, 167; Klara, *FDR's Funeral Train*, 170. Although Jackson did not mention talking to Black or Douglas on the return trip, he had previously noted that Black and Douglas (and their wives) had joined the Jacksons in their car when they drove to Union Station on Saturday morning to greet the funeral train. Jackson, *That Man*, 166.

339   **"clung to [Truman]":** Biddle, *In Brief Authority*, 364. Byrnes's emergence is chronicled in Klara, *FDR's Funeral Train*, 82–85, 98, 109–111, 120, 129–132.

339   **Murphy's award:** Associated Press, "Justice Murphy Cited for Brotherhood Work," *York (PA) Daily Record*, April 17, 1945, 2; Klara, *FDR's Funeral Train*, 175–176.

339   **Truman's speech to Congress:** Klara, *FDR's Funeral Train*, 182–189; Robert C. Albright, "New Chief Asks Congress' Help to Reach Every Roosevelt Goal," *Washington Post*, April 17, 1945, 1.

339   **"obviously nervous and upset":** Ray Tucker, "National Whirligig," *Charlotte Observer*, April 20, 1945, 12. Tucker speculated that the Justices were distressed because they viewed Truman's reference to a government based on "law and justice" as a criticism; his speculation on that point seems strained and unpersuasive.

339   **Reed told Frankfurter:** Frankfurter, memo, April 18, 1945, pp. 1–2, Felix Frankfurter Papers, Manuscript Division, Library of Congress, Washington, DC.

340   **Southern Conference for Human Welfare:** Newman, *Hugo Black*, 333; United Press, "Thomas Jefferson Award Presented to Justice Black," *Sandusky (OH) Register*, April 4, 1945, 7.

340   **"grossly improper":** Newman, *Hugo Black*, 333. Jackson's objection to the three lawyer-sponsors with cases before the Court is detailed in Dennis Hutchinson, "The Black-Jackson Feud," *Supreme Court Review* 1988 (1988): 236.

340   **"perfume of public praise":** "Eddie" to Frankfurter, April 12, 1945, Felix Frankfurter Papers, Reel 14, Manuscript Division, Library of Congress, Washington, DC.

340   **Roberts...dissenting 30 percent:** Pritchett, *Roosevelt Court*, 42.

341   **Roberts became convinced:** Bruce Allen Murphy, *Wild Bill: The Legend and Life of William O. Douglas* (Random House, 2003), 210; Richard Davis, *Justices and Journalists: The U.S. Supreme Court and the Media* (Cambridge University Press, 2011), 140; William O. Douglas, interview by Walter F. Murphy, December 27, 1961, cassette 4 transcript, 2–5, and cassette 5 transcript, 5–6, William O. Douglas Oral History Interviews, Public Policy Papers, Special Collections, Princeton University Library,

https://findingaids.princeton.edu/catalog/MC015_c01; Alpheus Thomas Mason, *Harlan Fiske Stone: Pillar of the Law* (Viking, 1956), 625n‡. The three cases were *Federal Power Commission v. Hope Natural Gas*, 320 U.S. 591 (1944); *United States v. South-Eastern Underwriters*, 322 U.S. 533 (1944); and *Bridges v. Wixon*, 326 U.S. 135 (1945).

341 **Roberts sent President Truman:** "The President's News Conference," July 5, 1945, Harry S. Truman Library and Museum, https://www.truman library.gov/library/public-papers/76/presidents-news-conference.

341 **Black objected:** Mason, *Harlan Fiske Stone*, 765–769.

341 *Jewell Ridge* **opinion:** *Jewell Ridge Coal Corporation v. Local No. 6167, United Mine Workers of America*, 325 U.S. 161 (1945).

342 **rehearing petition:** Petition for Rehearing, *Jewell Ridge Corporation v. Local No. 6167, United Mine Workers of America*, 325 U.S. 161 (1945) (No. 721), May 31, 1945.

342 **Court…recusal decisions:** Mason, *Harlan Fiske Stone*, 642–645; Hutchinson, "Black-Jackson Feud," 203–243.

342 **denied the company's rehearing petition:** *Jewell Ridge Coal Corporation v. Local No. 6167, United Mine Workers of America*, 325 U.S. 897 (1945).

342 **meeting between Jackson and Rosenman:** Jackson, diary entry, April 27, 1945, box 95, folder 4, Robert H. Jackson Papers, Manuscript Division, Library of Congress, Washington, DC. Jackson also noted Rosenman's statement that "President Truman had expressed the view" that the prosecutorial position "would not require resignation" from the Supreme Court. Truman had "indicated that it if did require resignation it would be too large a price to pay." Diary entry, p. 3.

343 **Jackson…war crimes:** John Q. Barrett, introduction to *That Man: An Insider's Portrait of Franklin D. Roosevelt*, by Robert H. Jackson, ed. John Q. Barrett (Oxford University Press, 2003), xvii–xviii.

343 **"relief from the frustration at being in a back eddy":** Hutchinson, "Black-Jackson Feud," 209.

343 **"Work, of course, is not any less":** Harlan F. Stone to Charles Burlingham, November 30, 1945, folder 10, box 7, Harlan Fiske Stone Papers, Manuscript Division, Library of Congress, Washington, DC.

343 **"Jackson is over conducting his high-grade lynching":** Harlan F. Stone to Sterling Carr, December 4, 1945, folder 8, box 9, Harlan Fiske Stone Papers, Manuscript Division, Library of Congress, Washington, DC.

344 **"grim determination to fight on":** C. P. Trussell, "Blackout Lifted on Capitol Dome," *New York Times*, May 9, 1945, 14.

344 **"We beat not only the German Army":** "Address by Justice Douglas Opening Indiana Bond Sale Campaign," May 11, 1945, *Congressional Record* 91 (1945), p. A2443.

344   **Black wrote his sons:** Hugo Black to Sterling Black, April 30, 1945, box 6; and Hugo Black to Hugo Black Jr., May 10, 1945, box 3, folder 4, both in Hugo LaFayette Black Papers, Manuscript Division, Library of Congress, Washington, DC.

344   **Stone jubilantly exulted:** Harlan Fiske Stone to Marshall H. Stone, May 2, 1945, box 2, folder 10, Harlan Fiske Stone Papers, Manuscript Division, Library of Congress, Washington, DC.

344   **"bedlam that broke loose":** Newman, *Hugo Black*, 311.

344   **"Twenty minutes after":** "President Takes White House Bow Before 10,000," *Washington Post*, August 15, 1945, 1.

344   **"We beat [Japan]":** "Address of William O. Douglas, Missouri Bar, Columbia, Missouri," September 21, 1945, 4, box 692, folder 9, William O. Douglas Papers, Manuscript Division, Library of Congress, Washington, DC.

344   **Reed had hosted Truman:** Helen Essary, "Trumans All Wool and 100 Per Cent Americans," *Knoxville (TN) Journal*, April 17, 1945, 4.

345   **"The country boy was at home":** Newman, *Hugo Black*, 339–340.

345   **Frankfurter's efforts with the Truman Administration:** Brad Snyder, *Democratic Justice: Felix Frankfurter, the Supreme Court, and the Making of the Liberal Establishment* (W. W. Norton, 2022), 460–462, 467. As Snyder recounts, Frankfurter was one of the few individuals who had advance knowledge of the atom bomb, likely through conversations with New York University physicist Irving S. Lowen and Danish physicist Niels Bohr. Frankfurter raised concerns about a possible arms race with FDR and then, through intermediaries, with Truman. Snyder, *Democratic Justice*, 443–444, 460–462.

345   **Stone's death:** Mason, *Harlan Fiske Stone*, 806.

345   **"Washington adores a funeral":** Newman, *Hugo Black*, 341; Hutchinson, "Black-Jackson Feud," 243.

345   **"inside track":** David Lawrence, "Lawrence's Daily Dispatch," *Daily Press* (Newport News, VA), April 25, 1946, 4.

345   **Drew Pearson's column:** Hutchinson, "Black-Jackson Feud," 215.

345   **"blood feud":** Doris Fleeson, "Court Feud May Force Naming of Outsider as Chief Justice," *Boston Globe*, May 17, 1946, 21. Fleeson's column first appeared in the *Washington Star* and was frequently referred to as "the *Washington Star* column" during the controversy.

346   **Jackson sent…to the chairmen of…Judiciary Committees:** "Text of Jackson's Statement Attacking Black," *New York Times*, June 11, 1946, 2.

346   **critical commentary of both Jackson and Black:** Hutchinson, "Black-Jackson Feud," 221. The *New York Times* editorialized, "It seems to us that Justice Jackson has committed an error in taste and that Justice Black has

committed the worse offense of lowering judicial standards." "Quarrel on the High Bench," editorial, *New York Times,* June 12, 1946, 26.

346 **"I'm sure lucky":** Harry S. Truman to Bess W. Truman, June 12, 1946, Papers of Harry S. Truman Pertaining to Family, Business, and Personal Affairs, Folder: June 12, 1946, Harry S. Truman Library and Museum, Independence, MO.

347 **Stone's position:** In Stone's opinion for the Court in *United States v. Carolene Products,* 304 U.S. 144 (1938), he included a famous and influential footnote (footnote 4) that distinguished economic regulation, on which courts should be deferential, from other circumstances, such as "prejudice against discrete and insular minorities... which tends seriously to curtail the operation of those political processes ordinarily to be relied upon to protect minorities, and which may call for a correspondingly more searching judicial inquiry." 304 U.S. at 153 n.4.

347 **Frankfurter, Black, Douglas, and Jackson:** Noah Feldman, *Scorpions: The Battles and Triumphs of FDR's Great Supreme Court Justices* (Grand Central Publishing, 2010).

348 **"the Saturday sessions...ended promptly":** Chamberlain, "Nine Young Men," 80.

348 **"not a very effective administrator":** Robert Jackson, Columbia Oral History interview, p. 976, folder 2, box 191, Robert H. Jackson Papers, Manuscript Division, Library of Congress, Washington, DC.

348 **"the great extreme of detail":** William O. Douglas, interview by Walter F. Murphy, December 20, 1961, cassette 1 transcript, 6–7; cassette 2 transcript, 1; cassette 3 transcript, 5, William O. Douglas Oral History Interviews, Public Policy Papers, Special Collections, Princeton University Library, https://findingaids.princeton.edu/catalog/MC015_c01.

348 **"mass the Court":** Barry Cushman, "The Hughes Court Docket Books: The Late Terms, 1937–1940," *American Journal of Legal History* 55 (2015): 361, 423.

349 *Skinner* **and reproductive freedom:** As Justice John Paul Stevens explained, *Skinner* and *Roe v. Wade* reflect "a consistent view that the individual is primarily responsible for reproductive decisions, whether the State seeks to prohibit reproduction, [as in] *Skinner v. Oklahoma*" or "to require it, [as in] *Roe v. Wade." Thornburgh v. American College of Obstetricians,* 476 U.S. 747, 778 n.6 (1986).

350 *Shelby County* **decision:** *Shelby County v. Holder,* 570 U.S. 529 (2013); *Brnovich v. Democratic National Committee,* 141 S. C+ 2321 (2021).

351 *"a Constitution* **we are expounding":** *McCulloch v. Maryland,* 17 U.S. 316; 407, 415 (1819).

EPILOGUE

353   **Murphy's death:** Greg Zipes, *Justice and Faith: The Frank Murphy Story* (University of Michigan Press, 2021), 282–283; Sidney Fine, *Frank Murphy: The Washington Years*, 589.

353   **Rutledge's death:** John M. Ferren, *Salt of the Earth, Conscience of the Court: The Story of Justice Wiley Rutledge* (University of North Carolina Press, 2004), 416–417.

353   **Rutledge dissent and Guantanamo:** *Ahrens v. Clark* 335 U.S. 188, 193 (1948) (Rutledge, J., dissenting); *Rasul v. Bush,* 542 U.S. 466, 476–479 (2004).

354   **Jackson's death:** John Q. Barrett, introduction to *That Man: An Insider's Portrait of Franklin D. Roosevelt,* by Robert H. Jackson, ed. John Q. Barrett (Oxford University Press, 2003), xix; Noah Feldman, *Scorpions: The Battles and Triumphs of FDR's Great Supreme Court Justices* (Grand Central Publishing, 2010), 403–405; Brad Snyder, *Democratic Justice: Felix Frankfurter, the Supreme Court, and the Making of the Liberal Establishment* (W. W. Norton, 2022), 599–600.

354   **seizure of the nation's steel mills:** *Youngstown Sheet & Tube Co. v. Sawyer,* 343 U.S. 579, 634 (1952) (Jackson, J., concurring). As the Supreme Court has explained, "In considering claims of Presidential power, this Court refers to Justice Jackson's familiar...framework from *Youngstown Sheet & Tube Co. v. Sawyer.*" *Zivotofsky v. Kerry,* 576 U.S. 1, 10 (2015).

354   **Reed was the Court's last holdout:** Richard Kluger, *Simple Justice: The History of* Brown v. Board of Education *and Black America's Struggle for Equality* (Alfred Knopf, 1994), 698–699; John D. Fassett, "Mr. Justice Reed and *Brown v. Board of Education,*" *Supreme Court Historical Society Yearbook 1986* (Supreme Court Historical Society, 1986), 48–63.

354   **Reed's death:** J. Y. Smith, "Retired Supreme Court Justice Stanley Reed Dies at 95," *Washington Post,* April 4, 1980, B6.

355   **Byrnes...ardently defended:** David Robertson, *Sly and Able: A Political Biography of James F. Byrne* (W. W. Norton, 1994), 502–522.

355   **Byrnes...became a vigorous supporter:** Robertson, *Sly and Able,* 530–542.

355   **Frankfurter's outrage at...*Baker v. Carr*:** J. Douglas Smith, *On Democracy's Doorstep: The Inside Story of How the Supreme Court Brought "One Person, One Vote" to the United States* (Farrar, Straus and Giroux, 2015), 92.

355   **"Tell the whole story":** Max Freedman, ed., *Roosevelt and Frankfurter: Their Correspondence, 1928–1945* (Little, Brown, 1967), 744.

356   **Black's dissent from First Amendment case:** *Tinker v. Des Moines Independent Community School District,* 393 U.S. 503, 514 (Black, J., dissenting).

356 **Truman offered Douglas:** Bruce Allen Murphy, *Wild Bill: The Legend and Life of William O. Douglas* (Random House, 2003), 238–243, 256–265; James F. Simon, *Independent Journey: The Life of William O. Douglas* (Harper & Row, 1980), 273–275. According to Murphy, Douglas heard the "second fiddle" line from Tommy Corcoran and appropriated it as his own (254–255). Douglas also may have been concerned that Truman would lose his reelection bid, as many people believed (Simon, 273).

356 **Douglas suffered from illness:** Bob Woodward and Scott Armstrong, *The Brethren: Inside the Supreme Court* (Simon and Schuster, 1979), 367–368; Carla Hall, "Cathy Douglas—the Woman Beside the Man," *Washington Post*, December 9, 1979, K1.

Selected Bibliography

Abraham, Henry J. *Justices and Presidents: A Political History of Appointees to the Supreme Court.* 2nd ed. New York: Oxford University Press, 1985.

Bannai, Lorraine K. *Enduring Conviction: Fred Korematsu and His Quest for Justice.* Seattle: University of Washington Press, 2015.

Biddle, Francis. *In Brief Authority: From the Years with Roosevelt to the Nürnberg Trial.* Garden City, NY: Doubleday, 1962.

Boyle, Kevin. *Arc of Justice: A Saga of Race, Civil Rights, and Murder in the Jazz Age.* New York: Henry Holt, 2004.

Brinkley, David. *Washington Goes to War: The Extraordinary Story of the Transformation of a City and a Nation.* New York: Alfred A. Knopf, 1988.

Byrnes, James F. *All in One Lifetime.* New York: Harper and Brothers, 1958.

Commission on Wartime Relocation and Internment of Civilians. *Personal Justice Denied.* Seattle: University of Washington Press, 1997.

Cushman, Clare, ed. *The Supreme Court Justices: Illustrated Biographies, 1789–1993.* Washington, DC: Congressional Quarterly, 1993.

Danelski, David J. "The Saboteurs' Case." *Journal of Supreme Court History* 61, no. 1 (1996): 68.

Daniels, Roger. *The Japanese American Cases: The Rule of Law in Time of War.* Lawrence: University Press of Kansas, 2013.

Delmont, Matthew F. *Half American: The Epic Story of African Americans Fighting World War II at Home and Abroad.* New York: Penguin, 2022.

Dobbs, Michael. *Saboteurs: The Nazi Raid on America*. New York: Vintage, 2005.

Douglas, William O. *The Court Years, 1939–1975: The Autobiography of William O. Douglas*. New York: Random House, 1980.

Driver, Justin. *The Schoolhouse Gate: Public Education, the Supreme Court, and the Battle for the American Mind*. New York: Pantheon, 2018.

Fassett, John D. *New Deal Justice: The Life of Stanley Reed of Kentucky*. New York: Vantage, 1994.

Feldman, Noah. *Scorpions: The Battles and Triumphs of FDR's Great Supreme Court Justices*. New York: Grand Central Publishing, 2010.

Ferrell, Robert H. *Choosing Truman: The Democratic Convention of 1944*. Columbia: University of Missouri Press, 1994.

Ferren, John M. *Salt of the Earth, Conscience of the Court: The Story of Justice Wiley Rutledge*. Chapel Hill: University of North Carolina Press, 2004.

Fine, Sidney. *Frank Murphy: The Washington Years*. Ann Arbor: University of Michigan Press, 1984.

Fisher, Louis. *Military Tribunals and Presidential Power: American Revolution to the War on Terrorism*. Lawrence: University Press of Kansas, 2005.

———. *Nazi Saboteurs on Trial: A Military Tribunal and American Law*. Lawrence: University Press of Kansas, 2003.

Fleming, Thomas. *The New Dealers' War: F.D.R. and the War Within World War II*. New York: Basic, 2001.

Freedman, Max, ed. *Roosevelt and Frankfurter: Their Correspondence, 1928–1945*. Boston: Little, Brown, 1967.

Goldsmith, Jack. "Justice Jackson's Unpublished Opinion in *Ex parte Quirin*." *Green Bag* 9, no. 3 (2006): 223.

Goodwin, Doris Kearns. *No Ordinary Time: Franklin and Eleanor Roosevelt, the Home Front in World War II*. New York: Simon and Schuster, 1994.

Howard, J. Woodford, Jr. *Mr. Justice Murphy: A Political Biography*. Princeton, NJ: Princeton University Press, 1968.

Irons, Peter. *Justice at War: The Story of the Japanese American Internment Cases*. New York: Oxford University Press, 1983.

———, ed. *Justice Delayed: The Record of the Japanese American Internment Cases*. Middletown, CT: Wesleyan University Press, 1989.

Jackson, Robert H. *That Man: An Insider's Portrait of Franklin D. Roosevelt*. Edited by John Q. Barrett. New York: Oxford University Press, 2003.

———. *The Struggle for Judicial Supremacy: A Study of a Crisis in American Power Politics*. New York: Vintage, 1941.

James, Rawn, Jr. *The Double V: How Wars, Protest, and Harry Truman Desegregated America's Military*. New York: Bloomsbury, 2013.

Jordan, David M. *FDR, Dewey, and the Election of 1944*. Bloomington: Indiana University Press, 2011.

Karski, Jan. *Story of a Secret State: My Report to the World.* New York: Houghton Mifflin, 1944. Reprint, Washington, DC: Georgetown University Press, 2013.

Klara, Robert. *FDR's Funeral Train: A Betrayed Widow, a Soviet Spy, and a Presidency in the Balance.* New York: St. Martin's, 2010.

Lash, Joseph, ed. *From the Diaries of Felix Frankfurter.* New York: W. W. Norton, 1975.

Leuchtenburg, William E. *The Supreme Court Reborn: The Constitutional Revolution in the Age of Roosevelt.* New York: Oxford University Press, 1995.

Mason, Alpheus Thomas. *Harlan Fiske Stone: Pillar of the Law.* New York: Viking Press, 1956.

———. "Inter Arma Silent Leges: Chief Justice Stone's Views." *Harvard Law Review* 69, no. 5 (1956): 806–838.

McKeown, M. Margaret. *Citizen Justice: The Environmental Legacy of William O. Douglas—Public Advocate and Conservation Champion.* Lincoln, NE: Potomac, 2022.

McMahon, Kevin J. *Reconsidering Roosevelt on Race: How the Presidency Paved the Road to* Brown. Chicago: University of Chicago Press, 2004.

Meacham, Jon. *Franklin and Winston: An Intimate Portrait of an Epic Friendship.* New York: Random House, 2003.

Murphy, Bruce Allen. *Wild Bill: The Legend and Life of William O. Douglas.* New York: Random House, 2003.

Newman, Roger K. *Hugo Black: A Biography.* New York: Fordham University Press, 1997.

Nourse, Victoria F. *In Reckless Hands:* Skinner v. Oklahoma *and the Near Triumph of American Eugenics.* New York: W. W. Norton, 2008.

Peters, Shawn Francis. *Judging Jehovah's Witnesses: Religious Persecution and the Dawn of the Rights Revolution.* Lawrence: University Press of Kansas, 2000.

Pritchett, C. Herman. *The Roosevelt Court: A Study in Judicial Politics and Values, 1937–1947.* New York: MacMillan, 1948.

Rachlis, Eugene. *They Came to Kill: The Story of Eight Nazi Saboteurs in America.* New York: Popular Library, 1962.

Robertson, David. *Sly and Able: A Political Biography of James F. Byrnes.* New York: W. W. Norton, 1994.

Robinson, Greg. *By Order of the President: FDR and the Internment of Japanese Americans.* Cambridge, MA: Harvard University Press, 2001.

Rosenman, Samuel. *Working with Roosevelt.* New York: Harper and Brothers, 1952.

Shesol, Jeff. *Supreme Power: Franklin Roosevelt vs. the Supreme Court.* New York: W. W. Norton, 2010.

Snyder, Brad. *Democratic Justice: Felix Frankfurter, the Supreme Court, and the Making of the Liberal Establishment.* New York: W. W. Norton, 2022.

Stone, Geoffrey R. *Perilous Times: Free Speech in Wartime*. New York: W. W. Norton, 2004.

Tyler, Amanda L. *Habeas Corpus in Wartime: From the Tower of London to Guantanamo Bay*. New York: Oxford University Press, 2017.

Urofsky, Melvin I. *Division and Discord: The Supreme Court Under Stone and Vinson, 1941–1953*. Columbia: University of South Carolina Press, 1997.

———, ed. *The Douglas Letters: Selections from the Private Papers of Justice William O. Douglas*. Bethesda, MD: Adler and Adler, 1987.

Wood, E. Thomas, and Stanislaw M. Jankowski. *Karski: How One Man Tried to Stop the Holocaust*. Rev. ed. Lubbock, TX: Texas Tech University Press, 2014.

Zipes, Greg. *Justice and Faith: The Frank Murphy Story*. Ann Arbor: University of Michigan Press, 2021.

Index

Cliff Sloan is a professor of constitutional law and criminal justice at Georgetown University Law Center. He has argued before the Supreme Court seven times. He has served in all three branches of the federal government, including as Special Envoy for Guantanamo Closure, and is the author of *The Great Decision: Jefferson, Adams, Marshall, and the Battle for the Supreme Court*. His commentary on the Supreme Court and legal issues has appeared in the *New York Times*, *Washington Post*, *Slate*, and other publications, and on television and radio networks.

PublicAffairs is a publishing house founded in 1997. It is a tribute to the standards, values, and flair of three persons who have served as mentors to countless reporters, writers, editors, and book people of all kinds, including me.

I. F. STONE, proprietor of *I. F. Stone's Weekly*, combined a commitment to the First Amendment with entrepreneurial zeal and reporting skill and became one of the great independent journalists in American history. At the age of eighty, Izzy published *The Trial of Socrates*, which was a national bestseller. He wrote the book after he taught himself ancient Greek.

BENJAMIN C. BRADLEE was for nearly thirty years the charismatic editorial leader of *The Washington Post*. It was Ben who gave the *Post* the range and courage to pursue such historic issues as Watergate. He supported his reporters with a tenacity that made them fearless and it is no accident that so many became authors of influential, best-selling books.

ROBERT L. BERNSTEIN, the chief executive of Random House for more than a quarter century, guided one of the nation's premier publishing houses. Bob was personally responsible for many books of political dissent and argument that challenged tyranny around the globe. He is also the founder and longtime chair of Human Rights Watch, one of the most respected human rights organizations in the world.

•   •   •

For fifty years, the banner of Public Affairs Press was carried by its owner Morris B. Schnapper, who published Gandhi, Nasser, Toynbee, Truman, and about 1,500 other authors. In 1983, Schnapper was described by *The Washington Post* as "a redoubtable gadfly." His legacy will endure in the books to come.

Peter Osnos, *Founder*